Essentials of Real Estate Economics

SIXTH EDITION

Dennis J. McKenzie

Richard M. Betts
MAI, SRA, ASA (Real Estate) Property Analyst

Carol A. Jensen
Cabrillo College, Aptos and City College of San Francisco

CENGAGE
Learning™

Australia • Brazil • Japan • Korea • Mexico • Singapore • Spain • United Kingdom • United States

Essentials of Real Estate Economics, Sixth Edition

Dennis J. McKenzie, Richard M. Betts, and Carol A. Jensen

Vice President/Editor-in-Chief: Dave Shaut

Acquisitions Editor: Sara Glassmeyer

Developmental Editor: Arlin Kauffman, LEAP Publishing Services, Inc.

Editorial Assistant: Michelle Melfi

Senior Marketing and Sales Manager: Mark Linton

Senior Art Director: Pamela A. E. Galbreath

Senior Frontlist Buyer, Manufacturing: Charlene Taylor

Production Manager: Jean Buttrom

Content Project Management: PreMediaGlobal

Production Technology Analyst: Starratt Alexander

Permissions Acquisition Manager/Photo: Deanna Ettinger

Permissions Acquisition Manager/Text: Mardell Glinski Schultz

Cover Designer: Jeff Bane, CMB Design Partners

Cover Image: © shutterstock images/ Paulpaladin/Tuckerb34/Jerryb8

For product information and technology assistance, contact us at **Cengage Learning Customer & Sales Support, 1-800-354-9706.**

For permission to use material from this text or product, submit all requests online at **www.cengage.com/permissions**. Further permissions questions can be e-mailed to **permissionrequest@cengage.com**.

Library of Congress Control Number: 2010928361

Student Edition:

ISBN-13: 978-0-538-73969-6

ISBN-10: 0-538-73969-X

Cengage Learning
5191 Natorp Boulevard
Mason, OH 45040
USA

Cengage Learning is a leading provider of customized learning solutions with office locations around the globe, including Singapore, the United Kingdom, Australia, Mexico, Brazil, and Japan. Locate your local office at **www.cengage.com/global**.

Cengage Learning products are represented in Canada by Nelson Education, Ltd.

Purchase any of our products at your local college store or at our preferred online store **www.cengagebrain.com**.

Printed in the United States of America
1 2 3 4 5 6 7 14 13 12 11 10

Brief Contents

PART III   MAJOR INFLUENCES ON REAL ESTATE DEVELOPMENT   333

PART IV   REAL ESTATE INVESTMENT   427

Contents

13 LAND-USE CONTROLS 360

14 REAL ESTATE DEVELOPMENT 388

15 REQUIRED GOVERNMENT REPORTS 410

19 ANTICIPATING CHANGE 496

Preface

This text was written to provide the basics of real estate economics. The text is intended for real estate students who have little or no background in formal economics. Thus, the approach is direct and practical. The book is an outgrowth of years of teaching real estate economics at California community colleges and private schools.

CONTENT SUMMARY

The emphasis is on the factors that cause real estate uses or value to change. Our intent is to present this complex subject in as simple and practical a manner as possible. The focus of the book starts with the big picture, an overview of economics and money, and then the general issues of real estate economics. The focus then narrows down to city patterns and growth, followed by an examination of neighborhood concepts. The view then turns to the markets for, and key characteristics of, the various property types. Next come chapters examining governmental impacts on real estate, through property taxes, planning and zoning, and environmental impact reporting. The last section of the book turns to the economics of the individual property: investment analysis, income tax effects, and the uncertainties of the future.

SPECIAL FEATURES

Each chapter in the book is self-contained, allowing instructors to adapt the book to various course formats. Instructors and students alike will appreciate the multiple-choice questions and the questions for discussion—designed for testing, learning, and reviewing the material covered in each chapter. Vocabulary and terms surrounding real estate economics have grown more complex with the new regulations. While the economics language can at first seem complicated, as you progress through the chapters, you will find that the text makes it easier to understand. The glossary will add to your understanding and is a great asset when you need to check the meaning of a word or term.

There is an appendix for most chapters, called "Case & Point," covering a variety of topics, such as the life of Adam Smith, the graphic presentation of supply and demand, the pros and cons of allowing homeowners to deduct mortgage interest, the Laffer curve, national migration patterns, and the changes in retailing. Other Case & Point topics include discussions of whether government should be involved in neighborhood preservation, and the question of whether gated communities are a form of American apartheid. These hot-button topics will catch many readers' interest! Many chapters contain boxed "Special Interest Topic" material, to stimulate interest, and classroom discussion.

NEW TO THIS EDITION

This sixth edition is a complete update of the fifth edition. The general format of the book has been retained, except that the Key Terms have been moved to the beginning of each chapter. Many new topics and illustrations have been added, as many economic issues are much more clear in an illustration than in words. The sections on cash flow analysis and federal income tax rules for real estate investments have been updated. All other material has been reviewed, revised, and updated, with an eye to improving clarity whenever possible. In short, this new edition presents the current information needed for a successful course in real estate economics for real estate agents, appraisers, lenders, and investors.

Additional changes in this sixth edition include:

- Chapter 1: Explanation why real estate economics is so interesting.
- Chapter 2: No Economic System Is Perfect, as well as new figures on Theoretical Economic System Characteristics, Factors of Production, and The Circular Flow of Economic System Is Perfect, as well as new figures on Theoretical Economic System Characteristics, Factors of Production, and the Circular Flow of the Economy, Simplified Model, excluding Government's Role and Imports and Exports.
- Chapter 3: New Special Interest Topics on "Early Monopolistic Markets," and "What Ever Happened to GNP." Discussion on How Government Economic Intervention Changed as well as Phases of the Business Cycle. New figures and tables focusing on GDP in 2000 Dollars, Gross Domestic Product by Industry, Person Savings Rate, Civilian Unemployment Rate, New Housing Units Started, and Changes of the Business Cycle.

- Chapter 4: New box features on What Is a Depository Institution, Reserve Requirements as of January 1, 2009, and Calendar of the Crisis 2007–2008. Discussion on Panic and the Fed's Response, and the LIBOR Rate. Also new to this chapter are figures and tables showing FDIC Insured U.S. Commercial Banks by Bank Charter Type, and What happens when the Fed changes the Reserve percentage.

- Chapter 5: Analyzing Demand and Supply Using Graphs.

- Chapter 6: Expanded discussion of the sources of Community Growth, the importance of productivity, and discussion of data sources and Web sites for growth forecasts. Also updated data on fast-growing areas. New figures on Central Valley Towns, Los Angeles-Long Beach Harbors, Basic and Local Employment, Economic Base Study, and an Input–Output Study.

- Chapter 7: Extensively revised for better clarity, and more examples are given. Expanded discussion of illustrations. New topics on Modern City Growth Patterns: Adding in Technology. New Addenda: Future Issues in City Layout.

- Chapter 8: New discussion on Learning to Fight Decay. New figures showing Mortgage Delinquency, Homeowner Equity, and One Reason for Studying the Neighborhood.

- Chapter 9: Expanded discussion of the effect of time on housing demand. Discussion on income, its effects on housing demand, and the types of income. Expanded the discussion of inflation, and income in relation to home prices. Also discussed condo conversions and other rent-ownership changes. Updated data on new housing units authorized. New topic on Available Supply Section 9.3, The Government and Housing was rewritten and substantially expanded. Finally, new topics include What About Rental Housing, Choosing Housing Location, Choosing Housing Type, The Importance of Confidence, and New Topic, The Future of Construction. New figures include Real Disposable Personal Income Per Capita, First-Time Home Buyer Affordability Index, Median Price to Median Household Income Rate, Home Ownership Rate, Total Consumer Credit Outstanding, Consumer Confidence Index, Housing Starts, Delinquency, Foreclosure, and REO Rates, Home Price Index, The Shadow Housing Inventory, and Development Prospects for For-Sale Housing in 2010.

- Chapter 10: Expanded discussion of the categories of income property, supply cycles and their causes and effects, financing and tax impacts, power centers and big-box stores, and the impact of Internet sales. Also updated ranking of major shopping centers.

New topics added are Investors Versus Users, The User Viewpoint, and The Investor Viewpoint. New figures on A Mixed-Use Building, Live-Work Industrial Conversion, Average Vacancy Rates by Property Type, Price Indices, Loan Originations Index, Good Retail Tenant Mix, Power Center, and Downtown Billings Retail Market Study.

- Chapter 11: Updated data on leading agricultural states and counties. Expanded discussion of rural agricultural product storage and processing facilities, changes in farm size and income, rural solar and wind power facilities, importance of crop exports, government crop price supports and controls, and cycles in resource prices. New material added on contract farming, and new data on the major minerals and their value. New figures on Farm Real Estate Values by State, and CRB Index.

- Chapter 12: New special interest topic on Morton's Fork. Expanded discussion on Major Taxes and Expenditures, Evaluating the Property Tax, and Property Taxes and Land Usage. Updated table on Major Tax and Expenditure by Each Level of Government.

- Chapter 13: New Special Interest Topics on Health Codes, Eminent Domain Case, Limited Government Funding, and National Affordable Housing Act of 2007.

- Chapter 14: New Table on California Median Home Prices for the Period 1982 to 2009 by Region. New topic on Green Building.

- Chapter 15: New Special Interest Topics on Building Codes, Equitable Life Assurance Society, and Saving San Francisco Bay.

- Chapter 16: Rewritten for better clarity. New terms have been added and others, better defined.

- Chapter 17: Update topic on Investor Versus Dealer. Update Gain and Taxes Owed on Income Property.

- Chapter 18: Updated figures, Steps in the Scientific Method and Steps in Analyzing an Unimproved Property.

- Chapter 19: New section on Major Economic Issues for the decade, including the financial collapse and recovery from 2007. New topics on Homeownership and the Elderly, including new tables, political and legal issues, Global Warming, The State of Real Estate Industry. New tables on Compound Growth and Largest Petroleum Companies.

Supplements

Instructors who adopt this textbook receive access to an updated Instructor's Manual written by the authors. Each chapter is supported with learning objectives, review material from last session, instructor notes, and a 10-question review quiz. The manual also provides a 50-question mid-term exam for Chapters 1–8 and a 100-question final exam covering the entire book including answers.

Online *WebTutor*™ support for WebCT™ and BlackBoard® is also provided. Designed to accompany this textbook, WebTutor is an e-learning software solution that turns everyone in your classroom into a front-row learner. Whether you want to Web-enhance your class, or offer an entire course online, WebTutor allows you to focus on what you do best—teaching. More than just an interactive study guide, WebTutor is an anytime, anywhere online learning solution, providing reinforcement through chapter quizzes, multimedia flashcards, e-mail discussion forums, and other engaging learning tools.

Classroom PowerPoint® presentation slides support each chapter by outlining learning objectives, emphasizing key concepts, and highlighting real-world applications to help further engage learners and generate classroom discussion. These instructional support materials are available online from the text companion site at www.cengage.com/realestate/mckenzie.

Acknowledgments

This book was first written, some years ago, using the ideas developed at state-wide meetings of California community college teachers of real estate economics. The valuable insight of these instructors is deeply appreciated! It is not possible to individually acknowledge all of the many ideas, feedback, and assistance with the subsequent editions that we have received from our students, colleagues, and friends. We hope that we have successfully communicated the insights that they have provided!

We welcome your comments, questions, concerns, and ideas for improvement. You can email us at *betts.text@gmail.com*. We don't guarantee a reply, but we do guarantee your email will be read and carefully considered!

We would also like to express our appreciation to those who served as reviewers for this edition and who provided many insightful comments and valuable suggestions.

Corina Rollins
College of Marin

Arakel Arisian
California State University-Fresno

About the Authors

Richard M. Betts Mr. Betts is a California Certified General Real Estate Appraiser and consultant in Oakland, California. He was educated at the University of California, Berkeley, where he earned B.S. and M.B.A. degrees in Business Administration, with emphasis in Real Estate. Subsequent educational work includes a Real Estate Certificate; AIREA courses/exams I, II, IV, and VIII; and SREA Course 301. Mr. Betts has extensive experience as a fee appraiser and economist, including expert witness testimony before various superior courts, federal courts, tax court, arbitration panels, and assessment appeal boards. He has served as a member, and chair, of many arbitration panels on real estate issues.

Betts has taught numerous times for Merritt Community College; the University of California, Berkeley, Extension Division; AIREA; SREA; and the Appraisal Institute. He also taught for IAAO (Courses, 1, 2, and 3); the University of Southern California; and the University of California, Berkeley, School of Business. Mr. Betts holds the professional designations MAI, SRA, and ASA (Real Estate) and is a past president of both the Northern California Chapter 11 of AIREA and the East Bay Chapter 54 of SREA. For some years, Mr. Betts served on national committees of AIREA, including the National Editorial Board of *The Appraisal Journal*. Mr. Betts is the President of REAMUG, the appraisers' computer user group. He coauthored *Basic Real Estate Appraisal*, 7th ed., also published by Cengage Learning in 2007.

Carol A. Jensen, MBA, REALTOR® Ms. Jensen is a California Licensed Real Estate Broker and consultant in Finance/Accounting/

and Information Systems in San Francisco, California. She was educated at the University of California, Santa Barbara and Los Angeles, where she earned a B.A. degree in History and an M.B.A. degree in Management. Ms. Jensen presently serves as the Director of the California Community College Real Estate Education Center, dedicated to supporting quality real estate education in the State community college system.

Jensen is also an instructor of real estate at City College of San Francisco and Cabrillo College, Aptos. She teaches online, hybrid, and traditional classroom real estate courses as well as courses on small business management. Other instructor opportunities have included "Micro-Economics" for California State University, Monterey Bay; graduate "Human Resources and Organizational Leadership" for Brandman (Chapman) University; and graduate "Information Technology" for the University of Phoenix. Her experience includes developing academic, vocational, and continuing education course curriculum. She also participates in Academic Senate shared governance. In addition, she has written several books and journal articles, and has contributed to online publications.

Dedication

We dedicate this sixth edition to the memory of our late co-author, Dennis J. McKenzie. Denny was the chair for the many California Community College real estate teacher meetings that resulted in the first state content outline for the real estate economics course. In turn, this text was developed from that outline. Denny was responsible for mentoring many people into real estate careers. Even more notable were his many efforts in support of real estate teachers, for decades. He was widely respected and admired, and his passing leaves a big gap.

Richard M. Betts
Carol A. Jensen

PART 1

Basic Economic Background for Real Estate Analysis

1. INTRODUCTION TO REAL ESTATE ECONOMICS
2. REVIEW OF THE ECONOMIC PRINCIPLES OF CAPITALISM
3. GOVERNMENT'S ROLE IN THE ECONOMY
4. MONEY, CREDIT, AND REAL ESTATE
5. IMPORTANT ECONOMIC FEATURES OF REAL ESTATE

Chapter

1

Economics
Real estate
Real estate economics

PREVIEW

As you begin reading this textbook, you probably have certain questions in mind: What is economics? What is real estate economics? Why should you study real estate economics? What topics are covered in this book? How is the material organized? This introductory chapter answers these questions; so you will know what to expect from this textbook.

Introduction to Real Estate Economics

WHAT IS ECONOMICS?

Economics is a social science that is concerned with how individuals and societies choose to use scarce resources to produce, distribute, and consume goods and services. The demand for goods and services frequently exceeds the supply. How these scarce resources are allocated is the main interest of economists.

Economics is not the same as accounting, which only looks at what has happened in the past. And economics may *use* numbers and math, but it is much more than just math. It is the study of what causes the economy to change, and how it changes.

The study of economics can be broken into two main categories: macroeconomics and microeconomics. *Macroeconomics* is the study of the national, regional, or state economy and its various segments, such as national, regional, or state income, output, employment, and growth. *Microeconomics* is concerned with the individual units within the general economy, such as business firms and households. Whether the focus is macro or micro, the role of the economist is to analyze how resources are being used. The economist may suggest changes, or forecast economic trends.

WHAT IS REAL ESTATE?

Real estate means land and buildings. The formal definition is land, that which is affixed to the land, that which is appurtenant to the land, and that which is immovable by law. Anything that is not real estate is called personal property. The ownership of real estate carries certain rights, known as the *bundle of rights*. The bundle includes the right to use, possess, exclude, and dispose of the property. Land includes both the surface, the subsurface (including any minerals), and the air above. However, right to any water, oil, or gas is more limited. And ownership of the air above is generally limited to only that height that can reasonably be used. All of these rights are not absolute; they can be legally modified by private restrictions and by government regulations and laws. In short, real estate or real property is land and improvements, and the rights of use associated with the ownership.

WHAT IS REAL ESTATE ECONOMICS?

Real estate economics is about people and how their actions affect real estate use and values. A formal definition would be: Real estate economics is a study that uses economic principles, both macro and micro, to analyze the impact that national, regional, community, and neighborhood changes or trends have on real estate values and uses.

In our society, our desire for goods and services frequently exceeds the supply available. When an object is scarce, people will give money to obtain it. Scarcity creates value. Real estate economics focuses on the economic principles that create and change real estate values.

WHAT REAL ESTATE ECONOMICS IS NOT

Real estate economics is not the study of general economics. Nor is it a course in the practice of real estate. Rather, real estate economics is the link between general economic theory and applied real estate practice. A course in general economics concentrates on how society attempts to use limited resources to satisfy the wants of its people. However, such a course does not examine how this affects local real estate markets. On the other hand, a course in real estate practice concentrates on the specific knowledge and techniques needed to complete a real estate transaction, but spends little time discussing the economic factors that influence whether a home purchase or other real estate investment will be profitable over the years.

Real estate economics draws principles from both general economics and real estate practice. It then combines them to study changes in real estate use, value, and activity. The focus is on real estate *change*. The main reason to study real estate economics is to help understand issues and changes, and the impact these will have on local real estate use and values.

Figure 1.1 illustrates the relationships among general economics, real estate economics, and real estate practice.

FIGURE 1.1 The field of real estate economics draws principles from both general economics and real estate practice.

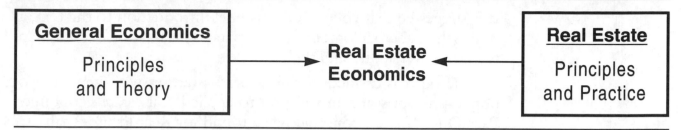

WHY IS REAL ESTATE ECONOMICS SO INTERESTING?

- Everything that we do involves economics! Does the price of gasoline concern you? What about interest rates on certificates of deposit? When corn is used to make ethanol to blend with gasoline, the price of corn goes up, and then the price of meat follows! This is economics at street level.

- But everything that we do also involves real estate: where we live, where we work, where we play, and more. And every real estate decision is also an economic decision! The American dream is to buy a home—but where? And how?

- Today, almost every other newspaper headline involves issues in real estate economics—mortgage problems, interest rates, the impact of unemployment, foreclosures, property values—all are issues that are discussed here!

WHY SHOULD YOU STUDY REAL ESTATE ECONOMICS?

Studying real estate economics helps people understand what causes fluctuations in real estate value, use, and activity. These fluctuations or changes in turn affect local real estate markets. Everyday, appraisers, investors, real estate agents, real estate lenders, voters, and others make real estate decisions that influence the shape, form, and value of property. In turn, real estate decisions made today will be reflected in real estate values in the cities and neighborhoods of tomorrow. Studying real estate economics helps people understand the impact today's real estate actions will have on future real estate values. In California, for instance, real estate economics is considered so important that state law requires that a course in real estate economics, or its equivalent, be completed before a person can become a licensed real estate broker. And real estate economics is a required education topic for everyone seeking a real estate appraisal license.

A GENERAL OVERVIEW

It is suggested that you review this brief introduction to the text, as well as the Table of Contents, to understand the relation of each chapter to the overall thrust of this book.

The book is divided into four parts, starting with general economic principles and moving on to applied real estate economics. Part One, "Basic Economic Background for Real Estate Analysis," contains five chapters, which review the major principles of economics and the reasons these principles are important to real estate students. Part One then explores the role of government and foreign interests in the economy, devotes a chapter to monetary policy, and discusses the economic characteristics of markets for real estate.

Part Two, "Understanding Real Estate Markets," devotes six chapters to regional, community, and neighborhood real estate analysis. The objective is to discuss why local and regional economies change and how these changes are reflected in the markets for each major type of real estate.

Part Three, "Major Influences on Real Estate Development," presents four chapters on real property taxation, land-use controls, real estate development procedures, and required government reports. These subjects are among the most controversial issues in the field of real estate.

In Part Four, "Real Estate Investment: The Economics of the Parcel," four chapters bring together all the material previously presented to demonstrate how the principles of real estate economics can be used to analyze a specific property. Topics include investment principles, cash flow analysis, income tax aspects of real estate, and forecasting trends.

Figure 1.2 is the essence of the entire book, and course, condensed into one illustration. These steps are the building blocks needed to understand real estate economics, and to apply it to daily real estate issues, problems, and decisions. The illustration shows how this textbook advances from one level of understanding to the next. Every newspaper will have stories, where you will use this knowledge to help you understand and evaluate what is reported. Some articles will be about events at the local level, and others will be at the city, county, state, nation, or international level!

CHAPTER OUTLINES

Each chapter in this textbook begins with a short preview of the material, followed by a list of objectives that you should be able to meet by the end of the chapter. The body of the chapter comes next, divided into sections. After each section, there is a series of brief questions to

FIGURE 1.2 The stairway of real estate economics.

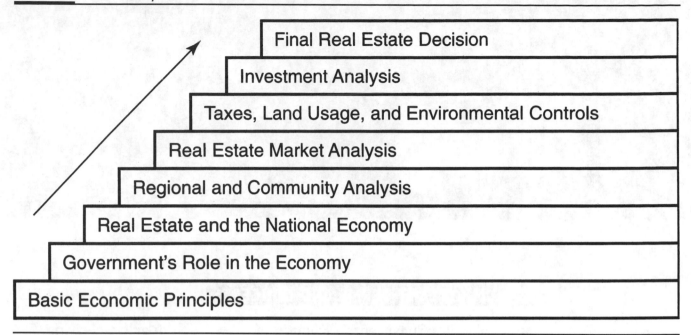

check your understanding of the material in that section. You should work methodically through each chapter, taking time to review each section for any points you have not understood.

At the end of each chapter, there is a brief summary, a list of the important terms and concepts in that chapter, and 25 multiple-choice questions. Answers are given at the back of the book. Once again, you can test your understanding of what you have read by studying the chapter summary, reviewing the terms and concepts, and answering the multiple-choice questions. This material is a valuable aid in preparing for examinations. Finally, a number of figures and other special-interest inserts have been included in each chapter to clarify some issues and provide variety in your reading.

A FINAL WORD

The study of real estate economics can be approached from the mathematical view, called *econometrics*, or from the non-mathematical perspective, using verbal descriptions. Econometrics combines economics, mathematics, and statistics, in order to express economic relationships with mathematical equations. The verbal approach uses words, rather than equations, to describe economic relationships.

This textbook uses the verbal approach wherever possible! Special emphasis has been placed on a clear and simple explanation of economic concepts. Students who wish to pursue economic principles in more detail are encouraged to contact their local college and obtain information about course offerings in economics, economic geography, and urban planning.

Chapter

2

IMPORTANT TERMS AND CONCEPTS

Balance of payments

Balance of trade

Capitalism—pure and mixed

Change in demand

Change in supply

Command economy

Communism

Comparative advantage

Demand

Economics

Equilibrium point

Effective demand

Factors of production
— land
— labor
— capital
— entrepreneurship

Flow of the economy

Free trade

Income

Law of demand

Law of supply

Market: perfect and imperfect

Market-clearing price

Market economy

Opportunity cost

Product market

Rate of exchange

Rent, wages, interest, profits

Resource market

Socialism

Supply

Traditional economy

PREVIEW

This chapter reviews the basic principles of an economic system, focusing primarily on capitalism. Section 2.1 examines the purpose of any economic system, the major types of economic systems, the issues with each type, and the characteristics of a pure capitalist economy. Section 2.2 describes the factors that any economic system uses to produce goods and services, and includes a model showing the flow of goods, services, and income in a

Review of the Economic Principles of Capitalism

capitalistic economy. Section 2.3 explores what a market is, why it is so important, and how prices and output are established in a competitive market. The Case & Point at the end of the chapter sketches the life of Adam Smith, an important figure in the development of economic theory. When you have completed this chapter, you will be able to:

1. Describe why every society must have some form of economic system.

2. List the basic characteristics of the pure capitalistic economic system.

3. List the factors of production that are used in our economy, to produce goods and services.

4. Describe how prices are established in a competitive market.

2.1 BASIC ECONOMIC CONCEPTS
Economics Revisited

As stated in Chapter 1, **economics** is a social science concerned with how individuals and societies choose to use scarce resources to produce, distribute, and consume goods and services. A science that is concerned with human behavior is frequently called a social or behavioral science. Therefore, economics is a social or behavioral science that studies how people allocate scarce resources, in order to satisfy their needs for food, clothing, housing, recreation, etc.

The desire for material goods and services usually exceeds the supply available. Economics studies how scarce goods and services can be distributed efficiently. For example, imagine how many people would like to live on a 10- to 15-acre ranch within an easy 20-minute commute to their jobs in a large city. When such a mini-ranch becomes available, who gets it? Who decides which person(s) gets the land and the opportunity to enjoy a rural setting and who must continue to live in the congested city? Should names be drawn out of a hat? Should it go to the highest bidder? Should the land be subdivided? Should the government make it into a park? As you can see, this is a problem involving scarcity. There is simply not enough land to satisfy all of the people who might wish to live on mini-ranches that are close to work!

Choice and Opportunity Cost: No Free Lunch

Two key concepts in economics are choice and opportunity cost. Resources are always more or less scarce. Individuals and societies must choose between competing uses of these limited resources. Once a choice is made, the alternative that was given up, or not selected, is the trade-off, or **opportunity cost**, that one must pay in return for a particular choice. For example, if a person works in a large city but chooses to live in a quiet suburban area, the trade-off or opportunity cost of living in the suburbs is the expense, time, and frustration of a long daily commute. In short, every choice incurs a cost! There is no free lunch! It is the role of the economist to examine alternate solutions to scarcity problems, pointing out the advantages and opportunity costs of each possible solution.

Economics Is an Inexact Science

As a social science, economics is concerned with human behavior, not with just physical objects. A chemist can predict with great accuracy what will occur when certain chemicals are mixed. But an economist cannot predict very accurately what will occur when certain economic ingredients are mixed. For example, if a country is in a recession, reducing income taxes should stimulate the economy, because people and businesses will have extra dollars to spend. But a tax cut will not immediately stimulate the economy if people and businesses decide to save, rather than spend their newfound dollars. The key point is that people can change their behavior patterns, and these changes add uncertainty to economic predictions. However, by constantly studying human behavior and upgrading their analytical tools, economists attempt to improve the accuracy of their forecasts.

Economic Solutions May Contain Value Judgments

Frequently, economists can agree on the nature of an economic problem. However, because of data interpretation and their own personal beliefs, they can disagree over which is the best solution. For example, suppose that a nation is in the middle of a very strong boom, resulting in a rapid increase in consumer spending. Businesses cannot increase the supply of goods fast enough, so there are shortages. Prices are rising rapidly, causing inflation. Most economists would agree that inflation should be reduced. But what actions should be taken to reduce inflation? Should the government increase taxes, to cut consumer spending? If so, whose taxes should be increased? Or should the government cut back on its own spending? If so, which government programs—welfare, defense, highways, low-income housing—should be cut?

Students should not be surprised by disagreements among economists. Disagreements among experts exist in most fields of study. How can two equally qualified real estate experts arrive at different conclusions as to the ideal use for the same parcel of land? Is there not just one ideal land use? Or does the interpretation of the ideal land use depend in part on the interests and experiences of the person proposing the solution?

As trained social scientists, economists attempt to minimize the number of personal value judgments that enter into their analyses, but students should recognize that some bias does exist. When disagreements arise among experts, students should carefully listen to all sides and then form their own opinions.

The Different Economic Systems

What will be produced? How will it be produced? For whom will it be produced? These are the economic questions that every society must answer! Economists have agreed that there are three general categories of answers to these questions. If the society chooses to continue doing things as they have been done before, we call its system a **traditional economy**. A child follows the parent's trade, a farmer uses age-old methods, and social stratification remains fixed. These are the hallmarks of a traditional economy, like that of medieval Europe and found today in some underdeveloped countries. If the great majority of decisions about production and distribution are made by private individuals in competitive markets, the system is called a **market economy**, or **capitalism**. If it is the government that makes most of the economic decisions in society, the system is a **command economy**, more commonly known as **socialism** or **communism** (see Figure 2.1).

Some of the underdeveloped world still has a traditional economy, and there remain some economies controlled by a dictator. Our concern here will only be with the *market* and *command* alternatives to the basic questions of production and distribution. The major

FIGURE 2.1   Span of economic systems.

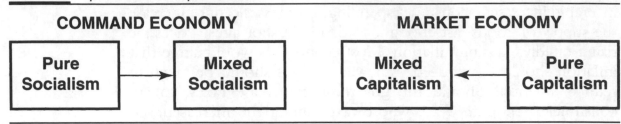

distinction between these two systems is the role of the government. In a "pure" market or capitalist society, the government provides only defense needs and a judicial system that will protect the rights of individuals and foster competitive markets. Private individuals own the property and resources of the society. They produce goods and services and distribute them according to supply and demand, using a competitive market system. *It is the ability to pay, not the need to have,* that determines who gets what in this system. On the other hand, in a "pure" command or socialist society, the government owns the major resources, as a trustee for the people. The government produces all of the goods and services, and distributes them according to its interpretation of its citizens' needs.

Real World Economies

In the real world, there is no such thing as pure capitalism or pure socialism. Although in recent years there has been a worldwide decline in the importance of socialism, all large economies have some mixture of the two systems. The United States is primarily a capitalistic country, but its economy has many features of the command system: look at the uses the government makes of tax dollars. Whether citizens like it or not, the U.S. government builds missiles, supports various social services, builds roads, and gives food to developing nations. On the other hand, countries with more socialistic economies nevertheless may allow farmers to have private plots of land, encourage some individuals to own and operate businesses, follow public buying patterns to help decide what consumer goods to produce, and create profit incentives for some categories of workers.

No Economic System Is Perfect

No country uses an economic system of pure capitalism or pure socialism. Instead, they all feature systems that are some mix of the two. It is also clear that the mix in use in any country changes, over the years. Sometimes, the mix moves toward the socialist or command economy side of the line. Other times, it will swing back toward a stronger emphasis on capitalism. The reason is that each system has built-in

FIGURE 2.2 Theoretical economic system characteristics.

SYSTEM	GOOD FEATURES	BAD FEATURES
CAPITALISM		
	Rewards efficiency	Hard on the old and sick
	Rewards productivity	Hard on the weak
	Rewards innovation	Rewards those who cheat
		Increases the rich-poor split
SOCIALISM/COMMAND ECONOMY		
	Protects the old and sick	Stifles innovation
	Protects the weak	Reduces productivity
	More even income distribution	Encourages bureaucracy
	More equal opportunities	Encourages bribery

issues or problems. Countries swing back and forth, trying to avoid the problems that they currently face, and hoping to work around the problems of the alternative economic system.

There is much debate about the advantages and disadvantages of each type of economic system. And there is no research that is likely to provide reliable answers. In part, this is because economic leaders can make mistakes, and these can make a bad feature of one system become worse. Nevertheless, there may be some general statements that we can make. These might be described as probable benefits and problems of each system. These are summarized in Figure 2.2. Each could be expanded to several pages of discussion!

Basic Principles of Pure Capitalism

The present economic system of the United States has its roots in the principles and theories of pure capitalism. Therefore, it is important to understand certain key elements that are known as the principles of capitalism.

Principles of Capitalism

1. *Private Property*: The right of the individual to own, control, and dispose of property.

2. *Private Enterprise*: The major resources and businesses are owned and controlled by private citizens, who have relative freedom of choice in the use of these resources.

3. *Competitive Markets*: Markets in which numerous buyers and sellers are pitted against one another, as they bargain for the exchange of goods and services. No one buyer or seller has enough power to manipulate prices. Ultimately, the bargaining process results in goods and services being allocated at the lowest possible price.

4. *Profit Motive*: The desire for personal gain or profit motivates individuals to take risks, and form businesses to produce the goods and services demanded by society. Failure to produce what society wants, at the correct price, will cause personal bankruptcy, whereas success will generate profits and personal wealth.

5. *Laissez-faire* (hands off): A philosophy that the government should minimize all interference in the basic economic affairs of private citizens.

How Pure Capitalism Answers the Questions *What, How,* and *for Whom*

In a pure capitalistic economy, how does society answer the critical questions of what, how, and for whom to produce? The answers are determined by the interaction of supply and demand—what Adam Smith, the famous capitalist, called the "invisible hand." **What to produce** is determined by businesses, as they try to produce goods and services to satisfy the demands of buyers and make a reasonable profit. Do you remember the Pontiac Aztek? General Motors built it, but there was insufficient demand and the Aztek went out of production after a year. On the other hand, illegal drugs continue to be produced and distributed, in spite of government efforts to prevent the flow of these harmful substances. Why? Because demand drives up prices, and high prices in turn stimulate the supply, even if the supplier runs the risk of imprisonment and/or death from gang wars.

The question of *how to produce* is answered by the pressure to have the lowest possible production cost. To remain competitive, a manufacturer or service provider must constantly seek ways to produce at lower costs. According to pure capitalistic theory, these lower costs should ultimately result in lower consumer prices.

For whom shall the items be produced? Who gets the goods and services, and who must do without? According to the theory of capitalism, goods and services will go to those who have something of value to offer in exchange. Usually the medium of exchange is money. In short, goods and services go to those who can pay for them. Others must do without them, in a pure capitalistic world.

Modern Mixed Capitalism in the United States

It should be clear from your understanding of American economic society that the United States does not have a pure form of capitalism. Economists refer to the American economy as a mixed capitalistic system. Although most goods and services are produced by private enterprise, the government plays an important role, either directly or indirectly, in controlling the economy.

The government in a mixed capitalistic system attempts to correct what it and the majority of its citizens consider to be the faults of pure capitalism. Especially since the Great Depression of the 1930s, the government has played a major role in attempting to maintain full employment, create general economic stability, and promote a reasonable level of economic growth. Other governmental interventions in the economy involve regulation of business, income redistribution, and welfare programs.

Famous Capitalist Adam Smith (1723–1790)

THEORIES AND THEORETICIANS

From the Warren J. Samuels Portrait Collection, Duke University.

In 1776, in addition to the American Revolution, another event took place that would have a profound effect on the world: Adam Smith wrote *The Wealth of Nations*. This book described an economic system that was based on the concept of private ownership of property and free competitive markets, without government interference. Smith used the term *laissez-faire* (hands off) to describe what he saw as the government's ideal role.

Smith stressed that an economy free of government interference, where individuals were motivated by profit and self-interest, would unknowingly provide for the efficient allocation of resources.

Modern-day capitalistic theories spring from the ideas set forth by Adam Smith in 1776. See the Case & Point section at the end of this chapter for more details on the life of Adam Smith.

As befits a democratic society, we hear voices of gloom on the right and doom on the left preaching, respectively, the adoption of a less or more active governmental role in preserving the fundamental essence of the American system.

THEORIES AND THEORETICIANS

Famous Socialist Karl Marx (1818–1883)

From the Warren J. Samuels Portrait Collection, Duke University.

In 1867, another important book on economics was published that would also have a profound effect on the world. Karl Marx, an impoverished philosopher living in England, wrote a book entitled *Das Kapital* (Capital).

In his book, Marx predicted that capitalism was doomed to fail, because capitalists were motivated only by profits, and would force workers to take less money, thus lowering wages to the subsistence level. In time, a few rich capitalists would have all the wealth, while

the workers would be living in misery. Angry workers would then
revolt, overthrow the capitalists, and seize the wealth on behalf of
their fellow workers.

Marx believed that this revolution would lead to a new, classless
society. All would willingly work according to their abilities, and
receive goods according to their needs. Some modern-day socialism
and much of today's communism stem from the ideas of Karl Marx.

In the field of real estate, you might hear voices asking for less
regulation over land use. A few minutes later, the same voices are
demanding that the government do something to lower interest
rates, to make housing more affordable! Today, there are many
spokespersons for the current system of economic compromise. This
mixed capitalistic system has evolved over many decades, and the
voters have made it abundantly clear that nothing approaching either
pure capitalism or pure socialism is acceptable.

Before taking a closer look at the American economy to see how
goods and services are produced, how income is generated, and the
importance of land, review the questions below.

REVIEWING YOUR UNDERSTANDING

Basic Economic Concepts
1. What is the definition of economics?
2. What does an economic system attempt to do?
3. What is government's role under capitalism? Under socialism?
4. Explain the following: private property, private enterprise, competitive
   markets, profit motive, and laissez-faire.

2.2 ECONOMIC PRINCIPLES IN ACTION

This section provides a simplified model of the U.S. economy. At this
point, we only want to look at how goods, services, and income flow
through the economic system. We will add more elements to the
model, as we go forward.

The Factors of Production

According to economists, in every economy, there are four essential resources, called **factors of production**, which are needed to produce goods and services: **land**, **labor**, **capital**, and **entrepreneurship**.

The Factors of Production

1. **Land** refers to all of the natural resources: trees, minerals, air, and water—as well as the surface of the earth. The land provides the raw materials or resources needed to manufacture goods, grow food, and provide shelter. The sun is a part of this pool of resources.

2. **Labor** is the human effort used to transform raw materials into finished products or to perform services.

3. **Capital** is any manufactured thing, instrument, or device that is used to increase production, such as machinery, tools, and buildings. Although *money capital* is needed to purchase *capital equipment*, money itself cannot extract resources or produce goods and services. The role of money capital in the real estate market is discussed later.

4. **Entrepreneurship** is the assembling or organizing of the other factors of production, in a systematic manner, to produce goods or services. This activity is performed by the owner, or entrepreneur, and is commonly known as "going into business." For simplicity, we can call this "business owner skills."

These four elements (Figure 2.3) come together to produce and distribute goods and services in the U.S. economy.

Rent, Wages, Interest, Profit, and Income

In a pure capitalistic economy, private individuals own essentially all of the factors of production, and they insist upon payment for the use

FIGURE 2.3   Factors of production.

- • **Land**
- • **Labor**
- • **Capital**
- • **Business Owner Skills**

of their "property." Owners of land receive **rent** for the use of their land. Workers sell their labor for **wages**. Lenders of money receive **interest** from borrowers who want to purchase capital equipment. And successful entrepreneurs earn **profits** from the operation of their businesses. (Unsuccessful entrepreneurs, of course, incur losses or go out of business.)

Rents, wages, interest, and profits constitute **income**. Everyone receives some income. In turn, if you are like most people, you spend a major portion of your income buying goods and services from businesses. Thus, *our economy has a circular flow*. Business buys land, labor, capital, and entrepreneurial or business owner skills from individuals. Individuals then use this income to buy goods and services from business. The money flows one way around the circle, and the goods and services flow in the opposite direction.

The Circular Flow of the Economy

Figure 2.4 illustrates the circular flow of the U.S. economy. The role played by government and businesses and people in other countries will be discussed in the next chapter. For now, assume that the government and other countries do not participate in the economy.

The solid inner lines in Figure 2.4 show the flow of resources and goods. The outer dotted lines show the reverse flow of money or income. As you see, the individual is both buyer and seller. He or she sells land, labor, capital, or business skills in the resource market and buys goods and services in the product market. Businesses buy land, labor, capital, and business skills in the resource market and sell goods and services in the product market. Check your understanding of this circular flow by answering the following questions.

REVIEWING YOUR UNDERSTANDING

Economic Principles in Action: The Circular Flow of the Economy

What will happen to this circular flow if the following occurs?

1. Business experiences a decline in sales, and decides to cut back on production. Will the economy expand or contract? Will employment rise or decline? Will household income increase or decrease?

2. What will happen to this flow if the reverse takes place, and high profits motivate business to expand its output? You should be able to trace the changes through each section of Figure 2.4.

FIGURE 2.4 The circular flow of the economy, simplified model, excluding government's role and imports and exports.

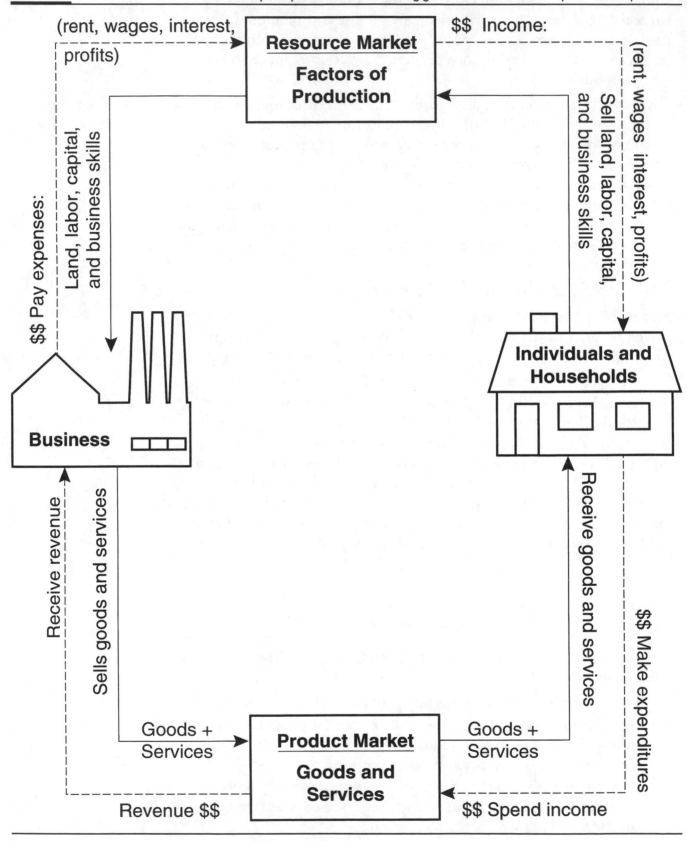

2.3 MARKETS AND PRICES

This section defines the critically important term **market** and describes how prices and output are established in competitive markets. We will focus on the factors that cause prices and output to change.

What Determines Prices and Output?

What determines the rent charged for land? The interest rate charged for money capital? The wage level charged for labor? The price of goods and services? The amount of goods produced? In the U.S. economy, most of these questions are answered in the marketplace. A **market** is defined as a place where buyers and sellers meet to bargain and exchange goods and services at negotiated prices. If you have ever been to a flea market, or a big farmer's market, then you know what a market is!

The characteristics of a market can influence the level of output, as well as the prices that are paid for goods and services. Markets can be defined by the two extremes: markets with *perfect competition* and markets with *imperfect competition*.

Perfect versus Imperfect Markets

It is important to understand **perfect** and **imperfect markets**. When conditions of perfect competition prevail in a market, there are many buyers and sellers, who are bidding against each other for the available goods and services. No one buyer or seller can exert influence over the market or control the prices. The goods or services being offered are similar enough so that the buyer will select the lowest-priced offering. The bargaining between buyers and sellers establishes prices.

If either the buyer or the seller exercises some control over the market, then conditions of imperfect competition start to prevail. If there are several sellers and one buyer, a lower price will result. If there are several buyers and one seller, a higher price will result. Consider the previous example of the mini-ranch in the suburbs: If there is just one property for sale and demand is strong, the many prospective suburbanites will drive the price up by bidding against each other. But if 500 mini-ranches suddenly came on the market, the price of most mini-ranches in the area should level off or fall. Consider times when you have personally observed a market for some product where sellers dominated, or one where buyers dominated!

Demand and Supply: The Classic Answer to Price Determination

The U.S. economy has become so complex that it is difficult to find examples of perfect competition. However, it is easier to understand the market forces that influence prices by viewing them with perfect competition. Therefore, the following discussion assumes a perfectly competitive market. Later, the principles discussed below will be modified to analyze prices in the imperfect real estate market.

Prices in a market economy are determined by the interaction of buyers and sellers, as they compete against one another for goods and services in the marketplace. *The total quantity that buyers are willing to buy at a given time at certain prices is called demand. The total quantity that sellers are willing to sell at a given time at certain prices is called supply.*

Demand

We must be careful not to confuse desire or need with demand. Demand is the presence of desire or need, coupled with the ability and the willingness to spend. For example, Family A wants a $500,000 home but cannot afford it. Family B wants the same home and can afford it, but does not want to make the necessary high monthly payments. Family C wants the house, can afford it, and will make the high monthly payments. Only Family C causes or creates a real demand for this house. Families A and B are lookers, not buyers. Some economists use the term **demand** for desire or need, and when ability to pay is joined to desire or need, they use the term **effective demand**. It does not matter which term is used. It is effective demand, not wishful desire or need, that influences the marketplace.

The Law of Demand

As stated earlier, economists do tend to agree on some things. One of these common points is the existence of a few economic laws. An important one is the **law of demand**, which states: The lower the price, the more consumers will buy. The higher the price, the less they will buy.

At lower prices, consumers will buy more goods, because they can afford more and because a lower price may entice them to buy more after their initial purchase. For example, you may buy one can of Brand A for $1.00, but to entice you to buy more, the grocer may lower the price to two cans for $1.75. However, at higher prices, consumers will buy fewer goods, because they cannot afford as much and because each additional unit purchased will give less satisfaction than the first unit purchased.

Changes or Shifts in Demand

Note that changing circumstances may cause a **change in demand**, by causing an increase or decrease in the number of available buyers. Some of the causes of a change, or shift, in demand are listed below:

1. *An increase or decrease in population.* Demand for most products and services rises or falls with changes in population. As the number of people increases, demand increases; as the number of people declines, demand declines. The presence of more people increases the demand for housing, whereas a drop in the number of people decreases the demand for housing.

2. *An increase or decrease in per capita income.* Demand also rises and falls with the level of per capita (per person) income: The higher the level of income, the greater the demand; the lower the level of income, the smaller the demand.

3. *Changes in consumer taste and substitute products.* If consumers favor smaller cars over large SUVs, demand for the former grows and demand for the latter diminishes. The same is true in housing: If city dwellers increasingly decide to move to the suburbs, then the demand for city apartments will decline and demand for suburban homes will grow.

4. *Changes in the amount of credit available.* Easy or inexpensive credit tends to increase demand, whereas tight or expensive credit tends to reduce it. Of course, you must pay back later what you borrow now, and this will affect future demand.

5. *The effect of advertising.* The well-written newspaper ad or the catchy TV commercial can create desires that may eventually lead to purchases and increased demand.

Supply

Demand represents the buyer's side of the market. **Supply** represents the seller's side of the market. The total quantity that sellers are willing to sell at a particular time and at a certain price is called supply.

The Law of Supply

The **law of supply** states: Producers will offer more products and services for sale as prices increase and fewer as prices decrease. Higher prices may mean higher profits, so businesses increase output. As prices decline, profits usually decline, and businesses cut back on output.

Changes or Shifts in Supply

Supply, like demand, changes over time with changing circumstances. Some of the causes of a shift or **change in supply** are:

1. *Changes in the cost of the factors of production.* If land, labor, or capital become more expensive, some producers will be unable to make a profit and may have to drop out of business, thereby reducing the supply. If the factors of production become cheaper, perhaps because of better technology or global access, some producers might seek a profit by moving into that particular business or expanding, thereby increasing supply.

2. *A change in demand for one product can cause a change in supply of another product.* For example, if people decided to live in apartments, instead of houses, you could expect to soon see a cutback in the supply of new homes and an increase in the supply of apartments.

3. *Business anticipation of future prices and profits can change the amount of goods supplied.* Sellers will increase output if they think future prices and profits will increase. They will decrease output, or even go out of business, if they think future prices and profits will decrease. This was very visible during the 2004–2006 boom, and 2007–2010 recession!

Supply and Demand Together Determine Output and Price Levels

If all the sellers and buyers of goods and services were to come together, there would eventually be an auction-like agreement among them, which would set the selling (buying) price of the goods and services. If sellers were to insist on prices that are too high, some buyers would refuse to purchase. Not wanting excess goods on hand, sellers would then lower prices until they sold the merchandise. If buyers offer prices that are too low, sellers would not be able to make a profit. They would stop production, and the buyers, not wanting to do without the products, would gradually increase their bids until sellers were enticed back into production.

After much movement back and forth, prices eventually settle at the point where the quantity that buyers are willing to purchase equals the quantity that sellers are willing to sell. This is called the **equilibrium point**. Here, buyers and sellers are matched, and the goods and services for sale in the market are sold. This point is also known as the **market-clearing price**: the price at which all of the goods in the marketplace are sold. Rents, wages, interest rates, and prices of all goods and services are established by this interaction of supply and demand, in perfectly competitive markets.

But in a dynamic economy, things never stay the same for very long. The changes that were noted previously cause both supply and demand to shift, and these shifts change the equilibrium point. For example, if supply remains the same while demand increases, would you expect prices to increase or decrease? Would supply remain at the same point or would it change in response to the increase in demand? Prices would of course increase: More buyers are after fewer goods. Suppliers would then increase production and the quantity supplied, to take advantage of the higher prices. Then, the increase in demand and supply would create a new equilibrium point, to clear out the market.

And what would happen if demand remained constant, while supply increased? Prices would go down as sellers tried to liquidate their stocks, but this trend might force some sellers out of business. Soon, the supply would decrease, to reach a new equilibrium point with the new level of demand.

Elasticity

The term *elasticity* refers to how much the price changes as the quantity changes. And the reverse: How much does the quantity change with changes in price? Demand for some products, like milk, is relatively *inelastic*, because the quantity purchased doesn't change much as prices change. Demand for other products, like deluxe chocolate truffles, is relatively *elastic*, because the quantity purchased is much more sensitive to price changes. Supply, too, can be elastic or inelastic, depending on the product and how easy it is to supply more or less.

The Flow of the Economy Revisited

Figure 2.5 shows the flow of the economy again, but this time, we have added labels for supply and demand. You can see that the individuals and households in the **resource market** represent supply; they are the sellers of land, labor, capital, and business management or entrepreneurial skills. How much business must pay, and how much individuals and households receive as income, depend on the price and quantity, as established by supply and demand. In the **product market**, the roles are reversed. Business is now the supplier, selling goods and services to individuals and households.

Impact of International Trade

Up to this point, our overview of a pure capitalistic economy has illustrated a closed economy, ignoring the impact of foreign imports and

FIGURE 2.5   The circular flow of the economy.

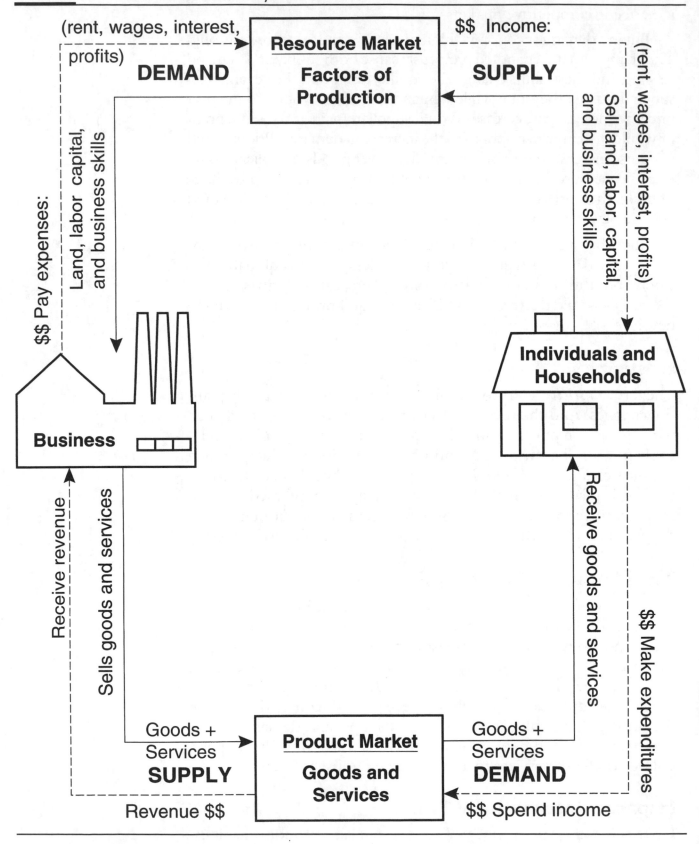

exports. In reality, most economies are somewhat open, allowing some imports and exports. This flow of imports and exports complicates both supply and demand, and directly affects domestic incomes and prices.

International Trade Concepts

1. **Free Trade**: When restrictions, quotas, and tariffs are removed, and all goods and services can flow between countries without restriction, in an open competitive market.

2. **Comparative Advantage**: Assuming free trade, this principle states that the entire world's standard of living will be increased, if each nation specializes in producing those goods and services for which it has the lowest cost of production.

3. **Balance of Payments**: A record of all transactions of the citizens of one nation with another, or with all other countries. Compare with *Balance of Trade*, which is different!

4. **Balance of Trade**: A record of the merchandise (goods, but not services) transferred between one nation and another, or with all other nations. An unfavorable balance of trade means that imported goods exceed exported goods. A favorable balance of trade means exports exceed imports.

5. **Rate of Exchange**: The rate or price at which the currency of one nation can be converted into the currency of another. Example: dollars for pounds, euros, or yen. A "strong dollar" means that a dollar buys more of a foreign currency. A "weak dollar" means that a dollar buys less foreign currency. A weakness in one currency means an automatic strength in another currency. If the dollar is down, the yen is up, and so on.

International Trade: Is Self-Sufficiency Better?

International trade between countries has an important impact on the domestic economies. The flow of imports and exports directly affects domestic incomes and prices.

Some people believe that a nation is better off economically if it can become self-sufficient, by producing all of its own goods and services. However, economic theory states that a nation that attempts to be self-sufficient will cost its citizens higher prices than if the nation had entered into free-trade agreements with other nations. Example: The climate of Costa Rica is ideal for growing coffee, whereas the United States has the resources and capacity to produce computer software. If the United States wishes to become self-sufficient and grow its own coffee, it can do so only by creating massive hothouses at tremendous cost. This in turn will drive up the price of coffee for U.S. citizens. In the process, resources will be drawn away from the production of computer software, reducing output and raising the price of computer software. Therefore, it makes more sense for Costa Rica to concentrate on coffee and the United States to concentrate on computer software and for each to trade. The result will be higher quality coffee and computer software, at lower prices, for *both* Americans and Costa Ricans.

The theory of free trade makes economic sense, but political and other forces within nations tend to restrict international trade, in an effort to protect special interest groups. Here are two examples: (1) The oil-producing export countries (OPEC) form cartels to regulate the production of oil and boost oil prices, and (2) the United States establishes tariffs and quotas to protect some domestic industries, such as sugar, from foreign competition. This prevents U.S. citizens from purchasing foreign imports at the lowest prices. If free trade were allowed, the price of all goods and services would be lower. Will low-priced foreign goods cause some Americans to lose their jobs? Yes, in the short run, inefficient American companies and their employees will be displaced, as low-priced foreign goods displace higher priced domestic goods. However, in time and/or with training, the locally displaced resources would flow into industries in which America has a comparative advantage, and these industries will expand and absorb the displaced resources. It is the *change* that causes the backlash!

Some people support self-sufficiency, on the grounds that national defense requires a country that is able to stand alone, and not depend on other countries for vital products. Other people counter this argument by stating that no nation can become truly self-sufficient in all products, and that any attempt to do so would result in an inefficient and weak national defense.

In today's world, the reality is that each country attempts to maximize its own welfare, by cooperating with other nations on some occasions and not cooperating at other times. The result is an international economy that is constantly in flux, as political and economic events cause alliances to shift. This in turn causes national economies to shake and roll, as international events unfold. These unfolding international events cause national and local real estate markets to feel the impact.

For example, the lower value of the dollar versus other foreign currencies should attract many foreign investors to what seem to them to be bargain prices for U.S. real estate. This investment by foreigners stimulates the U.S. real estate market, driving up prices and adding to U.S. profits and commissions.

Question:	What should happen to this process when the value of the dollar rises?
Answer:	Investments by foreigners should slow down, because prices of U.S. real estate will appear too high in other currencies. This is because the foreign investor must put up excessive amounts of foreign currency to convert to the high-valued dollars needed to purchase U.S. real estate.

The result should be a drop in demand and a drop in real estate prices, profits, and commissions.

The Economic Theory Sounds Good, But ...

Thus far, this chapter has stressed the interaction of supply and demand in perfectly competitive markets and in a pure capitalistic system. But the real world is not so simple. Most of the markets in the United States are somewhat imperfect, either because of trade restrictions or because the buyer or the seller is in a superior position and can influence price and output. The automatic corrections that take place in a perfectly competitive market do not always work in imperfect markets. Furthermore, the U.S. mixed capitalistic system grants a role to the government that also disturbs the pure capitalistic concept of supply and demand.

Nevertheless, the study of a "perfect" system creates an understanding of the basic mechanics of capitalism. Especially important is to understand how markets set prices and volumes. Even in an imperfect market, supply and demand are still varying, and influencing prices. Although the United States has imperfect markets and some government control of resources, it must be stressed that the main economic philosophy in the United States is still capitalism. Individuals do have the right to own property, run businesses, compete, and earn profits. But these rights are not absolute: The principles of pure capitalism have been modified to reflect social as well as private rights. This point is discussed in the next chapter, which examines the role of the government in the economy.

REVIEWING YOUR UNDERSTANDING

Markets and Prices

1. In the short run, if supply stays the same but demand decreases, what will happen to price? In the long run, to the amount supplied?

2. If the demand remains the same but supply increases, what will happen to price? To the amount supplied?

3. If the main industry in your town goes out of business, what short-term effect will this have on the price of homes?

CHAPTER SUMMARY

Economics is a social science that examines how people use and allocate scarce resources. There are several ways of solving the three central problems of *what* will be produced, *how* it will be produced, and *for whom* it will be produced. A capitalistic economy leaves the decisions to private individuals, operating in competitive markets. Command or socialistic systems look toward government for the decision making. The United States operates under a mixed capitalistic system, using a verifying mix of government and private enterprise to make economic decisions.

All economies need four elements, known collectively as the *factors of production*, in order to produce goods and services: land, labor, capital, and entrepreneurship. In a capitalistic economy, these factors are privately owned and must be paid for in order to be used. The payment for land is called *rent*, for labor it is called *wages*, for capital it is called *interest*, and for entrepreneurship it is called *profit*. When rent, wages, interest, and profits are received, they are called *income*. Income is earned by individuals when they sell the factors of production. The earned income is then spent to purchase the goods and services that are produced by these same factors of production. Thus, the U.S. economy has a circular flow, of which imports and exports from international trade are a part.

The prices paid in a competitive economy are determined in markets, through the interaction of supply and demand. *Demand* is the total quantity that buyers are willing to purchase at a given set of prices, in a particular market, at a particular time. *The law of demand* states that the lower the price, the more consumers will buy; the higher the price, the less they will buy.

Supply is the total quantity that sellers are willing to sell in a particular market, at a particular time, at given prices. The *law of supply* states that producers will offer more products for sale as prices increase, and fewer as prices decrease. The law of supply is based on the profit motive.

It is the interaction of supply and demand that determines the prices paid and the quantity produced, in a competitive economy. Certain influences can cause either supply or demand to change. When this occurs, prices and output also change. Understanding how market changes will influence price and output is essential for real estate investors!

REVIEWING YOUR UNDERSTANDING

1. A social science concerned with how people produce, distribute, and consume goods and services is:
   A. history
   B. economics
   C. geography
   D. political science

2. Famous capitalist who wrote *The Wealth of Nations*:
   A. Karl Marx
   B. John Stuart Mill
   C. Thomas Jefferson
   D. Adam Smith

3. The major economic decisions are made by a government committee, but minor economic decisions are left to private individuals. This describes:
   A. pure socialism
   B. mixed socialism
   C. mixed capitalism
   D. pure capitalism

4. All of the following are principles of pure capitalism, *except*:
   A. private property
   B. laissez-faire
   C. public ownership of basic resources
   D. open and competitive markets for goods and services

5. The payment for entrepreneurship is called:
   A. profit
   B. wages
   C. interest
   D. rent

6. In the circular flow of the U.S. economy, individuals go to the resource markets as sellers and to the product and services markets as buyers.
   A. true
   B. false

7. According to the *law of demand*, the higher the price of homes, the more likely it is that:
   A. the number of homes built will increase
   B. people will buy new homes
   C. the number of home sales will decline
   D. the number of homes built will decline

8. In a purely competitive real estate market, if demand by renters for apartments increases, while the number of apartment units available for rent remains the same, apartment rents should:
   A. increase
   B. decrease
   C. remain in equilibrium
   D. become static

9. Under pure capitalism, goods and services are produced primarily for people who:
   A. need them
   B. desire them
   C. wish for them
   D. effectively demand them

10. In international trade, the price that the currency of one nation brings in terms of the currency of another nation is known as:
    A. balance of payments
    B. rate of exchange
    C. balance of trade
    D. principle of comparative advantage

11. "No free lunch" is best explained by the concept of:
    A. diminishing returns
    B. opportunity costs
    C. highest and best use
    D. excess demand

12. Solutions to economic problems may be:
    A. influenced by value judgments
    B. considered an absolutely precise answer
    C. reproduced uniformly with computers in a lab
    D. uniformly considered correct by all citizens

13. If individuals and societies make economic choices based on the way things have always been done, the economy is considered:
    A. communistic
    B. capitalistic
    C. socialistic
    D. traditional

14. According to the theory of pure capitalism, how goods and services are produced is determined by:
    A. buyer's demand
    B. the lowest possible production cost
    C. who has the most money to spend
    D. government committees

15. Which economist predicted that capitalism was doomed to fail, because profit motivation would lower wages to a subsistence level, leading workers to overthrow the capitalistic system?
    A. Karl Marx
    B. John Stuart Mill
    C. John Maynard Keynes
    D. Adam Smith

16. A command economy is commonly called:
    A. traditionalism
    B. capitalism
    C. socialism
    D. opportunism

17. Regarding the circular flow of the economy, which of the following is true?
    A. Individuals and households sell goods and services and receive income.
    B. Business supplies resources and receives wages.
    C. The product market is where the factors of production are exchanged.
    D. In the resource market, land, labor, capital, and business skills are exchanged for income.

18. A place in which buyers and sellers meet to bargain and exchange items of value at negotiated prices is called:
    A. a market
    B. an economy
    C. gross domestic product
    D. derived demand

19. A change or shift in supply is caused by a change in:
A. the cost of the factors of production
B. population
C. consumer tastes
D. the amount of advertising

20. In a given real estate market, if the demand for commercial office space declines and the supply of office space also declines at the same ratio, market rent per square foot should:
A. increase
B. decrease
C. remain the same
D. shift to the right

21. That point at which supply and demand are matched at a price that will clear the market is called:
A. open
B. equilibrium
C. comparative advantage
D. surplus

22. The total quantity that buyers are willing to buy at a given time at certain prices is called:
A. supply
B. demand
C. equilibrium
D. perfect competition

23. A summary of all transactions between the citizens of one nation and the citizens of all other countries is called:
A. free trade
B. rate of exchange
C. balance of trade
D. balance of payments

24. In the short run, the lower the value of the U.S. dollar versus the Japanese yen, the:
A. more attractive are American products for the Japanese
B. less likely Japanese investors will buy U.S. real estate
C. more likely U.S. citizens will purchase Japanese products
D. more likely the price of U.S. exports will rise in the Japanese market

25. Economic theory states that the United States can become self-sufficient, with no need for international trade, if the United States is willing to:
A. drive up the price of domestic consumer goods and services
B. limit the economic choices of U.S. citizens
C. cancel all trade agreements
D. do all of the above

CASE & POINT

Adam Smith, Economic Philosopher

Adam Smith was born in 1723 in the town of Kirkcaldy, on the east coast of Scotland. His father, a lawyer, died before his birth. His mother, a local woman named Margaret Douglas, had married Adam Smith's father in 1720.

After attending the local school, Adam Smith entered the University of Glasgow in 1737, at the age of 14. Unlike today's standards, entering college at 12–14 years of age was quite common in the 1700s. While studying at the university, Smith was greatly influenced by Francis Hutcheson, a professor of moral philosophy. This influence would be reflected in Smith's future literary works. After completing his studies at the university, Smith studied for six more years at Balliol College in Oxford, England.

When his studies at Oxford were completed, Smith returned to Scotland, where a few years later, he began to give a series of public lectures on rhetoric, civil law, and what was called belles-lettres. These lectures were well attended, and Smith began to gain fame. In 1751, at the age of 27, Smith was appointed professor of moral philosophy at the University of Glasgow, the position previously held by his mentor, Hutcheson, who had retired several years earlier.

Smith remained at the University of Glasgow for 12 years, during which he wrote the first of his books, *The Theory of Moral Sentiments* (1759). In this book, Smith presented a theory on why people behave ethically. The book was an instant success, giving Smith fame not only in Scotland but also throughout Europe.

In 1764, Smith was enticed to resign from the University of Glasgow, to tutor the young Duke of Buccleuch while they went on a grand tour of Europe. The tour lasted until 1766, during which Smith spent time in Paris and became friends with many famous people, such as Voltaire, Dupont de Nemours, and Francis Quesnay, the famous French economist. In addition, one of Smith's closest friends in Scotland was the famous philosopher, David Hume.

Upon completing this grand tour in 1766, Smith returned to his hometown of Kirkcaldy and began writing his most famous book, *An Inquiry into the Nature and Causes of the Wealth of Nations.* Smith lived in Kirkcaldy until *The Wealth of Nations* was published in 1776. The book's main thesis was that the economic system common in Britain and Europe at the time, called mercantilism, which stressed the need to store up wealth in the government treasury, was doomed to fail and that a better economic system was needed. Smith then went on to outline what we now consider some of the basic principles of a capitalistic system. Much of Smith's material was not original, but his ability to organize and explain the working of a capitalistic economy was outstanding for that time. Like his earlier work, *The Wealth of Nations* became an immediate bestseller, giving Smith even more fame during his lifetime.

In 1777, Smith moved to Edinburgh to become the Commissioner of Customs and Salt Duties for Scotland. This government position assured Smith of a lifetime job, while he issued updated editions of his famous works.

Smith never married, although he is reputed to have fallen in love several times. He became ill and died July 17, 1790, and is buried in Canongate churchyard, Edinburgh. Unfortunately for the world, on his deathbed, he instructed his friends to destroy his volumes of working papers. Today, there is very little of Smith's original work for scholars to view. His gravestone reads:

> Here
> are deposited
> the remains of
> ADAM SMITH
> author
> of the
> Theory of Moral Sentiments
> and
> Wealth of Nations
> &cc &cc &cc
> He was born, 5th June, 1723
> And he died, 17th July, 1790.

On the next pages are photographs of Adam Smith landmarks in Scotland.

Bust in Adam Smith Theater, Kircaldy, Scotland.

Plaque marking the site where Adam Smith lived while writing The Wealth of Nations, *from 1766 to 1776, Kirkcaldy, Scotland.*

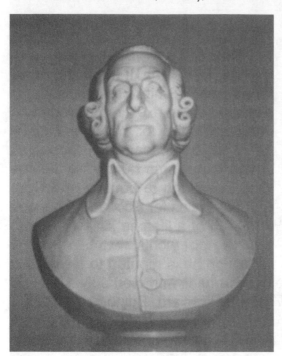

Present use of the site where Smith lived while writing The Wealth of Nations *from 1766 to 1776, Kirkcaldy, Scotland.*

House where Adam Smith lived at the time of his death in 1790, Edinburgh, Scotland.

Adam Smith's grave at Canongate Church, Edinburgh, Scotland.

Epitaph on Adam Smith's gravestone, Canongate Church, Edinburgh, Scotland.

Chapter

3

Asset bubble

Automatic stabilizers

Balance of payments

Balance of trade

Business cycles

Cyclical
   unemployment

Depression

Discretionary
   income

Disposable personal
   income

Employment data

Fiscal policy

Gross domestic
   product (GDP)

Imperfect markets

Lagging indicators

Leading indicators

Long-term secular
   trends

Monetary policy

Personal income

Real GDP

Recession

Seasonal
   fluctuations

Structural
   unemployment

Unemployment rate

PREVIEW

This chapter summarizes the role played by government in the U.S. economy. Section 3.1 explains the major reasons why the government has joined with business and consumers as a full partner in the operation of the economy. Section 3.2 shows how economists measure the performance of the economy, using national income accounting, employment and other data, and the impact of foreign investment. Section 3.3 explores changes in business activity, the business and real estate cycles, and the purpose of economic forecasts. Section 3.4 introduces fiscal and monetary policy, which

Government's Role in the Economy

are tools used by the government to fight the ills of inflation, recession, and unemployment. The Case & Point at the end of the chapter discusses the *Laffer Curve*.

When you have completed this chapter, you will be able to:

1. Discuss why the government's role in the U.S. economy has been expanding.
2. Define *gross domestic product* and label the phases of a *business cycle*.
3. Describe the types of national real estate cycles.
4. Define and explain the two main tools used by the government to fight economic problems.

3.1 THE REAL WORLD OF MARKETS AND GOVERNMENT

The pure capitalism of Adam Smith, which was discussed in the previous chapter, is not the capitalism that exists in the United States or in any other country. Instead, some form of mixed economy is common, part capitalism and part socialism. There are many reasons for this, as noted in the prior chapter.

To repeat, one major reason is that pure capitalism provides no protections for the old or weak. Only charitable organizations are there to help them, and they can only do so much. Indeed, even in a pure capitalistic system, we still need police and the courts, to protect us from criminals.

A second major reason is that pure capitalism works best with perfect markets, those that are fully competitive. Many of the resources in the United States are manufactured and sold in *imperfect markets*.

Imperfect markets arise when a group of buyers or sellers is able to directly influence the price or output of a good or service. This control may be in the form of an exclusive patent, ownership of a scarce commodity, or control of a transportation route. Control or dominance of a market may also be obtained through extensive advertising or by other means.

A seller or small group of sellers who can eliminate or dominate competitors can manipulate the market for that product and generate abnormally high profits. On the other hand, when a buyer or small group of buyers can manipulate a market, profits may be driven so low that sellers fail to realize any return on their investments.

Government Intervention in the Economy

Government spending, regulatory agencies, welfare programs, zoning, planning, and environmental constraints are a few examples of current government intervention in economic affairs, explored further in Section 3.4. Chapter 4 explores government intervention in the money and credit markets. The chapters in Part Three expand the related topics of taxation, land-use controls, and required government reports.

Some of the reasons given by those who favor taxation and regulations, to justify why the government should become a full partner in the operations of the U.S. economy, are:

1. Capitalism has a tendency to create imperfect markets; if they remain unchecked, a misallocation of resources can occur. Government intervention is needed to assure a reasonable degree

---

Special Interest Topic

Types of Imperfect Markets

Monopoly—A market in which there is only one seller.

Oligopoly—A market in which there are only a few sellers.

Monopolistic competition—A market in which a large number of sellers compete, but through advertising and promotion, each attempts to convince consumers that one brand is better than another. If successful, the seller then can charge a slightly higher price for his or her product.

Monopsony—A market in which there is only one buyer.

Oligopsony—A market in which there are only a few buyers.

of competition, to prevent one economic group from dominating others.

2. Terrorist threats and international peacekeeping require that the government controls some economic resources and personnel for dcfcnse needs.

3. We the people have agreed on standard social goals for our society. Most of these goals include care for those who are unable to adequately provide for themselves: the aged, the infirm, and the disadvantaged. Perfect markets do not allocate any resources at all toward these goals. If the government is to achieve these social goals, it needs more economic resources, or other controls.

4. Citizens want the government to reduce economic instability. They want the government to fight inflation, recession, and unemployment. To do this, the government needs some control over the economy.

5. Finally, some observers note that more and more voters are turning to the government for services once provided by private enterprise or charitable organizations. Examples range from medical care to product testing. To provide such services, the government must expand its economic activity.

On the other hand, those who oppose more regulation believe that the market is more efficient at allocating resources to good use, than government politicians and bureaucrats. They cite numerous unnecessary costs imposed on business by government regulations. If these wasted resources could be dirccted toward business expansion, more economic growth and jobs could be created. The pros and cons of government regulation are still another example of an economic topic that is deeply rooted in political philosophy.

Again, some suggest it simply is trying to find a good balance between an efficient and vibrant economy, and the social goals that the voters want. It is very important for real estate agents, appraisers, lenders, and investors to monitor these changes. Regulation and taxation can have a significant impact on real estate values, so markets can change quite rapidly, in anticipation of regulatory or tax changes.

How Government Economic Intervention Changed

The early years of our country featured a relatively unregulated capitalistic economy. Nearly all businesses were very small! Over time, businesses grew larger. In the 1890s, to help balance the growing problems created by imperfect markets, the U.S. government passed antitrust legislation, and created regulatory agencies to enforce the new laws. The Sherman Antitrust Act, passed in 1890, forbade businesses from forming combinations, or making agreements, that restricted competition between businesses. The Interstate Commerce Commission, created in 1897, regulated the practices of any monopolistic sellers of products that were moved from one state to another, or sold in more than one state (*interstate commerce*). The general trend from the 1890s to the 1970s was for increased government regulation over business activities.

Beginning in the 1980s, some deregulation occurred, to reverse what many felt had become too strong a government role. Some argued that overly tight government regulations put a damper on businesses' ability to expand output and create jobs. The airline, trucking, and other transportation industries were somewhat deregulated, as were many areas of the banking industry. In the 1990s, government regulations once again began to increase, for example, in the controversial areas of gun control and increased regulation of the banking and savings and loan industry.

The trend then reversed in 2000, and there were a series of major deregulatory steps, primarily in banking and financial industries. Unfortunately, in hindsight, the deregulatory movement may have gone too far. The result was a wave of excessively risky financial transactions, which resulted in the financial crisis of 2007, the collapse of Wall Street, and the collapse of real estate values during 2007–2010.

It seems clear that modern markets need limits, or serious abuses will result. The Savings and Loan Crisis of the late 1980s and the mortgage and financial crises of the late 2000s should be convincing evidence. The question, then, is what level or type of regulation or control is needed. This is a heavily debated issue, both politically and economically.

Special Interest Topic
Early Monopolistic Markets

Early American monopolies included water wheels, then the barge canals, followed by the railroads. One of the largest monopolies was John D. Rockefeller's Standard Oil Company, founded in 1870. By 1900, it dominated nearly all aspects of the oil industry. It was attacked as a monopoly. After years of litigation, it was broken into 34 independent companies in 1911, by order of the U.S. Supreme Court.

Flow of the Economy—The Government Included

Figure 3.1 takes the prior illustration of the flow of the economy, and adds the government. It is important to understand how the government participates with individuals and businesses, in the flow of money, goods, and services.

In Figure 3.1, note that individuals and households pay taxes to the government, and in return receive government services. Businesses also pay taxes, and receive government services. To provide the needed government services that are demanded by individuals and businesses, the government must purchase factors of production from the resource market and goods and services from the product market. The money for these purchases comes mainly from the taxes paid by households and businesses (plus government borrowing, fines, and fees). Students should look at Figure 3.1 as showing a continuous flow of money and goods, an economic system that is always moving and always changing.

REVIEWING YOUR UNDERSTANDING

1. How does a monopoly differ from pure competition? Why are most monopolies regulated by the government?

2. If most real estate brokers charge the same commission rate, does that mean that real estate brokers do not compete on price? How do real estate brokers compete?

3. Why does the government intervene in the economy? Does politics play a role?

4. If the government increases taxes, what impact will this have on the flow of the economy?

3.2 MEASURING THE PERFORMANCE OF THE ECONOMY

Just as a mechanic measures the condition of an automobile by checking various factors, the economist uses a number of tools to check the condition of the economy. When all the reports are in, the economist, like the mechanic, recommends any needed repairs. However, economists may differ about what to do to bring the economy back to good working order. As pointed out earlier, economics is not an exact science, and economic decisions frequently carry political overtones.

Local real estate markets are heavily influenced by economic changes in the immediate area. However, local economies are in

FIGURE 3.1   Simplified flow of the economy showing government's role.

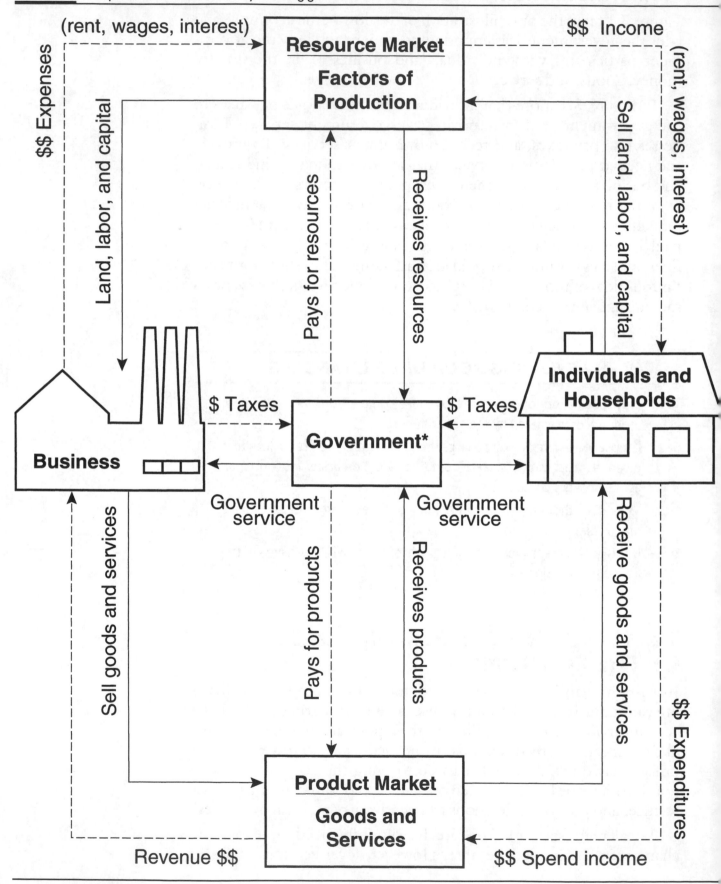

turn influenced by the general trend of the national economy. Understanding the causes of changes in the national economy helps people to understand what impact these national changes have on local communities, local real estate markets, and individual properties.

National Income Accounting

One way to measure the national economy is to compare the output and income that was generated in one year to that of past years. To do this, economists have developed several measurements, including the measurement called *gross domestic product*, frequently referred to as *GDP*. It is defined as *the total market value of all goods and services produced domestically in the United States during a given time*, usually in one year. Most countries, states, or regions also calculate their GDP.

If you add up the final retail price of all goods and services that are produced in a year, the total dollar amount would be the GDP. The calculation of gross domestic product does not consider whether the business producing the goods and services is foreign or domestically owned. If the goods and services were produced in the United States, they count toward GDP. **Gross domestic product** is compiled by the U.S. Department of Commerce and is reported on a monthly and annual basis. When comparing GDP in one year with past years, one must be sure whether the figures have been adjusted to omit the distortion of inflation. For example, if the GDP increases by 2 percent but prices have inflated by 6 percent, the real GDP has decreased by 4 percent. GDP adjusted for inflation is commonly called **real GDP**.

Special Interest Topic
What Ever Happened to GNP?

Well, it got pulled off the field, and replaced by *GDP*. GNP stands for *Gross National Product*, and it measures almost the same elements of the economy as GDP. The difference is that GNP starts with the GDP number, *adds* income earned by citizens working in another country, and *subtracts* income earned by citizens of other countries working in the country being measured. So, we could say that GDP measures the output of a region, while GNP measures the output of the *citizens* of a region. As a measure of the economic activity of the region, GDP is now accepted as the better measure.

The Details Behind the GDP Totals

The gross domestic product of the United States is acquired by consumers, business, government, and foreign markets. Goods and services purchased by consumers are called *personal consumption expenditures*. Business buying is called *gross private domestic investment*. Government purchasing of GDP, simply called *government*, includes federal, state, and local government buying.

Other nations also purchase a portion of our GDP, which is called *exports*. The United States, in turn, purchases a portion of the GDP of foreign nations, and this is called *imports*. If the United States exports more than it imports, foreigners have purchased more GDP from us than we have purchased from them. This net amount is called *net exports*.

In recent years, the U.S. purchase of imports has exceeded the sale of exports, so GDP showed a minus balance in this category. With the ongoing controversy regarding foreign trade, it should be noted that net imports or exports only represent a small percentage of GDP. Table 3.1 shows the breakdown of GDP for selected years.

Note that *net exports* only include goods and services. It does *not* include the effects of investment dollar flows. When analyzing how exports of goods and services compare with imports, we call it the **balance of trade**. This is an important number, because it shows how competitive a country's exports are! In the long run, however, exports and imports tend to balance, or else the purchasing power of the country's currency will shift to re-price exports and bring the two into balance.

In the short run, the purchasing power of a currency reflects not just the balance of trade (exports and imports), but also the effects of investment dollar flows. When investment dollar flows are combined

TABLE 3.1   GDP Expenditures (billions)

Gross Domestic Product—Current Dollars	1990	2000	2008
Total	5,803.1	9,817.0	14,264.6
Components:			
Personal Consumption Expenditures	3,839.9	6,739.4	10,057.9
Gross Private Domestic Investment	861.0	1,735.5	1,993.5
Government Purchases of Goods and Services	1,180.2	1,721.6	2,882.4
Net Exports	−78.0	−379.5	−669.2

Source: U.S. Department of Commerce, Bureau of Economic Analysis, www.bea.gov

with the balance of trade, we see the *total* flow of money in and out of a country. This is called the **balance of payments**.

Looking at the components of GDP, as we have just done, is not the only desirable step. We also need to consider what effect inflation is having on the numbers! As shown in Table 3.1, GDP increased between 1990 and 2008. This table shows the figures in *current* dollars, that is, without adjustment for inflation. When adjusted for inflation, however, the increase is less than what the raw figures indicate.

If real GDP increases, the national economy is growing, and optimism and spending are adding to prosperity. However, it should also be noted that increases in real GDP measure only the total growth in physical output and income. They do not measure the quality of life or the equality of the distribution of output and income. They also do not show if the GDP per *person* increased or declined. GDP per person is called *GDP per capita*. Table 3.2 shows real GDP and real GDP per capita for the same time periods. More recent data is readily available from the Department of Commerce, Bureau of Economic Analysis, at www.bea.gov.

Other Income Measurements

In an effort to study the performance of the economy in detail, economists have devised many other measurements. A few of the most important measurements for real estate purposes are personal income, disposable personal income, and discretionary income.

Personal income is the total income earned by all individuals, after business taxes have been paid, but before personal taxes are paid.

Disposable personal income is personal income after the payment of personal taxes. It is often called *take-home pay*. Disposable personal income is watched closely, because it is an important measure of consumer purchasing power for all basic needs, including housing. If take-home pay increases faster than the rate of inflation, consumers may have more money to spend on various items, including housing.

Discretionary income is the amount of money that people have after paying for necessities. Payments for basic housing, food,

TABLE 3.2 GDP in 2000 Dollars (Adjusted for Inflation)

	1990	2000	2008
GDP (Billions)	7,112.5	9,817.0	11,652.0
GDP per Capita (Dollars)	28,429	34,761	38,262

clothing, and transportation are subtracted from disposable personal income, leaving income that can be spent any way people wish.

An increase in discretionary income means that society is becoming more affluent, and that people are in a position to spend more on luxuries. The successful operation of travel and leisure facilities, such as restaurants, theaters, motels, vacation homes, health clubs, and tourist attractions, is tied to adequate levels of discretionary income.

However, a key issue with discretionary income is this: do consumers choose to spend it, or save it? Spending it increases demand for goods and services, which helps employment and the economy. However, savings decline. This means less money for a cushion in sickness or retirement, and less money available to be loaned out as capital, which means interest rates go up. Figure 3.2 shows how the personal savings rate as a percent of income has varied since 1960. The steep decline since 1980 has meant that the United States has turned more to other countries for capital. It has also meant that we have consumed more of our income, since we have saved less. Notice the sharp increase in the savings rate, starting in about 2008. This increase was a result of the financial concerns that many of us had during the Fall of 2007 financial panic. But this increase in savings, while desirable, reduced consumption, slowing the economy! Figure 3.2 is from the Federal Reserve Bank of Saint Louis, which maintains an excellent and relatively easy to use economic data bank, known as *FRED*, at http://research.stlouisfed.org/fred2/.

FIGURE 3.2   Person savings rate.

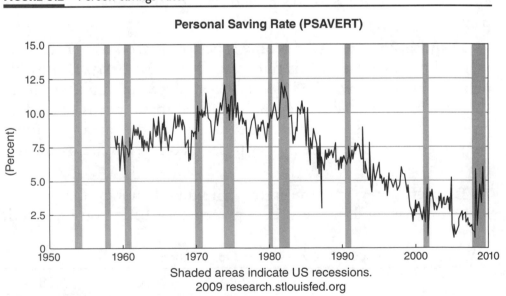

Source: U.S. Department of Commerce: Bureau of Economic Analysis

Another Issue With GDP
What About Unpaid Economic Activity?

Nearly always, GNP calculations exclude unpaid economic activity. The Wikipedia.com entry for *GDP* notes that "a paid nanny's income contributes to GDP, but an unpaid parent's time spent caring for children does not, even though they are both carrying out the same economic activity." Volunteer labor, a significant source of labor for many non-profit organizations in the United States, also does not get counted! Goods that people make and donate are also not counted.

So, two countries might have the same GDP per capita, but one country has a long-standing tradition of volunteerism. Clearly, the well-being of the population of that country will show the impact of the volunteer labor.

Keeping Up with National Income

Changes in GDP, personal income, disposable personal income, and discretionary income are important issues for real estate appraisers, agents, and investors. An increase in personal disposable income could mean that consumers are better able to qualify for mortgage loans, or that tenants can afford higher rent levels.

An increase in discretionary income could mean that raw recreational land might be more in demand and that tourist-oriented real estate, such as ski facilities, could be developed. Increases in real GDP mean that industrial and commercial properties will be in demand as business activities expand. And all changes in the various income categories must be reviewed with the rate of inflation in mind. Inflation is effectively reducing the impact of any increases in income.

Information about these changes can be found online at Web sites noted here, as well as in such publications as *Business Week* or *The Wall Street Journal*.

The Importance of Employment Data

In addition to monitoring various categories of income, economists study data on employment and unemployment. The analysis does not just count the *numbers* that are employed and unemployed. Data are collected on those who are working less hours than desired, those who want work but have at the time stopped looking, the number of workers by industry and by job title, and the hours worked per week.

Two Interesting Controversies

Does GDP really stand for gross domestic pollution?

Environmentalists point out that any economic growth represented by an increase in GDP does not take into consideration the increased pollution caused by the manufacturing of more goods. They argue that a really good measure of our standard of living should consider the quality of life, not just material possessions. At least two dilemmas arise: How to increase the GDP without increasing pollution, and how to measure the quality of life. Clearly, we would prefer to increase GDP while decreasing or not increasing pollution!

Does an increase in GDP mean more goods and services per person?

What matters more: GDP or GDP per person? The advocates of zero population growth argue that if real GDP remains the same while population declines, the standard of living per person will rise rapidly, with a minimum increase in environmental damage. Looking at the equation below, what will happen if real GDP increases, but the U.S. population increases at a faster rate?

$$\frac{\text{Real GDP}}{\text{Population}} = \begin{array}{l}\text{Goods and}\\\text{services}\\\text{per capita}\\\text{(standard}\\\text{of living)}\end{array}$$

There are several reasons why employment data is especially important. First, much of this data is available every month, and some of it is issued, on a preliminary basis, within a few weeks after the end of the month. As a result, employment data is often the most recent, and is watched closely for signs of economic change. Second, employment levels respond quickly to changes in economic activity. And third, a count of the number of jobs does not get distorted by inflation, as many other economic measures do.

Figure 3.3 displays the civilian *unemployment rate*, which is a closely watched economic indicator. The data is collected by the U.S. Department of Labor, Bureau of Labor Statistics (www.bls.gov). The unemployment rate is a percent of the *civilian work force*. It excludes people who have become discouraged and stopped looking for work (currently about 3.6 percent of those counted in the workforce).

FIGURE 3.3   Civilian unemployment rate.

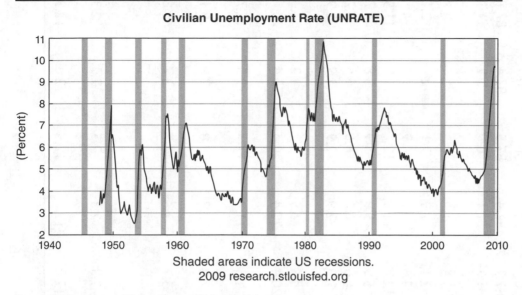

Shaded areas indicate US recessions.
2009 research.stlouisfed.org

Source: U.S. Department of Labor: Bureau of Labor Statistics

The most striking characteristic of the unemployment rate is how much it varies. U.S. recessions are shown on Figure 3.3 as shaded vertical bars. As we should expect, the unemployment increases during a recession. Typically, the unemployment rate drops very gradually after a recession, reaches its low point just before the next recession starts, and then climbs rapidly.

However, notice how low the unemployment rate was in the 1950s, and how high it was in the 1980s. Clearly then, there are a lot of complex issues at work.

Other Economic Data

Nearly any economic activity that you can think of is monitored: data is collected, tables and graphs created, and pages of analysis written! Construction, for example, is one economic activity that is monitored closely, because it varies relatively quickly. Table 3.3 shows the value added by industry as a *percent* of GDP, from 2000 to 2008. The construction category was at its low point in 2008, reflecting the real estate collapse, and its highest during the boom years of 2005 and 2006. In dollars, adjusted for inflation, the construction category fell from a high of $646 Billion in 2006 to $581 Billion in 2008. It is also notable how much manufacturing declined, as a percent of GDP, over the time period shown.

TABLE 3.3   Gross Domestic Product by Industry

Gross-Domestic-Product-by-Industry Accounts
Value Added by Industry as a Percentage of Gross Domestic Product
[Percent]
Release date: April 28, 2009

		2000	2001	2002	2003	2004	2005	2006	2007	2008
1	Gross domestic product	100	100	100	100	100	100	100	100	100
2	Private industries	87.7	87.6	87.2	87.1	87.2	87.4	87.5	87.4	87.1
3	Agriculture, forestry, fishing, and hunting	1	1	0.9	1	1.2	1.1	0.9	1.2	1.1
6	Mining	1.2	1.2	1	1.3	1.5	1.8	2	2	2.3
10	Utilities	1.9	2	2	2	2.1	1.9	2.1	2	2.1
11	Construction	4.4	4.6	4.6	4.5	4.6	4.9	4.9	4.4	4.1
12	Manufacturing	14.5	13.2	12.9	12.4	12.2	11.9	12	11.7	11.5
34	Wholesale trade	6	6	5.9	5.8	5.9	5.8	5.9	5.8	5.7
35	Retail trade	6.7	6.8	6.9	6.9	6.6	6.6	6.6	6.5	6.2
36	Transportation and warehousing	3.1	2.9	2.9	2.9	2.9	2.9	2.9	2.9	2.9
45	Information	4.7	4.7	4.6	4.5	4.5	4.5	4.2	4.2	4.4
50	Finance, insurance, real estate, rental, and leasing	19.7	20.3	20.5	20.5	20.4	20.4	20.4	20.4	20
59	Professional and business services	11.6	11.5	11.4	11.4	11.5	11.8	11.9	12.3	12.7
68	Educational services, health care, and social assistance	6.9	7.3	7.6	7.8	7.8	7.8	7.8	7.9	8.1
74	Arts, entertainment, recreation, accommodation, and food services	3.6	3.6	3.6	3.6	3.7	3.6	3.7	3.7	3.8
81	Other services, except government	2.3	2.4	2.4	2.4	2.3	2.3	2.3	2.3	2.3
82	Government	12.3	12.4	12.8	12.9	12.8	12.6	12.5	12.6	12.9

FIGURE 3.4 New housing units started in the United States.

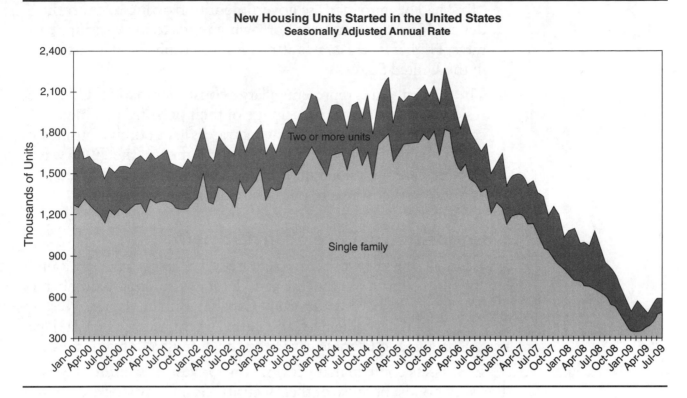

Housing starts are also watched, because the data is available every month, and quickly reflects economic changes. Figure 3.4 shows monthly new housing starts, both single family and two-plus units, from 2000 to July 2009. The monthly variation is quite noticeable, as is the huge drop since the peak in April 2006. Notice that this peak was well before the financial meltdown in the Fall of 2007. What lesson should economic observers draw from this?

Foreign Ownership of U.S. Businesses and Real Estate

The amount of foreign ownership of U.S. businesses, real estate, and other assets increases and decreases over the years. Some reasons are:

1. The flight of capital out of countries that are facing political instability, declining during periods of relative calm.

2. The decline in value of the dollar relative to other currencies in some years, followed by a stronger dollar in other years. If the dollar is declining, U.S. prices to foreigners appear to be a bargain. If the dollar is rising, the opposite is true.

3. Politically, the U.S. Congress and the president have, for the most part, been unwilling to face the reality of the budget deficit, by

cutting government spending or raising taxes. The easy short-run "fix" had been to increase government borrowing to cover the deficit. Heavy government borrowing tends to increase interest rates. Higher interest rates attract foreign capital and investment in the United States.

4. The United States represents a large consumer market. U.S. residents spend a large percentage of their personal income: consumption is high and the savings rate is low. Foreign businesses wish to gain a foothold in this large consumer market. One way is to increase the shipment of foreign products to the United States. Another way is to purchase existing U.S. businesses.

Composition of Foreign Investment

Investors all over the world have acquired U.S. assets since the founding of the country. Within the last decade, the largest number of foreign investors have come from Canada, Britain, Japan, Western Europe, Asia, the Middle East, and Latin America. In California, Japanese, Koreans, and Chinese have been the dominant foreign investors.

U.S. assets come in many form. Some investors want to buy U.S. Treasury bonds, because of their security. Some buy stocks or bonds issued by U.S. companies, simply as investors seeking good returns. Some seek to buy U.S. businesses, to combine with their business in another country. And others buy U.S. real estate as investments.

The ability to move funds from country to country varies over time. Some countries only allow citizens of that country to own real estate. Some countries do not allow *any* private ownership of real estate. And, from time to time, countries have frozen bank accounts, or have forbidden transfer of money out of the country. All of this makes the U.S. an investment haven, because of the relative ease of making investments and moving money, and the relatively low risk of arbitrary government seizure.

Not only does the volume of investment flows between countries vary over time, the type of asset that is purchased also varies. In recent years, the Chinese government, companies, and investors have purchased large amounts of Treasury notes and bonds. More recently, there has been an increase in stock and bond buying, as they get familiar with American financial instruments and markets. Real estate purchases have been limited. Japanese were once major real estate investors, but recently we have seen increasing investment in U.S. manufacturing facilities.

There is very poor data on the total ownership of U.S. real estate by citizens or businesses headquartered in other countries. Some good studies of agricultural land exist, but little else. Part of the problem is defining where money comes from, because capital can be moved from one country to another relatively easily. It is also difficult to separate flows of money that are simply payments for goods imported or exported from money that is being invested in assets.

With all the publicity regarding foreign ownership of U.S. businesses, it should be pointed out that Americans also have been buying the assets of other countries for many decades. The flow of international investments works to connect available funds with available investment opportunities. In turn, this helps the world economy to be more efficient and to prosper.

3.3 CHANGES IN ECONOMIC ACTIVITY

GDP does not stay the same, from month to month, or year to year. These changes are very important, because they usually impact real estate values. Some changes cause major real estate problems, as in 2007–2009. Since the Great Depression of the 1930s, real GDP has generally been on the rise, although this upward movement has not been constant. The up-and-down movement in economic activity results from either a seasonal fluctuation, a business cycle, or a long-term secular trend.

Seasonal fluctuations are short-term changes in business and economic activity that occur within the year, resulting from either weather or custom. For example, housing construction declines in the winter months, retail sales increase for back-to-school and at Christmas time, and travel increases in the summer.

Business cycles are the recurrent expansions and contractions in general business activity that take place over a period ranging from three to six years.

Long-term secular trends refer to economic changes that occur over an extended period of time, perhaps 50 years or more. Some examples of secular trends include a reduction in family size, a shorter work week, an increase in per capita income, and an increase in spending on recreation.

As real estate agents, appraisers, and investors observe the economic changes around them, it is important to try to consider if the change is seasonal, cyclical, or secular. If a person acquires real estate in a community that has severe seasonal changes, he or she must be prepared to support the investment when vacancies rise in the off-season. Apartments in college-dominated communities must generate enough income in nine months to help offset the loss of income in the summer recess. Ski resorts must generate enough extra income during the winter and spring to pay necessary expenses during the summer and fall.

Cyclical changes are especially important for a real estate investment. Business cycles refer to the economic activity changes that occur over a three to six-year period (see Figure 3.5). Business cycles cause changes in employment, income, output, and prices. All of these have a significant influence on the success of a real estate investment. For real estate, vacancy ratios, operating expenses, and rental rates are closely tied to changes in employment, income, and prices. Thus, in buying investment real estate, the results over the first few years will be very different if bought at an economic peak, versus buying in the trough of a recession.

Long-term secular changes or trends are also important for real estate purposes. The time span of secular trends can run 50 or more years. Secular changes will be the major influence on long-term value changes. In addition, there appear to be long-term real estate cycles, discussed below.

The Phases of the Business Cycle

The business cycle swings from a peak of economic activity down to a trough or bottom, as shown in Figure 3.5. From the trough to the peak is defined as the *expansion phase*, as the economic activity is expanding or increasing. During this phase, employment and incomes are rising. At the peak is the most prosperous time, but also the most common time for inflationary pressures to rise.

From the peak down to the trough, or bottom, is defined as the *recession phase*, and most economic activity levels are receding. Employment and incomes are declining, and inflationary pressure usually

FIGURE 3.5   The phases of the business cycle.

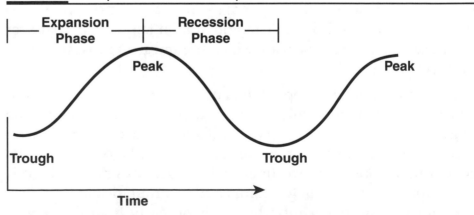

declines as well. The usual definition of a recession is at least two months of decline in GDP.

Business cycles vary in length, in how rapidly the economy improves or declines, and in how high the peak goes or how low the trough. The higher the trough, the greater is the risk of inflation. Residential home markets demonstrated this in the 2003–2006 time period. But higher peaks usually are followed by deeper troughs, as with home markets in 2007–2009. A shallow trough is called a **recession**, and a deep trough is called a **depression**.

The peaks and troughs of the business cycle in the United States are, by custom, determined by the National Bureau of Economic Research (NBER), a private non-profit research organization (www.nber.org). Usually, the exact dates cannot be determined until some months later, when all of the economic data have been collected and analyzed.

Often, the cycle is commonly viewed as having *four* phases: prosperity, the decline, the bottom, and the recovery. However, the technical standard that is used by NBER is the two phases as shown in Figure 3.5.

Causes of Business Cycles

There are many theories about the cause of business cycles. Although economists are continually debating the merits of each theory, most agree that no single factor is the sole cause of business cycles. Instead, cycles are caused by a combination of the factors listed below, and the combination or "mix" varies with each swing in business activity.

Business cycles can be caused by the following:

1. War and other international conflicts.
2. *The introduction of innovations that create new industries.* Examples include radio in the 1920s, television in the 1950s, computers in the 1960s, electronics in the 1980s, digital technology in the 1990s, and biotechnology in the 2000s.
3. *Erratic spending patterns of consumers, businesses, and government.* There is a tendency for consumers, businesses, and government each to have periods of spending, followed by periods of saving. This causes irregular supply and demand patterns.
4. *Changes in the amount of money and credit in circulation.* When money is plentiful and interest rates are low, spending tends to increase. When money is scarce and interest rates are high, spending tends to decline. Interest rates are heavily influenced by

government fiscal and monetary policies, discussed in Section 3.4. Most economists believe that incorrect monetary policy causes some business cycles.

5. *The psychological frame of mind of businesspeople and consumers.* If people are optimistic about the future, investment and spending will usually occur. If people should become more pessimistic, caution will prevail and business activity declines.

Real Estate Cycles

If we have national business cycles, do we also have national *real estate cycles?* Does real estate activity move through phases of prosperity, recession (or depression), and recovery? Real estate markets clearly do have their ups and downs; however, the patterns are irregular.

A review of U.S. economic history shows that until the 1940s, real estate construction activity fluctuated severely, experiencing great booms and deep depressions. On the average, these cycles took approximately 18 years to move through expansion and recession. This 18-year cycle is known as the *long real estate cycle*.

For the years since the 1940s, economists have not been certain as to clear signs of this long real estate cycle. However, they have identified another, much shorter real estate cycle that takes perhaps three to six years to move through all four phases. This newer cycle and its ups and downs is called the *short real estate cycle*.

There are also real estate trends to be considered. *Long-run trends* in real estate activity appear to be influenced by gradual changes in population, age distribution, marriage rates, income levels, construction costs, taxes, and transportation patterns. One of the more significant long-run changes is the large drop in births during the Great Depression (1929–1940), followed by the very large increase from 1945 to about 1955: the "Baby boom." As the years pass, the large group gets older, and its demand for real estate changes. Now, the "boomers" are facing retirement. How will that affect real estate?

Short-run changes in real estate markets are heavily influenced by the availability and cost of mortgage money and the current state of the national and local economy. Most real estate purchases require the use of borrowed funds. If these funds are available at reasonable interest rates, real estate activity increases. If the interest rates increase, real estate activity declines. Most drops in housing construction since World War II are partly due to the availability and cost of mortgage money. In addition, in order to qualify for a real estate loan, people must have jobs and businesses must have profits. If the national or local economy is in a recession, with high unemployment, the demand for real estate loans will decline.

During periods of high real estate activity, prices tend to rise for most categories of real estate. Demand is increasing, and it takes time to develop new real estate, to meet the increased demand. However, there have been times when prices of some categories of real estate escalate dramatically. This happened with home prices in the late 1980s, and again in the early 2000s, for example.

When this happens, instead of demand declining as one expects, demand can increase! This seems to be because people rush to buy while they still can afford it! And some buy property as investments, anticipating *further* price increases. Such a rush to buy creates what is called an **asset bubble**. Real estate asset bubbles are an important topic that we will explore later. They appear to be related to the long real estate cycle in some manner.

Increasingly, it appears that the old long real estate cycle is not dead. There is no definite answer, and economists are still debating the question. It is obvious that national real estate activity since 1945 has been closely tied to changes in the mortgage market and employment trends. More details on this important topic can be found in Chapter 4, "Money, Credit, and Real Estate."

Using Economic Indicators

There might be as many as 10,000 different economic indicators! Which ones should we be aware of? Indeed, why do they matter to people working as real estate agents, appraisers, loan brokers, or investors?

There are many reasons why these indicators matter. The first is simply for the information that one can get. Imagine that you are an appraiser who has been requested to appraise a five-unit apartment, in a more remote suburb of Los Angeles. You check your sales data sources, and find no sales. Is this because none are selling, or this is the only one in town? This difference is important, because it will affect what you report, and how you do the appraisal. The first reason suggests the buyers and sellers disagree on price, so prices are likely to move, either up or down. The second reason—it is the only one in town—means that you will need to widen your data search and will have clear justification to do so. A check with the local building department, or with the County Assessor's Office, should give you a good idea of the number of five-unit apartments in that suburb. The *change* in the number is not important here, the *number* is.

The second reason why economic indicators matter is signs of economic change. Imagine that you are a broker or an appraiser, looking at a parcel of vacant land, zoned for offices. Is this parcel likely to be sold for immediate development, or sold to a speculator, to hold until conditions improve? The answer is in knowing how much floor area of office space has been built recently, how that compares to past time periods, if office rents are increasing or declining, and how the office vacancy rate has changed over the past 12 or 24 months.

These examples have used very specific, local economic indicators, specific to a particular real estate problem. However, there are many other economic indicators that people in the real estate industry watch, because they help us understand the "big picture," the *macro-economic* view. Nearly always, it is change that we are looking for, or trying to understand.

Remember that it takes time to collect, analyze, and publish all economic indicators. Therefore, they always reflect change that has already happened. But it is even worse than that! Some economic indicators tend to lag behind an economic change, such as the business cycle. These are known as **lagging indicators**. An example is the unemployment rate. It continues to rise, for 2 or 3 quarters after the economy starts to improve.

Some other economic indicators do not lag economic change, but rather tend to change earlier. These are called **leading indicators**, and are closely watched for clues to future economic change. A private, non-profit group, The Conference Board (www.conference-board.org) publishes the *Leading Economic Index*. It combines data on ten leading indicators.

The Index is not perfect. It has forecast recessions that did not happen. And the time period between when the index signals a recession and the actual economic downturn varies a lot. Nevertheless, the Index is one of the best single indicators of the direction of the economy.

Forecasting Changes in Economic Activity

What a person does today is greatly influenced by what he or she thinks will occur tomorrow. People's decision to purchase real estate today is influenced by what they feel will happen to rents and property values in the future. Indeed, one common definition of *market value* is "the present worth of future benefits." Future benefits, whether non-financial ones or financial ones, are key!

Economic forecasting helps us to reduce the inherent uncertainty in our decision making. If investors can anticipate the direction of economic change, they will have a better idea of what lies ahead. Then they can decide whether they should take steps to protect their real estate investments from a shortage in income or an increase in expenses. In addition, economic forecasting can help investors decide whether now is the time to take on a new investment opportunity.

Economic forecasting is an art, not a science. It is impossible to predict the future with accuracy. Nevertheless, educated guesses are possible and are almost always better than blind plunges. Real estate students are encouraged to follow forecasts that are published by government agencies, financial institutions, economic research companies, and major universities. The regional Federal Reserve Banks are also good sources. One can contact any of these institutions for monthly economic newsletters, or access the information online.

A good collection of data of many types is the Statistical Abstract of the U.S., online at www.census.gov/compendia/statab/. Another, even broader collection, with links to many data sources, is at www.oswego.edu/~economic/data.htm.

REVIEWING YOUR UNDERSTANDING

1. If you knew that in the next five years, the economy would experience prosperity with rapid inflation, would you invest in real estate today, or would you wait for a couple of years? Why?

2. Assuming fixed interest rate loans, does unanticipated inflation benefit mortgage borrowers or mortgage lenders?

3. What influences long-run trends in real estate activity? Short-run trends?

3.4 GOVERNMENT TOOLS TO FIGHT ECONOMIC PROBLEMS

One of the primary responsibilities of the federal government is to maintain economic stability, by limiting adverse effects from unemployment, inflation, and recession. This section discusses the major tools that the federal government uses to fight declines in GDP and economic activity: fiscal and monetary policy. The same tools can be used to fight inflation, caused by excessive spending.

Fiscal Policy

Fiscal policy is the government's use of *taxing and spending* power to help counteract recession, unemployment, and inflation. When the economy is in a recession, an increase in government spending for goods and services increases the demand for land, labor, capital, and business skills. This generates more income for individuals, in the form of rents, wages, interest, and business profits. Some of this added personal income will be saved, but much will be spent in the marketplace. This increase in individual spending should stimulate economic activity.

In addition to increased government spending, the economy can be stimulated if the government cuts taxes. A general tax cut will give consumers more disposable income and give businesses more after-tax profits. Some of this additional income and profit will be spent, thereby stimulating economic activity.

Increased government spending to fight recession should not be financed by an increase in taxes, because a tax increase would reduce private income, at the very time an increase in spending is needed. Instead, the government frequently finances additional spending by going into debt. When government spending exceeds government income, it is called *deficit spending*. This tends to stimulate the economy.

However, when the U.S. economy is producing at full capacity and employment is high, it is in the prosperity phase of the business cycle. If consumers, business, and government continue to spend, pushing demand beyond the economy's ability to supply, then prices will rise, causing inflation.

Inflation is harmful, because it drives up prices without increasing output. The uncertainty about price changes causes business and consumers to act hastily and to become dismayed, discouraged, and confused. This eventually causes major disruptions in all segments of the economy. The government can fight inflation, by cutting back on government spending or by increasing taxes. Either step will reduce disposable income, which will reduce demand, thereby reducing the pressure on prices. The combination of reduced government spending and increased taxes can create a situation in which government income exceeds government spending, resulting in a *budget surplus*. This tends to slow down the economy.

One problem with using fiscal policy is that it usually requires an act of Congress to change tax rates, or to authorize an increase in government spending. This takes time, as a bill must be drafted, introduced, and sent to committee; committee hearings held; then floor debates, followed by the same process in the other house of Congress! Another problem is that politics can get in the way, turning good economic policy into a mess. Amendments to the bill can earmark spending that isn't needed, even to the degree that others vote to kill the entire bill.

A third problem is the difficulty funding a deficit when the economy is weak, which requires a borrowing. Or, not letting government spending grow excessively, when the economy is strong. This problem, in particular, appears to be growing.

A fourth problem is that use of the fiscal policy—changes in government spending and/or taxation—is very slow to cause economic change. A tax rate change will take several months to impact consumer spending at all. Changes in government spending can work faster, however. The "Cash for Clunkers" program in 2009 impacted auto sales immediately, and increased auto production within two months.

The "Cash for Clunkers" program in fact is an example of one of the good features of fiscal policy. Government spending can be designed to benefit a specific troubled industry, occupation, or region. In that sense, fiscal policy is a very flexible and adaptable economic tool. Note, however, that this tool can be used for political ends, instead of benefit to the economy. Some have argued that using corn to make ethanol as a replacement for gasoline was just that: a political payoff to the farm states, rather than a wise economic decision.

Monetary Policy

Either in addition to or instead of using fiscal policy, the government can use *monetary policy* to counteract recession, unemployment, or inflation. The government uses monetary policy when it *increases or decreases the supply of money* in an effort to stabilize the economy.

During periods of recession, the government may increase the supply of money, which in the short run should lower interest rates and increase the availability of credit. With easier and less-expensive credit, the government hopes that consumers and businesses will borrow for expenditures and business expansion. This could generate employment and help fight the recession.

However, in the long run, continued expansion of the money supply will eventually cause inflation! Remember that expansion of the money supply acts to increase demand. As demand continues to increase, it runs into limits on supply, causing prices to increase. This price inflation, or the fear of it, also causes lenders to increase interest rates, to offset the loss in value of their capital due to inflation.

On the other hand, during periods of inflation, the government can use monetary policy to curb spending, by reducing the supply of money and credit. A reduction in the supply of money will usually drive up interest rates. High interest rates discourage borrowing and make it more expensive, which in turn will reduce spending. As spending declines, the pressure is taken off prices, and inflation should recede.

Monetary policy is carried out by a government agency called the Federal Reserve Board. Chapter 4 is devoted to explaining the Federal Reserve System, how it controls the supply of money, and its effects on the real estate industry.

THEORIES AND THEORETICIANS

John Maynard Keynes (1883–1946)

From the Warren J. Samuels Portrait Collection, Duke University.

John Maynard Keynes, a British economist, is considered the founder of the "new economics." Keynes published his *General Theory of Employment, Interest, and Money* in 1936 and instantly started the "Keynesian Revolution."

Prior to Keynes, traditional economic theory held that there was a natural tendency for the economy to stabilize at full employment. Any unemployment would only be temporary, since the economy would soon adjust itself to a full employment balance. The Great Depression of 1929 challenged this.

Keynes's work pointed out that, contrary to traditional theory, the economy could reach a balance at *less* than full employment. Unless steps were taken by the government to stimulate the economy, the unemployment would become permanent. Thus, Keynes shocked traditional capitalists, by advocating the need for government intervention into private economic affairs, in order to preserve the capitalist system. Economists are still debating whether Keynesian theory is relevant in today's globalized, market-driven economy.

In his private life, Keynes was a successful and shrewd business investor. He is reported to have made over $2 million (in 1930 dollars!) by speculating in bonds and international currency, devoting one-half hour of his time, before breakfast, to these private business ventures.

Milton Friedman—Free Market Giant (1912–2006)

University of Chicago

Milton Friedman, formerly of the University of Chicago, was one of America's foremost economists of the 20th Century. A Nobel Prize winner in economics (1976), Friedman was a free market advocate, who believed that government's role should be limited to maintaining an environment where competition and free choice are allowed to flourish. His influence upon governments around the world was profound.

In Friedman's view, the free market is the most efficient allocator of social and economic well-being. Friedman stressed that the common person has fared much better throughout history under capitalism, than under any communist, socialist, or fascist regime.

Friedman was a monetarist, that is, he believed that the money supply is a prime determinant of economic stability, and that the Federal Reserve Board has caused chaos by constantly attempting to adjust the supply of money. He believed that a steady increase of the money supply, at a rate equal to the real growth of GDP, was the best way to wring out any inflationary pressure and maintain a stable economy.

The Theory Sounds Good, but There Are Some Problems

In theory, using either or both fiscal and monetary policy can fine-tune the economy, to prevent recession and inflation. However, in the real world, fiscal and monetary tools run into some problems. Most of these problems fall into two broad categories: political and structural.

Both fiscal and monetary policies are enacted by the government. The governmental process is essentially *political*, because governmental representatives must be elected. Critics point out that either Congress, the president, or both will often delay appropriate *fiscal* measures that conflict with current political realities. In times of high prosperity, for example, fiscal theory suggests that taxes be increased and government spending be cut, to create a budget surplus to help pay off previous budget deficits. But if an election is coming up, these actions may be delayed, for fear that higher taxes or cutting someone's favorite government program might prove unpopular at the polls. In fact, in prosperous times, government spending commonly is increased, as people believe that "we can afford to spend more!" Thus, budget deficits tend not to be reduced, but rather increased, even during a booming economy.

Moreover, the *monetary policy* of the Federal Reserve Board is not immune to political pressure, despite its theoretical independence. (See Chapter 4.) The Federal Reserve Board is a creature of Congress and, realistically, can be abolished or altered by an act of Congress. Thus, for better or worse, economics frequently must give way to politics.

The second major problem is *structural*. Neither fiscal nor monetary policies can be changed very rapidly. As discussed earlier, fiscal policy must be enacted by Congress and approved by the president. The legislative process is long and drawn out. By the time the policy is enacted, it is sometimes too late to be effective.

Monetary policy can be changed more quickly, because the Federal Reserve Board does not have to contend with congressional red tape. But monetary change, once enacted, takes time to work its way into the economy. Indeed, it may be six months or more before changes in the money supply start to influence economic decisions.

Automatic Stabilizers

Our economic system has some built-in **automatic stabilizers** that tend to dampen large swings in the business cycle, without waiting for governmental action. Two prime examples are the progressive income tax and unemployment insurance. During periods of prosperity, the total amount of income taxes that people pay rises at a faster percent than the increase in wages, because people's rising income is putting some of them in a higher tax bracket, and because the standard deduction stays the same. This slightly reduces the ability to spend, while building up a surplus of money for the government. Also, during prosperity, contributions to the unemployment insurance program increase, while unemployment claims fall, creating a larger surplus in that fund, a reserve.

When the business cycle is heading for a recession, the process reverses itself. As your income declines, the amount of income tax you pay drops by a larger percent, leaving you with proportionately more money to spend. Also, those left unemployed by the recession can obtain money by filing unemployment claims, drawing down the reserves in the unemployment fund.

Both of these processes apply economic forces that are opposite to the business cycle and are called *automatic stabilizers*, because they work without requiring any direct government action.

Special Interest Topic

Stagflation: Inflation During Recession

Traditional fiscal and monetary tools were designed to fight economic problems, such as rising prices and overemployment during periods of excessive prosperity, and declining prices and unemployment during periods of recession. But in the 1970s, a new economic phenomenon was identified—inflation during recession—and the term *stagflation* was coined to label it.

How do you fight stagflation? If you attempt to fight recession by increasing spending, you add to inflation. If you attempt to fight inflation by reducing spending, you prolong the recession. Stagflation disappeared in the 1980s, but economists are debating whether stagflation will return.

The Measurement Problems

Before Congress, the president, or the Federal Reserve Board decides to help the economy, each must have reliable evidence that help is needed. For example, they watch for any changes in the **unemployment rate**.

The government uses two surveys to estimate the unemployment rate. A monthly survey, called the *Household Survey*, asks a large statistical sample of *individuals* two main questions: (1) Are you employed? (2) If not, are you looking for work? From this, the government calculates and publishes an unemployment rate. But another monthly survey, called the *Payroll Survey*, asks *businesses* one main question: How many people work for you? From this, an employment rate is calculated and published. The two surveys do not always give the exact same picture. In economic recoveries, the Household Survey usually shows more employment than the Payroll Survey, because the Payroll Survey initially misses new business starts, and a faster recovery in the self-employed market. But as the recovery phase of the business cycle turns to the prosperity phase, the two surveys tend to join ranks.

Other measures of the economy have similar flaws. Thus, even if Congress, the president, and/or the Federal Reserve Board are prepared to act when the economy needs help, they may not get a clear signal *soon* enough to quickly stabilize the situation.

But even when the unemployment rate clearly is changing, the necessary action may not be clear. Is the increased unemployment *cyclical* or *structural*? **Cyclical unemployment** is caused when the economy slips into a recession and jobs are lost because of this slowdown. Once the business cycle recovers, the jobs are regained. **Structural unemployment** occurs when there are some fundamental changes in the economy that are not related to the normal ebb and surge of the business cycle. Recent examples include the elimination of defense jobs attributable to the end of the cold war, cuts in employment because of technological innovations, and certain U.S. jobs made obsolete by foreign competition resulting from globalization of the economy. Structural unemployment does not recover as the economy grows. Thus, structurally unemployed workers must shift to tomorrow's new jobs or run the risk of being chronically unemployed.

A further problem is in defining which economic problems are undesirable, and to be resisted. Increasing *unemployment* has been considered bad for many years. *Inflation* was not accepted as bad until the mid-1970s, when the economy was suffering after almost a decade of inflation. In recent years, inflation was by far the major concern. But *asset bubbles* were of concern only to economists, until the major real estate asset bubbles of the 2000s collapsed. It is not yet at all clear that asset bubbles have definitely been added to the list of economic changes to be resisted by government action!

REVIEWING YOUR UNDERSTANDING

Use fiscal and monetary tools to answer the following:

1. If the economy is in a recession, should the government increase or decrease taxes? Government spending? Money supply?

2. When should the government have deficit spending? Why? Should the government ever have a budget surplus (take in more taxes than it spends)? If so, when?

CHAPTER SUMMARY

Today, the government is deeply involved in private economic affairs. Imperfect competition, international conflicts, social goals, and a desire to maintain economic stability are some of the reasons why the government has become a full partner in the operations of the U.S. economy.

Economists have tools to measure the state of the economy. The most common measurement is gross domestic product (GDP), which measures the total value of goods and services produced domestically in a year. Other measurements include personal income, disposable personal income, and discretionary income. These measurements may be on a total or per capita basis. Any measurement in money may be in current dollars, or in real dollars, adjusted for inflation.

The GDP does not stay level, or change at a constant rate, but rather changes in irregular up-and-down movements. These fluctuations in economic activity are either seasonal, cyclical, or long-term secular changes. Most attention centers on business cycles. To date, no single theory is universally accepted as explaining the causes of business cycles.

In addition to business cycles, there are real estate cycles, which can be classified as either long or short. Since the 1940s, the short real estate cycle, caused by changes in the availability and cost of mortgage credit and in current business conditions, has been the most obvious. It is important for real estate appraisers, agents, and investors to understand business and real estate cycles and to forecast their swings, because these cycles give a better idea of what lies in the future. Appraisers can then reflect this understanding in their analysis. Agents can better advise clients. And investors can then decide whether they should take steps to protect their investments.

Fiscal and monetary policies are the tools that the government uses to fight the problems of inflation, unemployment, and recession. Fiscal policy means the use of government spending and taxation to counteract economic ills. Monetary policy refers to changes in the supply of money to encourage or discourage consumer spending and business investments.

REVIEWING YOUR UNDERSTANDING

1. A market in which there are only a few sellers is called a(n):

   A. monopoly

   B. oligopoly

   C. monopsony

   D. oligopsony

2. In the flow of the economy, government needs to generate money to pay for the benefits that society demands from government. Government raises revenue by all of the following *except*:

   A. borrowing

   B. taxes

   C. fees

   D. labor

3. The total market value of all goods and services domestically produced in the U.S. economy in a given year is called:

   A. gross domestic product

   B. personal consumption expenditures

   C. net export

   D. gross private domestic investment

4. The slope downward from the peak of a business cycle is called:

   A. depression

   B. recovery

   C. recession

   D. prosperity

5. Which of the following best describes a cause in the increase of foreign ownership of U.S. assets?
   A. very high value of the dollar
   B. disorganized U.S. consumer markets
   C. reduction in the U.S. budget deficit
   D. flight of capital seeking a safe haven

6. In the short run, real estate cycles tend to be most influenced by changes in:
   A. mortgage interest rates
   B. death rates
   C. age brackets
   D. cost of construction

7. The government's use of spending and taxing as a tool to control swings in the business cycle is called:
   A. automatic stabilizers
   B. fiscal policy
   C. monetary policy
   D. foreign policy

8. The government's use of money, credit, and interest rates as a tool to control swings in the business cycle is called:
   A. automatic stabilizers
   B. fiscal policy
   C. monetary policy
   D. foreign policy

9. During times of recession, the government can attempt to stimulate the economy by:
   A. decreasing government spending
   B. increasing taxes
   C. increasing interest rates
   D. increasing the supply of money

10. During times of rapid inflationary prosperity, the government can attempt to slow down the economy by:
    A. increasing government spending
    B. decreasing taxes
    C. decreasing interest rates
    D. decreasing the supply of money

11. A market consisting of a single buyer is called a:
    A. monopoly
    B. monopsony
    C. oligopsony
    D. oligopoly

12. Which of the following is a reason given to justify government intervention in private economic affairs?
    A. capitalism has a tendency to create imperfect markets
    B. citizens consistently vote for fewer government programs
    C. the market is the most efficient allocator of resources
    D. international peacekeeping is no longer needed

13. According to the circular flow of the economy, government:
    A. provides land, labor, and capital
    B. taxes businesses and households
    C. generates profits
    D. provides a vast array of consumer products

14. In measuring GDP, net exports refer to:
    A. foreign currency
    B. balance of payments
    C. comparative advantage
    D. balance of exports and imports

15. Real GDP is GDP adjusted for:
    A. taxes
    B. government expenditures
    C. inflation
    D. unemployment

16. After-tax income (take-home pay) is called:
    A. personal income
    B. disposable personal income
    C. discretionary income
    D. taxable income

17. Fluctuations in economic activity, usually running from peak to peak in two to six years, are called:
    A. seasonal fluctuations
    B. secular trends
    C. business cycles
    D. GDP deflator

18. Unanticipated inflation tends to benefit buyers/borrowers:
    A. who wait to purchase real estate
    B. who acquire bonds
    C. with fixed interest rate loans
    D. with adjustable rate loans

19. According to fiscal theory, a tax decrease should:
    A. increase private spending
    B. decrease private savings
    C. fight inflation
    D. create unemployment

20. A famous economist, considered to be the founder of "new economics," who advocated using government fiscal policy to offset unemployment:
    A. Adam Smith
    B. Milton Friedman
    C. John Stuart Mill
    D. John Maynard Keynes

21. In the short run, a reduction in the supply of money should increase:
    A. taxes
    B. government spending
    C. interest rates
    D. real estate construction rates

22. When government revenues exceed government spending, there should be a budget:
    A. deficit
    B. balance
    C. decline
    D. surplus

23. The type of unemployment that recovers as the economy recovers is called:
    A. cyclical
    B. structural
    C. chronic
    D. stifled

24. Progressive income taxes and unemployment benefits are examples of the use of:
    A. monetary policy
    B. pure capitalistic theory
    C. automatic stabilizers
    D. Federal Reserve policies

25. Fiscal and monetary policies run into problems because of structural difficulties, measurement problems, and:
    A. uniform applications
    B. political difficulties
    C. computer difficulties
    D. contractual applications

CASE & POINT

Laffer Curve

Economists continually debate what government taxation policy should be. However, economist Arthur Laffer points out that there is no economic theory, be it conservative or liberal, that states that a tax increase will stimulate the economy. Instead, economists appear to agree that tax increases slow down the economy. According to Laffer's research, history indicates that total tax revenue as a percentage of GDP is relatively constant, regardless of the level of tax rates.

Lowering tax rates at first glance should lead to lower government revenues. However, lower tax rates do stimulate business activity, and also encourage more people to report income. This increases government tax revenue and makes up for the revenue lost because of lower tax rates, Laffer points out.

On the other hand, higher tax rates at first glance should increase government revenue. However, higher tax rates depress business activity, and also cause more people to hide income, seek tax shelters, or substitute non-tax leisure for taxable work, Laffer contends. This decreases tax revenue and offsets the increases the government hoped to collect when it enacted the higher tax rates. Therefore, regardless of the tax rate level, government tax revenue tends to remain somewhat constant. This is illustrated in Figure 3.6, the Laffer Curve.

FIGURE 3.6   The Laffer Curve.

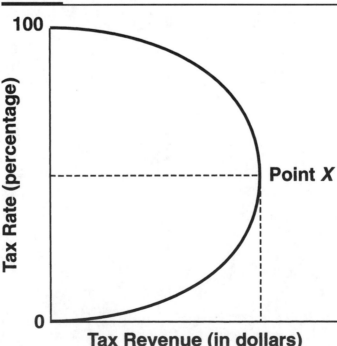

CASE & POINT

0% tax rate = No tax revenue
100% tax rate = No tax revenue
Point X is where tax rates should be set to maximize tax revenue.

At a 0 percent tax rate, Laffer notes, government will receive no tax revenue at all, as no one will need to pay taxes. At the other extreme, at a 100 percent tax rate, government again will not receive any tax revenue, as no one would work just to pay taxes. At some point, where the curve reaches its apex (point X), that tax rate will produce the maximum government revenue. Unfortunately, no one knows where that point is!

Many proponents of the Laffer Curve theory believe that historically tax rates were set too high, not at the most efficient point. Therefore, if the government lowered tax rates, government revenue would rise. They have argued that this is the best way to attack the government budget deficit. This lead to substantial reductions in estate, income, and capital gains taxes during the 1990–2008 time period. The argument then turned to the question of whether the reductions had reduced taxes to *below* the optimum point of maximum revenue.

Chapter

4

Counter-party risk

Deflation

Demand deposits

Depository institution

Discount rate

Disintermediation

Easy-money policy

Federal funds rate

Federal Open Market Committee

Federal Reserve System

Fractional reserve banking

Inflation

Measure of value

Medium of exchange

Open-market operations

Prime rate

Reserve requirements

Secondary markets

Standard of deferred payment

Store of value

Tight-money policy

PREVIEW

Money and credit have a critical effect on real estate activity. This chapter expands the previous explanation of economic principles and the role of the government, by examining money's role in economic transactions. Section 4.1 discusses the functions of money and how it is created. It also examines how the money supply interacts with inflation, and its impact on real estate markets. Section 4.2 reviews the way that the Federal Reserve System controls the money supply, in an effort to maintain economic growth and full employment, without inflation. Section 4.3 emphasizes the impact that changes in the money supply have on real estate activity. Section 4.4 explores how financial

Money, Credit, and Real Estate

markets and the Federal Reserve responded to the financial panic of 2007–2008. The Case & Point at the end of the chapter discusses the savings and loan (S&L) crisis of the 1980s and its successor, the mortgage securities collapse of 2007. When you have finished this chapter, you will be able to:

1. Explain what money is, and describe how banks and other depository institutions create money.
2. Understand the purpose of the Federal Reserve System, and describe three main tools it uses to regulate the flow of money and credit.
3. Discuss the impact that Federal Reserve policies have on real estate activity.

Understanding money and credit will allow agents, appraisers, investors, and others to understand the relationship between current real estate market conditions and shifts in the money supply. In turn, that improves the ability to anticipate changes in real estate markets.

4.1 THE SUPPLY OF MONEY

There is more to making money than just inking the printing presses. Most money in America is not in coins or bills! Instead, most of the money supply is created by banks and other depository institutions, in the form of demand deposits. This section explains the uses of money, the different types of money, and how money is created. Understanding the money supply, and how it is created, is an important tool for understanding real estate change. We start by looking at the general meaning of the word "money."

What is Money?

1. *Money is a* **medium of exchange**. It allows people to exchange goods and services, without the need to revert to a barter (or swap) system.

2. *Money is a* **measure of value**. It is used to measure or compare the worth of unlike items. What is a home worth in relation to an automobile? What are the services of a physician worth, as compared to the services of a plumber? Under a barter system, it might be said that 25 automobiles equal 1 home or 2 plumbers equal 1 doctor. Under the U.S. monetary system, each item is measured in dollars: an automobile, $20,000; a home, $500,000; a plumber, $80,000; a doctor, $160,000; and so on.

3. *Money is a* **store of value**. It is a way to store or save up wealth. If you choose not to buy goods and services immediately, you can store your right to spend, by saving money to spend later. But there are some risks. For example, what happens to your money during periods of inflation? Does it increase or decrease in value? The key is to understand what happens to its purchasing power!

4. *Money is a* **standard of deferred payment**. It is used to describe what a debtor owes a creditor. If you buy now and pay later, the amount that you owe is expressed in money.

What Makes "Good" Money?

Gold, silver, corn, cattle, and sea shells have been used as money at one time or another. Contrary to popular belief, money does not have to be a precious metal. In theory, anything that is universally accepted by a society can be used as money. In a practical sense, money should be *portable*, so it is easy to carry; *durable*, so it will not lose its value by wearing away; *divisible*, so it can be broken down into smaller units; and *stable*, so it will not radically change in value. This is the general meaning of the word "money." But money has a more specific meaning to economists, which is the meaning that we are interested in.

Money Today

Today, there are three types of money in the United States: *coins*, *paper currency*, and *checking accounts*. Pennies, nickels, dimes, quarters, half-dollars, and dollar coins make up the U.S. coin system. The metallic value of coins needs to be less than their face value. If the value of the metal should exceed the value of the coin, people would tend to hoard the coins and then illegally melt them down, and sell the metal.

Coins account for approximately 2 percent of the total value of the U.S. money supply.

Paper currency ($1, $5, $10, and other bills) makes up approximately 25 percent of the total value of the U.S. money supply. These bills, issued by the Federal Reserve, are essentially promissory notes. Federal Reserve notes circulate as money and will continue to do so, as long as people have faith in the strength of the government. Contrary to popular belief, U.S. paper money is no longer backed, dollar for dollar, by gold stored in Fort Knox, Kentucky. The only thing backing U.S. currency is the strength of the government.

The rest of the U.S. money supply, approximately 73 percent, consists of checks drawn against checking accounts—bank money. *In economic terms, checking accounts are called* **demand deposits**. When you write a check, you are transferring a portion of your bank deposit to a third party. The bank must pay this money upon demand. No time delays are allowed; hence, the term *demand deposit.*

Credit Cards Are Not Money

Money and credit cards are frequently used interchangeably by people, but economically, they are not the same. *Money* means currency and checks, a medium of exchange, or an assignment of assets from a buyer directly to a seller. *Credit cards*, on the other hand, consist of a loan. A credit card company issues what effectively is the same as a line of credit to a borrower, who then uses the line of credit to make a purchase. The business, which accepts the credit card, is paid by the credit card company for the goods and services given to the buyer. The credit card company then collects from the credit card user (buyer of the goods and services). Both money and credit cards are used to acquire goods and services, and this leads people to incorrectly think that money and credit cards economically are the same thing. They are not. Economists frequently refer to credit cards as "near money." On the other hand, bank *debit cards* are true money, in the sense the funds are deducted directly out of the user's checking account. The checking account funds are transferred directly (and almost immediately) from the buyer to the seller, so no loan is involved.

Depository Institutions Create Money

Only the federal government may legally mint coins and print paper currency, but a **depository institution**, such as commercial banks and savings banks, can legally create demand deposits or checks. At one time, only commercial banks could issue checks and create money. But the Depository Institutions Deregulation and Monetary Control Act of 1980, plus other laws, now allow various depository

Currency and Portraits

Denomination	Face	Highest Federal Office Held
$1	Washington	1st President (1789–1797)
$2	Jefferson	3rd President (1801–1809)
$5	Lincoln	16th President (1861–1865)
$10	Hamilton	Sec. of the Treasury (1789–1895)
$20	Jackson	7th President (1829–1837)
$50	Grant	18th President (1869–1877)
$100	Franklin	Ambassador (1776–1785)
$500*	McKinley	25th President (1897–1901)
$1,000*	Cleveland	22nd & 24th President (1885–1889) and (1893–1897)
$5,000*	Madison	4th President (1809–1817)
$10,000*	Chase	Chief Justice (1864–1873)

* Note that printing of these bills was discontinued in 1945.

What is a Depository Institution?

A depository institution is a company that is allowed by federal law to accept deposits, against which its customers are able to write checks. The institution is required to hold a percentage of its total deposits as reserves, and is allowed to loan the rest out. The primary types of depository institutions are listed below.

- Banks with a Federal Charter. Example: Bank of America.
- Banks with a state Charter, member of the Federal Reserve due to holding stock in the regional Federal Reserve Bank. Example: most medium-sized state banks.
- Banks with a state Charter, not Federal Reserve members. Example: most smaller local banks.
- Savings Banks. Example: most were former savings and loans.
- Credit Unions. Either state or Federal Chartered. A member-owned association.

An *insurance company*, such as MONY, is not classified as a depository institution. Its customers might deposit funds, but cannot write checks (except through an affiliated bank). The company can make loans using customer funds. However, the customer funds are not guaranteed by the U.S. Government.

An *investment bank*, such as Morgan Stanley, is not a depository institution. (It might also own a bank which is one!) Instead, investment banks buy and sell stocks and bonds and other investments, for their own account or for their customers. They also provide investment advice to companies and individuals. Investment banks can accept funds from consumers, and can make loans. However, again, customers cannot write checks against their funds, and their funds are not guaranteed by the U.S. Government.

institutions, namely, savings banks and credit unions to also issue checks and create money. For simplicity, all depository institutions will simply be referred to here as "banks." Figure 4.1 is a bar graph, showing the types of depository institutions that are insured by the

FIGURE 4.1   FDIC-insured U.S. commercial banks by bank charter type.

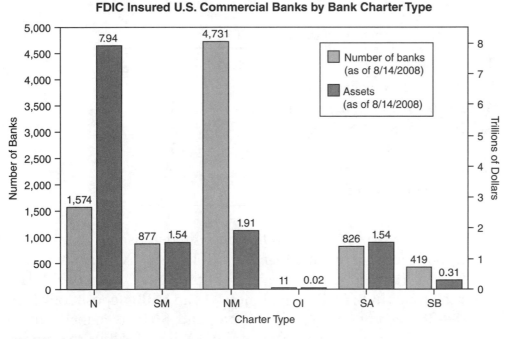

Legend:

N	Commercial banks with a federal charter
SM	State chartered banks, members of the Federal Reserve System
NM	State chartered banks, not members
OI	Insured U. S. Branch of a foreign-chartered institution
SA	Savings associations, state or federal charter
SB	Savings bank, state charter

Source: Federal Reserve.

Federal Deposit Insurance Corporation (FDIC), www.fdic.gov, a unit of the U.S. Treasury, and the number and assets of each type. This does not include the 8,101 Federal or State chartered credit unions, with $560 billion of assets, insured by an arm of the National Credit Union Administration, www.ncua.gov.

Banks create money because of a very important concept known as **fractional reserve banking**. Federal law requires that the bank must set aside a reserve for each deposit received. These reserves cannot be used to make loans, but rather assure that banks have some cash on hand (liquidity), and also give the Federal Reserve Board control over the money-creating ability of banks.

How Fractional Reserves Create Money

To see how banks actually create money, let us assume that federal law requires that 20 percent of each deposit in checking accounts must be kept as a reserve. The remaining 80 percent can be used by the bank to make a loan. (Actual reserve requirements are considerably less than 20 percent, and they vary with the size of the institution's deposits. They also are varied from time to time by the Federal Reserve to control the economy. Twenty percent is used here because it is easy to divide.)

Reserve Requirements as of January 1, 2009

Type of Liability	Reserve Percentage
Net transaction accounts:	
$0 to $10.3 million (M)	0
$10.3 + M to $44.4 M	3
$44.4 + M	10
Non-personal time deposits	0
Eurocurrency liabilities	0

Now let us assume that $1,000 is deposited in Bank A. Bank A will put $200 in its reserves, and loan out $800 to Mr. X. Mr. X will take the $800 and spend it. The receiver of this money will probably deposit the funds in Bank B. Bank B now has an $800 deposit, of which $160—20 percent—is kept in reserve, and $640 is loaned out to Ms. Y. Ms. Y spends the $640, and the receiver deposits the money in Bank C. Bank C now has a $640 deposit, of which $128 is kept in reserve and $512 is loaned out. In theory, this process continues on, until all funds are exhausted. Table 4.1 illustrates this process.

A single $1,000 bank deposit, under a 20 percent reserve requirement, can expand in this manner, to create $5,000 of total deposits,

TABLE 4.1 How Banks Create Money

Banks	Deposits	Reserves	Loans
Bank A	$1,000.00	$200.00	$800.00
Bank B	800.00	160.00	640.00
Bank C	640.00	128.00	512.00
Bank D	512.00	102.40	409.60
Bank E	409.60	81.92	327.68
All other banks together	1,638.40	327.68	1,310.72
Totals	$5,000.00	$1,000.00	$4,000.00

$4,000 of which is loaned out. In essence, the banking system has created additional purchasing power (demand deposits). This has exactly the same effect on spending as increasing the amount of coin and paper money.

In the real world, does this process that banks use to create money always occur at a constant, smooth rate? Not usually! Banks differ in their reserve policy (choose to hold more reserves than required by law), and the amount of loans available from each deposit varies among banks. In addition, "leakage" occurs whenever people fail to deposit money in banks. Going back to Table 4.1, what would happen if the borrower of the $640 from Bank B buys merchandise, and the store owner puts the $640 under the mattress, instead of depositing the money in Bank C?

Federal Deposit Insurance

With only a fraction of the actual deposits held in reserve, won't a bank or other depository institution fail, if depositors panic and create a *run on the bank*, by trying to withdraw all their savings? Prior to the establishment of the FDIC in 1933, this was a distinct possibility. The FDIC is a federal agency, funded by banks and backed by the "full faith and credit" of the U.S. government, that insures depositors, currently up to $250,000. If a bank or S&L association fails, the FDIC will pay insured depositors the full amount of their deposit, up to the ceiling. The FDIC charges each depository institution an amount that funds the deposit insurance program. When an insured depository institution is judged by its regulatory agency to be failing, the agency notifies the FDIC. The FDIC usually has two choices. The first is the "purchase and assumption" method, where the FDIC sells the deposits, branches, and good loans to another institution for the best possible price, and then tries to collect as much as possible from the bad loans. This is the preferred method. The second method is for the FDIC to close the institution, pay off all of the depositors, up to the maximum insured, close the branches, and sell the assets and good and bad loans to other institutions or investors.

The key here is *insured deposits*. Some securities that are issued by banks and thrift institutions are not insured by the FDIC. A subsequent institution failure could result in a total loss of money invested in these types of securities. See the Case & Point, "The Savings and Loan Crisis of the 1980s" at the end of this chapter.

Classifications of the Money Supply

For monitoring and analysis, the Federal Reserve classifies the money supply as follows: *M1* refers to coins, paper money, and demand deposits. *M2* is M1 plus investments that can quickly be converted to money, such as small savings accounts, CDs, and money market accounts. *M3* is M2 plus large CDs of over $100,000. Economists monitor changes in the level of each category, and debate which is more significant. Note that money invested in other liquid investments, such as gold jewelry, small precious stones, etc., is not counted as part of the money supply.

Too Much Money Can Cause Inflation and Cause Harm

When the money supply expands, there is more money available to make loans. As a result of this increased supply of money, the price of money, the interest rate, declines. Also, loans usually become easier to get. This stimulates spending, and increases the demand for resources, goods, and services. But a point can be reached where additional increases in the money supply will stimulate additional demand, beyond the ability of the economy to increase supply. The result will be **inflation**—a rise in general prices—caused by too much money chasing too few goods.

Inflation hurts people on fixed incomes, because their expenses increase, but their income doesn't. Inflation usually hurts creditors (lenders), because they will be paid back with dollars that don't buy as much as when the loan was made. And inflation can hurt workers who are unable to gain wage increases to offset inflation. Inflation also harms real estate markets, explored later. However, the federal government could gain during inflation, because inflation raises many peoples' incomes, which pushes people into higher income tax brackets. This is, in effect, a "hidden" tax. To offset this problem, the income brackets for each federal income tax rate are adjusted each year for inflation.

Real Estate Markets and Inflation

In periods of inflation, real estate mortgage lenders are hurt, like other lenders, because the money they receive from loan repayments is worth less than the money they originally loaned. Thus, to protect themselves during periods of rapid inflation, mortgage lenders

DEMAND-PULL INFLATION

COST-PUSH INFLATION

Two Types of Inflation

Demand-Pull Type

"Too much money chasing too few goods." Sellers are producing at full capacity, and in the short run, find it impossible to expand supply. Additional demand, fed by easy money and liberal fiscal policy, drives up prices. This type of inflation is curbed by reducing government spending and by reducing the money supply, in order to slow down demand to the point where supply and demand are balanced.

Cost-Push Type

Prices are pushed up because production costs (land, labor, and capital) are increasing. Controversy: Do strong labor unions force wages up, causing businesses to raise prices? Or do businesses raise prices, forcing unions to seek higher wages? Economists are still trying to find a solution to this type of inflation. Government wage and price controls have been used, but their success is debatable.

increase interest rates. But an increase in interest rates causes monthly payments to increase, thereby preventing some potential buyers from qualifying for loans. This reduces the demand for real estate.

In addition, if space is leased for a fixed rent, the owner (lessor) will receive money each month that is worth less than before. This causes the lessor to try to only agree to leases with increasing rent. But not all tenants have incomes that are increasing. In this way, inflation increases the uncertainty in all real estate markets.

Inflation can cause investors to seek higher returns, sometimes in hidden corners of the money market. This sometimes reduces the money available for mortgages.

Also, during times of inflation, the cost of the components of construction (land, labor, and materials) rises. This increases the cost of construction and can price some people out of the housing market, or out of markets for other types of real estate.

Increased prices also drive up the cost of purchasing the basic necessities of life. In effect, this reduces discretionary income—money for luxuries and leisure. A decline in discretionary income has harmful effects on the recreational and leisure real estate markets, such as vacation homes, motels, and tourist attractions.

Finally, inflation strikes at the core of all decision making. Uncertainties about future price change cause businesses and consumers to act hastily, to become dismayed, discouraged, and confused. Often, greater uncertainty causes investors to postpone investments. Ultimately, inflation causes major disruptions for all sectors of the economy.

On the other hand, deflation is equally bad. **Deflation** means that prices and wages are declining. Companies and people face problems making any payments that are fixed. These might include leases, fixed loan payments, and any others set by contract. Because of this, defaults, foreclosures, and bankruptcies become more numerous. New construction and investment in new machinery drops, because the future income may not justify the present expenditure. Many postpone purchases, in the hope of cheaper future prices. Unemployment gradually climbs, as the economy slows down.

The Importance of Controlling the Supply of Money

As discussed in the previous chapter, an increase or decrease in the money supply can be used to counteract fluctuations in the economy. However, there is always the danger that too great an increase in the supply of money can cause inflation, whereas not enough money can bring on a recession, and even price deflation.

Special Interest Topic
Tangibles in Times of Uncertainty

During a time of rapid inflation and/or political unrest, some people reduce their holdings of money and seek refuge in tangible assets, such as precious stones or metals, art, antiques, and real estate. The key is to find some item that has a limited supply that cannot be easily expanded. As people swarm to these tangibles, their prices skyrocket. If the panic subsides, the price of the tangible levels off or declines.

This trend has occurred in some South American countries. There, runaway inflation drove many South Americans to acquire tangibles outside their own country, such as U.S. real estate.

Speculators capitalize on the trends, by attempting to purchase on the low side and then ride the upswing and sell just before the market declines. If, on the other hand, prices continue to rise, the tangible may become a good long-term hedge against inflation.

In times of deflation or disinflation (inflation at a slower rate), the opposite tends to occur. People tend to abandon tangibles and seek a refuge in coins and paper money. The longer that people hold coins and paper money during deflation, the greater the purchasing power that it commands. Then, the phrase becomes: "Cash is king!"

Section 4.2 discusses who controls the U.S. money supply and how it is done. Before you proceed, review your understanding of the following.

REVIEWING YOUR UNDERSTANDING

The Supply of Money

1. How has the FDIC strengthened our banking system?
2. If all banks keep 10 percent of deposits in reserve, and if a new $1,000 deposit is taken into the system, how much can the bank receiving the deposit loan out? If that loan is deposited in another bank, how much can that second bank loan out?
3. If the economy is in a recession, assuming you had the power, would you increase or decrease the percentage of reserves that banks must keep to back each deposit? Why?
4. How can too much money create inflation? What problems does inflation cause for real estate brokers?

4.2 THE FEDERAL RESERVE SYSTEM

The Federal Reserve System regulates most of the U.S. money supply. This section explains the tools available to the Federal Reserve, and illustrates how these tools can counteract economic imbalances.

Purpose and Structure of the Federal Reserve System

The primary purpose of the **Federal Reserve System**, www .federalreserve.gov (hereafter referred to as "The Fed"), is to regulate the supply of money and credit, in order to achieve economic growth without inflation and unemployment. In short, The Fed views itself as a "money doctor," attempting to cure or prevent economic sickness, by controlling the flow of money and credit. (It is important to note that The Fed does not yet appear to include resisting asset bubbles as part of its duty. Asset bubbles are explored below.)

The Fed serves other functions as well. One is to operate the system that clears checks and other payments between financial institutions, and between the United States and other countries. A second function is to supervise and regulate banking institutions, both to protect the nation's financial systems and to protect consumers' credit rights. A third function is to keep the financial system stable, and not allow financial panics to grow.

FIGURE 4.2 Ben Bernanke—Chair, Federal Reserve System.

Source: The Federal Reserve.

The Fed was established by Congress in 1913. The system is over-seen by a seven-member *Board of Governors* that is located in Washington, D.C. Each governor is appointed by the President, sub-ject to confirmation by the Senate. Each serves one 14-year term, in the hope that long-term appointments will insulate the governors against political pressures, when making important economic deci-sions. The President designates, subject to confirmation by the Senate, two members of the Board to be Chair and Vice-Chair, for a four-year term. The current Chair is Ben Bernanke, shown in Figure 4.2. The seven Board members also serve on the 12-member **Federal Open Market Committee** (FOMC), which makes most policy decisions regarding monetary policy. See Figure 4.3 for a view of the overall structure.

The country is divided into 12 Federal Reserve Districts, shown in Figure 4.4. Each district is headquarters for a *Federal Reserve Bank*. Each bank is privately owned by the member banks operating within that region. However, the stock cannot be sold or used as security for a loan. Each bank has a nine-member board of directors, six elected by the member banks and three designated by the Board of Governors. Each regional Federal Reserve Bank elects its own president, subject to approval of the Board of Governors. Each of the district banks (except New York, Boston, and Philadelphia) has branch banks. There are a total of 25 branches, each with its own board of directors.

All of the district bank presidents attend meetings of the FOMC. The president of the New York Federal Reserve Bank is a permanent voting member. There are four more voting positions on the FOMC, which are filled by 4 of the 11 other district bank presidents, rotating

FIGURE 4.3   The Federal Reserve System.

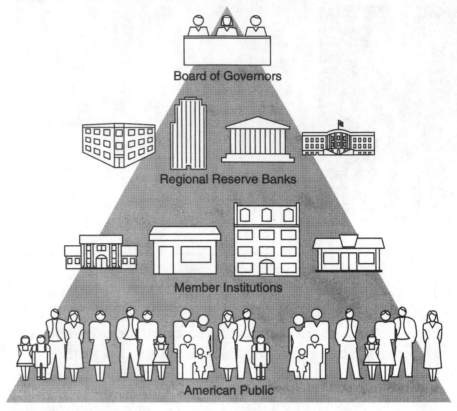

Source: The Federal Reserve.

at two- or three-year intervals. The FOMC usually meets eight times per year, with eight more meetings by conference call.

The overall structure of the Federal Reserve System is surprisingly complex. Much of the authority lies with the regional banks, which have close ties to the banks and business people in each region. The Governors serve long, staggered terms, making them in theory quite independent. However, the Chair and the Vice-Chair are appointed by the President, confirmed by the Senate, and only serve four-year terms. This causes them to be very aware of the political winds. In practice, too, the Chair has far more authority than the other members of the Board of Governors.

How the Federal Reserve Attempts to Control the Money Supply

Section 4.1 described how depository institutions create money by using fractional reserve banking. From reading that section, you will recall that the legal amount that banks must hold as reserves cannot be loaned out. Control over the legal percentage of reserves, therefore, constitutes control over the money supply: An increase in

FIGURE 4.4 Federal Reserve map of the United States.

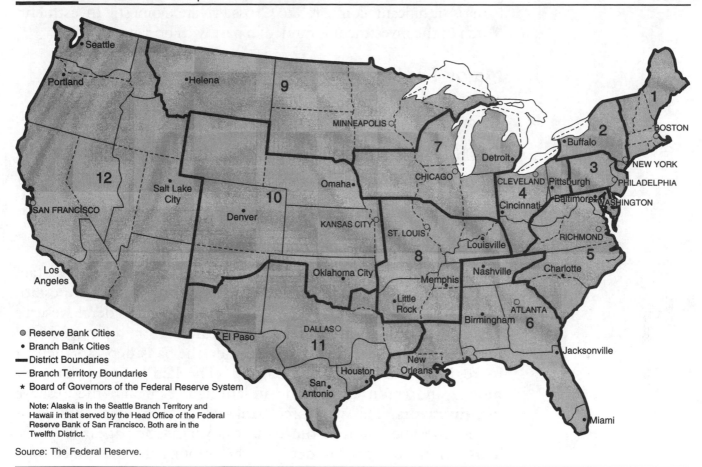

Source: The Federal Reserve.

the required percentage of reserves causes a decrease in the money supply, and a decrease in reserve percentages results in an increase in money and credit. This is exactly how The Fed operates. Using specific tools (frequently referred to as "weapons"), The Fed attempts to control the U.S. money supply and economy, by manipulating bank reserves.

Table 4.2 illustrates how a change in the reserve requirement affects the economy. The exact impact will not be as shown. The reserve requirement is not one uniform rate, but rather varies with the size of a

TABLE 4.2 What Happens When the Fed Changes the Reserve Percentage?

Assume that total deposits are about $10 Trillion.
Assume that only one uniform reserve percentage applies to all deposits.

Reserve:	10%	11%
Maximum Loans:	$9 Trillion	$8.9 Trillion
Reduction in Total Loans:	$100 Million.	
Percent of Gross Private Domestic Investment:	5%	

particular institution's total deposits. Notice that the impact on total loans is significant, compared to Gross Private Domestic Investment. Much of the investment is funded in part with borrowed funds.

Major Tools of the Federal Reserve

The Fed routinely controls bank reserves by using the following three major tools, discussed below:

1. Changes in the reserve requirements
2. Open-market operations
3. Changes in the discount rate

Changes in the Reserve Requirements

As noted, all depository institutions are required to keep a certain percentage of each deposit as reserves. The percentages are established by law, but the Board of Governors of the Federal Reserve has the right to vary the percentages within a certain range. These reserves are not kept at the bank. Rather, the bank deposits them at its regional Federal Reserve Bank. If The Fed believes that easy money and credit are feeding inflation, it can raise the **reserve requirements**. This will force banks to restrict their lending, as money must be diverted from loans to cover the shortage in reserves. This action is designed to decrease the amount of money in circulation, drive up interest rates, and eventually lessen inflation by slowing down spending.

What will happen if The Fed *decreases* the reserve requirements? Will this increase or decrease the money supply? Will this raise or lower interest rates? Trace the steps to check your understanding. Generally, changes in the reserve requirement primarily impact short-term interest rates.

Open-Market Operations

As part of its money-management tools, The Fed is authorized to buy and sell U.S. government securities, in **open-market operations**. These might be short-term U.S. Treasury Notes, or longer-term bonds. The public (private citizens and financial institutions) also regularly buy and sell government securities, as a form of investment. When The Fed buys government securities from the public, the seller of these securities (the public) receives The Fed's check, which the seller then deposits in a local bank. The local bank forwards the check to The Fed for payment. When The Fed receives its own check, it increases the reserves of the local bank by the amount of that check. The local bank now has more reserves than are required and therefore can grant more loans. *Thus, when The Fed buys government securities from the public, it increases the money supply by increasing bank reserves, which in turn will support more loans.*

What happens to the money supply when The Fed *sells* government securities to the public? The money supply tightens up, which increases interest rates and discourages borrowing. To help review your understanding, let us trace what happens when The Fed sells government securities.

When The Fed sells government securities, an individual purchases them by writing a check on his or her local bank. The Fed receives the buyer's check, and subtracts it from the reserve account of that local bank. The local bank now has fewer reserves and therefore must constrict its lending. *So when The Fed sells government securities, it decreases bank reserves, which in turn decreases the bank's ability to grant loans.*

Open-market operations primarily impact short-term market interest rates. Long-term rates tend to be influenced more by inflation fears than by Fed actions. This is also true of long-term fixed mortgage rates. However, The Fed can influence long-term rates somewhat, by aggressively buying or selling long-term bonds and securities. The Fed did this in 2008 and 2009, buying large amounts of long-term mortgage securities. At one point in 2009, the *Wall Street Journal* reported (September 22) that The Fed was buying 80 percent of all new mortgages, keeping interest rates low to aid the housing market recovery.

Once again, notice that the ultimate effect is to change the money supply by manipulating bank reserves. But The Fed has still a third important tool—changes in the discount rate.

Changes in the Discount Rate

When you need a loan, you might go to your bank. Where does a bank go when it needs a loan? One possible place is the Federal Reserve. The Fed is considered a banker's bank. When you borrow from your bank, you pay interest. When a bank borrows from The Fed, it is charged an interest rate that is known as the **discount rate**.

By decreasing the discount rate, The Fed can encourage banks to borrow. The borrowed funds increase the local bank's deposits and reserves, which allows the bank to make more loans. On the other hand, if The Fed increases the discount rate, banks become more reluctant to borrow, which will decrease the amount of money available for loans. The discount rate usually applies to overnight loans. Its impact is mostly on short-term interest rates.

Federal Funds Rate

Although not technically listed as one of the major tools of The Fed, the **federal funds rate** is one of the most closely watched indicators of the current thinking of the Federal Reserve. What is the federal funds rate? When a bank has loaned all of its available funds and only its reserves are left, it cannot grant additional loans to expand business until its reserves are increased. Or if the bank has granted too many loans relative to its existing reserves, it must by law either call in some loans, or increase its reserves. One way for a bank to solve these problems is to borrow excess reserves from another bank that currently has surplus reserves. The *federal funds rate*, then, is the rate of interest one bank charges another, for the overnight use of excess reserves.

The federal funds rate should not be confused with the prime rate. The **prime rate** is the rate of interest that a bank charges its large, better customers, such as major corporations. The federal funds rate is what one bank charges another bank for overnight use of excess reserves. The actual rate is negotiated between the two banks.

The Federal Reserve, in its effort to fight inflation or recession, increases or decreases the money supply, in order to try to keep the federal funds rate in a certain trading range. If The Fed wishes to encourage the economy to expand, it may expand the money supply, and allow the federal funds rate to drop. This will encourage one bank to borrow the excess reserves of another, and use the reserves to grant more loans, which should expand the economy. If The Fed wants to slow the economy, it may tighten up the money supply, and force the federal funds rate to rise. This discourages one bank from borrowing excess reserves from another bank, thereby discouraging the granting of additional loans. This will tend to keep the economy from expanding, or slow down the expansion.

The LIBOR Rate

Banks can also borrow funds directly from other banks, for a short period or longer. There is a very large market for overnight loans directly between large banks. It was given a formal structure by the British Bankers Association (BBA) in the 1980s. BBA now releases, through Thomson-Reuters, the *London Interbank Offered Rate*, or *LIBOR*. It is an index of the average interest rate submitted by a panel of banks. It represents the banks' view of the interest rate for loans between banks on the London wholesale money market. An index is published for a range of different loan maturities, from overnight to one year, in ten different currencies. *Note* that it is not an average of actual transactions, but rather the average of the opinions of a panel of bankers.

Increasingly, the LIBOR rate is used in other contracts, including variable-interest-rate home loans in the United States and the United Kingdom. Some people speculate on future interest rate changes, by buying interest-rate futures contracts based on LIBOR rates.

The LIBOR rate is widely viewed as reflecting the confidence that bankers have in other banks. Thus, the "spread," or difference, between the overnight U.S. dollar LIBOR rate and the federal funds rate will vary, as banker confidence varies. When confidence falls, banks are less able to easily borrow from one another, and the financial system becomes less liquid, a sure sign of financial stress.

A Review of the Major Federal Reserve Tools

Changes in the reserve requirement, open-market operations, and changes in the discount rate allow The Fed to control the supply of bank money. Of these three tools, the most commonly used is that of open-market operations.

To increase the money supply, The Fed will decrease the reserve requirement, buy government securities, decrease the discount rate, or use some combination of all three.

To decrease the money supply, The Fed will either increase the reserve requirements, sell government securities, increase the discount rate, or use some combination of all three.

The Fed keeps a close eye on the federal funds rate, and attempts to raise or lower this rate, using one or more of the three tools. Thus, the federal funds rate is a major indicator of The Fed's economic goals.

REVIEWING YOUR UNDERSTANDING

The Federal Reserve System
1. Why does the Federal Reserve System view itself as a "money doctor"?
2. Why are the governors of the Federal Reserve System appointed for 14 years? Who is the current chairperson of the Federal Reserve System?
3. If the Fed wishes to stimulate demand in an effort to fight a recession, would it increase or decrease bank reserves? What should it do regarding open-market operations? Regarding the discount rate?
4. What is the definition of the federal funds rate? Prime rate?

Special Interest Topic
U.S. Addiction to Foreign Capital

As noted earlier, the U.S. Congress and the president have been unwilling for political reasons to face the reality of the large budget deficit. The deficit can only be reduced by severely cutting government spending or drastically raising taxes, or some combination of the two. The easy short-run "fix" has been to increase government borrowing to cover the deficit. Remember how much the U.S. savings rate has declined in the past decade or so. As a result, a growing percentage of this borrowing has come from foreign investors. Foreign purchases of U.S. government and private securities have moved the United States from being a creditor nation to a debtor nation. This need for foreign capital gives rise to a couple of questions: Does the dependence on foreign capital reduce The Fed's ability to influence U.S. interest rates? If so, does this mean that The Fed's ability to use monetary controls to adjust the U.S. economy has been weakened? Although it is too soon to tell for sure, it appears that trends in the financial markets in Asia and Europe (both large buyers of U.S. bonds) have a strong influence on U.S. interest rates. This in turn makes The Fed's job more difficult. High or low interest rates in foreign markets help determine what U.S. interest rates must be, in order to attract foreign investors to finance the U.S. budget deficit. High interest rates could be counter to The Fed's wishes. For example, the U.S. economy could be in a slump. Monetary policy calls for lowering interest rates, to stimulate production and jobs in such a situation. But lower interest rates would discourage foreign investors, thereby forcing Congress and the president to cut government spending or raise taxes. This would tend to depress the economy even further. On the other hand, if The Fed maintains high interest rates, to attract foreign investors to cover the U.S. budget deficit, this will reduce the ability of U.S. companies and consumers to borrow for domestic economic expansion. This is just another example of the major impact that the globalization of financial markets has on domestic economies in today's world.

4.3 HOW THE ACTIONS OF THE FEDERAL RESERVE AFFECT REAL ESTATE

This section explains how The Fed's attempts to regulate the money supply influence real estate markets. This section also points out that the cyclical movement of real estate markets will not always be in perfect step with general economic trends.

Tight-Money Policies and Real Estate

The Fed usually institutes a **tight monetary policy** in order to combat inflation. Inflation itself is frequently caused by excessive private demand, government deficits, or a swollen money supply.

When The Fed fights inflation, it tightens up the money supply, which in turn causes interest rates to rise. Government agencies and corporate borrowers increasingly bid against one another for the shrinking money supply. Higher interest rates have a number of impacts on real estate. Most importantly, higher interest rates increase loan payments. This reduces the number of home buyers who have enough income to qualify for a loan to purchase a house. In turn, this reduces the demand for homes. The increased loan payments also impact purchases of income property. The increased loan payments mean some properties do not sell, or else the price may have to drop, to reduce the loan payments.

A second major impact of higher interest rates is that investors who have money try to increase the earnings on their own investments. Often, they move their money. Historically, depository institutions granted the biggest share of home mortgages, but paid low rates to depositors. When banks and savings institutions lost funds, mortgage lending decreased, and the residential real estate market went into a recession. The economic term for this historical outflow of funds from depository institutions into corporate and government notes or other investments is called **disintermediation**.

With the introduction of adjustable rate mortgages (ARMs), money market certificate accounts, and a vastly improved secondary mortgage market, depository institutions have become somewhat insulated against disintermediation. By **secondary market**, we mean that the company that originates a mortgage loan no longer usually holds on to the loan as an investment. Instead, the loan is sold to investors on the secondary market, with the original lender collecting an origination fee. The original lender could be guaranteeing the investors against loss on the loan, but often not.

What happens in the secondary market when The Fed causes interest rates to rise? Investors may prefer other investments with higher yields, reducing the demand for mortgage investments. The lender has to raise the interest rate on new mortgages. And the market prices of existing mortgages have to fall, in order to increase the effective interest rate, or yield, to the buyer. As a result, when The Fed tightens money to combat inflation, housing is one of the first economic sectors to feel the pinch. The income real estate sector follows close behind.

This frequently brings cries of "discrimination" from the real estate industry.

Does The Fed Discriminate Against Housing When It Tightens Money?

Does The Fed really discriminate against housing? In the purest sense, the answer is no. When The Fed decreases the money supply, it does not single out the real estate market, and it does not only squeeze housing funds. Historically, real estate mortgages are usually unattractive investments in tight-money markets. This is because they are long-term loans, and historically had low to moderate fixed interest rates.

During periods of prosperity and inflation, interest rates for other investments tend to rise. Some institutional lenders and investors may refuse to invest in low-paying, fixed-rate, long-term mortgages. Instead, they are attracted to high-yield, short-term government notes and business loans. As the demand for funds continues to exceed the supply, interest rates on Treasury and federal agency instruments also increase, and disintermediation may take place. The values of existing long-term fixed-rate mortgages and mortgage securities fall. The Fed does not specifically discriminate against housing; rather, the structure of the mortgage market tends to defeat itself in tight-money situations.

Easy-Money Policies and Real Estate

During periods of economic slowdown, The Fed shifts to an **easy-money policy**, as it attempts to head off a recession by easing the money supply. An increase in money and credit, in time, usually causes spending to increase, and this expansion will bring a gradual increase in employment.

As money and credit become more plentiful, interest rates tend to decline. These lower interest rates do not immediately attract business borrowers, because the economic turndown still leaves a lingering feeling of pessimism. Meanwhile, private savings may increase, as uncertainty causes people to become cautious and to restrict their spending.

Wall Street and financial institutions find that savings are piling up. The Fed is making more money available, but few businesses are borrowing. So investors and lenders look more favorably at real estate mortgages as an outlet for their funds. As money moves back into the mortgage market and interest rates decline, the demand for housing, which was previously suppressed by higher interest rates and a lack of credit, begins to pick up, and the real estate market slowly recovers.

The hard part of The Fed's job is timing. The Fed tries to lower interest rates early enough to soften the fall of the economy. And then The Fed tries to avoid leaving rates too low too long, so that no inflationary bubble is started.

Recovery in the Real Estate Market Normally Precedes a Recovery in the National Economy

The volume of real estate sales, as it increases, generates income for all segments of the real estate industry: sales, loans, escrow, and appraisal. As sales volume grows, prices begin to recover. In turn, the strengthening demand and firmer prices cause new construction to increase. Because of the size and impact of the construction industry, an increase in home and other building helps to lead the economy out of a recession. As construction picks up, employment, income, and spending increase. This in turn generates even more activity, and the general business cycle heads for recovery.

The real estate market (cycle) in the short run may travel somewhat opposite to the general business cycle. When the general economy is at the top of a boom, real estate activity is usually already declining because of higher interest rates and a tightening of credit. When the general economy starts to slow down, real estate activity may increase, as interest rates drop and funds flow back into the mortgage market. Starting in the mid-1970s, both the general economy and the real estate market prospered simultaneously, for the first time since World War II.

Mortgage Market Reforms

It is often said that correcting one problem only leads to another. Major financial reforms were introduced after the Savings and Loan Crisis of the late 1980s. Financial institutions increasingly sold new mortgage loans on the secondary market, instead of holding them as investments. The cost of producing loans became more important than ever before. Banks turned to temporary contracts with outside loan brokers and outside appraisers, instead of using salaried personnel. The rapid growth of loan origination by loan brokers followed, along with growth of the secondary market. This led to increases in packaging mortgage loans into securities, like bonds, to be sold to investors. A group of loans was considered much safer than any one loan. In turn, the securities were broken into pieces, called *tranches*, with the first tranch getting paid first, followed by the second, etc. In some cases, the poorer quality tranches were bundled into a new security, which was also sold in tranches. Many of the securities were also insured against default. The securities were all reviewed and rated , as to quality and risk, for a fee, by one or more of the three recognized rating companies. These ratings gave the securities more credibility to investors all over the world.

In hindsight, lenders (all types—banks, Wall Street, etc.) changed to only making money by processing loans, instead of investing. This reduced the emphasis on quality and shifted it to volume—making more loans and selling them faster. Now, we must clean up the resulting financial mess, and figure out how to change the system, to improve mortgage loan quality.

REVIEWING YOUR UNDERSTANDING

How the Actions of the Federal Reserve Affect Real Estate

1. How do tight-money policies of the Federal Reserve System influence the real estate market?

2. What causes disintermediation from savings institutions? How does this affect real estate markets?

3. Why does a recovery in the real estate market usually precede a recovery in the national economy?

4.4 THE FED'S EMERGENCY POWERS

We noted earlier that one of the major functions of The Fed is to keep the financial system stable, and halt the spread of financial panics. The Fed was created in 1913, primarily in response to a serious financial panic, a "run on the banks," in 1907, and several runs in prior decades. Its powers and duties increased after the stock market crash of 1929, which was followed by another major bank run.

What causes bank runs or financial panics? The answer is a *loss of confidence,* or trust, in financial institutions. Every business transaction involves some degree of trust. For example, will the customer at a fruit stand grab the bananas and run, or pay? Prior to federal bank deposit insurance, only some trust in the bank could justify anyone keeping money on deposit. When people lost confidence, they lined up to try to get their money out. However, the bank had loaned much of the funds out, could not possibly pay off all of the depositors on short notice, and was at risk of failing. Deposit insurance essentially eliminated that problem.

Trust and Counter-Party Risk

Today, financial transactions have become much more complex than when The Fed was established in 1913. Every bank, stock brokerage firm, major corporation treasury, mutual fund, and pension fund has hundreds of agreements with others, seeking to transfer the risk of a change in interest rates, wheat prices, stock prices, even weather to some other party. Sometimes, companies sell assets— stocks, bonds, real estate, and more—to others, with an option to buy them back in the future at a fixed price, hoping to profit from a future price increase.

The bundling of many thousands of home loans into mortgage-backed securities was behind another part of this growing complexity. (College loans, car and boat loans, credit card debt, and others were also bundled into securities. Commercial mortgages were also securitized.) As described earlier, each security was usually split into *tranches*, or levels of priority to receive loan payments. The top tranches got paid first, were rated as extremely secure, and were bought as investments by institutions and investors all over the world. These investments were considered so secure that many were used as security for loans, used to make more investments. The total volume of securitized loans increased rapidly in 2005 and 2006. Underlying all of this was trust—trust in the credit rating of the original mortgage borrowers, trust in the value of the homes securing the mortgages, and trust in the rating agencies.

The key point is the number of layers that eventually built up. Many mortgages were sold several times, before finally being bundled into a security and split into tranches. Most tranches were sold and then traded, just like stocks. Some tranches were bundled into new securities that were also split into tranches and sold! And many tranches were used as security for loans, which were used to buy more tranches, which were used as security for loans, which were used … Do you get the picture? See Figure 4.5! Meanwhile, in 2007, the Securities and Exchange Commission (SEC) sharply reduced the level of equity assets that investment banks were required to hold, allowing them to borrow *far more* money than before. Most did so.

As long as there was trust, this incredibly complex web of contracts and agreement seemed workable. Each party trusted the others, so **counter-party risk** seemed low. Everyone was making money, so how could there be a problem? But problems emerged. First, it turned out that the credit ratings of the original home loan borrowers were not as reliable as believed. Some mortgage brokers or borrowers had lied, or forged documents. Next, a small but growing number

FIGURE 4.5   The house of cards.

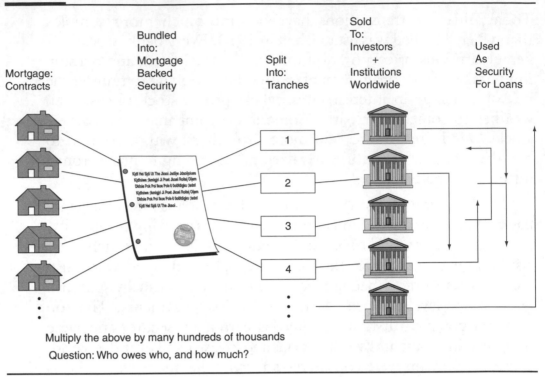

Multiply the above by many hundreds of thousands

Question: Who owes who, and how much?

of loans appeared to be based on inflated or even forged appraisal reports. Defaults and foreclosures started growing. The rating agencies noted the rising default rate and lowered the ratings of a few tranches, which dropped in value. Trust started to erode.

As trust deteriorated, investors tried to sell the tranches that were viewed as more risky. The demand to buy tranches declined, and the supply that was offered to sell began climbing. Market prices of more tranches declined. Institutions which were required to report the market value of their investments reported that values were declining. Those who had borrowed, using tranches as security for the loan, found that the value of the security had declined, forcing them to pay down the loan or put up more security. A few banks that had invested very heavily in tranches of mortgage-backed securities were closed by regulators. Trust eroded further. The LIBOR rate started to rise, as confidence declined.

Because some securities loans had complex documents, it was not always clear who was at risk. There was a loan, with a tranch as security. But the tranch had been sold several times. Perhaps another company agreed to guarantee the loan for a fee. Still another institution had borrowed the tranch, for a fee, so they had temporary ownership.

Some tranches could not be sold for any reasonable price. The tranch might still be rated highly, because its performance was insured. But markets started to see that they could not figure out how reliable the insurance really was. This type of insurance often was not regulated by any of the usual state insurance regulators or any federal agency. Trust continued to erode.

The LIBOR rate continued to inch up. More institutions reported declines in the value of their assets. Regulators expressed concern. Institutions tried to "unwind" some of the complex asset swaps, guarantees, and other agreements that they were wrapped up in. More institutions failed. Many others hinted of problems. Suddenly, a full financial panic arose.

Calendar of the Crisis: 2007–2008

Aug. 1, 2007	- BNP Paribas announced good earnings, pleasing investors because the very large European bank owned a lot of mortgage-backed securities.
Aug. 7	- The Fed announced that the Board had unanimously voted to continue a bias toward tightening, despite some "trouble in financial markets."
Aug. 9	- BNP Paribas reportedly halted withdrawals from several funds, as the values of the assets could not be determined.
	- Inter-bank overnight loans declined sharply.
	- The European Central Bank (ECB) provided over $200 billion of low-interest overnight bank loans.
Aug. 10	- The Fed announced that it also would provide overnight bank loans of $39 billion.
Aug. 13	- The ECB made another $65 billion of short-term bank loans.
Aug. 14	- The ECB added $34 billion more.
Aug. 17	- The Fed lowered the discount rate from 6.25% to 5.75%.
Sept. 1	- Funding for commercial real estate loans were reported to be unavailable, and interest rates for business loans were climbing, shutting off new loans.
Sept. 18	- The Fed unanimously voted to lower the discount rate to 5.25%.
	- Mortgage lenders reported increasing write-offs on sub-prime mortgages.
Oct. 26	- Countrywide Financial reported a huge and unexpected loss for the third quarter, but said it was "transitory."
Oct. 31	- The Fed cut the discount rate to 5%, with 1 of 12 voting for no cut.
Nov. 28	- Fed members stated opposing views on what to do with rates.

Dec. 11	- The Fed cut the federal funds target rate from 4.5% to 4.25%, with 1 of 12 voting for a greater cut.
Late Dec.	- The Fed announced Term Auction Facility (TAF) loans, allowing banks to bid on low-interest short-term loans, to improve year-end liquidity (and balance sheets!).
Jan, 11, 2008	- Bank of America to buy Countrywide, with financial assistance from the Fed.
Jan. 21	- By video conference, The Fed cut the federal funds target rate from 4.25% to 3.5%, followed by the Bank of Canada.
Jan. 30	- The Fed cut the federal funds target rate to 3% and cut the discount rate to 3.5%.
March	- Speculators started a run on Bear Sterns investment bank, dropping its stock from $100 to $70 per share in three months.
March 17	- J. P. Morgan Chase to buy Bear Sterns for $10 per share, with the Fed taking over $30 Billion of illiquid mortgage assets.
March 18	- The Fed cut the federal funds target rate to 2.25%.
April 30	- The Fed cut the federal funds target rate to 2%.
May	- The checks for $150 Billion in stimulus funds to consumers were mailed.
July 11	- The Office of Thrift Supervision closed IndyMac Bank.
Sept. 8	- The Treasury took control of FannieMae and FreddieMac.
Sept. 11	- Lehman unexpectedly filed for bankruptcy, after failing to obtain a government bailout.
Sept. 16	- The government stepped in to protect AIG from bankruptcy.
Sept 21	- Washington Mutual is taken over by JP Morgan Chase with government assistance, after a "run on the bank."

Source: Diane Swonk, "Diary of a Crisis: Two Years and Counting", *Themes on the Economy*, August 11, 2009 and September, 10, 2009.

The Panic and the Fed's Response

The initial indicator of the crisis was not the historical indicator of a run on the bank. Instead, all types of lenders seemed to reach the same conclusion at close to the same time: They did not know which of their borrowers were safe. *Counter-party risk* went from an obscure technical term to a roar! The result was a credit freeze in August 2007: No one wanted to loan to anyone (except national governments, of course).

The early actions by The Fed and other central banks were to keep banks liquid, by providing overnight bank loans. This was to substitute for the frozen LIBOR market. The authorized amounts were increased several times, over several days, especially in Europe. The problem initially was viewed as just a European problem! A week later, to encourage banks to borrow from The Fed, the discount rate was cut. The problem was still viewed as a temporary liquidity issue. Eight separate rate cuts were ultimately made. Note that these actions were all made using the standard tools of The Fed.

At year-end 2007, The Fed made short-term funds available to banks. Overnight loans were no longer enough. And, as financial institutions began to fail, The Fed worked closely with the Treasury and FDIC, to find buyers and keep panic from spreading. Often, this involved federal guarantees of some assets, or actual purchases of blocks of assets.

It took two years for the financial panic to gradually subside. The underlying problems for financial markets, however, consisted of investments that were not as risk-free as expected, and companies that had borrowed too much, relative to their equity capital. Neither problem had been solved.

Borrowing is always dangerous, because it nearly always must be paid back dollar-for-dollar. But the assets purchased or investments made with borrowed funds often do not perform as well as hoped. The loan usually must be paid off in full, so all of the loss impacts the company's capital. This is exactly the same as buying a home at the top of the market, using a low-down payment home loan. The initial problem was with the investment banks (e.g., Bear Sterns) that sharply increased borrowing after the SEC allowed it in 2007.

Given that bank and investment bank loans and investments declined in value, the pressure on the equity was extreme. As noted, Bear Sterns' common stock dropped, from over $100 per share, to $10 per share, in perhaps four months! What choices did institutions have? One was to raise more equity capital. AIG "sold" preferred stock to the Treasury, turning over control of the company in order to avoid collapse. Some banks were able to sell stock to investors, both here and abroad.

Another option is to sell assets, and use the sale proceeds to pay down loans. In the worst of the credit crisis, however, there were very few buyers and they only wanted to buy things at bargain prices. Remember the saying that applies in times of financial panics: "Cash is king!"

Most institutions were left with large amounts of securitized loan investments, for which there were very few buyers. Remember our analysis of supply and demand? The Treasury started buying significant numbers of home loan mortgages, which had two effects. First, it provided liquidity to investors who were holding mortgages that were not in default, but hard to sell. Second, it provided a major increase in

Too Big To Fail?

When financial institutions make bad loans or investments, the regulators are supposed to recognize the problem during their periodic examinations, and get the institution straightened out before it is too late. The regulatory agencies have broad power to force needed changes. If the regulators catch the problem too late, and cannot turn it around, then the institution is supposed to fail. The FDIC then takes over, as explored earlier, and disposes of the remains.

However, financial markets have long felt that some financial institutions were "too big to fail." The belief was that the government would have no choice but to prop them up somehow, and keep them running. These institutions were considered too big for another institution to take them over. The combination would have been so large, it would cause anti-trust, monopoly concerns among other institutions and the public. And a big bank could not just be shut down and liquidated, due to the billions of contracts with other institutions. These contracts are *not* insured by FDIC, so the liquidation would cause massive confusion and ultimately panic.

This theory was not conclusively tested in the Savings and Loan Crisis of the 1980s. As the 2007 panic grew, markets considered this theory to be another element of risk. The government stepped in to rescue FreddieMac and FannieMae, which the market expected would happen. A few days later, the government allowed Lehman Brothers to collapse. This was a huge market shock, as most felt that the government would step in, and there had been no hints to the contrary. A few days after that, the government had no choice but to rescue AIG. Note that AIG was an insurance company, not a bank nor an investment bank. It was its size and number of contracts with others, not the type of institution, which dictated the rescue. Soon after, Washington Mutual was taken over by Chase, Wachovia by Wells Fargo Bank, and Merrill Lynch by Bank of America. The picture became clear: Some institutions, indeed, are too big to fail!

demand for mortgage securities, which lowered interest rates on federally insured mortgages.

The Treasury also set up a similar program, the Term Asset-Backed Securities Facility (TALF), to buy existing commercial mortgage-backed securities (CMBS). Commercial real estate values did not drop at the same time as home values. Rather, they lagged. As home prices fell, construction slowed down, lenders collapsed. The economy started to weaken. Unemployment started to rise. Retail sales then started to fall. This was a train wreck, occurring in a very slow motion. By 2009, it was clear that commercial real estate was also in trouble. Many commercial loans and securities were also in trouble. The TALF authorizes low–interest-rate loans to investors, with the loans to be used to purchase existing or new CMBS. This is expected to allow lenders to sell troubled loans to investors, and generate cash to improve lenders' balance sheets.

In a financial panic, then, The Fed has a wide range of powers. Some require the cooperation of the U.S. Treasury and/or the FDIC. Some require special authorization from Congress. The primary tools are to (1) maintain liquidity of financial institutions at all times, and (2) step in to improve financial institution balance sheets, either by buying assets (which generates equity cash), or by loans or purchases of shares of preferred or common stock.

REVIEWING YOUR UNDERSTANDING

The Fed's Emergency Powers

1. Why is confidence so important to financial markets?
2. Is an understanding of risk important to investors, agents, appraisers, and lenders? Why?
3. Why is liquidity important to financial institutions?

CHAPTER SUMMARY

Money acts as a medium of exchange, a measure of value, a store of value, and a standard for deferred payment. There are three types of U.S. money: coins, paper currency, and demand deposits (checking accounts). Demand deposits are by far the most important part of the U.S. money supply.

Although only the federal government may legally mint coins and print currency, U.S. banks and other depository institutions create checking account money. Banks are legally authorized to create this money by means of fractional reserve banking.

The amount of money in circulation has a tremendous influence on the performance of the economy. Too much money and credit will create inflation, whereas too little will cause a recession. In an effort to control the flow of money and credit, Congress established the Federal Reserve System (frequently referred to as The Fed).

The Fed attempts to control the money supply by using three main tools: changes in the reserve requirements, open-market operations, and changes in the discount rate. All of these tools control the credit-creating ability of banks, by manipulating the amount of money banks must keep as a reserve. If a bank's reserve requirement is high, the bank can lend less money. If a bank's reserve requirement is low, the bank can lend more money. The Fed watches the federal funds rate, to monitor how well its tools are working.

If The Fed believes that there is too much inflation, it will attempt to tighten up the money supply. It does this by increasing the reserve requirements, raising the discount rate, or selling government securities in the open market. As the money supply tightens, one of the hardest-hit areas is the real estate market. Tight money and higher interest rates make mortgage credit scarce and expensive. This makes it difficult to buy or build a home or other real estate, so that activity in the real estate markets declines.

On the other hand, if the economy is heading for a recession, The Fed will increase the money supply. This encourages more spending and helps to slow the recession. An increase in the money supply is called an easy-money policy. During the early periods of easy money, activity in the real estate market picks up, as interest rates decline and mortgage credit becomes more plentiful. Because of the size and impact of the real estate and construction industries, an increase in real estate sales and in building helps to lead the economy out of a recession.

However, if spending and demand rise beyond the economy's short-term ability to supply goods and services, inflation reoccurs. If this happens, the Fed may again tighten up the money supply, so that interest rates rise and funds flow out of investments in mortgage securities. This will cause a drop in real estate activity, and once again it becomes more difficult to buy and sell homes and other real estate. It is very important for appraisers, agents, lenders, and investors to understand the impact that changes in the money supply have on local real estate activity.

Confidence in others—counter-party risk—is always an issue in markets. In a financial panic, trust disappears, and deal-making stops. As a result, everything is frozen—an absence of liquidity. The Fed tries to provide liquidity to financial institutions through alternate channels. Some forms are short-term loans; others are asset purchases.

REVIEWING YOUR UNDERSTANDING

1. Which of the following is *not* considered a function of money?
   A. medium of exchange
   B. measure of value
   C. standard of deferred payment
   D. standard of tangible asset

2. The greatest percentage of the U.S. money supply is represented by:
   A. checking accounts
   B. coins
   C. paper currency
   D. certificates of deposit

3. If the banking system is using a 10 percent reserve requirement, an initial $1,000 deposit can expand to a maximum of how much in new loans?
   A. $1,000
   B. $5,000
   C. $9,000
   D. $10,000

4. If the Federal Reserve wishes to expand the money supply, it could:
   A. increase the reserve requirements
   B. raise the discount rate
   C. buy government bonds
   D. increase the federal funds rate

5. The rate of interest that one bank charges another for the overnight use of excess reserves is called:
   A. prime rate
   B. discount rate
   C. federal funds rate
   D. commercial rate

6. The flow of funds from depository institutions to the general money market is called:
   A. reintermediation
   B. disintermediation
   C. run on the bank
   D. recapitalization

7. Which of the following actions by The Fed tends to raise interest rates?
   A. selling government securities
   B. lowering the discount rate
   C. decreasing reserve requirements
   D. reducing the federal funds rate

8. The increase in the use of foreign capital tends to motivate Congress and the president to solve the U.S. budget deficit problem.
   A. true
   B. false

9. Which government agency insures savings accounts at approved depository institutions?
   A. Federal Reserve System
   B. Federal Home Loan Bank
   C. Federal Deposit Insurance Corporation
   D. Federal Trust Association

10. Which of the following is true?
   A. U.S. paper currency is not backed by gold.
   B. Inflation is always good for real estate because prices go up.
   C. Government deficits decrease the government's need to borrow.
   D. All economists agree that monetary policy is better than fiscal policy for controlling the economy.

11. Money has various functions. When money is used to describe what a debtor owes a creditor, this function of money is called a:
   A. medium of exchange
   B. measure of value
   C. standard of deferred payment
   D. store of value

12. Depository institutions create money as a result of a concept known as:
   A. fractional reserve banking
   B. demand deposits
   C. reintermediation
   D. capitalization

13. A decrease in the rate of inflation is called:
   A. deflation
   B. disinflation
   C. disintermediation
   D. disintegration

14. Rapid unanticipated inflation is most harmful to real estate:
   A. lenders who grant ARM loans
   B. lenders who grant fixed rate loans
   C. borrowers who have fixed rate loans
   D. purchasers who pay cash

15. For monitoring and analysis, the Federal Reserve classifies coins, paper money, and demand deposits as:
   A. M1
   B. M2
   C. M3
   D. M4

16. "Too much money chasing too few goods" is what kind of inflation?
   A. cost-push
   B. spiral-up
   C. twist-down
   D. demand-pull

17. The Federal Reserve System contains how many regional reserve banks?
   A. 5
   B. 7
   C. 12
   D. 14

18. The Federal Reserve's control over the economy is called:
    A. fiscal policy
    B. monetary policy
    C. fractional reserve policy
    D. market policy

19. When The Fed buys and sells government notes and bonds, it is called:
    A. change in reserve requirements
    B. change in discount requirements
    C. supply of money operations
    D. open-market operations

20. To decrease prevailing interest rates, The Fed:
    A. sells government notes
    B. lowers the discount rate
    C. increases reserve requirements
    D. increases the federal funds rate

21. Recovery in the real estate market frequently begins before a full recovery in the general economy.
    A. true
    B. false

22. When interest rates rise, the:
    A. demand for housing declines
    B. supply of housing increases
    C. demand for commercial real estate increases
    D. supply of commercial real estate increases

23. Historically, in tight-money markets, real estate mortgages are attractive investments.
    A. true
    B. false

24. A decrease in mortgage interest rates tends to increase:
    A. home sales
    B. refinances
    C. home prices
    D. all of the above

25. Which mortgage market reform has insulated depository institutions from excessive disintermediation?
    A. adjustable rate mortgages
    B. money market certificate accounts
    C. an improved secondary mortgage market
    D. all of the above

CASE & POINT

The Savings and Loan Crisis of the 1980s and Its Successor, the Mortgage Securities Collapse of 2007

Background

By the early 1980s, excessive inflation during the previous decade had placed the savings and loan (S&L) industry in a financial bind. High interest rates were being paid by banks and money market funds to attract depositors, but savings and loans were prohibited by law from paying interest above a low passbook account rate. Thus, deposits were flowing out of S&Ls into other investments. In the meantime, the S&L industry was saddled with a huge inventory of low fixed interest rate mortgages that were made in earlier years. The resale value of these loans was low, because of the discount needed to increase the yield to the level demanded by investors. In short, the asset value of the entire industry was declining, and it looked like the real estate market, which was closely tied to the S&L industry, was heading for trouble.

The Proposed Solution

The proposed solution was to deregulate the S&L industry, and allow its owners and managers to compete in the general marketplace, as did banks and other financial institutions. The thought was that this would stimulate the general economy and boost the real estate market. The following major events set this proposed solution in motion:

1. In 1980, Congress passed the Depository Institutions Deregulation and Monetary Control Act. This law, in phases, lifted interest rate ceilings for S&Ls, and allowed the industry to issue checking accounts and certificates of deposits, grant commercial real estate and consumer loans, acquire stocks and bonds, and own and operate real estate development companies, mutual funds, and many other ventures. In short, they could operate similarly to commercial banks.

2. In 1981, Congress passed the Economic Reform Act to stimulate the economy, which was in a recession. One of the main provisions of this act was a favorable accelerated depreciation rate for real estate investors. This in turn started a boom in new

residential, commercial, and industrial development. The S&L industry was heavily involved in financing these projects. Many projects were built on speculation, without a buyer or tenant under contract. This was especially true in the rapidly expanding mountain states and the Southwest.

3. In 1982, Congress passed the Depository Institutions Act (Garn Bill), which continued the trend of deregulation. Another important feature of this law allowed real estate lenders to enforce due-on-transfer clauses, whereby lenders could call their existing low interest rate loans when a property was transferred to a new owner, rather than be stuck with a loan assumption at a low interest rate.

4. After much promotion, real estate lenders convinced the public to accept the concept of adjustable rate mortgages (ARMs). This helped to protect the value of the lender's portfolio, by passing the risk of future inflation to the borrower and away from the lender. In addition, increasingly sophisticated secondary markets allowed lenders to package and resell their existing mortgages faster, and avoid being saddled with unwanted inventory.

These events, plus others, placed savings and loan associations on an equal footing with other financial institutions, and gave S&L owners and managers the economic freedom to go to the marketplace and generate profits.

What Happened?

Why did we have a savings and loan crisis? Why did Congress need to pass the "bailout" legislation known as the Financial Institutions Reform Recovery and Enforcement Act of 1989 (FIRREA)? Did deregulation fail? Did the free market theory fail to work?

These questions may never be answered fully, but here are some concepts to consider:

1. The collapse of oil prices led to an economic crash in the "oil patch" and mountain states (Texas, Louisiana, Oklahoma, Colorado, and Utah), which in turn led to massive real estate foreclosures and other business failures. After a decade of oil shortages, who in the late 1970s and early 1980s dreamed that we would have an oversupply of oil in the mid-1980s? Had oil prices remained stable, might the savings and loan associations in these regions still be solvent?

2. Did deregulation really create a free market? Savings and loan managers were able to use government-insured deposits

CASE & POINT

to invest in various ventures. Thus, a case can be made that there was not a free market. If government deposit insurance was not available, a depositor would scrutinize the financial background of the savings and loan association before depositing savings, just as a prudent investor would in any other nonguaranteed investment. With no government insurance, it is likely that savings depositors would have avoided the weak, poorly managed institutions, thereby depriving those institutions of the funds needed to make investments. Instead, depositors placed money with institutions, knowing that it did not matter if they were good or bad, because the government would guarantee deposits up to the insured maximum, then $100,000.

3. If the government intended to maintain the deposit insurance program, would it not have been prudent for the president and Congress to provide adequate funds for the inspection and examination of savings institutions? Instead, the budgets of the bank and savings and loan examiners reportedly were cut during the early and mid-1980s. This made it easier for crooked S&L owners and managers to loot the institutions. It also allowed incompetent, but not necessarily dishonest, managers to operate longer.

4. Did pressure from savings and loan association trade groups, along with their political action committee (PAC) fund contributions, generate political favors that added to the crisis?

5. It must be pointed out that many savings and loan associations were financially solid and profitable throughout this period. Apparently, deregulation and free market forces worked for these institutions.

As with many economic issues, there are no clear-cut answers to the questions posed by the S&L crisis. Economic historians will be debating its causes for many years to come. But in the end, the U.S. taxpayer footed most of the bill for this financial folly.

Liberal Housing Finance Programs of the 2000s: Another Crisis in the Making

One method used to help pull the United States out of the post 9/11/01 recession was to lower interest rates and liberalize home financing terms. Traditional programs that required 10–20 percentage down payments faded. Instead, no money down (100 percentage) financing programs, coupled with interest-only loans, increased in popularity. This allowed people who were not qualified to own a home under the traditional lending programs to become homeowners. These liberal financing programs also increased the demand for homes, which provided the fire to drive up home prices. Rising home prices generated larger commissions for mortgage and real estate agents, while providing home sellers with large tax-free gains, due to the liberalization of income tax laws passed in 1997.

As noted earlier, at the same time, mortgage loan origination had shifted to mortgage brokers, selling loans into pools that were bundled into securities, split into tranches, and sold as investments all over the world. The many parties in the process were paid based on the volume of transactions, and loan quality was given less emphasis.

The result was an asset bubble—home prices rose rapidly in almost every market. Loan defaults initially were very low, because rising prices bailed out those who couldn't keep up their payments. Investors bought massive amounts of securitized real estate mortgages.

However, all asset bubbles end, as prices cannot increase faster than income for very long. As home price inflation slowed down, the loan quality problems became more apparent, and the loan default rate soared. The market for securitized loans collapsed, dragging much of Wall Street down with it: the collapse of 2007–2008.

Unfortunately, all of this was foreseeable. Industry observers in 2004 and 2005 prominently warned of the coming collapse. Will we learn this time? Can economists resist political pressure? Can Congress? Or are we doomed to these cycles?

So the question becomes, "Are we setting the stage for another real estate housing crisis down the road?" What if interest rates rise, the economy tanks, unemployment rises, and incomes drop? Will the demand for housing then decline, lowering home values and leaving many homeowners "upside down" or "underwater," meaning that they owe more than the home is worth? What if the homeowner then needs to sell and finds out that the lender is owed more than the home is worth? What will be the choices? Add money as a seller to close the sale? Walk away and let the lender foreclose? Ask the lender to forgive part of the loan to avoid foreclosure? What about the tax law that says if the lender forgives part of the loan, that part of the loan must then be declared by the borrower as taxable ordinary income, under the "debt forgiveness rule"? Will this become a crisis equal to the savings and loan crisis of the 1980s? Will the taxpayers be faced with footing the bill for another financial folly? By 2006, signs of this problem were showing up in various real estate markets, especially in California and Florida.

Chapter

5

Demand

Fixed land supply

Fixed short-term
land use

Intensity of land use

Supply

PREVIEW

This chapter explores the basic economic features of real estate. A more in-depth analysis of residential, commercial, industrial, and rural real estate markets will be presented in later chapters.

Section 5.1 discusses the major differences between a perfectly competitive market and typical real estate markets. Section 5.2 outlines how real estate markets react when the demand for real property changes. Section 5.3 introduces the use of graphs to analyze the interaction of supply and demand. The Case & Point at the end of the chapter expands the topic of graphic analysis of supply and demand in the real estate market.

Chapter 5 completes Part One, "Basic Economic Background for Real Estate Analysis." When you have completed this chapter, you will be able to:

1. List five reasons why a real estate market is considered to be imperfect.

2. Discuss why the supply and use of land is considered relatively fixed in the short run.

Important Economic Features of Real Estate

3. Describe why real estate markets need the services of real estate professionals.

4. Describe how an increase or decrease in demand influences the value of real estate.

5.1 ECONOMIC CHARACTERISTICS OF REAL ESTATE MARKETS

A market was previously defined as a place where buyers and sellers meet to exchange items of value. The market for each product or service is somewhat different. The nature of a particular market influences the level of prices paid. In a perfectly competitive market, there are numerous buyers and sellers, each assumed to be knowledgeable and free to move in or out of the market at will. Neither party has any control over the market. Because the products being sold are assumed to be nearly alike, buyers will usually select the one offered at the lowest price. In such a perfect market, prices would be established purely by the principles of supply and demand.

Another important feature of a perfect market is that prices move relatively quickly, either up or down, with minor changes in demand or supply. Both *real and perceived changes* cause prices to change. Buyers who anticipate a drop in supply will, in the short run, bid up prices, even when supply really is not changing! And, with perfect markets, price movement is equally smooth in both the up and down directions. Prices in the stock market (for actively traded stocks) display such a pattern of price movements.

In practice, most markets are *imperfect*. Some of the characteristics of a perfect market are either missing or distorted, preventing the principles of supply and demand from operating efficiently.

What can we say about *real estate market characteristics*? Are real estate markets perfectly competitive or are they imperfect? The answers may be found in Table 5.1, which compares the characteristics of a perfect market and a typical real estate market.

TABLE 5.1 Perfect Markets versus Typical Real Estate Markets

Characteristic	Perfect Market	Typical Real Estate Market
1. Number of buyers and sellers	Many participants; no monopoly, oligopoly, or monopolistic competition	Few participants; seller controls during a "seller's market," and buyer controls during a "buyer's market."
2. Product knowledge and ease of exchange	Buyers and sellers are knowledgeable; exchanges take place with ease.	Buyers and sellers are not always knowledgeable; the exchange is legalistic, complex, and expensive.
3. Standardized products	All products are alike and interchangeable; little difference between products of different sellers.	Each parcel of real estate is unique and separate from all others; no two are exactly alike
4. Mobility	Products can be moved elsewhere to sell at a better market.	The location is fixed; a parcel cannot be moved to another, more profitable location; a real estate market is local, not regional or national.
5. Size and frequency of purchase	The item purchased is small and relatively inexpensive; it is purchased frequently.	Real estate is purchased infrequently (rarely more than four or five times in a lifetime); for example, a home is the largest single investment for an average family.
6. Government's role	Government plays little if any role; laissez-faire prevails.	Government plays a dominant role in encouraging or discouraging real estate development, with fiscal and monetary tools and zoning, environmental, and health codes.
7. Prices	Prices are established by the smooth action of supply and demand.	Prices are influenced by the interaction of supply and demand, but this interaction is not smooth; a lack of knowledge by either the buyer or seller can distort the prices paid.

Table 5.1 shows that real estate markets are very imperfect! Characteristics of the imperfect real estate markets include the following: real estate buyers and sellers are frequently relatively uninformed about real estate issues, values and market trends; the transfer of real property requires a legal and technical knowledge not possessed by the average citizen; each real estate parcel is separate and unique from all other parcels; and the location of the land cannot be moved to benefit from better market conditions in other geographic areas.

Does This Mean That the Principles of Supply and Demand Do Not Work in Real Estate Markets?

No, the principles of supply and demand are still important influences on the value of real estate. However, it is important to recognize that supply and demand operate differently in real estate markets. In a perfectly competitive market, supply and demand react quickly to changes in market conditions. *In real estate markets, supply is fixed in the short run and cannot respond quickly to changes in market conditions.* Under the best of circumstances, it takes a minimum of several years to subdivide raw land, develop lots, and build the first house. With very complex properties, it can take a decade. Even with a supply of vacant buildable lots, it can take a year for a builder to buy a lot, obtain financing and permits, and complete construction. Real estate supply can be very slow to change.

The Total Supply of Land Is Fixed

One of the most fundamental principles of real estate economics is the recognition that there is a **fixed land supply**. The land surface cannot be increased or decreased according to the whims of demand. At any point in time, every inch of land is being used for some purpose. It might be vacant land that is not being farmed, but only held in anticipation of higher prices. Nevertheless, that is its current use! Any use of land can be changed to another use, but that can take time. A change in use could require annexation to the local city, or to a sewer or water service area. Rezoning might be required. Sometimes, an environmental impact study is needed. These issues are explored further in Chapter 15. The **intensity of land use** can also change, and in time this will act to increase or decrease the supply of real estate. For example, it may be impossible to increase the number of acres within the city limits, but it can be easy to increase the number of housing units per acre. This can generate an increase in the supply of homes, without any increase in the supply of land.

However, any change in the *intensity* of land use usually also takes time. If the demand for residential or other real estate projects was suddenly to increase, developers would need considerable time to acquire land, get it rezoned to a higher intensity of use, and obtain permits and financing. The state and local permit process could take years. And environmental groups and unhappy neighbors might sue, seeking to block further development. So, in a practical sense, there is a **fixed short-term land use**.

Once a building is constructed, it tends to have a long life, regardless of any short-run changes in the real estate market. This keeps supply from declining. For example, if the demand for homes within a community declines, a builder with an unsold supply of new houses will not demolish them, simply because the demand for the homes has diminished! Instead, the homes will sit vacant on the market until they are sold. If they remain unsold very long, the lender will foreclose, and then sell the inventory at discount prices. (Note that when houses are foreclosed before construction is completed, the damage from the weather could result in their demolition!) If demand continues to be less that the existing supply, buildings could simply sit vacant. This happened to a few poorer neighborhoods of New York City in the 1980s, and Detroit in the mid-2000s. Many mining towns just turned into ghost towns, when mining no longer was profitable.

If demand shifts to another use, there will be an over-supply of buildings designed for the old use. It may be possible to adapt an existing building to another use. Many large older residences have been converted into apartments or even rooming houses. And many residences located along streets that have become arterial roads, with heavy traffic, have been converted into offices, stores, or even small churches. See Figure 5.1. However, most buildings are not that easy to adapt to a new user. Rezoning might be required. Costly remodeling may be necessary. Both take time, making any change in use of existing buildings a slow process. This again can act to keep supply somewhat fixed in the short run.

But real estate supply can be complex to figure out. Consider the supply of homes. At any one point in time, there are only so many existing homes. So, we can say that supply is fixed. But the key issue in pricing is not the total number of homes. Instead, it is the supply of homes for sale. That number is not fixed in the short run.

What would happen if, for example, a new government program lowers interest rates for home loans? The lower interest rate would mean that monthly payments would be less (if prices do not change.) Lower payments mean that more people would qualify for a loan. This would increase demand! With more demand, prices

FIGURE 5.1 House converted to an office.

would rise. With higher prices, the supply of homes for sale is likely to rise! Here is why.

Speculators holding houses are more likely to sell. People renting out "the old family home," but living elsewhere, are more likely to decide to let go. Some will decide that the increase in their equity will allow them to sell and retire to the country, or sell and move up to a better home, better school district, or more convenient location.

Therefore, the supply of homes for sale is not really fixed in the short run. This is also true of homes or apartments for rent. What if a small town is to host some large gathering? There aren't enough hotel rooms within a reasonable travel time. Every vacant housing unit will quickly be converted to house the guests. As all available regular units books up in advance, overnight rental rates for the week in question climb! Some people offer a room in their home, or fix up an unused mother-in-law unit. Others move in with family, and offer their unit for rent. The supply grows, in a very short time, with no new construction!

Commercial property has the same supply pattern. The total number of income property of any type is fixed, at any one point in time. However, the *number for sale*, or for rent, can increase quite rapidly, when prices increase.

5.2 HOW REAL ESTATE MARKETS REACT TO CHANGES IN DEMAND

What happens with a *real estate demand change*? An increase in demand for a particular type of real estate, at a particular location, will generally have the following consequences:

1. An increase in demand will reduce the number of existing real estate vacancies, be it in office space, stores, apartments, or in the inventory of homes for sale.

2. This reduction in vacancies will be followed, relatively quickly, by an increase in rents and prices (assuming no rent controls) as more people continue to bid for the existing supply.

3. As demand pushes rents and prices up, a point is reached at which investors and builders, motivated by profit potential, are drawn into the construction market.

4. Assuming favorable economic and governmental conditions, new construction takes place slowly, and the supply of real estate gradually increases.

5. However, as this new construction grows, eventually it overtakes the increase in demand, and vacancies begin to rise.

6. This increase in vacancies causes a decline in rents and prices. Price and rent declines may not be readily apparent at first, but instead often initially show up as rent concessions, or favorable seller-aided financing.

7. With lower rents and prices, the difference between building costs and sales prices begins to narrow, and developer profits decline and then disappear. This change in developer profits is rapid, because the increased construction activity forces up building costs, catching builder profits in a fast-moving squeeze, between rising costs and falling sales prices.

A decrease in the demand for a particular type of real estate, in a particular location, will generally have these consequences:

1. A decrease in demand causes an increase in vacancies in offices, stores, apartments, or a larger number of unsold homes.

2. The increase in vacancies will cause rents and prices to decline.

3. With lower rents and prices, people can now obtain more spacious quarters, at no increase in costs. This may absorb the vacancy. If not, the continued vacancy will eventually force owners to demolish structures and reuse the land.

4. The real estate market will remain in this state until demand once again increases.[1]

The 2007 Mortgage Crisis contained many superb examples of supply and demand in practice. For example, there were many home loan mortgages in the processing pipeline, between the time of a loan commitment, through close of escrow, sale on the secondary market, bundling into a security ("securitization"), and the time of final sale to investors as tranches. Once a loan commitment was made, all parties were committed, *except the ultimate tranche buyer*! When the market for mortgage-backed securities froze, the securitizers—usually investment banks—had a supply of securities, but no demand for them. Prices collapsed, followed by company bankruptcies.

And as home prices no longer climbed rapidly, many people who had paid deposits on new homes defaulted or cancelled. The absence of buyers left many completed unsold homes—supply without demand. Completed lots lacked builders willing to build, and lenders willing to lend—supply without demand. Prices fell, drastically in some overbuilt areas.

Ultimately, prices fell far enough to interest buyers. Figure 5.2 shows the steep build-up in unsold homes between 2004 and 2008. Notice the equally sharp decline afterwards, as price drops attracted large numbers of buyers! In addition to price drops, demand was increased by Congress, passing several significant stimulus measures, including the first-time homebuyer credit. This noticeably increased demand in 2009. Actions by The Fed lowered interest rates, as well, which further increased demand.

---

[1] Based in part on *A Teacher's Guide for Real Estate Economics*, California Department of Real Estate, prepared by Dr. William Hippaka, 1974, Sacramento, CA.

FIGURE 5.2   Unsold inventory index.

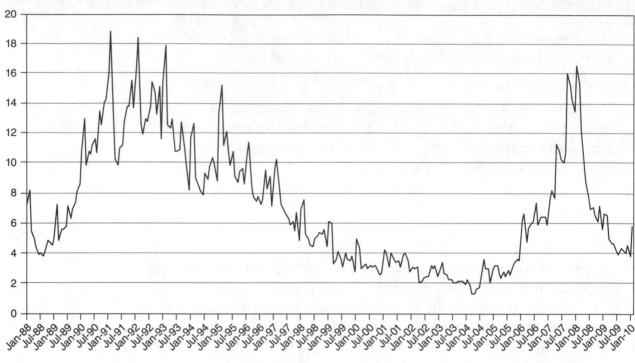

Source: California Association of REALTORS

What Causes Supply and Demand for Real Estate to Change?

Changes in real estate demand can be caused by real or expected changes in population, income, availability of mortgage credit, personal lifestyles, or governmental actions. Recall the discussion, above, and in prior chapters about the impacts of governmental actions and economic change. Long-run changes in supply, on the other hand, result from changes in the rate or cost of construction, conversion to another use, or demolition, and from how governmental actions impact these three alternatives.

The cause of a change can vary for each type of real estate market and location. The reasons for a change in the supply or demand for residential real estate are often different from the reasons for changes in commercial, industrial, or rural real estate markets. The causes for changes in supply and demand for specific types of real estate will be examined in detail in Chapter 9, "Housing Markets"; Chapter 10, "Commercial and Industrial Markets"; and Chapter 11, "Rural and Recreational Real Estate Markets."

Where does *cost* enter into this? For demand, the cost to build it is not a direct factor. It would cost a lot of money to build a modern computer chip manufacturing facility in the middle of the Sahara

Desert, in Africa. But that high cost would not change the reality that there is no demand at that location for such a plant, at any price.

However, cost could be a demand factor, if the choice to meet demand was to either purchase an existing home, or buy a lot and build a new one. Everything else being equal, and if time to build the new home is not an issue, the price for the existing house is likely to be less than the total cost for the new one. This assumes that the new one is more desirable, because the materials, colors, layout, and appliances can exactly match the buyer's preferences! And cost of a new home would not be relevant if the buyer wanted to buy an older or historical building. The supply curve, on the other hand, can be closely tied to the cost to supply the product. In an older neighborhood with no vacant lots, there is little connection between the supply of homes and the cost to build a new home. In areas with available vacant lots, however, there is a close connection. Sometimes, producers end up selling below their cost; other times, they make a larger profit than expected. Over time, however, they have to cover all of their costs, including a reasonable profit, or they will go broke. *In the short run*, however, real estate supply has no close connection to cost at all: What is for sale simply is there.

At all times and all locations, however, cost does not determine price or value. One can see a mansion, listed for sale but in escrow, that seems absolutely perfect to a buyer. Since it is no longer on the market for sale, why not find a lot, and have the same builder build another? The next town over is closer to work, so the next step is to buy a lot there. The best lot is rather small, but will do. When completed, can it be sold, or appraised, to cover its costs (assuming that markets have stayed stable during this time period)? Not necessarily! For this town, the mansion may be too big, the school district not as favorable, or the neighboring houses not attractive enough for mansion buyers. The best house in an area almost always is penalized in this way, because it is not *in balance with* its surroundings. On the other hand, the worst house in an area usually will sell at a good price relative to its costs.

Foreign Ownership of U.S. Real Estate[2]

Clearly, foreign investors form part of the demand for U.S. real estate. Investors, agents, lenders, and appraisers need to recognize this impact on demand, and when it changes. In the 1980s, major segments

[2] Information based in part on Lawrence Bacow, "The Internationalization of the U.S. Real Estate Industry," Cambridge: Massachusetts Institute of Technology, 1989. For a copy and price, contact Director of Publications, MIT Center for Real Estate Development, Building W31 310 Cambridge, MA 02139.

of real estate gradually shifted, from being controlled by local developers, investors, lenders, and agents, to a global business, with many foreign investors playing a key role. Foreign investors initially acquired fully leased commercial properties with triple "A" tenants, at excellent locations in major U.S. cities. By the mid-1980s, foreign investors were perceived to be overpaying for the properties, and driving up prices in the local real estate market. Some foreign investors either purchased or founded U.S.-based real estate companies, to acquire and manage their properties. Later, foreign development companies created projects from the ground up, rather than depend on finding existing buildings for sale at reasonable prices.

With the crash of commercial real estate market prices in the early to mid-1990s, many foreign investors took heavy losses on their U.S. real estate. Using the accuracy of hindsight, it appears that many U.S. real estate owners sold at the peak of the market to foreign buyers, getting out just before the crash. By the early 2000s, some foreign property owners had resold their buildings at a loss to U.S. interests.

The rise in prices in the mid-2000s caused a mixed flow of overseas investment capital. The decline of prices in the late 2000s, however, lead to an increase in overseas investors, seeking to buy at what was perceived to be a cyclical bottom in the real estate price cycle. This reflected the growing understanding of American real estate markets by foreign investors and their advisors and money managers.

Foreign investment is heavily influenced by factors besides the prices of U.S. real estate. A second major influence is the exchange rate between the U.S. dollar and other currencies. When the dollar falls in value, relative to other currencies, then U.S. real estate looks less expensive and foreign investors tend to buy more. The exchange rate for the dollar does not move the same for all other currencies. Some go up; others go down. This means that buyers will come from varying countries, depending on changes in the exchange rate for each currency.

A third major influence arises from the political, social, or economic issues in each country. For example, around the time when the British turned over control of Hong Kong to China in 1997, some well-to-do Hong Kong investors purchased U.S. and Canadian real estate, to diversify their investment, out of concern for future Chinese actions. In the 2000s, well-to-do Russians became major buyers of high-end New York and Miami condominiums. South Americans have also been major buyers of Miami condominiums. In the San Francisco Bay area and Seattle, Asian buyers have become more numerous. This factor or motivation has existed for centuries.

It just varies, from decade to decade, depending where there is money, combined with some instability.

The entire issue of foreign ownership of U.S. businesses and real estate has had emotions running high. Here are some of the advantages and disadvantages frequently cited.

Advantages of Foreign Ownership

1. Generates income for U.S. real estate owners who sell. This income is reinvested, which stimulates the economy and leads to additional employment.
2. Provides tax revenue to the government from the profits on the sale. This helps cover some of the budget deficit, without raising income tax rates or cutting government spending programs.
3. Generates commissions and fees for the real estate industry.
4. Increases the number of prospective buyers, which strengthens demand and helps to maintain or improve prices.

Disadvantages of Foreign Ownership

1. Makes the United States less self-sufficient and more dependent on foreign investment. In short, it constitutes a "selling of America."
2. Gives the U.S. government less incentive to solve the budget deficit problem, by providing a short-run "quick fix" using foreign capital, instead of reducing government spending or raising taxes.
3. High prices paid by foreign investors replace local investors in the real estate market.

No matter where a person stands on the issue of foreign ownership, it should be pointed out that U.S. citizens have been buying assets of other countries for many decades. Americans supported free trade when they were buying into foreign countries; when the reverse became true, some U.S. citizens lobbied for restrictions!

Why Have Real Estate Professionals[3]

What is the *real estate professional's role*? In perfectly competitive markets, there is no need for the services of a real estate professional or any other third party. Buyers and sellers are considered to be fully

---

[3] Based in part on A Teacher's Guide for Real Estate Economics, California Department of Real Estate, prepared by Dr. William Hippaka, pp. 142–143, 1974, Sacramento, CA.

knowledgeable, and are able to handle transactions themselves. However, because the real estate market is imperfect, the real estate professional's role is to help buyers, sellers, landlords, tenants, lenders, and others overcome these market imperfections.

Many people are involved in real estate transactions. This includes obvious examples, like real estate brokers and agents, escrow agents, and title insurance companies or title researchers. Lenders are also involved, including loan brokers or loan bankers, underwriters, and appraisers. Now, there also are secondary market investors, and people to bundle mortgages into securities. In addition, there are wood-destroying organism inspectors, roof inspectors, building inspectors, and septic system inspectors. Property managers are active with properties that were purchased as investments. Working behind the scenes are people who post and remove the "For Sale" signs, those who take pictures of the property for the Multiple Listing Service (MLS), and the people who handle the advertisements, print the brochures, and run the MLS. Some consult on "staging" a property, so that it shows well. And behind it all are the numbers of invisible but indispensable support people.

Real estate professionals fill gaps in market knowledge, by providing the following services:

1. Improve a property's exposure to buyers, by marketing, including MLS listing, advertisements, flyers, brochures, and open houses.

2. Improve buyer's awareness of alternative properties, by use of the MLS, property tours, and research.

3. Increase buyer and seller knowledge by:

   a. Providing current market information regarding selling prices, rents, and market trends.

   b. Advising clients and customers on investment opportunities, property characteristics, and market issues.

   c. Providing information on sources and alternative methods of financing.

   d. Helping the parties to negotiate an agreement, and close the real estate transaction.

4. Increase the number of market participants, by persuading owners to offer their property for sale, and by encouraging people to overcome concerns and acquire real estate. These efforts can increase the number of buyers and sellers, and help to reduce one of the major imperfections of a real estate market: too few participants.

Impact of the Internet

The Internet is a means of communicating information. As such, it improves the ability of markets to change, as supply and demand change. As more data becomes available on the Internet, the traditional role of all real estate professionals is being changed. With a few clicks on a search engine, consumers can find nearly all properties that are currently offered for sale, estimate market prices, and find sites that tell you step by step how to buy, finance, or sell a home. A good example is Zillow.com, a leading online real estate marketplace to find and share vital information about homes and mortgages. When you view their Web page, notice the tabs at the top of the page, and all of the information sources that are immediately available. There are thousands of useful websites! A few good "starters" are listed below.

As more and more consumers utilize the Internet, many of the information functions of the real estate professional outlined above will fade away. Some, however, will remain. Because market conditions change, Web sites often lack good information on the most recent price trends, and the currently used local listing and buying strategies. In turn, Web sites offer agents, appraisers, lenders, etc., new ways to reach out to customers. The primary role of all real estate professionals is evolving. Buyers and sellers will be more knowledgeable than in the past, but often will still need real estate professionals for advice on current trends and issues at that particular location and on listing or

---

Some Useful Websites

www.Realtor.com	www.car.org	www.move.com
www.craigslist.org	www.city-data.com	www.bankrate.com
www.floodsource.com	www.mtgprofessor.com	www.nolo.com (legal)
www.buildings.com	www.inman.com	

Useful Categories of Sites

Association of REALTORS® brokerage companies

Associations of all types lenders

City, county, state or federal agencies title companies

Useful Real Estate Publication Sites

Wall Street Journal (www.wsj.com)	www.workingre.com
www.realtytimes.com	www.globest.com

buying alternatives, for transaction negotiations, and to handle the time-consuming follow-up, needed to close a real estate transaction.

Overall, one of the major economic impacts of the Internet has been to reduce the role of the so-called "middleman." Use of the Internet has noticeably reduced the needed number of travel agents, stock brokers, insurance agents, mortgage brokers, and so on. Consumers can log on and then buy direct, cutting out the middleperson. However, real estate, as emphasized earlier, is an unusually complex product to buy or sell. Only the future will show what impact the Internet will have on the needed number of real estate appraisers and agents, and on real estate practice.

REVIEWING YOUR UNDERSTANDING

How Real Estate Markets React to Changes in Demand

1. If the demand for apartments increases, what will happen to vacancy rates? The price of apartment buildings?

2. Will an increase in real estate demand raise mortgage interest rates in the short run? In the long run?

3. If contractors build too many homes, what will happen to sales prices? Why?

4. As a broker, you have been asked by a consumer group to justify the need for the services of a real estate agent. What are some things you should point out?

5.3 ANALYZING DEMAND AND SUPPLY USING GRAPHS

According to economic theory, prices and output in perfect markets are established by the smooth interaction of demand and supply. To show this visually, economists use lines on graphs. For theory purposes, straight lines are commonly used. In the real world, demand and supply lines are usually curved, which is why they are referred to as "curves."

Demand

Demand is the total quantity that buyers are willing to buy, at a given time and location, at certain prices. Figure 5.4 illustrates a downward slope of the demand curve to the right. This reflects the *law of demand*. The law of demand states that the lower the price, the more

FIGURE 5.3 Demand curve.

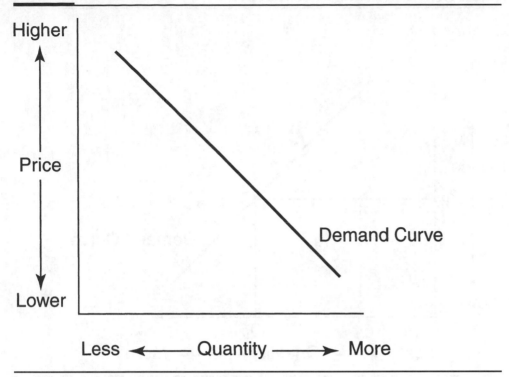

consumers will buy; the higher the price, the less they will buy. The price is always shown on the vertical axis or side of the graph. The quantity is shown on the horizontal axis or bottom side. By tradition, where the vertical and horizontal sides meet is always either *zero*, or else it is the lowest number on that line. Thus, any point on the demand curve has a matching price, and a matching quantity.

We analyze a graph, like Figure 5.3, by selecting a price on the vertical line, "Price." Next, from that price, we go across level, until we hit the demand curve. From where we hit, we look straight down to the bottom line, "Quantity." Now, we know the quantity that will be demanded at that price.

The graph can also be read in the other direction. If we are planning to build 200 condominium units, we would find "200" on the bottom "Quantity" line. From there, we would go straight up until we hit the demand curve. Next, we would look straight left, to see what price we need to have, in order to sell all 200 units in a reasonable time. Of course, almost never is there adequate data to do this in the real world!

If you are not familiar with analyzing graphs, it will be helpful to review each of the graphs in this section with its related text.

Now, look at Figure 5.4. Notice that, as you move along the demand curve from point X to point Y, the price declines, from Px to Py.

FIGURE 5.4   Movement along the demand curve.

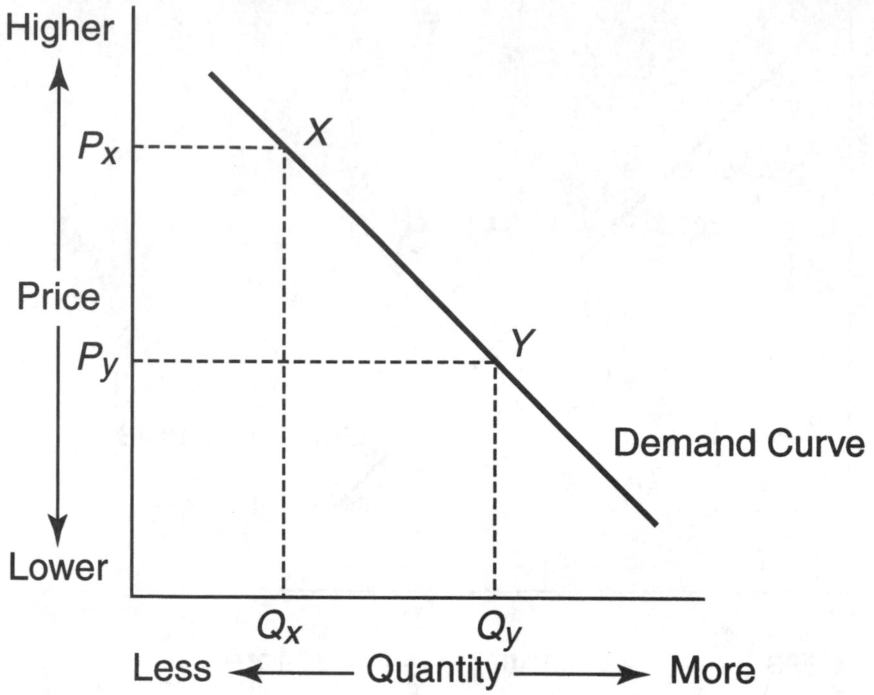

But the quantity increases, from Qx to Qy. At lower prices, the quantity that existing buyers are willing to purchase increases, just as the law of demand states. If you move back on the curve, from point Y to X, prices will increase, from Py to Px, and quantity will decline from Qy to Qx.

Therefore, a change in price does not move or shift the *demand curve* right or left. Instead, a change in price results in movement up or down, *along* the existing demand curve.

Supply

Supply is the total quantity that sellers are willing to sell at a given time at certain prices. Figure 5.5 illustrates the upward slope of the supply curve to the right. This reflects the *law of supply*. The law states that sellers or producers will offer more goods and services for sale as prices increase, and fewer as prices decrease.

Looking at Figure 5.6, notice that as you move from point A to B, prices increase from Pa to Pb. Quantity increases from Qa to Qb. As the prices increase, the existing suppliers, motivated by profits, will increase their output. If you move back from Pb to Pa, the decline in price will cause suppliers to cut back in quantity from Qb to Qa.

FIGURE 5.5 Supply curve.

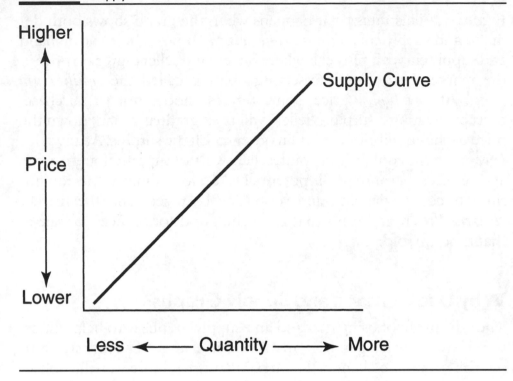

FIGURE 5.6 Movement along the supply curve.

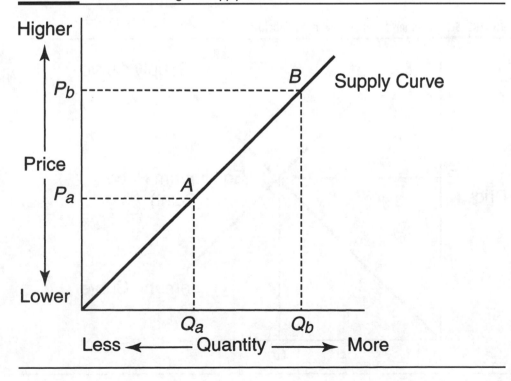

Equilibrium

Figure 5.7 illustrates what happens when the graph shows both demand and supply curves, at *any one point in* time. Where the demand and supply curves intersect is where buyers and sellers agree on price in the marketplace. This intersecting point is called the *equilibrium point*. At any *higher* price, some buyers choose not to purchase, thereby creating a surplus. Sellers will then gradually mark down the price to the equilibrium point, in order to sell the surplus. At any price *lower* than the equilibrium point, sellers will not supply enough goods and services, because profit potential is too low. Only at the equilibrium price will demand and supply be balanced, and the market *cleared*. This term means that all of the goods or services for sale at that time are sold.

Why Use Demand and Supply Graphs?

The advantage of using demand and supply graphs is to help understand what may happen with an economic change. The first step is to see the economic change. The next step is to figure out the consequences for supply, demand, and prices. You can consider this further, in the Addendum, which takes a deeper look at demand-supply graphs.

FIGURE 5.7   Demand and supply in equilibrium.

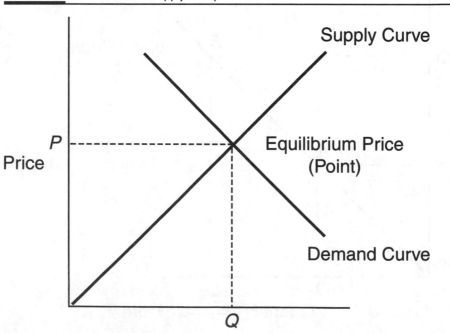

REVIEWING YOUR UNDERSTANDING

Analyzing Demand and Supply Using Graphs

1. Why does the demand curve slope downward to the right side of the graph? Why does the supply curve slope in the opposite direction?
2. Can the demand curve only be used to see what price would cause a particular quantity to be in demand?
3. Is the equilibrium point fixed for a time period?

CHAPTER SUMMARY

All real estate markets have unique economic characteristics that separate them from markets for most other products and services. For example, real estate buyers and sellers may not be fully informed about real estate values and market trends. In addition, the transfer of real property requires legal and technical knowledge not possessed by the average person. Each real estate parcel is unique, isolated, and tied to a single, fixed location. Real estate is purchased infrequently, and often represents the largest single investment an individual will ever make. Finally, once a real estate use is established, it tends to have a long physical and economic life.

These characteristics of real estate markets create a need for an expert to provide technical advice, and to advise the uninformed. The expert's role is filled by real estate professionals, who provide buyers and sellers with the market information needed to make rational real estate decisions. However, as more information becomes available on the Internet, the real estate professional's role will gradually change, from information provider to becoming more of a facilitator and strategic advisor.

The analysis of any real estate market requires understanding basic facts about the supply and demand of real estate. The supply of land in the short run is fixed—it cannot be expanded. The supply of land for various uses is also fixed, in the short run. Thus, in the short run, changes in current real estate values are usually the result of shifts in demand, not in supply.

Changes in demand result from changes in population, income, credit, lifestyles, and governmental action. Long-run changes in the supply of real estate structures are influenced by the rate of new construction, conversion to another use, and demolition. However, each segment of the local real estate market, whether residential, commercial, industrial, or rural, reacts differently, and therefore must be analyzed separately. Foreign ownership of U.S. real estate has created debates regarding the impacts on real estate markets.

Graphs of the demand and supply curves show how the quantity varies with price. Where the demand and supply curves intersect or cross is the market price, for that product or service, at that instant in time. These graphs are a useful tool, to help understand the impact of economic change on prices.

REVIEWING YOUR UNDERSTANDING

1. Which of the following is a characteristic of an imperfect real estate market?
   A. many and equal numbers of buyers and sellers
   B. highly knowledgeable buyers and sellers
   C. all products are alike
   D. fixed location

2. In a real estate "seller's market":
   A. supply exceeds demand
   B. prices are declining
   C. there are many qualified buyers but few properties for sale
   D. mortgage interest rates are very high

3. One of the key economic features of real estate is:
   A. short-run fixed supply
   B. fixed demand
   C. mobility
   D. low unit cost

4. An increase in demand will have what short-run impact on real estate prices and rents?
   A. prices and rents should decrease
   B. prices should decrease, but rents should increase
   C. prices and rents should increase
   D. prices should increase, but rents should decrease

5. The use of real estate brokers tends to make the real estate market:
   A. less than perfect
   B. more imperfect
   C. more nearly perfect
   D. does not influence the market one way or the other

6. Multiple listing services of a local real estate association tend to make the real estate market:
   A. less than perfect
   B. more imperfect
   C. more nearly perfect
   D. does not influence the market one way or the other

7. If the demand for commercial real estate increases, but "no growth" controls prevent new construction, rents per square foot in the short run should:
   A. increase
   B. decrease
   C. remain the same
   D. shift downward

8. All of the following can influence the demand for real estate except:
   A. population
   B. mortgage interest rates
   C. rates of construction
   D. lifestyles

9. "Six months free rent" as a concession is in reality a:
   A. reduction in rent
   B. sign of an increase in the need for construction
   C. sign of an increase in demand
   D. sign of a decrease in supply

10. Foreign ownership of U.S. real estate:
    A. provides needed capital for U.S. citizens
    B. in the short run, increases government revenues
    C. helps maintain real estate prices
    D. does all of the above

11. Numerous and knowledgeable buyers and sellers, and neither party has control, describes which of the following?
    A. perfect market
    B. imperfect market
    C. mixed economy
    D. command economy

12. In real estate, a "buyer's market" usually occurs when:
    A. demand exceeds supply
    B. numerous properties are for sale
    C. interest rates are low
    D. there are plenty of qualified buyers

13. The supply of land is fixed, but in time, the intensity of land use can be increased.
    A. true
    B. false

14. Overbuilding results when:
    A. demand exceeds supply
    B. lenders tighten up on construction credit
    C. government imposes "no growth" controls
    D. supply exceeds demand, but new construction continues

15. All other things being equal, if population increases and mortgage interest rates decline:
    A. office rents should decline
    B. more renters should start to buy homes
    C. the economy should be heading for a recession
    D. resale of existing homes should go down

16. Which of the following is considered a real estate supply variable?
    A. consumer tastes
    B. population
    C. income
    D. rate of construction

17. A change or shift in the demand for real estate can be caused by:
    A. changes in the availability of mortgage credit
    B. population changes
    C. income changes
    D. all of the above

18. According to the law of demand, as local home prices drop, the:
    A. demand for homes should decrease
    B. quantity of homes demanded should increase
    C. supply of homes will increase in the short run
    D. vacancy rate for homes should increase

19. Foreign ownership of real estate tends to increase when the:
    A. value of the dollar increases
    B. U.S. economy and the country of the potential foreign investor are in recession
    C. value of foreign currency increases compared to U.S. currency
    D. barriers to free trade are increased

20. Which of the following actions by real estate agents tend to make the real estate market more competitive?
    A. establishing uniform rates for sales commissions
    B. encouraging more owners to list their homes for sale
    C. member-only access to multiple listing information
    D. not explaining information about the various options for home financing

21. An increase in demand is illustrated by a:
    A. shift of the demand curve to the right
    B. shift of the demand curve to the left
    C. movement along the demand curve
    D. decrease in the quantity demanded

22. A decrease in supply is illustrated by a:
    A. shift of the supply curve to the right
    B. shift of the supply curve to the left
    C. movement along the supply curve
    D. increase in the quantity supplied

23. Price is set by:
    A. a movement along the demand curve
    B. a shift of the supply curve
    C. where the supply and demand curves cross
    D. where the supply and demand curves intersect the borders

Questions 24–26 are based on the Case & Point, "Demand and Supply Graphics"

24. In Figure 5.10, as demand increases, while supply remains the same:
    A. prices increase
    B. supply decreases
    C. equilibrium remains the same
    D. quantity decreases

25. Once in equilibrium, an increase in demand and supply at the same time by the same amount will:
    A. decrease price
    B. increase price
    C. increase quantity
    D. shift the demand and supply curves to the left

26. According to Figure 5.16, a short-run decrease in demand for real estate will:
    A. decrease prices and rents
    B. increase prices and rents
    C. decrease supply
    D. decrease quantity

CASE & POINT

Taking Demand and Supply Graphs Another Step

In Section 5.3, we introduced the idea that one could prepare a graph, showing how the demand for a product or service could change as prices change. And one can prepare a graph, showing how the supply of that product or service changes as prices change. When combined, the two lines illustrate how buyers and sellers negotiate over prices, and find a price that gets everything sold that is for sale, within a reasonable time. Higher prices leave some products unsold, while lower prices cause some sellers to take products off of the market. But the graphs in Section 5.3 only show the market at one instant in time. What happens later?

Increase or Decrease in Demand and Supply

In the real world, markets are dynamic! The equilibrium point is constantly changing, as buyers and sellers shift back and forth. The impact that these changes have on market prices will depend on the direction and intensity of the change in demand or supply.

Changes in demand are caused by changes in population, income, personal tastes, credit, substitute products, perception, and advertising. Changes in supply are caused by changes in the cost of production, new technology, and shifts in optimism or pessimism regarding the economic future. Figures 5.8 and 5.9 illustrate that any *increase* in demand or supply is shown by a movement or shift of the curve to the right.

Figures 5.10 and 5.11 illustrate that any *decrease* in demand or supply results in a movement or shift of the curve to the left.

Figure 5.12 illustrates the impact of an increase in demand, with the supply curve remaining the same. If demand increases while the supply curve remains unchanged or fixed, the quantity produced must increase from Q1 to Q2, prices must increase from P1 to P2, and a new equilibrium is established at E2.

On the other hand, if demand decreases while the supply curve remains unchanged or fixed, see Figure 5.13. The quantity produced must decrease from Q1 to Q2, prices decrease as a result from P1 to P2, and a new equilibrium is established at E2.

Figures 5.14 and 5.15 illustrate the impact, if supply increases or decreases, while the demand curve remains the same. If supply *increases* while the demand curve remains fixed, prices

CASE & POINT

FIGURE 5.8 Increase in demand.

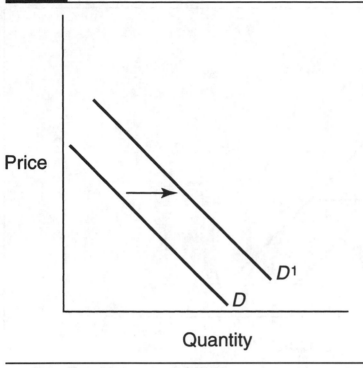

FIGURE 5.9 Increase in supply.

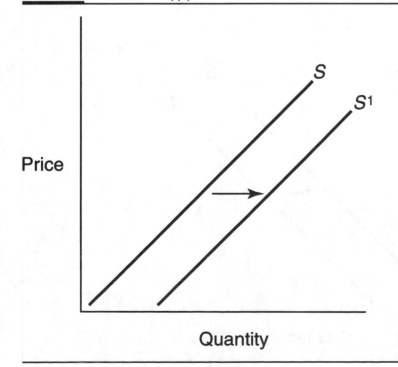

CASE & POINT

FIGURE 5.10   Decrease in demand.

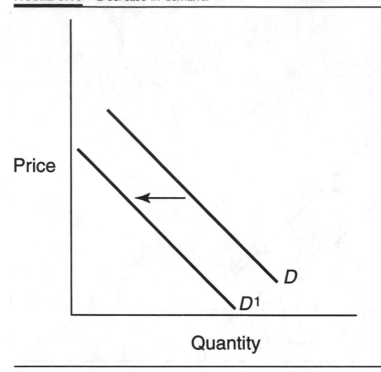

FIGURE 5.11   Decrease in supply.

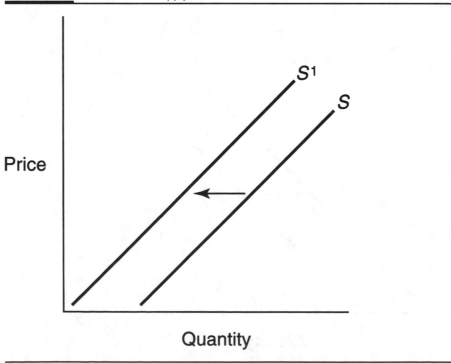

CASE & POINT

FIGURE 5.12   Increase in demand, with the supply curve remaining the same.

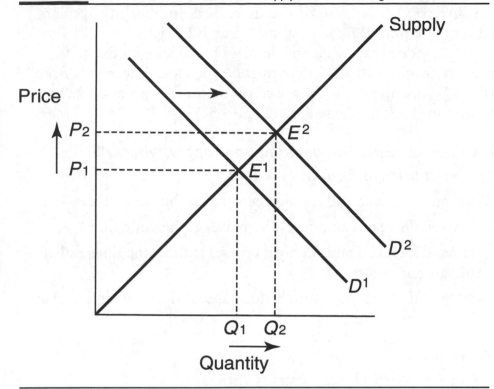

FIGURE 5.13   Decrease in demand, with the supply curve remaining the same.

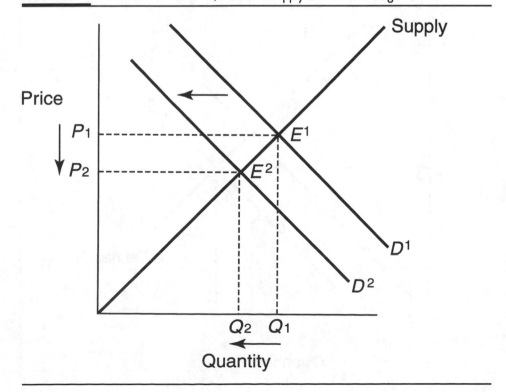

CASE & POINT

must drop from P1 to P2, as the quantity produced increases from Q1 to Q2, because of the increased number of suppliers, and a new equilibrium is established at E2 (Figure 5.14).

If supply decreases while the demand curve remains fixed, prices must rise from P1 to P2, as the quantity produced decreases from Q1 to Q2, because of the decreased number of suppliers, and a new equilibrium is established at E2 (Figure 5.15).

Test Yourself: Based on demand and supply, what will happen to price and quantity when:

1. demand increases and supply decreases at the same time?
2. demand decreases and supply increases at the same time?
3. demand increases and supply increases at the same time and at the same amount?
4. demand decreases and supply decreases at the same time and at the same amount?

Answers

1. You should get a large increase in price.
2. You should get a large decrease in price.

FIGURE 5.14   Increase in supply; demand curve remaining the same.

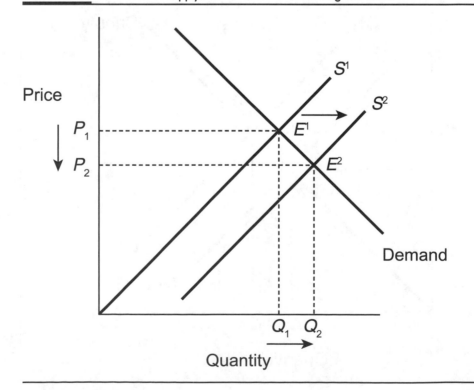

CASE & POINT

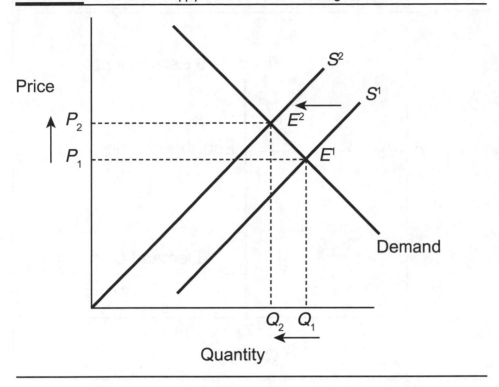

FIGURE 5.15   Decrease in supply; demand curve remaining the same.

3. You should get no change in price, but an increase in quantity.

4. You should get no change in price, but a decrease in quantity.

The Demand and Supply for Real Estate
Short-Run Impact

As mentioned earlier, a fundamental principle of real estate economics is the recognition that the total amount of land is fixed. The land surface cannot be increased or decreased, according to the whims of demand. However, the *intensity of land use* can change. In time, this will increase or decrease the supply of real estate units. Any change in the intensity of land use takes time. If the demand for residential or other real estate was suddenly to increase, a small increase in demand probably could be handled with the existing supply of buildings. But a big increase in demand essentially would face a fixed supply. To expand supply, developers would need considerable time to acquire land and obtain permits and financing. Figure 5.16 illustrates a down-sloping real estate demand curve, with a short-run fixed supply curve, intersecting at equilibrium.

CASE & POINT

FIGURE 5.16 Real estate demand curve with a short-run fixed supply.

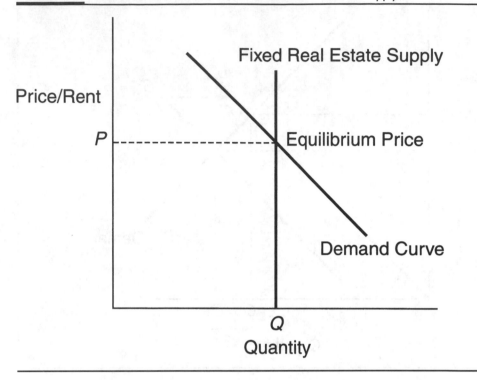

If the supply of real estate is relatively fixed in the short run, any change in current market prices and rents will be heavily influenced by local changes in demand for that type of real estate. When the demand goes up, and the demand curve shifts right, prices and rents must rise, as buyers and renters attempt to outbid one another for the fixed supply. Figure 5.17 illustrates how an increase in demand increases prices or rents, but this *short-run increase* cannot immediately increase the supply of real estate. Therefore, the price and/or rent levels of the existing real estate increase from P1 to P2.

However, when the demand goes down, and the demand curve moves or shifts to the left, prices and rents decline, because the decrease in demand creates some vacancies, and owners and landlords attempt to fill these vacancies by lowering prices and rents. Figure 5.18 illustrates how a decrease in demand decreases prices or rents, but this *short-run decrease* cannot immediately decrease the supply of real estate. Therefore, the price and/or rent levels of the existing supply decrease from P1 to P2.

FIGURE 5.17 Increase in the demand for real estate with a short-run fixed supply.

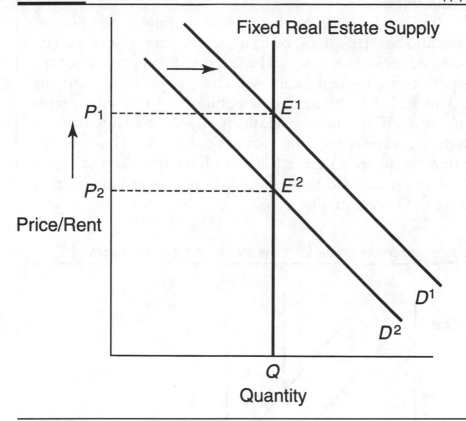

FIGURE 5.18 Decrease in the demand for real estate with a short-run fixed supply.

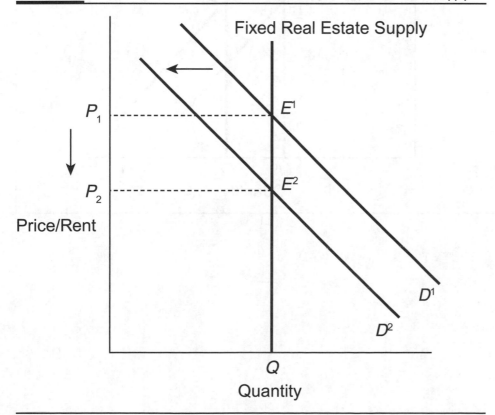

CASE & POINT

Long-Run Impact

In the long run, once financing and building permits are obtained and construction is completed, the supply of real estate units offered for sale or rent can be increased. When this occurs, the supply curve for real estate will change, by shifting to the right. This will then create a new equilibrium for prices/rents and quantity. If the new increase in supply matches existing demand, prices and rents should remain stable. (See Figure 5.19.) If the new construction exceeds demand, overbuilding will have occurred and prices and rents should decline as owners attempt to reduce the excess supply.

FIGURE 5.19   Increase in demand for real estate with an increase in supply.

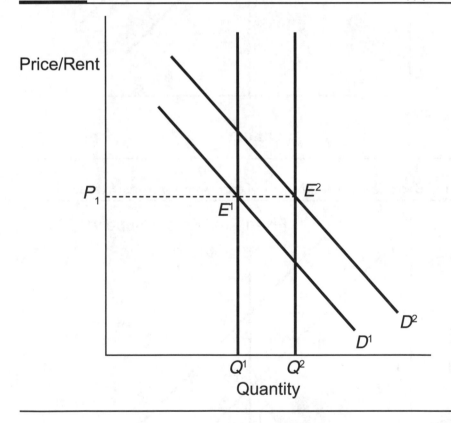

PART 2

Understanding Real Estate Markets

Chapter

6

IMPORTANT TERMS AND CONCEPTS

Basic employment

Break-cargo point

Central town

Economic base
  study

Input–output study

Multiplier effect

Nodes

Secondary
  employment

Transportation
  service towns

PREVIEW

Every parcel of real estate gets its value because of its connections to the other parcels around it, near and far. A new auto assembly plant in the middle of the Sahara Desert has no value. As a result, understanding regions and communities is essential to understanding the likely future use and value of any one parcel.

In a pure sense, there is a technical difference between a *community*, a *city*, and a *town*. In an effort to simplify, however, the three terms will be used interchangeably, to refer to a centralized location where people live and work. We use the term region to refer to a group of communities in a surrounding area.

This chapter examines the factors that contribute to the location and economic health of a community and a region. Section 6.1 explores the origins of communities, and how these origins strongly affect the development of the community. Section 6.2 studies the reasons that cause a city to either grow or decline. Section 6.3 outlines techniques that are used to forecast a region's economic growth. The

Regional and Community Analysis

Case & Point at the end of the chapter looks at the movement of Americans from region to region. When you have completed this chapter, you will be able to:

1. Discuss how communities are formed.
2. List the economic factors that cause communities to change.
3. Describe the major tools that are used to forecast a region's economic growth.
4. Locate data sources that help you understand your community's economic growth.

6.1 WHY AND WHERE COMMUNITIES FORM

Economic activity has a major effect on establishing the location of a community, shaping the pattern of its growth, and influencing the future value and use of real estate within the community. By looking at a community's past, agents, appraisers, investors, and others can better understand some of the changes, from then to now. Once the past changes are understood and current local economic trends interpreted, a better forecast can be made of what might happen to the value of real estate in any particular location within the community.

The History of Communities

Early human beings lived as nomads. They migrated with the seasons and the availability of natural foods or wild game. At some point, as agriculture initially developed, early people began to build small clusters of dwellings in particularly favorable locations. These were the earliest towns. Knowledge of these early people is very limited. It is believed that the first towns arose around 7000 B.C., in the valleys of the Tigris and Euphrates rivers, known as Mesopotamia, now part of Iraq. From studying the long history of communities, two important themes emerge: (1) the reason why the *original town location* was chosen and (2) the reasons for the *economic survival* of the town after its beginning.

What Determines Community Location?

Every community started with an initial decision of where to locate. The factors that influence the choice of a site depend on why the community is being formed. Among early nomads, important factors often included water, sources of food, and protection from enemies. Climate or weather often influenced both water and food. Later, the factors sometimes involved social reasons, such as sites chosen for their religious significance, or for governmental purposes like regional development.

The majority of community sites in America appear to have been chosen because of their commercial significance. Commercial influences result in the formation of the following three types of community origins. Note that, over time, the significance of any one factor may change, as a town grows and changes.

1. The central town
2. The transportation service town
3. The special-function town

Central Towns

A community that has its origin as a **central town** performs a variety of services for a *surrounding area*. The services that are provided usually include commercial, social, religious, and governmental. Such communities tend to be fairly evenly spaced throughout the productive countryside, each surrounded by the hinterland, or "tributary area," that it serves. Thus, when forest land is converted to agriculture, the growing population provides an opportunity for the start of a series of such central market towns. The California Central Valley and the American Midwest are examples of areas with many central market communities. Figure 6.1 is a map of a portion of the Central Valley of California. Notice that there are a few larger towns in this area, quite a few medium-sized towns, and a number of very small towns, like Tranquility (in the lower left.) This is a typical pattern in areas developed initially for agriculture.

FIGURE 6.1 Central Valley towns.

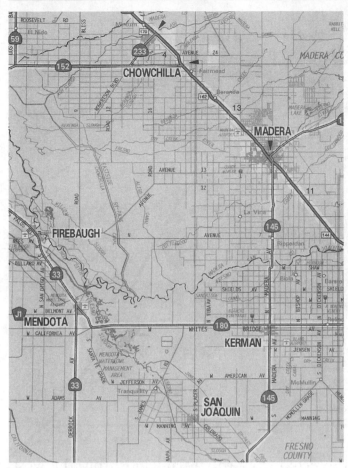

Source: CA. Road Atlas, Rand McNally.

Transportation Service Towns

In the second category were **transportation service towns**, performing services along transportation routes. These communities initially form at locations called **nodes**. Among the many types of nodes are those at a **break-cargo point**, which is a place where a shift in the transportation system or route, or an obstacle, requires the unloading and reloading of the transport vehicles. At this point, the goods being carried can be repackaged ("break-bulk"), processed, wholesaled, or otherwise manipulated more easily than elsewhere. Possible break-cargo points include ports, major rail intersections, freeway intersections, river forks, and mountain passes. Points at which transportation systems require some type of service act in a similar manner. Examples include the many former steam railroad watering stops in the western United States, such as Ogden, Utah, and San Bernardino, California.

Figure 6.2 is a map of the Los Angeles and Long Beach Harbor area of California. Because the harbors face to the south, they are

FIGURE 6.2 Long Beach Harbor.

Source: CA. Road Atlas, Rand McNally.

naturally somewhat protected from the usual winds from the west. And the size of these harbors allowed ample room for ships to anchor.

Special-Function Communities

The third type of commercial city owes its origins and early growth to a *concentration on one special function or service*, such as mining, government, or retirement. Examples of special-function towns are resorts (e.g., Palm Springs, California), lumbering centers (e.g., Eureka, California), government centers (e.g., Washington, D.C.), and university towns (e.g., Davis, California).

Reasons for American City Locations

A study of American cities indicates a range of reasons for community origin. Some towns, such as Fort Bridger, Wyoming, were originally protection sites. Rossmoor (a senior-citizen development in Walnut Creek, California) could be considered a more recent protection community. Salt Lake City was a religious community, created at a site chosen to provide protection by distance and isolation. Break-cargo points include such ocean ports as San Francisco Bay, Baltimore, Seattle, San Pedro, and San Diego. River forks were factors at

FIGURE 6.3 First plat of Los Angeles.

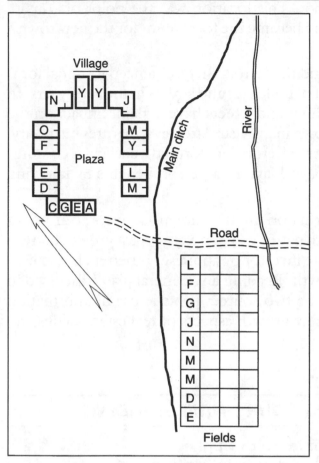

Source: Richard M. Hurd, *Principles of City Land Values*. New York, The Record and Guide, 1903, p. 39.

Pittsburgh, Pennsylvania, and Sacramento and Stockton, California. Denver, Colorado, and Truckee, California, owe their origins to mountain passes. The first plat of Los Angeles (Figure 6.3) suggests that both the river and the ford over it were important to the early town's location.

How the City's Origin Fits In

There are several keys to consider, in trying to explain a city's origin. *Topography* (the shape of the earth's surface) often influences where communities are initially located. For example, protection-type communities tend to be located at sites that offer some security, such as islands or mountaintops.

Moreover, all communities *must* have some contact with the world around them. The transportation systems that are in use at the time the location was chosen, combined with the local topography and the reason for the town's founding, determined where the initial town was sited. It may have been at the ship landing, the railroad station, or the stage depot. This location was the point of contact with the outside world and became the focal point for the new town's growth.

The origin of a city, and the factors that influenced its initial location, shape the placement of buildings and streets in the early years. In turn, these original buildings and streets have a major impact on the shape and layout of the town many years later, as it matures into a city. Therefore, to understand the factors that formed a particular community's current size, shape, and layout, a person benefits by knowing the reason for its origin.

Once the reasons for its origin are known, a person can better understand a city's growth pattern. When a city's past growth pattern is understood, a real estate investor or appraiser is better able to estimate future paths of growth. Reading any general plan (discussed in Chapter 13) will help. The two sources provide useful information when analyzing community growth aspects of real estate values and value change.

REVIEWING YOUR UNDERSTANDING

Why and Where Communities Form
1. What determines a community's original location?
2. What are the three types of commercial city origins? Give some local examples of each.
3. How does transportation affect the initial location of communities?

6.2 WHY THE COMMUNITY GROWS

The continued survival of all communities requires that the residents' needs for food, clothing, shelter, and other necessities are met. Few communities are completely self-sufficient. Nearly all communities need goods and services that are made or grown elsewhere. Therefore, each community must be able to pay for the goods that it buys from other areas. It must export goods to other areas, in order to earn money, and use the money to buy needed goods from these other areas.

The Community as an Economy

Economic success is essential to the continued existence of a community! As a result, economists frequently study and forecast the

FIGURE 6.4 Basic and local employment.

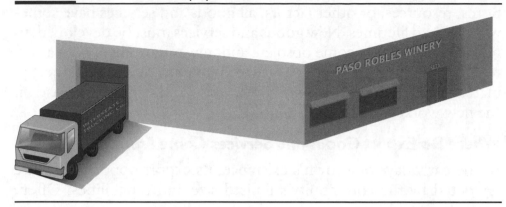

community's economic health. They pay particular attention to how a community develops "export" goods and services (those sold to other areas), to pay for its imported goods and services. This is very similar to the international trade that exists between countries.

In studying an area's economy, all businesses and employees are separated into two broad categories. Local companies that produce goods and services to be shipped outside the community or region are called *basic industries, export jobs* or **basic employment**. Local companies that produce goods and services for use by people within the community or region are called *local industries* or **secondary employment** industries or employment. Economists then analyze the trends within these two categories, to forecast the economic strength and growth potential for the community and its surrounding region. Figure 6.4 contrasts the two categories of employment. Here, one company has both types!

The Need for New Export Jobs

Economic success of a community can take several forms. The simplest would be continued survival of a fixed population, at a fixed standard of living. More complex forms would involve either growth in population ("volume" changes), growth in the economic welfare of individuals ("per capita" changes), or both.

Community survival without population or income change is not common in American society, because the rate of births and immigration historically has been higher than the rate of deaths. These increasing numbers of people must be housed and fed. Communities have expanded their economic capacities in order to provide these necessities.

Outside forces, moreover, tend to upset the stable economic existence of a community. For example, the advent of the automobile industry created new jobs in some areas, but eliminated jobs (such as making buggy whips) in others. As a result of changes in technology, tastes, resources, or other factors, all goods and services have somewhat limited lifetimes. New goods and services must be developed, to replace those that become obsolete and unwanted. Thus, even a currently stable city finds itself in a race to encourage new jobs. Projected increases in population require further job (and export) increases, if the new workers are to be employed.

Where Do Export Goods and Services Come From?

In the early days of a town's existence, its export opportunities are restricted by the community's limited size and capabilities. Often, the only possible export is some simple local resource, such as cattle, grain, ores, timber, or fish. For other communities, the only available export may be labor skills, exported for the day or the week or the year. When the workers bring their earnings back, the money supports the community. This is evident even today, as Mexican citizens work in the United States and return and/or send money to their families in Mexico. On a small scale, the same process happens when people live in a suburban area with few jobs, and commute to the city to work. The "export product" for the suburb is workers.

As the community grows, additional resources can be developed into export items. Often, some existing export resource requires processing that can be done locally, leading to the export of processed goods, instead of raw materials. In time, the processing develops local skills, which become a new marketable resource.

If the shift in exports from resources to processed goods is successful, cities that were originally formed for resource exploitation can still survive when the resource is exhausted, by having the raw materials shipped to local processing plants, to use their skilled work force.

A complex example is Detroit, which was originally a wheat-shipping port. Its workers learned how to repair broken steam engines of wheat ships, then how to make needed spare parts, and finally how to make entire engines. They became so expert at manufacturing steam engines and similar machinery that early automobile designers came there, for technical help with engine designs. Now, Detroit finds it necessary to reinvent itself again!

This analysis of community economic growth focuses on the products or services that are developed. Readers will find *The Economy of Cities*, by Jane Jacobs, a fascinating presentation of this type of analysis.[1]

---

[1] Jane Jacobs, *The Economy of Cities*. New York: Random House, 1969.

Jacobs suggests that two main community growth methods are important.

The first method is to use local raw materials and skills to generate *new export products*. Silicon Valley does this every year, creating new or better chips or devices. The Los Angeles entertainment industry essentially does the same thing, as each new song, movie, or TV show is a new export product. Many "new products," then, are not completely new, but just altered, improved, updated, or just rebranded!

Much of the growth in world trade today results from this same mechanism. Many of the products that we use every day are made or assembled in other countries. Business people saw products that their workers had the skills to manufacture, took a risk, and developed an industry.

The second method of growing a community's economy is to develop *local production* of goods that were previously imported. When this happens, the product is no longer imported, or the import quantities are reduced. In turn, this change frees export earnings that can be used to buy some other needed imports. In the Detroit example, workers learned to make spare parts that had previously been imported. This was a key step in the evolution of Detroit from a port to a manufacturing center.

In the past, nearly all of the cheese eaten in California came from other states or countries. Now, there are a number of very successful smaller cheese plants, primarily in the North Coast area. And chocolates were all imported into California, while today there are many small local producers. The same pattern, for various products, can be found everywhere. Some types of jobs are flowing into an area, while others are flowing out.

Production Efficiency

The *efficiency of production* is a third path to economic growth. A fixed workforce could export more goods, if local businesses could increase productivity. This would mean increasing output without added labor, by using better planning or more sophisticated equipment. However, this path to economic growth may be resisted by workers, because the increase in productivity acts to reduce the number of workers needed for a particular production level. This means firings, retraining, and *change*, which some firms and workers resist.

From society's view, however, increased productivity is very good, because the freed worker can be used to produce other goods and services. Thus, the total amount of goods and services available to the community can grow, without any increase in the numbers of workers or hours worked. Alternatively, the hours worked can be reduced, without a reduction in the standard of living. Either way, welfare per capita is improved.

There are two marvelous examples that demonstrate how important productivity is to our well-being. The first is agriculture. Without the major improvements in farming productivity over the centuries, we would all have to work as farmers. We would have none of the goods and services that we enjoy every day. And we would face famines from time to time, where the crops failed, due to insects or weather, and many of our family and friends died.

The second is the telephone. Initially, every call had to be connected by hand. The telephone operators (initially all women) had to put a plug into a socket, to make the connection. Now, electronic switches do it all. It is said that, with the increase in the number of telephones, and in the number of calls, without the invention of the telephone switches, every woman in the entire world would be needed to work the switchboards! Or it might be all of the men! First were mechanical switches, then electrical ones, and now electronic.

Modern Regional and Community Growth

Studies show that two major factors currently influence regional economic change. The first factor is the growth rate of an area's existing export business base. As mentioned earlier, growth in the businesses that create export goods and services is the key. Often, there are actions that communities or regions can take, to strengthen existing export businesses. For example, there may be job skills that are critical, but scarce. Local community colleges can be funded to develop vocational training programs. Or it may be some desirable transportation improvement, to improve access to suppliers or to raw materials.

However, an existing export industry may be viewed as causing excessive pollution. It may be socially or politically difficult to support the industry. Sometimes, also, it will not be economically feasible. Many industries have their day, and then decline. Some wagon and buggy makers, however, were able to survive, and continued to grow, by changing into automobile body manufacturers!

The second major factor impacting regional economic change is the shift of businesses from one area to another. This shift can occur whether a particular company's national or worldwide business is growing or declining. When a company moves to a new area, it will generate new jobs and income for that area—even if the company is in a stagnant industry. Of course, the area the company leaves then suffers the loss of jobs and income. The shift in businesses from the Midwest to the South, Southwest, and West is a modern-day example.

TABLE 6.1   Business Location Factors

Raw Materials	cost____ availability ____		
Selling Markets	near ____ far ____		
Transportation	cost ____ availability ____		
Labor	cost ____ quality ____ quantity ____		
Water	cost ____ quality ____ quantity ____		
Energy	cost ____ quantity ____		
Community Attitude	positive ____ negative ____		
Taxes	high ____ low ____		
Site Cost	high ____ moderate ____ low ____		
Environmental Controls	restrictive ____ moderate ____		
Employee Housing Cost	low ____ moderate ____ high ____		

When considering locations, businesses generally seek the least expensive access to the needed inputs and outputs. This means access to the inputs of land, labor, capital, and entrepreneurship, and access to its output markets.

For each community, the availability of land, skilled labor, raw materials, business skills, and final markets is fairly fixed at any one time. Many communities will not have the resources or skills that particular industries need, but over a period of years, changes in technology, natural resources, population, and community attitude can alter the desirability of any community for business locations.

Changes in technology, population base, and availability of resources have been the main reasons for this shift. In recent times, the emphasis has been on "glamour" businesses. These are companies with rapid growth potential and low pollution emissions. For example, every community that wishes to grow has attempted to attract high-tech, digital, and biomedical companies. A notable example here is the shift of businesses from the high-cost, high-tax, and occasionally not so business-friendly California, to low-cost, low-tax, business-friendly Nevada. Table 6.1 lists several factors that businesses look for when seeking a new location. This issue is explored further in Chapter 10.

Setting Community Goals

Each community or region should review its economic future: *to decline, to hold stable, or to grow*. The choice of one or the other is sometimes made politically, as when the area votes for or against new roads or water, or other issues that affect community growth. At other times, the decision is an economic one, as the demand for the products and skills of the local area either increases or decreases.

Growth in Population

One community choice concerns the level of future population growth. An increase in export production is the most common path toward population growth. However, issues of land use, congestion, pollution, and changes in lifestyles are often raised.

Clearly, no product or service can continue to be in demand at the same level forever. Everything changes, or is replaced, over time. Every community must encourage new ideas, new products, and/or new fields of work, to replace those that decline. In the process, it is hard to stop with *just enough* replacement jobs. Indeed, the small town, with a rapidly growing new-employment category, may find population growth all but impossible to stop. On the other hand, an area that has historically exported natural resources may find it difficult to maintain a healthy economy, once the resource becomes depleted. California's lumber towns face that issue.

Growth in Welfare

The second type of economic change for a community is to improve its income per person—its per capita welfare. There are wide variations across communities and states, in per capita income. Some of these variations are explained by differences in population composition, such as comparing the ages of people in the area. Per capita income could be lower in a community with many young children than in a community with mostly older couples. A population composed of workers with limited skills or limited education, for example, has a lower per capita income than one with advanced skills.

However, the type of employment in the area is the main cause of differences between the *existing* per capita incomes of communities. The higher per capita incomes are found in communities with high-salaried occupations. These are usually in businesses with a large amount of machinery, technology, and other capital investment, in relation to the numbers of workers. On the other hand, businesses that are labor intensive—those that use a lot of labor—usually seek out existing low-wage locations. This means that *past differences* in community income levels tend to get reinforced in the future. Low-income communities tend to be chosen as locations for companies that need low wages, whereas higher-income communities often have skills or facilities that attract high-wage companies.

The factors that influence the types of new jobs in a community are important. Many factors, such as technology or transportation changes, can produce major new higher-income opportunities in low-income areas. With recent cutbacks in high-tech digital and software companies, former high–cost-of-living communities have been losing jobs to lower-cost communities as these companies relocate. Examples include shifts of the manufacturing operations of technical companies from California to Arizona, New Mexico, and Nevada. For the individual community, the important issue, in both *population growth* and *per capita growth*, is an awareness of the community's weaknesses and strengths as a business location, and a willingness to respond to opportunities.

Trying to Diversify

Finally, a community may choose to have other economic goals, besides those involving population growth or per capita growth. One example is where a single firm or industry becomes so successful, at a particular location, that it dominates the entire area. Think of Hershey's, Pennsylvania, or Pontiac, Michigan! If the dominant industry ages and declines, it could drag the city down with it.

As communities developed skills that were needed to deal with their early resources, their businesses tended to specialize in these resources and skills. This is desirable, because these skills become major exports. However, if these skills become obsolete, because of new materials or processes, entire cities can be put out of work. Thus, most communities today prefer not to be one-industry towns. They prefer a *diversification* of companies, industries, and job types.

REVIEWING YOUR UNDERSTANDING

Why the Community Grows

1. Why must each economic community usually have some export trade? Why must there be new products or services to export?

2. How does a community generate new exports?

3. Explain the difference between growing companies and shifting companies. How do they choose locations?

4. What are the two primary factors influencing changes in per capita income?

6.3 HOW TO STUDY A COMMUNITY

The economic study of a community or a region can be approached informally or formally. Most businesspeople, real estate agents, appraisers, lenders, and investors are continually watching community progress, for signs of strength or weakness. Informally, they are watching the forces of supply and demand at work, when they observe population, employment, and income changes. Although keen observation and instinct are invaluable tools, concrete economic studies can provide a factual basis for better decisions. This section reviews the traditional ways to analyze community growth, stressing the two major techniques now used for regional study: *economic base analysis* and *input–output analysis*. The section ends with a discussion of sources of information on regions and communities.

Traditional Community Analysis

A number of supply and demand factors have traditionally been used to study communities. Analysis of supply factors has emphasized the inventory of each type of existing structure and their size, price, age, and condition. The cost of new construction, availability of suitable land, zoning, financing, and utilities have also been considered important.

In recent times, as noted earlier, attention has also focused on more subtle supply factors. These include the quality of education, recreation facilities like parks, cultural amenities such as concert halls and libraries, and religious facilities. The intent is to inventory all of the factors that might influence business owners to choose this location, or to decide to move elsewhere

The most important demand factor is population. The interest is both in the total numbers and also by age, education, or other categories (population demography). Population change is the focus. Nearly every state now prepares forecasts of future population growth. (For California, the Web site is http://www.dof.ca.gov/research/demographic/overview/.) These forecasts, in turn, are tied to U.S. Census Bureau national forecasts. Some regional planning agencies prepare data by county and by city. An example is the Southern California Council of Governments, at www.scag.ca.gov, or the Association of Bay Area Governments, at www.abag.org. Nearly every region now has some form of regional agency. Because people must have jobs, employment characteristics of the town are also studied, including wage rates, types of jobs, and unemployment rates. State employment departments often prepare studies of local employment by industry, and forecasted growth. For example, the California forecasts are prepared by the California Employment Development Department, at www.labormarketinfo.edd.ca.gov/. Income per household or per capita is also of interest, since people may have other income than what is earned at a job.

Often, the data about one area or community can best be understood by comparison. How do the characteristics of the area's population (demography) compare to the county, the region, the state, or the country? Are they younger? What about education levels, household size, or incomes? How is this area changing, compared to other areas, over the past few years? What about the changes over the past several decades? Are they the same as recent trends, or different? This type of data helps you see how this area is changing, and how that relates to state and national changes.

Basic Employment Reviewed

The most important long-term influence on a community's population and employment is its basic or export employment. Because basic employment differs from one community to another, towns can be classified according to the dominant type of basic employment. Some towns concentrate on industry, some on commerce, some on resorts, some on government, and some on resources. There are several classification systems; one, distinguishing towns as *central towns, transportation service towns,* or *special-function towns,* was introduced in Section 6.1.

These classifications indicate the major activity that is serving as the town's economic base. This information can be combined with data on community origin, to see how the basic employment has changed since the community was founded. In turn, it is important to discover what factors caused the changes in basic employment!

All this information is helpful, in order to better forecast the future of a region and its communities. Understanding past changes in the economic base will help predict future changes. Even knowing the current economic base may tell something about the area's future. This is particularly true of extractive resource regions, whose basic employment involves some local resource to be dug up or harvested. Here, the economic future depends on the size of reserves of the timber, oil, fish, coal, or other harvested resource. If it is used up, or becomes much more expensive to recover, the region's economy is at risk.

Regional Economic Studies

Most often, studies of an area's economy focus on population, education, and income changes. However, some formal regional studies are performed on occasion. The two main techniques used to conduct a regional economic study are (1) *economic base studies* and (2) *input–output studies.*

Economic Base Studies

The **economic base study** approach forecasts population growth by forecasting basic employment. These studies start with data on the

Special Interest Topic
The Multiplier Effect

As noted earlier, increasing the number of basic or export jobs is important to the growth of any community. And for every new *basic* job, some additional *local or secondary* employment is created, in schools, shops, and the like. The ratio of new local jobs for every new basic job is called the *multiplier effect*. Economists who study basic employment have found that all areas do not have the same proportion of workers in basic or export jobs. This proportion varies with the size of the community, as shown in the listing below.

Community Size	Number of Local Jobs Added for Each New Basic Job
Very large cities	2.0
100,000 people	1.0
50,000 people	0.5

This ratio—local to basic jobs—is significant. An addition of 100 new jobs in basic employment will actually have a greater effect on total employment. This is called the **multiplier effect.** It is easy to see why chambers of commerce want to obtain large, new manufacturing plants in their communities! The multiplier effect on total employment will result in an increase in such related areas as population and retail sales.

However, the increase in population also means more children in school and more cars on the road. An increase in basic employment affects the entire community! Everything feels the multiplier effect.

numbers of current jobs in the area, broken down by export and non-export companies. The first step is to forecast how employment in each basic industry in the region will change. This might be done by assigning to this location some fraction of the expected nationwide growth in that industry, or by projecting the past local trends of employment. The forecasts of employment by industry are then totaled, to make a forecast of basic employment for the region.

The next step is to convert the forecast of basic employment to a forecast of total employment, using the ratio or multiplier of export to local employment. Next, the forecast of total employment is converted to a population forecast for the total community, by using the ratio of workers to people (the *labor participation rate*; see Figure 6.5). In turn, population forecasts can be converted to land-use forecasts or other specialized studies.

FIGURE 6.5 The economic base study.

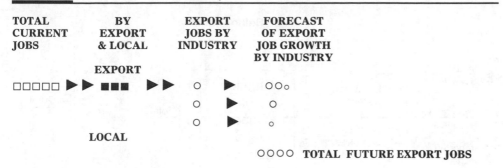

TOTAL FUTURE EXPORT JOBS	○○○○
TIMES: MULTIPLIER	× 1.8
EQUALS: TOTAL FUTURE JOBS	▢▢▢▢▢▢▢▫
TIMES: LABOR FORCE PARTICIPATION RATE	× 1.3
EQUALS: TOTAL FUTURE POPULATION	☺ ☺ ☺ ☺ ☺ ☺ ☺ ☺ ☺ ☺

These economic base studies require enormous amounts of data and analysis and are therefore quite expensive. They are not practical for small communities. Also, they would not be reliable in such cases, simply because a single new factory could move into a small town for reasons that are impossible to predict. For the large community or region, however, the studies have value.

Input–Output Studies

Another, but less common, approach is the **input–output study**. The steps are shown in Figure 6.6. In this type of study, researchers examine the resources that go into the economic activity of the community (inputs). This includes the raw materials, purchased parts, supplies, services, labor, and management. They then calculate the goods and services (outputs) of the producing sectors of the community, on the basis of where they are distributed or shipped. Outputs that are used locally, as inputs for other producers, must be identified separately.

Input–output analysis requires extensive amounts of data, which can be difficult to obtain. When the data are available (usually for very large regions), this method provides a full understanding of what happens in the economy of the region. For instance, the dollar amounts of all imports and exports can be determined. The production of various industries is totaled, as well as the breakdown of customers by product. In this way, one can see the flow of money through the community. This is one of the major features of input–output analysis.

FIGURE 6.6   An input–output study.

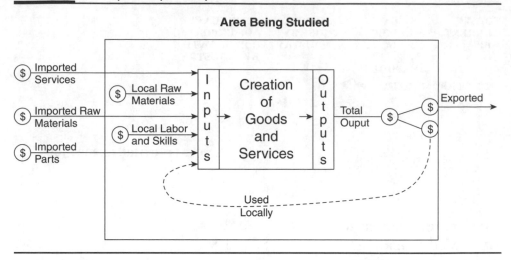

The Gatekeeping Syndrome

In rapidly growing areas, there often is a tendency for old-timers to resent newcomers. The many changes, and the environmental impacts of growth, generate opposition. Once the newcomers get in, they try to keep out "new" newcomers, on similar grounds. In another kind of gatekeeping, a large portion of Western land is owned by the federal government. Environmental groups attempt to minimize development of a vast portion of this land, in order to preserve the natural environment. These and numerous other factors create controversy over growth. There are hundreds of polarized groups, fighting one another to press their own viewpoint.

Sources of Data

The major sources of information about current and past regional and community conditions are the U.S. Census Bureau publications. These include the most recent census of population, housing, and manufacturing. Many specialized analyses are also generated by the Census Bureau, or from Census Bureau information, by universities, and by public and private data centers. State and federal labor and employment offices are good sources of additional data, as are state and local chambers of commerce. Research publications from banks, universities, and regional Federal Reserve banks are also very helpful.

In general, the larger areas have been more thoroughly studied and documented. However, the scope of this coverage is improving. Some county and city planning departments and regional planning groups now have, or are developing, elaborate and detailed data centers. A growing amount of data is available online.

Forecasts of regional growth have most often been available from state and federal agencies, or as regional studies. Regional forecasts of specific types (especially transportation and population) are now available for many regions, and they are being updated and expanded. Various specialized forecasts (transportation, land use, pollution, water demand, and sewage) are being combined. The errors of some earlier forecasts are also being reviewed, as planners seek to improve forecasting accuracy.

REVIEWING YOUR UNDERSTANDING

How to Study a Community

1. Why is the economic base important in studying a region?
2. What is an input–output study?
3. What is the multiplier effect?

CHAPTER SUMMARY

This chapter stressed that the purpose of regional and community analysis is to understand the economic activity in the area and its direct effects on real estate supply and demand.

The origin of community results from the combination of site characteristics and commercial or social factors. Commercial factors play a more important role in cities founded recently, both in America and throughout the world. The origin of a city is important, because it has a tremendous influence on the locations of major buildings and the layout of street patterns in subsequent years.

Community growth depends on economic factors, because communities are not self-sufficient. They need many goods imported from other areas. The economic growth of a city, practically speaking, is usually limited by the growth of jobs that produce goods or services for export. These export earnings, in turn, pay for the necessary imports. Exports at the time of a city's origin were usually related to the community's material resources, but in time the skills learned from handling these resources became more important.

Community studies examine such factors as basic employment, population, income, and other specific land-use factors. The two major types of such studies are economic base studies and input–output studies. There is a tremendous variety of source material available for persons wishing to understand a community.

REVIEWING YOUR UNDERSTANDING

1. A city that originally formed at a "break-cargo" point is called a(n):
   A. central town
   B. transportation service town
   C. special-function town
   D. economic town

2. Growth of a region is most closely tied to what kind of jobs?
   A. local
   B. secondary
   C. basic
   D. internal

3. In terms of economic base studies, a computer software company would be considered what kind of business?
   A. export
   B. import
   C. secondary
   D. local

4. In terms of economic base studies, a residential real estate brokerage business is what kind of business?
   A. export
   B. basic
   C. manufacturing
   D. secondary or local

5. If a region's population expands rapidly, while jobs and government spending decline, the per capita standard of living, as measured by goods and services, will probably:
   A. decrease
   B. increase
   C. remain the same
   D. escalate

6. If the multiplier effect for a local economy is that 1 export job creates 1.5 secondary jobs, an increase of 100 basic export jobs should create a total of how many new jobs in the area?
   A. 67
   B. 100
   C. 150
   D. 250

7. When selecting a new location for a factory, a company will usually check which of the following items?
   A. environmental requirements
   B. community attitudes
   C. transportation systems
   D. all of the above

8. The underlying principle of economic base studies states that for a region to grow economically, it must:
   A. export more than it imports
   B. import more than it exports
   C. increase secondary business faster than basic business
   D. decrease basic industries

9. For some people, the disadvantages of economic growth include:
   A. more people
   B. traffic congestion
   C. additional pollution
   D. all of the above

10. The advantages of economic growth include more:
    A. goods and services
    B. jobs
    C. financial security
    D. all of the above

11. To stimulate economic growth, an increase in local jobs must occur before there can be an increase in export jobs.
    A. true
    B. false

12. A group of cities or communities in a larger or surrounding area is usually called a:
    A. town
    B. region
    C. locality
    D. township

13. It is believed that the world's first towns and villages were located in:
    A. Europe
    B. Latin America
    C. the Middle East
    D. New Zealand

14. A "central town":
    A. is located midway between two large cities
    B. performs a variety of services for a surrounding area
    C. contains the central government offices for the region
    D. is usually located at a river fork, mountain pass, or ocean port

15. A community location selected to be convenient to a resource is described as a:
    A. special-function town
    B. resort town
    C. node
    D. break-cargo location

16. Original locations of cities tend to be influenced by:
    A. topography
    B. transportation
    C. both a and b
    D. neither a nor b

17. Two measures of community economic growth are:
    A. expansion and integration
    B. per capita and overall growth
    C. annexation and divestment
    D. local jobs and the multiplier

18. Greater productivity influences community growth by:
    A. allowing the same number of workers to produce more export goods
    B. reducing the number of jobs
    C. creating more instability through changes
    D. interrupting government efforts to limit growth

19. When a community learns to make objects that previously had to be imported:
    A. the loss of imports hurts the local economy
    B. additional earnings are generated to pay for imported goods and services
    C. added jobs are tied up in local employment, hurting growth
    D. there is no net effect on the local economy

20. In an economic base study, a population forecast for a region is estimated by using a ratio of workers (or jobs) to people. This is called:
    A. job multiplier
    B. labor participation rate
    C. demography
    D. topography

21. A city can grow in population, even if its export jobs are in industries that are not growing nationwide.
    A. true
    B. false

22. Moderate increases in productivity are considered socially desirable by many people, if the increase in productivity:
    A. lowers per capita living standards
    B. improves per-person welfare
    C. fulfills government objectives for slow growth
    D. eliminates private jobs

23. If a community's export jobs are mostly in one industry:
    A. such concentration is considered desirable
    B. diversification should be a key community goal
    C. real estate investment potential is enhanced
    D. the town's future is guaranteed

24. A shift of jobs in an industry from one city to another can cause some cities to grow, even when the industry's overall growth is in decline.
    A. true
    B. false

25. Input–output analysis examines:
    A. whether production efficiency can be improved
    B. which jobs should be reclassified from basic to export
    C. what resources go into community economic activity, what goods and services are produced, and where they are distributed
    D. how long it takes on average to convert inputs to outputs

CASE & POINT

"Where Are We Moving To?"

The Sunbelt Boom

The Sunbelt states of the South and West have experienced major growth since the 1940s. Reasons include their perceived pleasant climates and lifestyles, the desire of city dwellers to escape urban problems, excellent retirement communities, tourist attractions, and the shift in new employment opportunities. In the case of the South, the lack of unions, lower wages, and inexpensive real estate were initial factors. Today, the cost differentials are not as great as they once were, but still are an important factor. The Southwest states of Utah, Arizona, New Mexico, and Nevada are among the fastest-growing states in the union.

The losers in this shift were older industrial areas such as the Midwest Rust Belt (from Chicago east to Pittsburgh), farm states such as the Dakotas and Iowa, and some Northeastern states. In some cases, these "loser" states have drawn together to provide a more united political front, in an attempt to stem the flow of business and government projects to the Sunbelt states. At other times, these "loser" states fight over the shrinking job base. Since 2005, the Northeastern states have shown gains in population.

The Rocky Mountain High

Mountain states, such as Colorado, Utah, and Idaho, initially gained growth in the 1970 period and then suffered in the 1980s, when the resource extraction businesses (oil and oil shale) declined. During this period, overbuilding glutted the

CASE & POINT

residential and commercial real estate markets, resulting in foreclosures and a massive drop in real estate prices. By the mid-1990s to the late 2000s, these problems gradually were worked out, and the mountain states are once again attracting businesses and experiencing large percentage gains in population.

Pacific Northwest's Green Acres Beckon

Northern California, Oregon, and Washington, bountiful in forests and rain, have been attracting people and some businesses. The Seattle–Tacoma metro area of Washington has experienced especially rapid growth. Microsoft and Boeing have been the major employers. Several rating agencies have selected this area as one of the more "ideal" in the United States. However, by the mid-2000s, Boeing moved its headquarters to Chicago and severe competition from European-based Airbus Company, plus economic weaknesses in the airline industry, caused a drop in Boeing employment. The long-run economic impact of this is currently unknown. The lack of state income taxes in Washington and state sales taxes in Oregon could attract some retiring baby boomers later in the 2010s, as these retirees attempt to seek a more peaceful, rural setting, as well as stretch the money in their financial retirement plans.

U.S. Census Bureau Data

According to the U.S. Census Bureau, the fastest-growing large metro areas for 2000–2007, by percentage growth, were:

1. Atlanta, GA 24.3%
2. Houston, TX 19.4%
3. Dallas-Fort Worth, TX 19.1%
4. Washington, D.C. 10.6%
5. Minneapolis, MN 8.1%

For 2008, the fastest-growing areas with a population of 100,000 or more were:

1. New Orleans, LA
2. Round Rock, TX
3. Cary, NC

CASE & POINT

4. Gilbert, AZ
5. McKinney, TX
6. Roseville, CA
7. Irvine, CA
8. Raleigh, NC
9. Killeen, TX
10. Fort Worth, TX

Chapter

7

PREVIEW

This chapter describes how a community takes physical shape, how land use determines the community's layout, and where its population settles. Section 7.1 explains the factors that influence land-use patterns. Section 7.2 illustrates the basic city growth patterns. Section 7.3 describes what happens to growth patterns as the community population increases. The Case & Point at the end of the chapter explores future issues in city layout. When you have completed this chapter, you will be able to:

1. List the major forces that influence the shape, layout, and density of a community.

2. Describe how each force affects the future shape of the community.

Community Growth Patterns

3. List the basic patterns of community growth.

4. Explain how studying changing land-use patterns in a community helps forecast the path of growth.

7.1 LAND-USE PATTERNS

Appraisers often joke that there are three important factors in real estate values: location, location, and location! And *location,* in turn, consists of all of the characteristics of a particular spot. This includes all of the properties around that spot, their characteristics, and how they are used. That pattern of uses is a significant element is *location.* How does that pattern of land uses come to exist?

The initial reason for establishing a community often determines its shape, the pattern of land use, and even how land is allocated among users. In the many cities laid out by the church in medieval Europe, church leaders made most of the land-use decisions, primarily for religious reasons. Similarly, in cities whose original function was to protect the residents, military and police considerations dictated the location of shops, homes, and manufacturing sites.

However, as stressed in Chapter 6, if communities are to continue, they must become *economically successful,* whatever the reasons were for their initial location. Therefore, **economic influences** or motives will eventually influence how land is allocated among competing land users.

How Economics Determines Land Use

In a market economy, there is competition among the various buyers of each product. In the absence of government or private controls, all goods and services go to the highest bidders. There is a similar competition among potential users of a site, and land goes to the user who is willing to pay the highest price. Appraisal books call this the **highest and best use**.

According to the *principle of highest and best use*, the best use of land is the legal use that will produce the highest capitalized net income return to the land, after allowing for the cost of the building. In most cases, this means that the value of a site is determined by how much rent it will bring. Possible tenants are sorted out, by how much rent each could pay at that particular site. Or, if the site is vacant and for sale, the site will be captured by the user who pays the highest price. This usually is the user who will benefit the most.

Why Patterns?

Even though land use is mostly set by the rent-paying ability of different legal users, why do communities form patterns of land use? The answer seems to be tied to an interesting set of rules. Thus, similar users tend to cluster together at favorable locations, even when there is no government zoning. Commercial users cluster with other commercial users, homeowners locate near other homeowners, and so on. These clusters of uses are no accident!

What Are the Rules?

A series of rules appears to control the economic process of developing land-use patterns. We focus on the rules first, before looking at the patterns that they create.

Rule 1: Competition of Uses

Every available site faces a *competition of uses*. When a number of different potential users seek the same site, competition between them causes the asking price of the land to increase, until the highest bidder wins. The highest bidder's price was based on an expectation regarding the property's ability to produce a desired level of benefits to that user.

Rule 2: Economics of Succession

If a site is vacant and available to any legal use, the type of development will usually be determined by the most profitable use. However, if there is a building on the site, a user who can occupy the existing improvements has an advantage over other users. The improvements will be demolished *only* when a new use is profitable enough to pay for the site, the old building, the demolition cost, and the cost of the new building. This is the rule of **economic succession**.

Rule 3: Comparative Advantage

Each site has unique advantages and disadvantages for particular uses. Some locations may have favorable natural characteristics (raw materials, climate, topography, or water, for example). Other locations may have access to many customers, or to needed materials from nearby facilities. Still other locations might have good schools, suppliers, favorable government regulations, or other institutional advantages.

The advantages and disadvantages of a particular site will give a *comparative advantage* to whichever land use gets the greatest *net benefit* from that unique set of advantages and disadvantages.

Rule 4: The Rule of Imperfection

The ideal pattern of land use rarely exists, because the information needed to make a perfect decision is often not available. Unwise property development, or unusual social or political situations, will also impede the highest and best use. Sometimes, the community will interfere with the market (by zoning, for example) to avoid changes that market forces would otherwise cause. Thus, land-use patterns are never completely perfect or completely predictable. This is explored further, later.

Rule 5: Principle of Change

Nothing is static or fixed; **change** is the only constant! Therefore, the highest and best use of land is always changing. Technical, social, and economic changes continually alter the structure of the community and the pattern of ideal land use.

These five economic rules are major factors in land-use patterns. Every community furnishes repeated examples of each rule. The student should particularly think about *comparative advantage*—why each use is located where it is. Examples: Industrial users cluster together for many reasons. Sometimes, it is because favorable utilities and transportation routes are nearby. To locate elsewhere could incur additional costs that can cut into profits, or drive up prices with the danger of losing sales. Retail stores group together to form "one-stop" shopping convenience for customers. Homes are built near one another, because water and other needed services (including schools, shops, and transportation) are nearby and already in place.

The Noneconomic Factors in Land Use

In addition to *economic forces*, there are *social and political forces* influencing land-use decisions. **Political influences** take the form of decisions carried out by state and local authorities, executing the law.

Social influences operate more subtly, through group pressures. Political, social, and economic influences on land use often operate independently of each other.

Political or legal effects on land-use decisions result from community attitudes on land use, expressed through the police power and the power of eminent domain. **Police power** refers to the right of the community to regulate private behavior, in order to protect the public's health, safety, and welfare. **Eminent domain** is the right of the community to buy, for full value, any site that the community needs to use. Zoning laws provide one of the most noticeable examples of police power. This topic is so important that most of Chapter 13 is devoted to the many different political land-use controls, as is a part of Section 7.3.

Social controls on land use are less noticeable than political or economic ones. The past forms of social control often involved unwritten understandings, or common viewpoints, that certain land-use decisions would or would not occur. Past examples of such unwritten rules included ethnic neighborhood limits, the importance of downtown stores over neighborhood stores, and the superiority of detached homes over multiple-unit structures. Such social controls could influence both political and economic decisions. We have separated them, to point out that social controls are based on social notions, opinions, and/or biases, rather than on any kind of objective, established, factual bases. Social controls are becoming less influential, as political controls become more dominant.

REVIEWING YOUR UNDERSTANDING

Why There Are Land-Use Patterns
1. The three major community forces that influence the land-use system are economic, _____, and _____.
2. How does competition influence land use?
3. List the five rules of economic land-use allocation. Explain each.

7.2 LOOKING AT THE STRUCTURE OF COMMUNITIES

Given the forces that were examined in Section 7.1, patterns of land uses develop. This section examines the typical patterns of land use in small communities. Four dominant factors are analyzed: *accessibility*, *topography, transportation,* and *community origins.* A clear understanding of these four factors is necessary for the study of more complicated, larger communities, discussed in Section 7.3.

Why Study Community Land-Use Patterns?

Remember that the value of each individual real estate parcel is heavily influenced by its location. And location is almost always another way of saying the pattern of land uses around the parcel. Every time that we think of, look at, or analyze that parcel, we are seeing the effects of that location, those uses, and the pattern that they make.

Each of those nearby uses is changing over time, which changes the pattern. That changes the characteristics of that location, for better or for worse. The first step, then, is to understand the pattern, and then the changes.

Investors, agents, and appraisers look at the structure of land uses in a community, in order to understand what changed in the past and what caused this change. From this, a person will be better able to see what the future influences and changes might be. As James Vance wrote, "The more we understand the original purpose of a city's physical components, the more meaningful is its present pattern and the more we learn about the processes at work in the city's structure."[1]

For example, when an appraiser looks at comparable sales, to see what indications they give about the value of the subject property, the appraiser must consider differences in location. How does each of these sold properties fit into the patterns of land use? What locational advantages did each buyer see? Was it a *present* advantage, or a *future* one?

When an agent lists a property for sale, what are its key features? What will attract the right buyer, the optimum user? The building will be important, but so will the location. Are future locational changes a negative or a positive? Where does the property fit into the pattern?

Viewing the Small Community

How can a community's structure be examined? The answer depends on the tools available. We can use maps that show types of land use, land or property values, number of people per square mile, automobile traffic, pollution counts, telephones per square mile, crime rate per block, or any other factor that seems important. In addition to maps,

---

[1] James E. Vance, Jr., *Geography and Urban Evolution in the San Francisco Bay Area.* Institute of Government Studies, University of California, Berkeley, 1964, p. 3.

U.S. Census Tract data can be used to show tables of population, the number of households or houses, the ages of homes, conditions of structures, fire alarms per city block, and any other available data.

This information could relate to the community either at one point in time. Capturing a snapshot community shows how the parts of it differ at that instant. Tables and maps that show changes over time go one step further, and allow researchers to see differences as they emerge. Here, we will focus on land-use patterns.

Simple Circles—Accessibility

Accessibility is the single most important factor. One of the earliest concepts of how communities are arranged was developed in Bavaria by Johan von Thunen in 1826. von Thunen was the first to suggest that the shape of communities followed a predictable pattern. He wrote that if we simplify a town by choosing a flat, level site with farmland all around, the town would take the shape of a circle. In the center would be the land uses to which *everyone* needs access, such as community meeting places, churches, courtyards, and community food stores. Around these central uses would be a simple ring with the homes of the village people. von Thunen's concept of accessibility is fundamental to the study of land-use patterns.

In addition, von Thunen wrote that land uses beyond the city would be distributed in similar circles or rings. Closest to the town would be farms growing perishable produce, and farms requiring intensive, frequent care by farmers. Farther out would be farms with crops requiring less care or transport. The most distant lands would be used for grazing by animals that could transport themselves, and for growing timber.

Others have since applied von Thunen's ideas to American communities. Burgess presented the concept of concentric rings in 1920. In the inner ring of the community would be shopping centers, department stores, and offices for lawyers, bankers, accountants, and government. In the second ring would be older homes, undergoing a succession of uses as the first ring expanded. In addition, there would be warehouses, wholesaling activity, and on one side of the city, manufacturing. In the third ring from the center, Burgess suggested we would find low- and medium-cost housing, whereas higher-priced homes and shops would be located in the outer edges of the community. Figure 7.1 illustrates the concepts of von Thunen and Burgess. **Concentric growth** in such cities results in the rings gradually expanding, with older buildings being converted to a new use, or demolished.

FIGURE 7.1   A simplified pattern of land use in cities. von Thunen (1826): 1, central facilities; 2, homes; 3, crops; 4, grazing. Burgess (1920): 1, commercial and offices; 2, older homes, warehouses, and manufacturing; 3, low- and middle-cost housing; 4, higher-priced homes and shops.

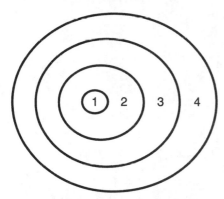

Sources: Park, Burgess, and McKenzie, eds., *The City*. Chicago University of Chicago Press, 1925; von Thunen, Der Isolierte Staat, 1826.

The Importance of Topography

The second of our four dominant factors is **topography**. von Thunen simplified everything, by assuming that villages were located on level or flat plains, and that they used the transportation systems of 1826: walking, pack animals, and slow carts. These two assumptions were important to his conclusions. His central concern was the importance of transportation cost or effort. His pattern of uses provided people with the easiest access to those places they had to go to most often or most urgently.

However, when a community site is not level, the round pattern begins to change. For example, if a city had its origins as a protection site, located on top of a ridge, with steep slopes on two sides, there will be little economic activity on these steep slopes. The city would be strung out along the ridge top in each direction, and its circular shape would become a ribbon. This is one example of the effect of topography on city shape. Topography—the shape and slope of the land— changes the shape of cities in several ways.

Topography may explain the community's original location. Similarly, topographical features can attract added development or impede growth. Features that are *attractions* to growth include pleasant lake shores, level land, and—for their views—gentle hills. Features that are *barriers* to growth include steep hills, ravines, marshes, swamps, and riverbanks. Effectively, topography acts to modify the important issue of accessibility! von Thunen's concept of a round city assumed a town on a level site. As we introduce topography, the shape changes. Figure 7.2 shows how topography modifies the round city shape.

FIGURE 7.2   The influence of topography on the circular city.

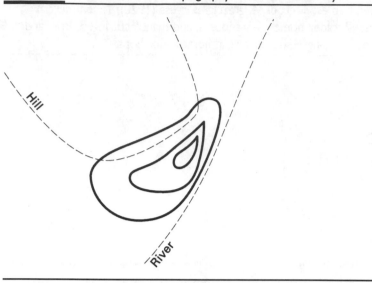

Transportation

Transportation is the third key factor, because it affects accessibility. Topography has an obvious effect on transportation. It is easier, cheaper, and faster to travel on level land, than up or down steep hills. The circular city developed in von Thunen's work was based on transportation by foot, pack animal, or cart. These are all transportation systems that we would describe as being (1) slow and (2) dispersed or *random*. Random means that one can go from any place to any other place with equal ease. People moving on foot or on horseback can travel equally well in any direction (unless blocked by the topography)!

Twentieth-century communities developed transportation systems that von Thunen did not foresee. The influence of each on city shape differs. The automobile on a city street is a relatively random transportation system, similar to a person on foot. However, the car is capable of moving far greater distances in a given time period. Automobile cities, therefore, tend to be circular, like von Thunen's, but extremely spread out, with much lower population density. Streetcars and subways, on the other hand, cannot move randomly; they must move along rail lines. They are "linear" or "axial" transportation systems. These create patterns of **linear (axial) growth**. Such rail systems, however, are strongly influenced by topography.

Freeways are a combination of the two types of transport: The car itself tends to give a circular shape to the city, but freeways produce a series of linear extensions. Simple examples of these are illustrated in Figure 7.3. When we add modern transportation systems to

FIGURE 7.3 Effects of transportation on city shape for four cities, each with 100,000 people. (a) Small size attributable to foot transportation, and the round shape to random access. (b) Large size attributable to auto transportation; round shape to random access. (c) Small size attributable to streetcar transportation and walking; star shape due to linear access. (d) Large size attributable to auto transportation with two freeways; linear shape due to linear access.

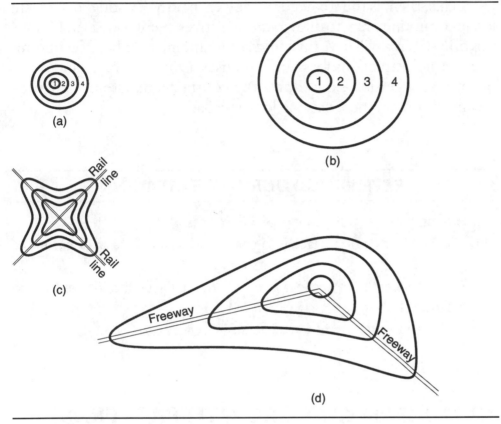

von Thunen's simplified model of a community, we see that *the transportation system or systems in use will affect the density of the town as well as its shape.*

The Existing City: Origins

The fourth factor that influences community structure is history: What and where was the *community origin*? How was the community first built? When the first building was erected, it influenced where the second building would be—probably close to the first, but not too close. When the first store was built, it is likely that it was located in or very close to the center of the existing housing cluster. Similarly, when the first government structure was built, it was usually located in the middle of the existing community. The town probably grew around its center—shops next to shops, homes next to homes, and offices next to offices.

This type of development occurred because there was a locational advantage for each type of land use at some particular location. Each new user wanted the same locational advantages that the existing competitive users had. This means that the community's origin continues to play a major part in the location of new buildings, because the new buildings (for a particular use) *tend to develop near the existing buildings*. This, then, is the tremendous power that the existing investment in the community has, to draw additional investment toward it. In time, this original area will have built up a commanding number of economic and cultural attractions for many land uses. Only very high land prices or traffic congestion slows down the constant pressure of new uses, seeking to obtain these existing locational advantages.

REVIEWING YOUR UNDERSTANDING

Looking at the Structure of Communities

1. List the four dominant factors in community shape. Give an example of each.
2. How does each of these four factors influence the population density of a city?
3. List four examples of how topography influences a city.

7.3 MODERN CITY GROWTH PATTERNS

We started with simple towns, in Section 7.2, so that we could understand the patterns that lie at the heart of a big city. Now, let us add size and complexity. This section combines the four factors (accessibility, transportation, topography, and origin) with the additional elements that appear in the larger community. The result is a fairly realistic model of the pattern of land use in American communities.

Proximity Versus Accessibility

If the community grows, the growing population exerts greater and greater pressures on the downtown central zone. These growing pressures involve larger numbers of people seeking to work, shop, and visit in this central area. Congestion increases (whatever the transportation system), until the advantages of the downtown area—its accessibility and central location—begin to disappear. For the person who lives on the edge of the community and needs to buy a few things, the shopping trip downtown becomes uneconomic. At some point, it becomes feasible for some types of downtown land uses to leave the downtown area, and move to the outskirts to gain better access to their outlying customers. This movement can be either a gradual *creep*, one store moving a little farther out than the last, or a sudden *leapfrog* to the city's fringe.

This process illustrates the continual tug of war between the two main influences. The first, **proximity**, comes from the original location of the city, the high investment in existing buildings, the central location of the city center, and its proximity to the entire community. These represent the established, the fixed, and the past. The second is *accessibility* (the original reason for the central core) and the influence of transportation and transportation change on accessibility. These speak for change, and the future.

Each land-use decision throughout the community involves a weighing, often consciously, of the relative benefits of proximity and accessibility. Should we put the building in the safe location, near where the last one was built? Or should we pioneer farther out, along the transportation routes that have emerged in recent years?

Quick investor response to the San Francisco Bay Area Rapid Transit System (BART), in the late 1960s, is an excellent example of a new transportation system, bringing shifts in the balance between proximity and accessibility, and the system's impact on real estate values. The Los Angeles transit system is having the same effects.

When new transportation systems are initiated in other metro areas, the same investor response and favorable impact on real estate values takes place. Outlying suburban areas tend to benefit most when a new transportation system is created, because of improved accessibility to the central core. All of the station locations along the route also benefit, because of the increased traffic exposure and accessibility.

The Complex City

As the community gets larger, it requires more than one transportation system. Most communities now combine some *linear types* of transportation with *random types*: subways and automobiles, for instance. Even in communities on level ground, with streets forming a grid, some streets will be one-way and some will be widened, arterial routes. These changes introduce linear features into an otherwise random street pattern. At the same time, the move to encourage walking, and bicycles, offers a contrary force, towards greater density and a non-linear development pattern.

FIGURE 7.4   (Top) The effect of a suburban shopping center on community shape. (Bottom) The added effect of a second freeway.

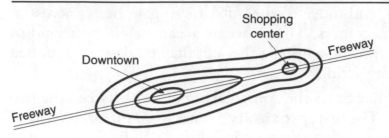

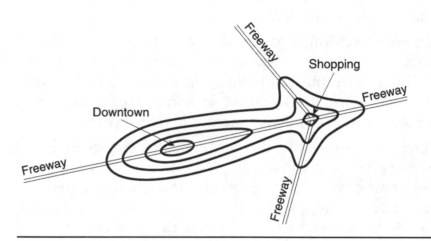

Each use that moves away from the downtown, along a linear route, pulls the circular shape of the community with it. Sometimes a use will leapfrog, or jump still farther out, as most shopping centers have done. This is also called "bursting." These outlying centers in turn become mini-downtown areas, with their own forces of *proximity* (also called "gravity" or "centrality") flowing out in mini-circles around them, as shown in Figure 7.4. Shopping centers, big box retailing, and outlet centers are our premier examples of bursting. Suburban office buildings, research parks, and manufacturing plants also illustrate the concept.

Because the leapfrogging retail users of land are primarily seeking better accessibility to customers, they usually locate near an intersection of two or more transportation routes. This may be where two arterials meet, at a major freeway off-ramp, or (best of all) at a freeway-freeway intersection. Such locations can become complete new downtowns, because of the drawing power that their growing mixtures of uses create.

Enter the Wedge

Our analysis so far has involved a community that has no better or worse side. Thus, we have assumed that you and I would live anywhere in the residential ring that lies on the outskirts of the city. This is not so in practice, and one example is our preference for locations that are easier to reach. Homer Hoyt's classic 1939 study, *The Structure and Growth of Residential Neighborhoods in American Cities*, concluded that higher-priced homes took the best acreage on the outskirts of the city. These houses tended to cluster into one segment of the outer circle. As the community grew, and as new houses were added in the suburbs, the higher-priced homes were added just beyond the existing high-priced areas. In this fashion, the higher-priced sector became a wedge. In Figure 7.5, observe this wedge pattern most clearly in the historical development of Minneapolis and Richmond. In Boston, while the fashionable area tended to stay to the same side of town, it did not form a wedge, but just moved outward.

Medium-cost and low-cost homes sorted themselves out into the segments not claimed for the high-priced homes.

The medium-cost homes typically sought to be near the prestige locations, leaving the poorest area for development of lower-priced homes. In fact, one author called these poorer areas "sinks," because they were often areas with poor drainage. Hoyt mapped the shifts in location of better residential areas in a number of American cities; several of his maps are reproduced in Figure 7.5.

Hoyt then pointed out that the retail district in the city followed the higher-priced homes. As these homes concentrated to one side of the city and moved out toward the suburbs in a wedge, the better residential shops moved to that side of the downtown core. The wholesale and manufacturing uses generally oriented themselves out of the way of such high-priced commercial uses. This sorting process often left manufacturing located on the side of the downtown core closest to the area of low-priced homes.[2]

Hoyt further found that the wedge shape of the high-priced home area endured for a long time. Its direction of movement was toward the higher ground, but it also moved away from areas that were impossible to build on or that involved such dead-end developments as extending to the end of a peninsula or toward a riverbank. He found that changes in the direction of high-priced home movement occurred very slowly, because of the long life of real estate improvements. He noted that

---

[2]Contrary to Hoyt's theory, in some industrial cities old abandoned factories have been turned into shopping malls and condominiums. The success of these projects has varied.

FIGURE 7.5   Shifts in location of fashionable residential areas in six American cities, 1900–1936. Fashionable residential areas indicated by solid black.

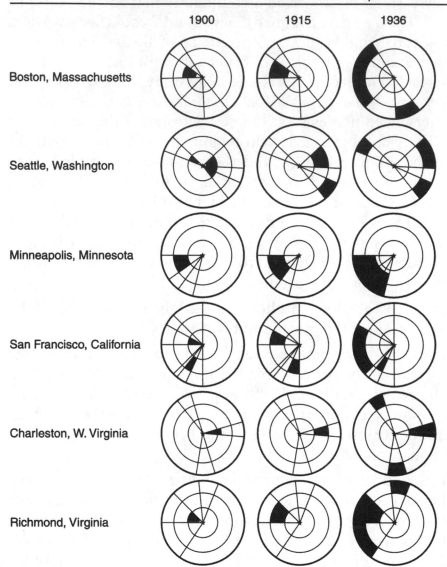

Source: Homer Hoyt, *The Structure and Growth of Residential Neighborhoods in American Cities*. Washington, DC, Federal Housing Administration, Government Printing Office, 1939, p. 115. This study is considered a classic by modern urban planners.

industry and manufacturing tended to be close to such transportation sources as waterfronts, railroads, airports, and highways. Retail business, on the other hand, might be found at highway intersections and at any similar population cluster away from highways.

Political and Social Factors

As indicated earlier, we rarely find an ideal community growth pattern. Part of the reason is that factors like topography have subtle effects, because they are based on people's *feelings* about topography. A good example is that hills and high ground can be an *attraction to growth*, especially of high-priced homes, and can also be a *barrier to growth*, because of the high utility and transportation costs associated with getting there. The question of whether a particular hillside will be an attraction or a barrier to growth is difficult to predict. Moreover, the amount of attraction may change as transportation, utility systems, and people's tastes change.

The process is also complicated by factors other than the "big four"—accessibility, transportation, topography, and community origins. Political factors also influence community location and direction of growth. In some instances, political boundaries of cities are absolute barriers to growth, with no construction permitted outside the city limits. Sometimes these limitations are county boundaries, and growth of the city or community in that direction may be blocked. In other instances, city and county boundaries are not the problem. Instead, growth is hampered by boundaries of sewer or water districts. Sometimes, environmental issues, or endangered species, will act to set a boundary.

Political factors are not limited just to the boundary problem. Communities establish general plans to express community feelings about land use, land-use patterns, and growth patterns. Increasingly, regional plans are impacting what cities are able to do. These planning decisions create land controls and restrict or direct growth patterns. For example, a community could pass an ordinance that reserves prime flat land for agriculture, so-called "green belts," despite its suitability for residential development. A community can also state what types of structures it desires, or the density at which development can occur. Thus, there may be insufficient land to meet market wishes for one type of structure, and excessive land for other types!

Community Attitudes

There are other *social influences* on the community's growth pattern and land-use pattern. One example is the community's attitude toward transportation systems, alternatives, and change. If voters in a dense urban area refuse to approve the financing of a rapid transit system, it probably means that the future transportation system will be more random and less linear or axial, than if the financing had passed. This will affect the overall density of the region, and the clusters of secondary downtowns, or secondary concentric centers, that occur in a large region. Social pressure to encourage pedestrians and bicyclists also clearly impacts density and use patterns.

Still another social influence is changing attitudes about where, and how, to live. During the 1950s, and for decades after, the dream was to own a detached single-family home in the suburbs. Close-in locations, and other types of housing, did not do well in the marketplace during this time period. That has gradually changed, as condominiums became more common in the 1990s. But in the late 2000s, we see a major shift toward close-in locations. So-called "in-fill" development has become a major factor. More variation in types of units emerged, with townhomes, duets, and zero-lot-line homes. These use in-fill sites to a higher density, but still provide fee-simple ownership of the lot.

More Information About City Issues

There are many sources of added information. Here are a few viewpoints.

www.smartgrowth.org

www.epa.gov/dced—the Environmental Protection Agency

www.nrdc.org—the Natural Resources Defense Council

www.cei.org—the Competitive Enterprise Institute

www.sprawlcity.org

www.planetizen.org—an urban planning news website

For an example of a good city site: www.cityplanning.lacity.org

For links to many city planning resources: www.lib.berkeley.edu/ENVI/cityweb.html

Even individual decisions can influence community growth patterns. An example is the farmer whose property is on the community's outskirts, in the path of development. Should this farmer hold and farm the land, well past the time developers seek to use it, development pressures will be directed toward other available lands to the sides or beyond. The farmer could create a large island or barrier to growth. In other cases, however, the farm owner whose land is somewhat remote from development may become eager to sell, and by skillful merchandising, vigorous promotion, and use of politics, the farmer may encourage development far earlier than would otherwise be the case.

The Results

Thus, there are many factors that influence community growth patterns. Their effects, and the end result, are complicated and interwoven. It is possible, however, to describe how these forces interact, and the best description is the widely quoted statement by the pioneer urban economist Richard Hurd in his Principles of City Land Values (1903):

> Cities originate at their most convenient point of contact with the outer world and grow in the lines of least resistance or greatest attraction, or their resultants. The point of contact differs according to the methods of transportation, whether by water, by turnpike or by railroad…. The influence of topography, all-powerful when cities start, is

constantly modified.... The most direct results of topography come from its control of transportation.

Growth in cities consists of movement away from the point of origin in all directions, except as topographically hindered, this movement being due both to aggregation at the edges and pressure from the center. Central growth takes place both from the heart of the city and from each sub-centre of attraction, and axial growth pushes into the outlying territory by means of railroads, turnpikes, and street rail-roads. All cities are built up from these two influences, which vary in quantity, intensity and quality, and resulting districts overlapping, interpenetrating, neutralizing, and harmonizing as the pressure of the city's growth brings them in contact with each other. Residences are early driven to the circumference, while business remains at the center, and as residences divide into various social grades, retail shops of corresponding grades follow them, and wholesale shops in turn follow the retailers, while institutions and various mixed utilities irregularly fill in the intermediate zone, and the banking and office section remains at the main business center. Complicating this broad outward movement of zones, axes of traffic project shops through residence areas, create business sub-centers, where they intersect, and change circular cities into star-shaped cites. Central growth, due to proximity, and axial growth, due to accessibility, are summed up in the static power of established sections and the dynamic power of their chief lines of intercommunication.[3]

Each sentence in this quotation has great significance. Reread the passage and take each sentence as a full, separate thought. Stop at the end of the sentence and ask yourself what it means, in terms of the cities and communities that you have known. It is striking that Mr. Hurd was so successful in capturing the dynamic combination of factors, in such clear language, so long ago.

Other Views

Comments by Burgess, Hoyt, and others do not seem to disprove or take a position opposing what Hurd said, but rather emphasize one view or another of the complicated whole. For example, Harris and Ullman suggested in 1945 that the dominant concept in city shape was that of **multiple nuclei**. Their thought was that each land use responds in a different way to topography, transportation, and other influences. Similar uses tend to cluster together in nuclei, illustrated in

---

[3]Richard M. Hurd, *Principles of City Land Values*, New York, 1903, pp. 15–16.

FIGURE 7.6   Multiple nuclei in city growth patterns.

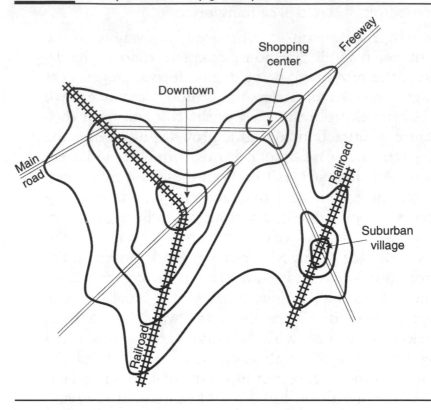

Figure 7.6. The city thus created appears to be star-shaped. The multiple-nuclei concept explains how uses become located in different places in the community.

Others have stressed socioeconomic linkages, and have pointed out that locational desires of families are the force in shaping cities. Families choose their residential location for social and economic needs. Businesses and public facilities follow them, in order to be of service. This humanistic viewpoint of community shape, however, falls short of analyzing the factors that influence family residential choices. These turn out again to be amenities of location, topography, transportation, and political and social constraints on growth. Again, we find a viewpoint that seems to restate Hurd.

Richard Nelson suggested in 1958 that there are four urban models. The largest is the metropolitan commercial center, which he calls Commerce City. Next in size is the medium-sized city, or Center Town. Third is the rural trading area (Countyville), and fourth is the dormitory suburb for a larger city (Forest Lake). He suggests that land-use patterns in Countyville are predominantly the circular-zone concepts of von Thunen and Burgess. Sector (wedge) theory seems to become more relevant or visible in the larger Center Town. The largest community, Commerce City, shows the patterns described by the sector theory, and also begins to demonstrate the multiple-nuclei concept. His fourth model, Forest Lake, is a satellite

FIGURE 7.7 The superblock grid system of city land use. Land use codes: I, industrial; C, commercial; A, apartments; H, houses.

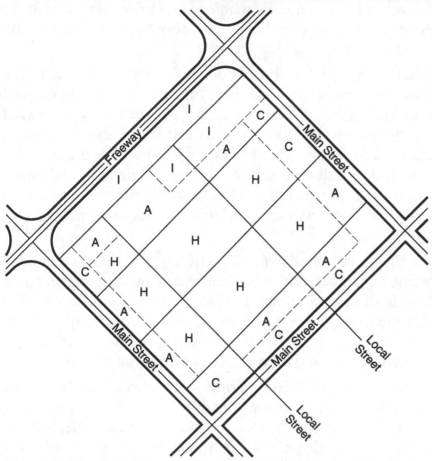

Source: After Barlowe, *Land Resource Economics*, 1972. Prentice Hall, Englewood Cliffs, N.J.

community, unlike the other three. It has a layout that will vary, as determined by its relationship to its parent city—the distance, topography, transportation systems, etc.

In 1972, Barlowe suggested that suburban areas surrounding large cities increasingly show a land-use pattern of large grids. In these grids, the major avenues and cross streets are lined with commercial and (sometimes) industrial uses or sites, whereas the enclosed superblocks and the interior streets are reserved for residential uses. Figure 7.7 illustrates this pattern. Both Nelson and Barlowe sharpened our perception of how communities are structured. Nelson's four cities, in particular, seem to agree with the California experience. Both Nelson and Barlowe are consistent with the model that Hurd presented.

The Effects of Transportation Change

Nevertheless, there are ways in which Hurd's language cannot help us understand today's city. One major change since his time has been the effect of transportation on manufacturing and wholesale activities. Air freight, trucks, and freeways have freed wholesalers from the need to locate close to their retail customers. Indeed, many wholesalers now service an entire state, a region, or sometimes an entire country from one warehouse. These shifts in wholesale location do not violate Hurd's general concepts, but his language about the specific location of wholesalers is generally no longer valid.

Manufacturing, too, has thrown off its former strong ties to the railroad line. As a result, most manufacturing units no longer need to locate in the center of the community, where the railroad yard and unloading spurs were located. Once freed from these constraints, manufacturing can follow other locational factors. One is a need for inexpensive land, as industrial factories shift to single-story buildings. The addition of worker parking heightens this need. Good access to freeways, for both workers and trucks, became much more important.

The ties that once bound many types of land use to the inner zone are now weak. In the past, both wholesale and manufacturing units had to be located in the central community, to have reasonable accessibility to their shipments, customers, and the technical assistance of patent lawyers and banks. The transportation revolution of the twentieth century has liberated these, and other, land uses from the central zone.

And better transportation, along with more flexible work schedules, have shifted housing locations. Fifty-mile commutes, or longer, are now fairly common. This has caused "leap-frog" housing—major growth or new towns on the outskirts of every major region. However, these have proved vulnerable to the economic impacts of higher gasoline prices. Pressure to reduce air pollution might be an additional problem in the future.

Adding in Technology

Another significant change, and one that is critical for the future, is the explosion in communication capabilities. In the past, many businesses required physical proximity to their customers, because interactions between people required a physical meeting. That era is at an end. Suburban movement of office buildings is one example of this change. Photocopying, fax machines, and computers were early steps. Now, the Internet, cell phones, instant messaging, and video conferencing continue to accelerate this major swing. In many downtown areas today, the remaining retail establishments consist primarily of specialty retail stores. Often, these retail stores market to an entire region, or even to tourists from other areas, states, or countries. Beverly Hills, San Francisco, and New York come to mind! Wholesale and office use now is for those that require face-to-face contact, such as jewelry or fashion clothes wholesaling. Lawyers, who often must negotiate directly, or must have access to local courts, also stay.

Special Interest Topics

Largest Cities by Population in the United States and California

United States	Rank	California
New York	1	Los Angeles
Los Angeles	2	San Diego
Chicago	3	San Jose
Houston	4	San Francisco
Phoenix	5	Fresno
Philadelphia	6	Sacramento
San Antonio	7	Long Beach
Dallas	8	Oakland
San Diego	9	Santa Ana
San Jose	10	Anaheim

Source: U.S. Census Bureau 2008;.

Since 2000, in the U.S. rankings, Phoenix moved up from #8 to #5, San Antonio from #10 to #7, and San Jose came on the list to replace Detroit. Philadelphia moved down from #5 to #6 and Dallas from #7 to #8.

In the California rankings, Fresno has moved up from #8 to #5, Long Beach moved down from #5 to #7, and Oakland moved from #7 to #8.

REVIEWING YOUR UNDERSTANDING

Modern City Growth Patterns

1. What is meant by proximity and accessibility as forces in shaping cities? Give an example of the influence of each in your city.

2. Explain how the home location preferences of high-income people influence the layout of cities.

3. Give five examples of how political and social factors can influence city shape and layout.

4. What does the concept multiple nuclei mean? What effect do they have on the shape of cities?

5. Give five examples of the ways in which the use of cars and trucks has changed the shape and layout of cities.

CHAPTER SUMMARY

This chapter has discussed how the community gets its shape, layout, and population density. The patterns of community development are important, because they tell what factors have influenced land uses and changes. In turn, property value rests on its location. Our understanding of these past and present forces and changes is our major tool in understanding locations, and value changes.

The major economic forces influencing community growth patterns are (1) accessibility, (2) transportation, (3) topography, and (4) community origins. For any given parcel of land, one specific use has a comparative advantage over all other uses, because of the effects of these forces. This comparative advantage is reflected by the amount of rent that the highest and best use is able to generate. Nearby sites, which have similar characteristics, attract similar uses to them. This leads to clusters or nuclei of similar uses.

In addition to economic forces, political and social pressures affect land-use decisions. Public land-use controls and eminent domain are the two most common types of political forces. Social pressures are varied, but are a main influence on land use. Economic, political, and social forces spring from "we, the people," but in different ways, with different effects and mechanisms.

Small communities tend to have simple land-use patterns, generally a series of concentric rings of different land uses. Larger cities develop pie-shaped wedges that expand through several rings. This results from the gradual development of a higher-priced side or sector, in the residential and commercial rings. When we turn to large metropolitan areas or complexes, we often see that a number of small concentric communities grow until they meet. The resulting pattern of land uses has a number of centers, both from suburban areas and from new clusters around major transportation intersections. Each center or nucleus has rings of uses around it, but each center may serve a specialized function.

In each case, the location of land uses seems to be the result of the competition between the drawing power of the existing buildings and the changing accessibility to people, resulting from growth of the community and changes in its transportation systems. The former is dominated by the origins and early transportation features of the town, and the latter owes much to topography, social and political influences, and the current transportation systems.

REVIEWING YOUR UNDERSTANDING

1. When land is allocated to the legal user who pays the highest price, economists call this the principle of:
   A. balance
   B. highest and best use
   C. economic succession
   D. change

2. The impact that zoning has on community growth patterns is what type of force?
   A. economic
   B. physical
   C. social
   D. political

3. The circular or concentric theory of growth has the city growing:
   A. around the downtown central core
   B. along transportation lines
   C. from several points such as suburban shopping centers
   D. from the highest to the lowest topographic point

4. The multiple nuclei theory of growth has the city growing:
   A. around the downtown central core
   B. along transportation lines
   C. from several points, including regional shopping centers
   D. from the highest to the lowest topographic point

5. The growth of a community along transportation lines, such as freeways or rapid transit routes, is best described as:
   A. spatial
   B. axial or linear
   C. sporadic
   D. circular

6. In real estate land use, accessibility means:
   A. similar zoning
   B. ability to get to a site, and from it to other places
   C. social factors that determine use
   D. nearness to other businesses

7. According to the classic study by Homer Hoyt, *The Structure and Growth of Residential Neighborhoods in American Cities*, higher-priced homes tend to be built:
   A. on flat land
   B. near transportation systems
   C. near industrial parks
   D. on hillsides

8. The physical shape of a city can be changed by:
   A. new transportation systems
   B. topography
   C. new technology
   D. all of the above

9. No-growth policies by city government-ments are an example of what type of force?
   A. political
   B. economic
   C. physical
   D. social

10. The future growth patterns of large U.S. cities will be heavily influenced by:
    A. transportation systems
    B. environmental concerns
    C. telecommunications systems
    D. all of the above

11. Which transportation vehicle or system is considered random?
    A. trains
    B. automobiles
    C. subways
    D. streetcars

12. Comparative advantage means the:
    A. increased benefit that a particular building gives to a particular site
    B. locational benefit to a user gained by a site being in the central area of a town
    C. increased benefit to a user that a particular property gains from the advantages it may have over less desirable properties
    D. locational forces that shift town growth away from desirable areas

13. When an existing building is demolished and a new, more profitable building is constructed, this is an application of:
    A. the economics of succession
    B. the principle of change
    C. highest and best use
    D. all of the above

14. The pattern of land use in cities is based solely on the interplay of private market forces.
    A. true
    B. false

15. The four dominant factors shaping land-use patterns for small cities are:
    A. origins, social issues, politics, and change
    B. topography, transportation, economics, and politics
    C. topography, transportation, social issues, and change
    D. origins, accessibility, topography, and transportation

16. Each land use tends to seek that location that has the best combination of benefits and minimal problems. This is called:
    A. zoning
    B. comparative advantage
    C. eminent domain
    D. concentric growth

17. Accessibility and topography have strong influences on land-use patterns.
    A. true
    B. false

18. In modern U.S. cities, land-use patterns are no longer influenced by major transportation systems.
    A. true
    B. false

19. After a town is formed, the forces of proximity and _____ are in a continual tug of war over the locations of new buildings.
    A. productivity
    B. import goods
    C. obsolescence
    D. accessibility

20. Leapfrogging is the label applied:
    A. when a new town is established
    B. when a new location is selected well away from existing central locations
    C. to the process of growth established by a new freeway
    D. when property is rezoned

21. The wedge describes the manner in which:
    A. a new transit system alters the pattern of land uses
    B. a shift of a major government building changes uses
    C. the principle of change influences government policies
    D. concentric rings of uses break into slices of different values

22. The ever-increasing use of electronic equipment such as the Internet, cell phones, and interactive TV could lessen the need for additional office buildings in downtown areas of major U.S. cities.
    A. true
    B. false

23. Without zoning laws, similar land uses tend to cluster together: residential with residential, commercial with commercial, manufacturing with manufacturing, because of the principle of:
    A. change
    B. substitution
    C. decreasing returns
    D. comparative advantage

24. Which main transportation system allows the most flexibility in the location of manufacturing plants?
    A. railroads
    B. trucking
    C. waterways
    D. airlines

25. The increased use of the Internet and other communication systems changes land-use patterns by:
    A. increasing the power of existing locations
    B. making cities more linear in shape
    C. reducing the need for physical proximity to other uses
    D. reducing the leapfrogging tendency

CASE & POINT

Future Issues in City Layout

We can see the major forces in city layout. Some, like topography, do not change much over time. Others are sure to change. What can we say about these possible changes?

Transportation

Will we continue to rely on the automobile to the degree that we now do? It seems probable that the cost for gasoline, or its replacement, will rise. But will it rise faster than inflation?

And what about public support for buses and other forms of mass transit? If we look back in time several decades and compare to now, funding for mass transit has increased but not by much more than the rate of inflation. The United States continues to lag behind most other industrialized countries in funding for mass transit. This is to be expected, given the low density of development in most of the United States. But, as population and congestion grow, will this change?

Commute Time

This involves two different issues: how far (or how long) are people, on average, willing to commute, and where do they want to commute to? Both, of course, closely involve transportation.

The move to the suburbs, starting in the 1950s, profoundly changed American cities. Today, in-fill development is changing most older downtowns. How far will this reverse wave go?

For a time, especially in the mid 2000s, many seemed willing to accept longer and longer commutes. Often, they appeared to be motivated by the desire for less-expensive home ownership opportunities with better schools. However, traffic congestion grew during the same period, making the same physical commute take longer, with more stress. Now, many of these deep-suburban areas have seen the worst house price drops, a result of the mortgage mess, as well as higher gas prices. Have we reached the peak of average commute times, or will the average start rising again?

Demography

One of the nice things about demographic change is its relative ease of forecasting. Whatever is the current age, skill, and

CASE & POINT

FIGURE 7A.1   U.S. births by year.

Source: www.census.gov

income makeup of the population of a state, experts can make very reliable projections for ten years in the future. Birth rates do not change rapidly. Barring a major medical crisis, neither do death rates. In and out migrations are more variable, but are usually not large enough to significantly change the results. The major demographic change that we face is the aging of the huge group of "baby boomers," born in the 1946–1964 time period. Figure 7A.1 shows the annual birthrate. Note the big increase from just over 220,000 births in 1935 to over 430,000 births in 1960. The annual rate dropped to about 315,000 births in 1973–1975, and then rose again to 420,000 births in 1990, as the baby boomers had children.

Where will baby boomers choose to live when they retire? Will this change as they age? Clearly, they are one factor in the recent in-fill wave. And what type of housing will they choose? Many inner-city luxury condominium projects appear to have targeted them. But some choose to move to rural areas, or to southern resort areas. So, we can say a lot about the numbers, but what the individuals will do is much less clear!

Chapter

8

IMPORTANT TERMS AND CONCEPTS

Change in use
Density of use
Deterioration
Forces for change:
   Economic
   Physical
   Political
   Social

Gentrification
Historical
   preservation
Location
Neighborhood
   boundaries
Neighborhood
   cycle

Neighborhood
   obsolescence
Neighborhood
Preservation
Rehabilitation cycle
Turnover rate

PREVIEW

Chapter 8 describes the clusters of similar land uses and values that are called "neighborhoods." Section 8.1 defines the neighborhood concept, shows the close connection to "location," and illustrates how to locate neighborhood boundaries. Section 8.2 explains the importance of the study of neighborhoods as a tool to identify changes that will influence individual property values. Section 8.3 analyzes neighborhood decay, and the tools used to reverse the decline. The Case & Point at the end of the chapter explores the advantages and disadvantages of government versus private decision making, regarding neighborhood preservation. When you have completed this chapter, you will be able to:

1. Define *neighborhood* and explain how to locate the boundary of neighborhoods.

Neighborhoods: Clusters of Land Use and Value

2. Discuss how neighborhoods influence real property values.
3. List the four forces that affect neighborhood change.
4. Describe the process of neighborhood decay.

This information will help you to analyze the strengths and weaknesses of neighborhoods in your local community. Agents, investors, and appraisers each use this understanding in their daily work.

8.1 THE NEIGHBORHOOD AS THE BASIS OF VALUE

Chapter 7 discussed how growth starts from the initial origins of the community and the forces that lead to a predictable pattern of land use and expansion. This section shows how neighborhoods make a bridge between these community land-use patterns and the values of individual parcels.

What Is a Neighborhood?

A **neighborhood** is a cluster of properties of relatively similar land use and value. Neighborhoods frequently have occupants with similar characteristics. In residential areas, occupants may have somewhat similar income levels, education, and status.

Neighborhoods exist because topography, transportation, and social and political influences have different effects on each type of land use. Thus, similar uses will be influenced in similar ways and will tend to cluster together. On the other hand, land uses can conflict, such as an airport locating in a residential neighborhood. This potential problem is usually addressed by zoning ordinances, which restrict land uses in a zone to a few narrow categories. Variances are granted only when applicants show that the proposed use is not injurious to the existing uses allowed in that zoning category. Similar controls can be achieved by the use of private deed restrictions. Chapter 13 explores zoning and other governmental controls in more detail.

Neighborhood, Location, and Property Values

There is an old saying that there are three factors that determine the value of a property—"location, location, and location!" This saying emphasizes that real estate has a fixed location, which means the value of any individual parcel is determined by, and cannot escape, the features or forces that surround it.

The value of a property is also a function of the physical property itself. That is, a large house on a large lot is worth more than a small house on a small lot, *assuming* that all other factors are the same. Other physical characteristics of the property (such as age, condition, quality, charm, renovation, mechanical features, and special equipment) are also part of what gives that property its value. However, the example of a brand-new automobile assembly plant in the middle of the Sahara Desert is used by many appraisal teachers, to illustrate the relative importance of the physical property versus its surroundings.

In this case, despite the newness, excellent condition, functional layout, and quality materials of the assembly plant, the plant is not worth much at all. It lacks all of the necessary features around it, such as utility and transportation systems and availability of skilled workers, raw materials, and markets for its products.

Another example is that of building identical homes on different sites. One site may be close to downtown, whereas another may be in an older suburb, on the last available vacant lot. A third site may be in a new suburb, surrounded by similar newer homes. Finally, a fourth site might be in a rural area, on a lot in a farmer's field. Although the houses are identical, and were built by the same builder at the same time, each will have a different market value, because of its individual location.

Defining Location

If property value is heavily influenced by location, the question is asked, what is location? Location is the sum of all the topographical, transport, and other influences on land use that characterize a particular neighborhood or nucleus. Location means almost the same thing as neighborhood. **Location** refers to the proximity to transportation, employment, shopping, and desired cultural facilities, and the influence of any nuisance that is found in the area. Location is also the sum of all the characteristics of the people who are present in the neighborhood. When people refer to the *neighborhood*, they are emphasizing the general characteristics of the area. *Location* refers to how these characteristics apply to a specific site.

Increasingly, people want to know more about the characteristics of a neighborhood. Home buyers are particularly interested! They might go for details to Web sites, such as:

- realestate.yahoo.com/neighborhoods
- www.neighborhoodfind.com/
- www.moving.com/real-estate/explore-cities-neighborhoods.asp
- neighborhoods.realtor.com
- www.eneighborhoods.com
- zipskinny.com

These sites are also used by real estate agents, to see how the neighborhood for a new listing is rated. Appraisers may use these sites, both for neighborhood data, and also to see if the neighborhoods of potential comparable sales are similar.

Neighborhood Boundaries

Where does one neighborhood end and another begin? **Neighborhood boundaries** occur where the location starts to change. In some cases, a neighborhood boundary will be sharply defined, as by a lake, river, marsh, freeway, or a similar distinct barrier to development. In other cases, neighborhoods lack such sharp boundaries; instead, there is a gradual merging of neighborhoods. Sometimes, two adjacent neighborhoods could be considered as one, because they differ only slightly in their characteristics. On the other hand, one could subdivide any neighborhood, by using minor differences among its several parts. You can see that *neighborhood* is not a precise term and that boundaries are usually not exact.

The type of boundary also varies for different types of neighborhoods. For example, the neighborhood for central financial district office buildings, in larger cities, may be set by the cluster of the existing financial office buildings.

Industrial developments tend to have defined boundaries. Often, the boundaries are set by the zoning ordinance, or at the point where the existing industrial park stops. However, if the industrial district contains a mixture of other uses, the boundary becomes uncertain.

For example, many older areas have industrial and residential buildings mixed together. This type of mixture has characteristics that could make it a neighborhood of its own, separate from adjoining areas that contain only industrial buildings.

A modern trend is for commercial use on the lower floor, with residential uses over. This is often called "new urbanism." Most commonly, these buildings are located on main roads, or else in very dense downtown areas.

Often, *mixed-use buildings* might be located on main roads. These main or arterial roads might be located every five or ten blocks. This forms what is sometimes called a *superblock*, with heavy traffic and commercial uses on the perimeter, and quiet streets and residential uses in the interior.

Thus, neighborhood boundaries are usually defined either by geographic features, by political boundaries of some kind, or by transitions in the existing pattern of land use. The boundaries are often vague and imprecise; however, many observers "on the ground" agree on what constitutes a local neighborhood.

Often, the best evidence of market rent or market value for a specific property will be the rents or sale prices of similar properties in that neighborhood. For that reason, real estate agents and appraisers learn to pay particular attention to the neighborhood.

REVIEWING YOUR UNDERSTANDING

The Neighborhood as the Basis of Value
1. What determines the boundary of a neighborhood?
2. How small can a neighborhood be? How large?
3. What do occupants of a neighborhood have in common?

8.2 NEIGHBORHOODS AS BAROMETERS OF CHANGE

We have said that a neighborhood is a collection of relatively similar occupants, structures, and uses of land. Nevertheless, there are slight differences among properties in the neighborhood. (Some neighborhoods will have a lot of variation!) These variations could be among the lots, structures, occupants, or locations. Over time, the forces that determine land use in the community will be changing. They will first affect the places that are most vulnerable to change. When the small changes over the months are similar, it indicates that the neighborhood is responding to the new forces pushing on it. An example would be gradual conversions of homes to small offices, along a busy street.

Forces for Change

All forces for neighborhood change can be divided into the categories of physical, economic, social, or political. Within these broad headings, there are different possibilities. Appraisers, agents, and planners monitor these changes.

Physical Forces

Physical forces or factors for neighborhood change include the effects of time and the elements. They include weather—from routine fading and settling to the sudden tornado or flood—as well as earthquakes, slides, soil creep, and fault creep. Fires also can be a physical factor for change, as can pollution.

Political Forces

Political forces or factors that cause neighborhoods to change range from taxation to education. They include the effects of a radical city council on a conservative neighborhood, and of a traditional city council on an unorthodox neighborhood. Examples of these effects can include the willingness or failure to provide the level and type of education, police, or fire support that the neighborhood seeks.

For nonresidential neighborhoods, taxation is often an issue that motivates change. Sometimes, strict zoning laws will make it difficult for slightly different uses to move in, as others move out. For example, there are many older arterial streets with commercial zoning. Retail uses may be declining, as stores move to better locations, perhaps for more parking. Service and office uses may want to move in. If the zoning is exclusively retail, they might not qualify, leading to increasing vacancy.

Political factors can combine with physical issues. One example is governmental land-use controls in residential neighborhoods that use septic tanks. Some areas were subdivided many years ago, using, say, 50- by 100-foot lots. But sanitary standards today (depending on the soil) might require that five or more lots be purchased, to get a building permit for using a septic tank. Or other homes, built with a septic tank, might be required to pay for a sewer line extension.

Social Forces

Social forces can consist of national or local factors, or a variety of lifestyle and age factors. Examples include the type of conflict faced by a residential neighborhood with predominantly older residents, when younger couples move in. The conflict can be over children playing, loud music, residence upkeep, or other issues that result from the differences in the characteristics of younger and older households.

Not all social changes involve such conflicts. One example is the increasing desire to minimize one's impact on the environment. Some seek to use a bicycle for as much of transportation needs as possible. This boosts demand for live and work locations that are closer together, on more level land, with safer bicycle routes. Demand is reduced for long commutes, hills, and crowded arterial commute roads. We already see an impact in where people live and work!

Social conflicts can be among the most destructive to neighborhood stability. They are exceeded only by physical catastrophes, such as fires and floods. At various times in the past, changes in the nationality, race, or religion of neighborhood occupants have panicked owners into hasty flight. Fortunately, as society becomes more comfortable with diversity, such an extreme reaction is expected to be rare in the future.

Social forces can combine with physical issues. As all buildings age, they require ongoing maintenance, or else they deteriorate. They require remodeling, from time to time, or else they become less up-to-date, and more obsolete. But people (and companies) have differing views. Some keep their home, office, or factory in top condition. Others choose not to do that, or lack the money to do so. Sometimes, neighbors encourage people to keep properties maintained. So social factors play a major role in how rapidly a neighborhood deteriorates with age.

Nonresidential neighborhoods can also be influenced by changing social forces or factors. One example is the impact on offices as a result of the work-at-home movement. Some companies have so many telecommuters that having a permanent desk is the exception!

Industrial neighborhoods have been impacted by workers' increased use of cars. Older industrial plants and warehouses sometimes have bought nearby parcels, solely to provide more worker parking. Some industrial areas have grouped together to fund shuttle buses, in order to make it easier for workers to commute without a car.

Economic Forces

The most obvious **economic force** that causes residential neighborhoods to change is the steady transition of a neighborhood to lower-income use as, its structures get older. Although this is not a hard-and-fast rule for all neighborhoods, it pertains to most neighborhoods. A second economic factor is that *locations vary in their economic stability*. Thus, most of the employment income in one neighborhood might be workers from nearby electronics factories.

A swing in the business cycle for electronics may cause more variation in the unemployment rate than in another neighborhood occupied by people with a varied mixture of jobs.

Transportation influences are a third economic factor. Income differences change the transportation choices of households. So, a bus strike will have different economic impacts on different neighborhoods. Closure of a bus company can have a permanent effect on one residential neighborhood's values, but have no effect on another neighborhood that is also served by the bus line. The residents of the latter might have the money to seek alternative transportation, whereas the others did not.

The effect of a transportation change on a neighborhood involves the social class of the occupants, as well as their income levels. For instance, in a downtown high-income apartment, the percentage of occupants owning an automobile may be as low as in a low-income residential neighborhood, leaving both areas dependent on various forms of public transit.

Economic factors influence nonresidential neighborhoods in many ways. We referred, above, to telecommuting as a social change. It involves social change because both workers and bosses need to adapt to the change. But this is also an economic issue, as it can save companies rent money. It can also save employees commute time and expense! In some cases, employees can reduce child care expenses and even clothing expense.

Transportation is a major economic force on nonresidential neighborhoods. Any change in transportation changes the access to the neighborhood, and to the properties in it. The impact on a retail area is the most obvious. But offices, warehousing, and other uses are also impacted by transportation change.

Combinations

Physical, political, economic, or social factors can become involved with each other, as we have noted above. Protection from floods is surely a political issue and social responsibility. Damaging civil riots may involve all four factors, in a most complex and distressing pattern. Nevertheless, it is helpful to categorize these factors, in order to understand the forces at work in a neighborhood. Table 8.1 summarizes these forces for neighborhood change.

Signs of Neighborhood Change

As stated earlier, what happens in a neighborhood is a sensitive barometer of change in a city. The effects of change will be different in

TABLE 8.1   A summary of the forces for neighborhood change

Physical	*Social*
Time	Conflicts
The elements	Age
Weathering	Lifestyles
Tornados	Demography
Floods	Ages
Earthquakes	Household sizes
Fires	*Economic*
Pollution	Job stability and diversity
Political	Aging of buildings
Facilities	Transportation cost and availability
Provided	
Omitted	
Taxes	
Amount	
Kind	
Philosophies	

residential, commercial, or industrial neighborhoods. Nevertheless, the following broad categories suggest what to look for, as signals of a changing neighborhood. See Table 8.1 for more information on neighborhood change.

Condition

Age is an inescapable physical force, creating change in every neighborhood. **Deterioration** or decay is always an issue. Regardless of the category of land use, there is a constant struggle to maintain the condition of the buildings. Stable neighborhoods almost always appear well-maintained. Other neighborhoods show signs of trouble, when the condition of buildings deteriorates and needed repairs accumulate. This is a warning that the deterioration must be halted, or else at some future time, more rapid change must occur.

Turnover

Surprisingly, a stable neighborhood does not necessarily mean stable, unchanging ownership. The reason is that, like buildings, owners and occupants age. If there is no turnover in owners (or occupants), then their average age gets steadily older. This increasing age is like watching a cliff approaching! It has implications for the future use, maintenance, and demand for neighborhood properties. Will there be adequate future demand, when owners' increasing ages force the sale of a larger number of properties? A reasonable level of annual turnover, then, is a sign of a stable neighborhood age balance. Too *much* turnover, however, may represent a response to some unpleasant neighborhood force!

What is a normal **turnover rate**? The level will differ for owners of different property types. Industrial properties usually have the slowest turnover rates. Downtown commercial properties typically are next. Residential districts vary widely, depending on the age, income, and employment characteristics of the occupants. In a few residential districts, turnover can be quite high, because of corporate relocations. Experienced brokers and appraisers tend to be aware of the local turnover rate.

After the collapse of credit markets in 2008, people started to watch the *foreclosure rate* in residential neighborhoods. The rate varied from one neighborhood to another. The variations between states were particularly noticeable. Foreclosures have become a major factor in the turnover rate for many neighborhoods. This is particularly true for areas that had the greatest price increases during the home price bubble of the early 2000s. And foreclosures are expected to remain relatively high into 2011. Figure 8.1 shows the delinquency rates for new mortgages issued each year.

Part of the pressure comes from the drop in home prices. As home prices fall, people find their home ownership equity dropping. Data calculated by First American CoreLogic, shown in Figure 8.2, indicates that in September 2009, only 5 percent of U. S. homeowners with a mortgage had positive equity. Almost 10 percent had a negative equity of 25 percent or more, meaning that the

FIGURE 8.1   Mortgage delinquencies by months since origination.

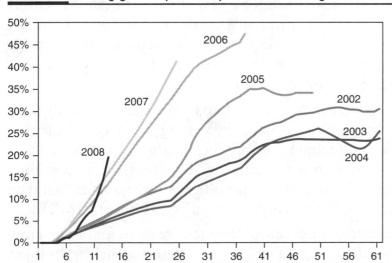

Source: Subprime ARMs 60+ Delinquencies, by John Silvia and Mark Vitner, Housing Chartbook, page 11, October 2009. Reprinted with permission of Wells Fargo Securities.

FIGURE 8.2   Distribution of homeowner equity.

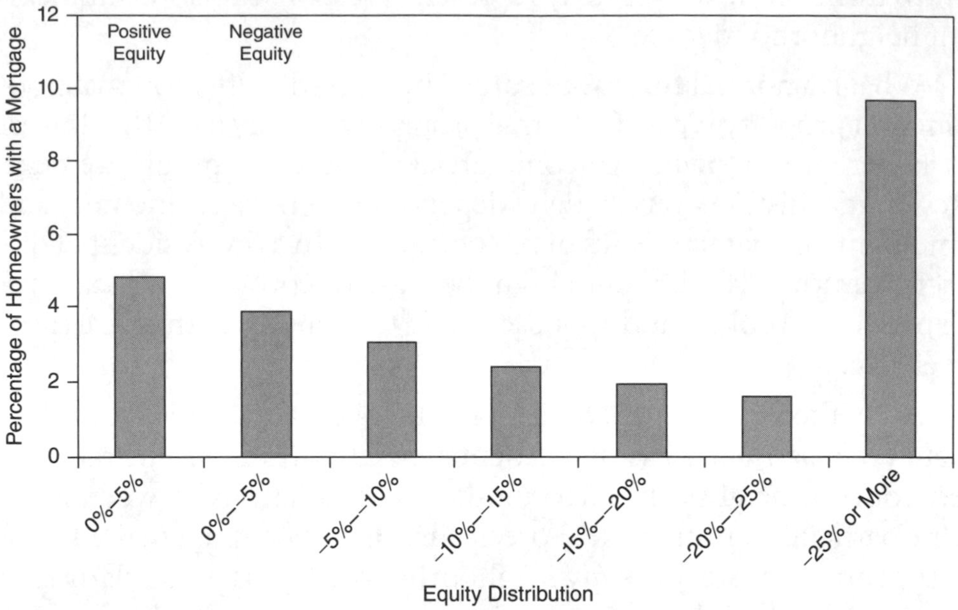

Source: New Negative Equity Report, 2009. Reprinted with permission of First American CoreLOGIC.

mortgage balance was at least 25 percent more than the home value. This imbalance and the resulting foreclosures sharply increase the turnover rate, impacting neighborhoods as well as the affected homeowner.

Use Change

Changes in property use cause neighborhoods to change. When a **change in use** starts to occur, the first changes are usually at the boundaries or edges of the neighborhood. They may involve demolition of a house for construction of a new store, for example. Often, however, the early changes do not involve demolition, but rather conversion to another use. In the above example, instead of demolishing the house, it might be converted to an office or to a light commercial use like a hair salon or a preschool nursery.

Not all changes can occur, even when they are economically feasible. Many use changes are regulated by zoning ordinance. A use permit, a variance, or rezoning would be needed. Some owners in neighborhoods try to resist change by blocking these new uses. They can appeal to local government officials and agencies that have approval power—the "not in my backyard" syndrome (NIMBY).

Figure 8.3 demonstrates one of the many reasons for understanding neighborhood change. The person interested in the "subject property" might be seller, buyer, broker, appraiser, lender, tax assessor, or insurer. The interest of each is with its value. If they only look at

FIGURE 8.3   One reason for studying the neighborhood.

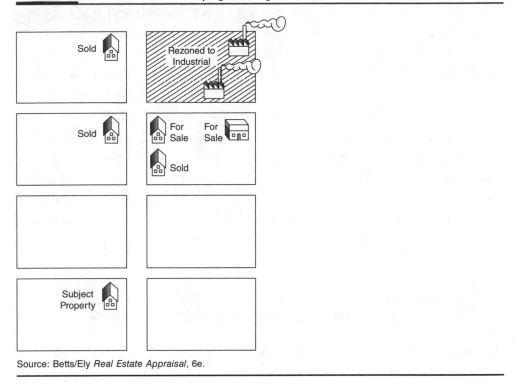

Source: Betts/Ely *Real Estate Appraisal*, 6e.

the cluster of nearby sales, without understanding what is going on in the neighborhood, they are each going to undervalue the home.

Density of Occupancy

Sometimes, when it is not feasible or legal to change the use, a more subtle change will occur—an increase in the **density of use**. A home-owner may rent out rooms; an industrial manager may sublease an unused portion of a plant; a store owner may sublease space for an affiliated venture; or an office tenant may seek someone to share space. Increases in density are another way to get more income from an existing structure. The desire to increase income suggests that the existing income of the structure is inadequate to cover its costs. This may happen because the existing use is no longer as successful as it once was, at this location. Density changes are usually temporary. In time, economic conditions will improve enough to justify a full conversion to a new use, or else a healthy economic return to the prior use. In either case, however, the meaning is clear: The neighborhood is changing its characteristics, for better or worse.

The Meaning of It All

What does all this change mean? How does it affect real estate markets and values? The most important point to realize is this: What matters most is not whether a change is for better or worse, but that a change is occurring. Once it is recognized that a neighborhood is changing, these changes can be studied, to estimate the forces causing the shift. Neighborhood changes should be viewed as signals for the future—predictors of the direction of real estate values. Common indicators of neighborhood change are turnovers, shifts in usage, increases in density, and increases or decreases in upkeep and maintenance.

The key is to start with an understanding of the patterns of city growth, outlined in Chapter 7. This should be combined with an understanding of the forces of neighborhood change. The combination helps investors forecast the investment potential of individual properties within the city and neighborhood. Real estate agents, lenders, and appraisers each need to understand neighborhood change.

REVIEWING YOUR UNDERSTANDING

Neighborhoods as Barometers of Change
1. List four forces that produce neighborhood change. Give two examples of each.
2. List five visible effects of neighborhood change.

8.3 AS NEIGHBORHOODS AGE

Aging is a constant force for change. The changes that age imposes will affect every neighborhood, regardless of its use.

Progressive Decay

The passing years expose property to the weathering effects of the elements and to wear and tear from use. Without care and maintenance, all buildings will deteriorate and decay with age. The comment has been made that houses do not wear out, but neighborhoods do. Do neighborhoods die? Like people, do neighborhoods have a life cycle of childhood, maturity, and decline? If so, what is the **neighborhood cycle**?

It is obvious that some type of a "life" sequence does occur in all neighborhoods. In its youth, a new neighborhood will have only a few new buildings. The remaining area will be vacant lots or older, pre-existing uses. As a neighborhood advances to adulthood, most of the land will have been developed, and the initially high rate of new construction will slow down. However, construction may continue for some years, as the last remaining lots are developed. During the maturing or middle-aged stage of a neighborhood, the condition of buildings generally remains good. Occupancy is typically stable, and the properties generate adequate income.

In time, however, the community can change. These changes begin to have their effect on the neighborhood, and decline sets in. Deteriorated buildings and other signs of decay are noticeable. This sequence can be observed in many neighborhoods.

However, the total age of the neighborhood does not seem to always match the sequence, in predetermined steps. Areas such as Georgetown in Washington, D.C., are several hundred years old and have never been more desirable than they are now. Other areas appear to reach maturity and turn downward in 25 years, as in some of the lower-priced residential subdivisions built in the early 1950s.

The End Result

We want to stress that the neighborhood life cycle does not lead inevitably to the same death. In some cases, a declining neighborhood is redeveloped for a new use. This might involve the commercial expansion of the downtown area, or expansion of a nearby industrial area. The conversion to a new use can be accomplished by private money, or it can be aided by governmental urban-renewal programs.

In other cases, a neighborhood simply continues to decline while **neighborhood obsolescence** grows. The dying process drags on, and produces a neighborhood that is truly a social horror. In some extreme cases, the neighborhood becomes so miserable that many city blocks of property are totally abandoned. But there is a third possibility!

Wow! What Happened?

Most interesting are the older deteriorated neighborhoods that neither change uses, nor slide into blight. At some point, some factor or group of factors emerges, to produce a slow, gradual stabilization of certain neighborhoods. It can even reverse their decline. Remember that the properties are still aging; weather and constant use are still beating them down. Therefore, the process that stabilizes such a neighborhood *must be positive* and forceful, to overcome the continuing pressures of time!

This process of **preservation** or stabilization is not well understood, but is very significant to the real estate community! Here is why. When a city's population is growing, there is ample economic pressure, to convert a deteriorating older neighborhood to new land uses. But when the city's population is not growing, or even is declining, there tends to be no demand for new land uses. (Detroit in the 2000s is an example.) So, the demand to convert an old decaying neighborhood to a new use would be weak, or not even present. Enduring the deteriorating slums, the other extreme, is an even worse answer. The process of neighborhood renewal, then, is *critical*, if society is to have pleasant, stable older neighborhoods, in cities with relatively stable population.

The Rehabilitation Cycle

What is this **rehabilitation cycle**? Evidence suggests that in a number of older American residential neighborhoods, property has repeated the same life cycle a series of times. Neighborhood life cycles reviewed: Each cycle starts with neighborhood properties that are well maintained, modernized, and occupied by stable uses. The cycle then turns, with age, to a gradual decay of the neighborhood. This leads to a period when the neighborhood has deteriorated and prices of homes have fallen. In some instances, home prices will sink quite far, before any recovery begins. The neighborhood has a high turnover rate, and occupants tend to have low incomes. Density is high, and maintenance is low. Illegal uses can be common, and abandoned homes are seen, often in the center or heart of the neighborhood.

The Recovery Period

The cycle then enters a *recovery period*, attracting new occupants. Typically, these are different in income levels and density of occupancy from the present occupants. These people are often called "urban homesteaders." The change usually appears first on one side of the neighborhood, toward the better-maintained or more attractive adjacent areas. These new occupants rehabilitate and remodel the structures that they buy and occupy (see Figure 8.4). They are pioneers, who show the way to additional buyers. A gradual renaissance of the neighborhood occurs. Prices begin to rise at this stage, and enthusiasm grows, often to an evangelical pitch! This is the rehabilitation phase of the neighborhood cycle.

However, over the following decades, the enthusiasm wears off. As the forces of aging continue, the neighborhood reaches a mature state again, and starts to deteriorate once more. This cycle of decay and rebirth can be repeated indefinitely, unless it is interrupted by a major change in land use.

This process of neighborhood revival is not free of any problems. During the recovery period, as the neighborhood improves, it becomes more desirable! Prices and rents increase; poorer residents are "priced out" and move to less-expensive areas. Because the new

FIGURE 8.4   Signs of neighborhood recovery.

Source: Boston Redemption Authority.

inhabitants are usually better off than the old ones, neighborhood revival is sometimes sarcastically labeled **gentrification**. A key point here is that, if the neighborhood can be *maintained* at a good level, this major turnover and its social tensions can be avoided.

The American Experience

Many older American cities have experienced these repeated rehabilitation cycles. In some cases, the cycle has had a very wide swing, from decayed slum to prestige address. Certain examples are well known, such as Georgetown in Washington, D.C., and Back Bay in Boston.

Others are not well known, and could even only be a few blocks in area. Some swings of the neighborhood cycle may be so small as to only be ripples—a small and unnoticed deterioration of some houses for several years or a decade, and then a gradual recovery. Nearly every major article on housing rehabilitation now mentions another neighborhood where this cycle has been observed.

History shows that residential neighborhoods need not deteriorate into slums—that deterioration, once begun, can still be stopped. However, there is still the question of *how* to halt or reverse deterioration! How is neighborhood decay arrested and rehabilitation encouraged? What is this magical process that can fight off the forces of aging? It is helpful to remember that American cities are far younger than those in some other areas of the world. Our understanding of the process of neighborhood aging and the feasible life of structures is less complete than those who have wrestled with the problem for over 2,000 years (as Rome has), or over 4,000 years (as Cairo has).

Not every decaying neighborhood can be preserved. To try would be to try to freeze change, or to deny that change exists! Neighborhood declines that should *not* be reversed might include areas on the fringe of a growing downtown commercial area, where land use conversion is feasible, or a neighborhood so influenced by a new transportation system that it is best to encourage change.

Imagine an older residential area that has had a new rapid transit station placed in the middle of it. The traffic, noise, and congestion from the station could destroy the residential amenities that single-family residential owners seek. The transportation shift also changes the characteristics of the neighborhood's location, by changing its accessibility. This could change the neighborhood's ideal use, from private homes to new apartments and apartment conversions. These uses are oriented to easy transportation access, and are historically more tolerant of congestion and noise.

Learning to Fight Decay

Sometimes, it is the people in a neighborhood who first become active. One neighbor, or a neighborhood group or association, may be the initial force. It is not uncommon for new occupants to be an active force. Other times, it begins with the city, or even a regional group. In a commercial area, it might be the chamber of commerce.

In all cases, it begins with a desire to improve the neighborhood, perhaps focused on a particular problem. However, any one problem often is completely tangled into the full complex of neighborhood problems that we have explored. So, attention soon turns to a broad look at the neighborhood. *Each force for neighborhood decay* really needs to be resisted!

Resisting Wear and Tear

It is clear that the effects of time are usually major issues in neighborhood decay. Weathering and normal wear never stop! If a neighborhood is to resist decay, or recover, deferred maintenance is a big issue! Both public and private actions are available. The city can increase code enforcement, street cleaning, and policing, and can create loan or subsidy programs for property repair. Neighbors can improve their own property, encourage others to do the same, and pitch in to help elderly owners. The subtle process of neighborhood pressure is often a *major force* for neighborhood improvement. Sometimes, there are organized neighborhood cleanup weekends, with flyers, newspaper publicity, and possible help from city workers. It is clear that wear and tear *can be reversed*! But it does take a major effort, continued for some time!

Destabilizing Forces

Age is not the only problem. Other forces also contribute to neighborhood decline. In many communities, for example, the general plan and zoning ordinance show older residential neighborhoods as intended for some other use. This is a policy statement that the neighborhood is to be changed. It is a serious error if, in fact, the community seeks to stabilize, and save the existing use of the neighborhood. General plans are commonly revised every five years or so. But the changes from one version to the next, for most neighborhoods, are quite minor. However, a group of neighbors can switch fairly quickly, from a passive acceptance of whatever the future brings, to a vigorous desire to shape and even control the future of the neighborhood. As a result, the general plan *need not reflect* the neighborhood consensus. Such a mismatch is a major issue: who gets to decide the future of a neighborhood? Investors may take one view; neighborhood activists another—both have real money at stake! It is important to recognize when there are differing opinions. Investors, appraisers, agents, lenders, property managers, and planners all need to be very aware of the range of opinions in the community.

Redevelopment plans have also been a major force for neighborhood change. Redevelopment appears to have been conceived initially to cope with a seriously deteriorated neighborhood, where no private renovation was occurring. A redevelopment agency would be formed, as authorized by state law, usually by the city. After study of all alternative possibilities, the agency would adopt a plan for the future use of the area defined in the plan. The agency would then acquire all of the property and transfer it to private developers. In some cases, the existing owners could keep their property, by agreeing to develop or rehabilitate it as set forth in the plan. The properties would then be rehabilitated or developed according to the plan, and then rented or sold.

There often is community opposition to redevelopment plans. The displacement of existing residents and businesses form the core of one objection. Destruction of historically significant buildings or communities is a second area of protest. A third objection is that some projects seem to be more focused on private developer profit or government tax revenues than elimination of "blighted neighborhoods." There clearly is much more public scrutiny and opposition to new redevelopment projects now than in the past.

Today, most cities are very aware of the neighborhood cycle. Increasingly, cities are focused on how to preserve and strengthen neighborhoods. Master plans are only one issue, and often only a minor one. Cities often try to increase the ties within a neighborhood. This might mean establishing an advisory council, or a specific area plan as a subset of the general plan. Many cities now have a formal neighborhood preservation element of the general plan, and staff committed to implement it.

Another tool that is frequently used to help maintain an area is **historical preservation**. As neighborhoods age, buildings develop more history—events with which they are associated. Sometimes, it is the architect or builder, or an owner. Other times, it may be the design of the building, or even its extreme age, relative to other buildings. Either the city or a historical preservation group may step in, and identify a building as deserving historical recognition. There are various ways of preserving historically significant buildings, explored further in Chapter 13.

In addition, many people have commented that property taxes often work against neighborhood stabilization. They point out that, in most states, a professional tax assessor is required to reevaluate a remodeled property, because of its increased value. However, this leads to a higher tax, which penalizes the person who remodels and continues to occupy the building. Assessors have also usually placed low values on slum properties, because the owner can easily demonstrate limited property income and major deterioration. Deteriorated property thus usually pays much lower property tax than rehabilitated buildings, in the same neighborhood. Some states have explored property tax alternatives, to minimize this type of penalty.

In many communities, the process of change has included population shifts. In some cases, extreme antagonism occurred between the group departing the neighborhood and the group entering. Such hostile transitions often hasten neighborhood deterioration during times of change. Both neighbors and cities can take steps to ease the hostility, making for reduced panic. This usually leads to a slower transition, with less impact on values and on owner upkeep.

With some effort, the community also could try to minimize the destructive effects of market pressures on the existing uses. If the land use in a neighborhood is going to gradually change, for example, from residential to commercial, the changes should be encouraged first at the very edges of the neighborhood, where the impact will be less noticeable. The heart of the neighborhood could be *fully protected* from the change for some time. In this manner, the new use can be gradually phased in, without years of growing blight and neighborhood problems.

A Summary of Preservation

The foregoing discussion highlights how the forces of change put pressure on a neighborhood, and what stabilizing actions are available. Fighting neighborhood decay involves locating the negative forces in time to correct the problem, or to fight the negative influences. Just who should fight decay—government or private enterprise—is debatable (see the Case & Point section). However, those who take action should understand neighborhood forces and effects, if they are to obtain the desired results. A thorough knowledge of urban land economics is the key to understanding the process of neighborhood stabilization.

There is a tremendous interest in these topics today. One can do an Internet search on topics such as "neighborhood preservation" or "neighborhood life cycle" and find huge numbers of links. The numbers of entries that are for individual city efforts are one of the surprises! The interconnections with affordable housing are also frequent. An example of a helpful Web site is neighborhoodpreservationcenter.org. Because of the massive foreclosure-related problems that some neighborhoods now face, it is more important than ever to improve every city's neighborhood preservation efforts.

REVIEWING YOUR UNDERSTANDING

As Neighborhoods Age
1. Why is age such an important factor in neighborhood change?
2. What are the phases of the neighborhood life cycle? What steps are involved in the rehabilitation phase?
3. Why is rehabilitation significant to the future of American cities?
4. Give examples in your community of deteriorating neighborhoods (not just residential uses) that have recovered, or of neighborhoods deteriorating because of negative factors that can be changed.

CHAPTER SUMMARY

This chapter has discussed the clusters of similar land uses called *neighborhoods*. As noted in Chapter 7, land uses tend to form clusters of similar uses, drawn together by their mutual need for the characteristics of a particular location or place in the pattern of the city.

Because real estate is not movable, its value is influenced by the location of the property, as well as the characteristics of the improvements. *Location* is the combination of all the influences on land use that are characteristic of a particular place in a community. A neighborhood is simply an area of relatively similar uses and similar locational influences.

Neighborhood boundaries are sometimes set by physical objects (freeways), or political borders (city limits). In other cases, one group of uses will blend into another, with no definable boundary. Neighborhood size varies with the use and location.

The study of neighborhoods is important, because changes that eventually affect individual values are first visible at the neighborhood level. Investors and homeowners need to interpret neighborhood changes early enough to protect their investments. And agents, appraisers, and lenders need to understand the influences on value.

Examples of forces that change neighborhoods include physical elements such as age and weather, political factors like school quality and taxation, social factors including group conflicts and group attitudes, and numerous economic influences. Often, the forces behind changes are complex or obscure. Thus, the *early effects* of these forces usually are the first indication of change.

The physical condition of properties is a sensitive indication of change, because both age and weather cause deterioration. The rate of turnover of occupants and owners is also a measure of stability. Other barometers of neighborhood trends are changes in uses and in the density of occupancy.

Aging of property is an especially important force, because of its constant negative pressure. Neighborhoods and properties start out new, become mature, and frequently decay in a predictable cycle. The length of time of the cycle varies and so does the end result. Some decayed neighborhoods are redeveloped to a new use, either by private or governmental effort. Others become stagnant slums. Some areas, however, neither change their major use, nor slide into blight. Rather, they extend the neighborhood cycle into a new phase: rehabilitation, which repairs and restores the old structures and brings the neighborhood back to its mature, stable stage again. Some American cities have older neighborhoods that have gone through a number of such rehabilitation and decay cycles.

Not every decaying neighborhood can be preserved. However, interest in neighborhood preservation is increasing. The process involves locating those forces that hurt the neighborhood and correcting them. Thus, aging is met by renovation efforts. Economic pressures for land changes can, rightly or wrongly, be blocked by zoning or redirected to limit the impact of change.

REVIEWING YOUR UNDERSTANDING

1. A cluster of properties of relatively similar land use and value is a:
   A. neighborhood
   B. location
   C. city
   D. block

2. The value of a property at a particular location is created by which force?
   A. political
   B. economic
   C. physical
   D. all of the above

3. A political factor that causes a neighborhood to change is a(n):
   A. earthquake
   B. change in lifestyles
   C. rezoning
   D. new transportation route

4. An economic factor that causes a neighborhood to change is a(n):
   A. earthquake
   B. change in lifestyles
   C. rezoning
   D. new transportation route

5. Which of the following can establish neighborhood boundaries?
   A. rivers
   B. zoning
   C. property use
   D. all of the above

6. An ideal stable residential neighborhood would have:
   A. no turnovers
   B. high turnovers
   C. reasonable turnovers
   D. high percentage of commercial properties

7. All neighborhoods will:
   A. decline
   B. age
   C. stabilize
   D. appreciate

8. High turnover, falling prices, and deferred maintenance are signs of which phase in the life cycle of a neighborhood?
   A. beginning
   B. stabilization
   C. deterioration
   D. rehabilitation

9. When an attempt is made to save a residential neighborhood from decay, which of the following requires the most money in construction costs?
   A. preservation
   B. prevention
   C. rehabilitation
   D. reconciliation

10. A study of changes in city growth patterns, coupled with shifts in neighborhood uses, helps to predict:
    A. changes in values of properties located in the neighborhood
    B. future appreciation rates
    C. good investment opportunities
    D. all of the above

11. The reason people say that "location, location, and location" are the three factors that determine property value is:
    A. people cannot find property without knowing its location
    B. real estate has a fixed location
    C. demand for real estate cannot move from place to place
    D. buyers typically must choose the particular location, regardless of other property characteristics

12. Proximity to employment is irrelevant in studying neighborhoods.
    A. true
    B. false

13. Many residential neighborhoods have boundaries that are defined.
    A. very clearly
    B. vaguely
    C. by deed restrictions
    D. by topography

14. Residential neighborhoods are typically considered to contain about 1,000 households:
    A. true
    B. false

15. Compared to the boundaries of residential neighborhoods, commercial neighborhood boundaries are:
    A. typically more precise
    B. typically much less precise
    C. more likely to be set by physical features
    D. much more influenced by social issues

16. The exact same home, built at three different locations in the same subdivision, will always have the same value.
    A. true
    B. false

17. A physical force that causes real estate values in a neighborhood to change is:
    A. population trends
    B. weather and the elements
    C. lifestyle changes
    D. business cycles

18. The greatest influence for neighborhood change usually comes primarily from:
    A. national trends
    B. regional factors
    C. local factors
    D. physical changes

19. Preservation refers to:
    A. maintaining a neighborhood
    B. rebuilding a neighborhood
    C. demolishing a neighborhood
    D. investing in a neighborhood

20. Neighborhood changes appear first at the:
    A. end of the neighborhood life cycle
    B. center of the neighborhood
    C. edge of the neighborhood
    D. recovery stage

21. The first phase of a neighborhood life cycle is:
    A. stability
    B. development
    C. decline
    D. rebirth

22. Assuming no redevelopment, the last phase of a neighborhood life cycle is:
    A. stability
    B. decline and/or slum
    C. steady maturity
    D. increasing values

23. Neighborhood change is usually:
    A. welcomed by all residents
    B. occurring in some manner at all times
    C. accomplished swiftly
    D. not reflected in property values

24. The value of a particular parcel of real estate is *most* influenced by:
    A. national trends
    B. state trends
    C. city trends
    D. neighborhood trends

25. The main reason real estate investors should take the time to study neighborhood trends is the impact these trends have on future cash flows and property values.
    A. true
    B. false

CASE & POINT

Neighborhood Preservation: Two Viewpoints

Viewpoint 1—Government Aid Approach

When a community decides that a neighborhood should be preserved, the entire community should put its resources to work. One could just wait to see if the neighborhood recovers by itself, but many do not want to just "wait and see." Instead, an active effort is required.

Aging and obsolescence can be countered by maintenance and remodeling. Property owners who are willing to do this should be encouraged, and provided with the necessary funds by loans or outright grants and other public assistance. Owners or tenants who refuse to maintain their properties must be persuaded to do so, by social pressure or legal force.

In addition, government resources must be focused to help stabilize the neighborhood. Examples include more frequent street sweeping, increased police patrol, more street lighting, diversion of through traffic, and added speed bumps or stop signs. Code enforcement may be increased, to reduce illegal changes in use or increases in density, as well as encourage renovation and maintenance. Government's use of tax dollars can result in a good return for the taxpayers.

Viewpoint 2—Free Market Approach

Keep government out of the neighborhood preservation business! The free market of supply and demand will be a better (more honest and more neutral) determinant of the highest and best use of land than will a government agency. Given a reasonable amount of time, the profit motive will stimulate maintenance of an existing use, or a transition to a more economically feasible use. Government's track record of mandated neighborhood preservation is a tale of waste, mismanagement, corruption, blown-up (razed) housing projects, and silly economics.

Indeed, because local government officials are more responsive to the opinions of local voters, they do not do what makes economic sense. Instead, they tend to be biased in favor of the existing land users, as opposed to a change to a higher and better use. This means government tends to resist change. But when a population is growing, or demographics are changing, or major transportation shifts are occurring, one cannot resist all change. Therefore, the government should leave neighborhoods alone, and let the forces of supply and demand do the allocation of land between competing uses.

Chapter

9

Affordability index
Condo conversions
Credit availability
Demand composition
Demography
Demolition

Discretionary income
Disposable income
Doubling up
Economic life
Filtering

Housing composition
Inclusionary zoning
New construction
Rent controls
Turnover rate

PREVIEW

Chapter 9 explores factors that influence residential property values. Section 9.1 looks at the demand for housing and the causes for changes in demand. Section 9.2 focuses on the supply of housing, including both new construction and existing structures. Section 9.3 reviews the effects of governmental actions on the market for residential property. The Case & Point at the end of the chapter discusses the political controversy over gated housing developments. When you have completed this chapter, you will be able to:

1. List the major forces influencing supply and demand for residential real estate.

2. Discuss how to obtain forecasts of national and local housing market trends.

3. List the major effects of governmental activity in the housing market.

Housing Markets

This information will help you to anticipate changes in residential markets in your area.

Housing Markets

As explored earlier, communities contain many different land uses, but the most common is residential housing. Housing land use includes homes, apartments, hotels, motels, and boarding homes. This chapter concentrates on homes and apartments. In previous chapters, you learned that the allocation of land in a mixed capitalistic economy occurs mostly in the marketplace. There, buyers and sellers interact, and eventually a price is determined and a real estate sale takes place. But governments also have a powerful influence on the final outcome of a real estate sale and on the future use of the property. In this chapter, attention is focused on two main topics: (1) How do the laws of supply and demand influence the residential housing market? And (2) What impact does government intervention have on the housing market?

9.1 THE DEMAND FOR HOUSING

The demand for housing should be studied from two points of view. The first view looks at total demand, or the numbers of housing units needed in a given market. The second (and perhaps more important) view looks at the composition of housing that is in demand. **Housing composition** means the mix of unit size, age, location, and condition, and whether the units are intended for owner occupancy or for rent. Thus, housing analysis involves both *numbers and preferences*!

Another way of looking at the demand for housing is to tie it to time. Are we interested in studying demand in the short run—where is it this month, for example—or are we considering total demand over a longer time, perhaps the next five years? Both views are quite important, but usually to different parties. For the broker, appraiser or home owner, facing a question about a particular property at a point in time, the major concern is with the market at that instant!

But for city planners, traffic engineers, investors, loan underwriters, and others reviewing the big picture, the longer time period is the concern. Of course, the appraiser might be working on an employee relocation assignment, perhaps one where the client wants an estimate of market value a year from now! There are just as many circumstances where we need to understand the long-term as for the short-term view!

The demand for housing is influenced by three major factors: (1) population and demographics, (2) effective income and related credit issues, and (3) tastes and lifestyles. *Each* can have short-term and long-term effects on the demand for housing.

Population

The most important influence on housing demand is the size of the population. Put simply, housing is for people, and their presence or absence affects housing demand. Thus, major growth in community population must create demand for more housing. And a decline in population, as in central Detroit, causes a decline in demand for housing. The structures are still there, so some might be abandoned and sit vacant. The economic definition of a "ghost town" is supply with no demand!

The causes of population change are many. Most start with changes in the number of jobs at that location. The decline in housing demand in Detroit has its roots in the decline in basic employment in the auto industry. Review Chapter 6, especially Section 6.2, for a refresher on community growth and decline!

Demography

The sheer numbers of people are not the only influence on the demand for housing. A second population issue is **demography**, which is the breakdown of the population according to age, sex, occupation, income level, and other variables. Demography is important, because people of different demographic characteristics have different housing needs. For example, young children live with their parents. By the time they are 18 or so, some have moved into their own apartments. But culture plays a role—some stay at home until they marry. By age 30, the great majority have moved into a housing unit of their own. And, as they age, their housing needs continue to change!

Therefore, two neighborhoods with the same total populations, but with different demography, will have different housing needs. One neighborhood might contain mostly older, retired people, living in apartments. Some might be couples and some single people. Only a few would have any children living at home. Another neighborhood might be made up of single-family homes, occupied by middle-aged, middle-income families. This second neighborhood would have far more children, and the average family size would be larger. Although the population is the same in both neighborhoods, the number of housing units would be less in the second, as a result of the larger average family size. The neighborhoods would also differ, in terms of the need for more or fewer schools, shops, and public transportation.

The Divorce Rate

The rate of divorce in the United States is another aspect of demography, and influences housing demand. With no increase in population, an increase in the divorce rate will create need for additional housing units. If the divorced person remarries, the additional demand is temporary; if the person decides to remain unmarried, the demand increase is permanent. Uncoupling by unmarried people living together can have the same result as a divorce.

In high divorce rate states, such as California, the divorce rate is a major factor contributing to the **turnover rate**, the percentage of housing units which change occupants each year. However, the overall impact on total housing demand is relatively small.

The Importance of Population Trends

Of all the factors that influence long-term housing demand, population is the most important. Luckily, population information is readily available. Demographic change is especially easy to follow, because of the time delay before babies become adults. Researchers can forecast the demography of the next ten years, by adding ten years to the present age composition of a population and then adjusting for births, deaths, and in-and-out migration, both domestic and foreign. Migration varies greatly by region, so these forecasts are more reliable in slowly changing areas than in rapidly changing ones.

Each area has its own demographic breakdown, and future changes in each will be different. In areas with lots of children, they will grow up and want apartments. In other areas, the middle-aged couples will grow older, find big homes burdensome, and put their houses up for sale. In another area, the young apartment dwellers may be marrying, having children, and seeking larger dwelling units.

For the nation as a whole, the 1980s had a strong housing demand, as the baby boomers of the 1950s became the homebuyers of the 1980s. However, many forecasted that the 1990s would be different, as the decline in the birth rate during the 1960s and 1970s was reflected in the declining number of people reaching homeowner age. The forecasted drop in the number of new household formations in the 1990s led some economists to calculate that, in some regions, the housing market would become a buyer's market, in sharp contrast to the seller's market of the 1980s. In some cases, this did occur. But it must be remembered that local real estate trends can differ from national trends. In certain areas, such as California, Florida, and Texas, massive foreign immigration generated a sharp increase in housing needs. By the mid-2000s, housing demand was strong in most of the United States (and world), due to an expanding population, and fueled by low interest rates and liberal financing.

Sources of Information about Population and Demography Trends

Population and demographic breakdowns and projections are frequently available from county or state planning offices. Their projection periods range from 10 to 50 years. The longer-range forecasts, however, are less reliable. Good information on population characteristics is compiled every ten years, when the national housing and population censuses are taken. The government tries to estimate and update the information each year. When attempting to gather this information, be sure to check with the U.S. Department of Housing and Urban Development, state planning departments, local universities, utility companies, regional, county or city planning departments, or private research firms. Much research may have already been done.

Income and Financing

The second of the three major items influencing housing demand is income. People who lack money cannot afford adequate shelter, however great their housing needs. When people have a housing need, and if their income is sufficient to pay the costs they create an *effective demand* for housing. Because the housing market today is totally based on loans, the availability and cost of loans are major issues in demand.

For some people, too many bills to pay or mouths to feed restrict the money available for housing. Thus, when analyzing income as a factor in housing demand, one focuses on that portion of people's total income that is available for housing use. There are many different measures of income. Generally, we start with total income, which includes wages, received interest, dividends, capital gains, cash awards, child support, and alimony. Gains that are only on paper, and promised payments, are usually omitted.

Most commonly, the next level is **disposable income**, which *usually* is defined as gross income, less all income taxes. Sometimes, this is considered the same as one's net paycheck. Figure 9.1 is from the U.S. Bureau of Economic analysis (www.bea.gov). It shows U.S. real disposable personal income per capita, by month, for 2006 through November 2009. The term "real" means that the dollars have been adjusted to eliminate the change due to inflation or deflation. The legend at the top left tells us that these are adjusted to be 2000 dollars, not current. And "per capita" tells us that this is the average income *per person*, which adjusts for any change in population over the time period in question.

Generally, the next income level is referred to as **discretionary income**. This is usually defined as gross income, less income taxes, and less necessary expenses. Clearly, "necessary expenses" is hard to define, so there is some confusion about it. What is generally understood to be included are: rent or mortgage payments, utilities, food,

FIGURE 9.1   Real disposable personal income per capita.

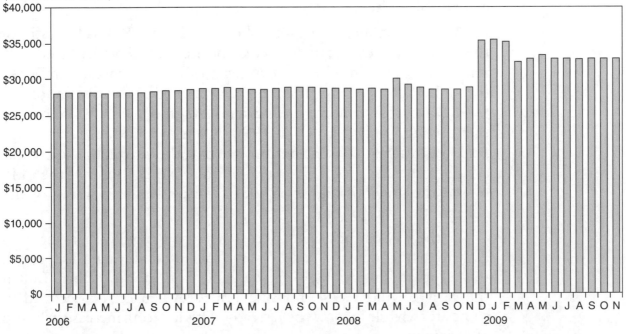

Source: U.S. Bureau of Economic Analysis.

work transportation, and other necessary expenses. These might include minimum credit card payments, child support, and alimony.

Income levels, like population, affect not only total housing demand, but also the composition of that demand. **Demand composition** means the mix of types of housing that is in demand. People with higher incomes often leave rental units, and buy homes or condominiums. People with lower incomes sometimes find they must share housing accommodations with their parents or other people, which is called **doubling up**.

Income Changes

A rise in income can cause a change in the *type of unit*, or in the *amenities* demanded. Examples include the addition of swimming pools, family rooms, extra bathrooms, and the like. A decline in income, however, leads to more modest housing and perhaps to doubling up. When income increases, they frequently move out and seek a dwelling of their own, a process called "undoubling."

Income changes must also be compared to the rate of inflation. Usually, the Consumer Price Index (CPI) is used. When personal income is increasing, but the CPI is increasing more, then *real income* is decreasing! Also, the CPI measures price changes in *all items*. Homes can change in price at a different rate, or even direction, than the CPI. This was very noticeable in 2003–2007. When this happens, people's ability to buy a home, on average, declines. One measure of this, shown in Figure 9.2, is the first-time home buyer **affordability index**.

A slightly different measure, shown in Figure 9.3, is the ratio of the median home price to the median household income. ("Median," remember, is the middle number in a list from the lowest number to the highest.) Since 1989, this ratio has averaged 6.1, with a low of 4 in 1996 (favorable to home buying) and a high of 10 in 2006. Notice that the ratio only got to 6 in 1990, when the previous home price peak was reached. This helps us to see that the year 2006 clearly was a highly unusual speculative price bubble! Note, too, that the ratio passed the previous high by 2003, a clear advance warning of the collapse that was to come.

In the 1980s, housing prices rose more rapidly than income. Although the demand for housing increased during this period, this affordability problem kept demand from rising further. But in the early to mid-1990s, housing prices leveled off or declined in some areas, while incomes held steady. This led to an increase in house affordability.

FIGURE 9.2 First time buyer housing affordability index.

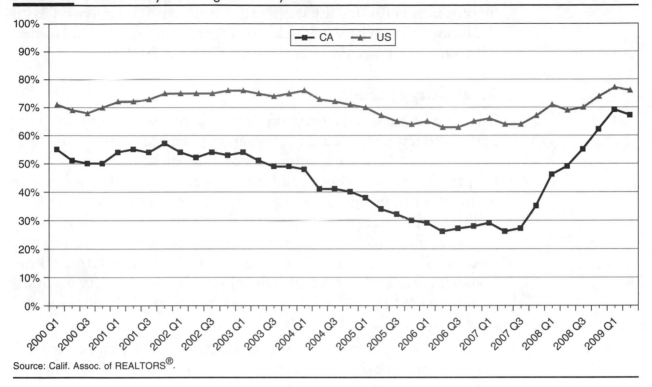

Source: Calif. Assoc. of REALTORS®.

FIGURE 9.3 Median price to median household income ratio.

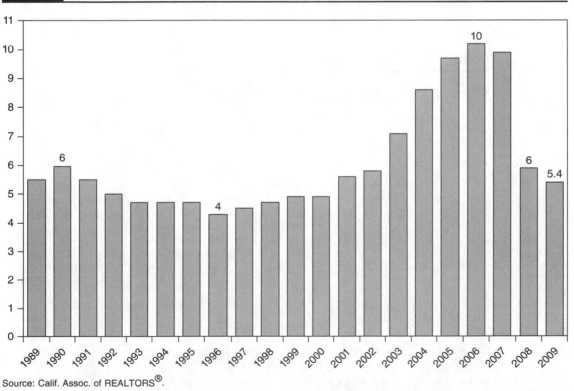

Source: Calif. Assoc. of REALTORS®.

Then in the mid-2000s, housing prices soared much faster than incomes, and affordability was a major problem. This reversed, with the home price collapse of the late 2000 era. This also teaches us that *affordability is cyclical*, as both affordability graphs show!

Availability of Credit

Buying a home is the largest single purchase that most people ever make, and few people have the resources to pay cash for a home. The availability and cost of mortgage credit has an important influence on people's ability to buy, and, therefore, it has an impact on the demand for housing. Lower mortgage interest rates (or easier loan terms) have the effect of increasing the demand for housing at any given level of income. Figure 9.4 shows the homeownership rate since 1987, versus the 30-year fixed-rate mortgage term. Home ownership rises whenever rates drop! **Credit availability** is critical to understanding real estate demand, and especially bubbles and other major shifts in demand!

A significant increase in housing demand in the past century has occurred because of liberal changes in mortgage credit. One hundred years ago, real estate loans were limited to a two- to five-year term, interest-only, and renewed at the lender's discretion. Now, 30- to 40-year fully amortized loans are common. In the 2003–2007 period, special loan features, such as below-market adjustable "teaser" rates, and interest-only loans allowed many people to acquire a home they

FIGURE 9.4   Home ownership rate.

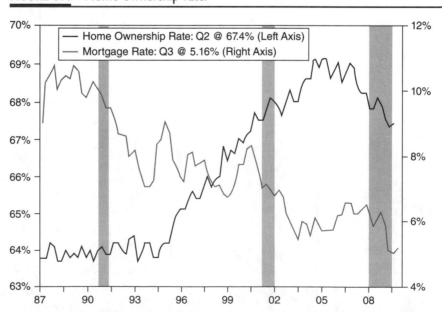

Source: Wells Fargo Securities LLC, Economics Group, Weekly Economic & Financial Commentary, 10/9/2009.

FIGURE 9.5 Total consumer credit outstanding.

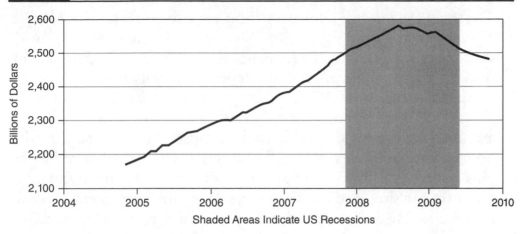

Shaded Areas Indicate US Recessions

Source: Federal Reserve Bank of St. Louis.

otherwise would not have been able to afford. Unfortunately, we now see that some loan features, especially teaser rates, encouraged people to buy homes that they could not hope to continue to pay for.

In Figure 9.4, we can see that mortgage interest rates vary. In fact, over longer periods, they clearly are cyclical, moving up and then down. But rates are not the only aspect of financing that is cyclical. For example, government-insured/guaranteed FHA or VA loans were just under 20 percent of the total in 1994, dropped to under 5 percent in 2006, and went up to 20 percent again in 2008. Another variable is how much debt consumers are willing or able to take on. Figure 9.5 shows the total consumer credit outstanding, from 2005 through 2009. The increase from late 2004 to the peak in late 2008 was a four-year 20 percent increase, followed by a one-year 5 percent drop!

It is clear that any future changes in mortgage credit will affect housing demand. Any U.S. capital shortages in the future will bring hard times to the real estate housing market. Economists closely watch the U.S. savings rate and the rate of foreign investment for signs of shifts. If the savings rate rises and/or foreign investment in the U.S. capital market increases, that will spell good news for the housing market. If the opposite occurs, hard times could hit the housing market. The size of the U.S. budget deficit also has an impact on the availability and cost of mortgage money. If the U.S. government must finance a large deficit, it can crowd out the private sector, driving up interest rates. If plentiful affordable housing is a national goal, society will need to establish capital priorities and reorganize financial institutions, so that mortgage credit can remain affordable.

Changes in Taste

The third major factor influencing housing demand is taste or lifestyle. The most basic need for housing is a roof and four walls, to provide shelter from animals and the elements. As people seek a better standard of living, they respond to their own desires or their friends' expectations of what life ought to be. Thus, where people choose to live is not only a function of income and credit, but also of personal preference. For example, some people choose to place most of their wealth in their home, whereas others might choose a modest principal residence, plus a getaway vacation home. Still others decide to spend the minimum on housing, and use the extra money for investments, leisure, or hobbies. Their confidence level also plays a big part in this decision!

Choosing Housing Location

As tastes and lifestyles change, housing demand changes. One variable is *where* people choose to live. We can live in a big city, a suburb, or a small town, as just one example. In the distant past, where we lived was dominated by where we could find work. Gradually, that bond was loosened, as roads (and trains) improved, allowing a longer commute to and from work.

Now, more people are also able to work at home, for some or all of their work time. And, because people live longer than they did 50 years ago, there are more retired people, whose residence is no longer tied to their job. In turn, these people buy food, gas, and services where they live, so that jobs are created in new locations.

Even more important is the growing flexibility for locating many basic industries. The Internet allows many businesses to access specialized services, such as patent attorneys, architects, insurance services, and others, without the need to locate in a big city. Improvements in trucking, rail, and air freight services allow many businesses to serve distant customers far better than before. All of these issues are making job location, and therefore housing location, far more flexible than before.

Another aspect of location choice is our choice of neighborhood. Neighborhoods vary in how desirable people perceive them to be. Sometimes, this is because of a remote location, perhaps poorly served by public transport or freeways. More often, this is because of perceptions of crime rates, or school quality.

But perceptions can change! New freeways or bus routes can open. Crime rates can improve, as can schools. And sometimes, prices in better neighborhoods increase, to where people are more willing to accept less desirable neighborhoods. Thus, neighborhoods can be fashionable, fall out of fashion, and come back in fashion.

Choosing Housing Type

Think back to what you know about the housing units you know that are over 100 years old. There were detached single family homes, in a range of sizes. There were attached row houses, some just two or three units, and others entire blocks. There were "flats", usually a duplex or triplex, with one unit per floor. And there were larger rental apartment buildings. Only a few condominium or cooperative buildings existed, mostly in the largest cities.

Today, there are some additions to that mix. There are many more condominiums, in configurations from duplex buildings to tall towers. Arguably, "zero-lot-line" designs are new. Buildings with a mix of residential and commercial uses existed in large cities then, but now are much more common. New mixtures are found: hotel/office/condo, for example. And sometimes, new names have emerged for old designs—townhouse for row house, duette for duplex.

But there also is more variation. Large subdivisions of similar homes were common in the 1950s and 1960s. Now, most large developments have a wide mix of housing types and of unit sizes! These reflect buyer demand for more variation, more choice, and more flexibility in how we house ourselves.

The Influence of Confidence

Four walls and a roof are the minimum requirements for housing. Our income usually allows for more, and we usually want more. How much housing we demand is partly determined by how confident we are about our job, income, health, relationships, and so on. Consumer confidence also varies over time. Figure 9.6 displays the cyclical changes in the well-known Consumer Confidence Index, released by the Conference Board (www.conference-board.org). Clearly, demand drops when confidence drops! The figure shows the year-to-year change in confidence, both monthly and in a 12-month moving average.

Can Consumer Taste and Lifestyles Be Forecasted?

No one can say how long a particular fancy will last, or how widespread it will become. The only certainty is change itself. However, real estate analysts should constantly monitor the market for change. Students of marketing suggest that changes in taste appear first in people who are fashion conscious, then trickle down to the general population. Will housing styles be as volatile as clothing fashion? Will Santa Fe and Mediterranean housing motifs be like the miniskirt? Are huge houses on small lots in, and condos out? No one knows for sure, but because of tradition and the long life of homes, changes in housing taste tend to occur slowly. This usually allows builders to adjust their inventory so as not to be stuck with unsold, unappealing

FIGURE 9.6   Consumer confidence index.

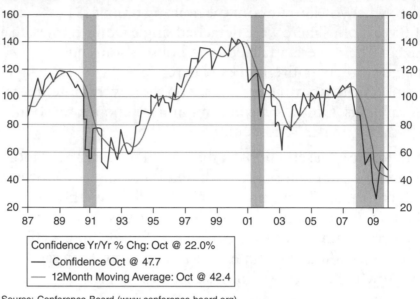

Confidence Yr/Yr % Chg: Oct @ 22.0%
— Confidence Oct @ 47.7
— 12Month Moving Average: Oct @ 42.4

Source: Conference Board (www.conference-board.org).

homes. For existing homes, updating and remodeling are ways to maintain appeal and value.

One additional note: A major reason for the increase in new home prices in the early 2000s was the buyer's desire for a larger home. If today's new homes were only 1,500 square feet, like the homes built in the 1970s, the cost would be considerably less than the 3,500+ square-foot homes of the 2000s. So, the demand for different-sized homes changes over time!

Special Interest Topic
$$$ Affordability Index $$$

The National Association of REALTORS® and the California Association of REALTORS® have constructed a housing affordability index. The index comprises these three basic elements:

1. Determine the median home price for the area. Median means that half of the sale prices were larger and half of the sale prices were smaller.

2. Select the prevailing interest rates on standard home loans. Usually defined as a 20 percent down, 80 percent conventional home loan, most often using fixed rate loans.

3. Determine the household income level for the area.

Calculating the Affordability Index

1. Determine the median price home, say $400,000.
2. Calculate the loan payment for an 80% loan at the current interest rate, at, say, 6%. Then $400,000 × 80% = $320,000 loan @ 6% for 30 years = $1,918.56 monthly payment for principal and interest. Then add in monthly property taxes and insurance, for a PITI monthly payment of, say, $2,500.
3. Calculate the monthly income needed to qualify for a monthly PITI payment of $2,500, using a 30% qualifying ratio (payment should not exceed 30% of monthly income). Then $2,500 divided by .30 = $8,333 × 12 mos. = $100,000 (actual $99,999) annual income needed to qualify for a $320,000 loan, and a $400,000 home.
4. Next, using census data, determine how many households have incomes of $100,000 or more, say 30,000 households. Next, determine the total number of households in the area, be it city, county, state or national; say the area has 100,000 house-holds. Then the affordability index is calculated as follows:

$$\frac{30,000 \text{ qualifying households}}{100,000 \text{ total households}} = 30\% \text{ affordability index}$$

This means that only 30 percent of the households in the area can afford to buy the median priced home. A high percentage is good news for the local housing market, while a low percentage is not. Current national and local affordability index ratings are published in REALTOR® magazines and available on their Web sites (www.realtor.com).

REVIEWING YOUR UNDERSTANDING

The Demand for Housing

1. What are three major forces influencing housing demand?
2. How does demography affect housing demand?
3. How does mortgage credit affect housing demand?
4. What do people's tastes have to do with housing demand?

9.2 THE SUPPLY OF RESIDENTIAL HOUSING

It is important to recognize that housing differs from many other economic commodities, because a very large percentage of the demand is met by the supply of units that are already in existence. In boom years, new construction has added around 2 percent per year to our national housing stock. Most local areas experience a similar percentage increase. The existing stock is thus 98 percent or more of all the housing supply in any particular year. As a result, economists consider the supply of real estate housing to be fixed in the short run. Therefore, a change in supply is viewed as a slow process, occurring over a long period of time. However, new construction provides jobs for many, so it is important to the overall economy. It also varies a lot, making it a sensitive measure of the economy. Figure 9.7 shows housing starts (seasonally adjusted) since 1987. The peak month reached a 2.3 million home annual rate in 2006, but dropped to an annual rate of 0.5 million in late 2008, a drop of almost 80 percent!

The supply of housing must be studied from two viewpoints: (1) the total number of units and (2) the quality or suitability of the units. *Suitability* involves the types of units, their condition, etc.

Evaluation of Supply

The supply of housing at any *future* date will consist of the units that existed at a prior date, minus those units lost as a result of fires, demolition, and conversions to other uses, and then increased by buildings converted to housing and by **new construction**. The process is illustrated in Table 9.1.

FIGURE 9.7   Housing starts.

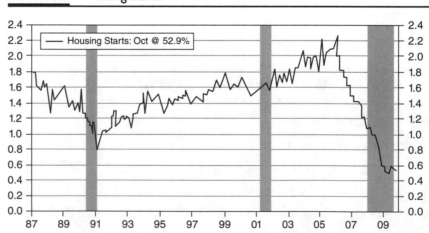

Source: Wells Fargo Securities LLC, Economics Group, Weekly Economic & Financial Commentary, 11/20/2009.

TABLE 9.1   Changes in Housing Stock, Sometown

	21,214	Existing stock, end of previous year
Less	− 137	Demolitions during current year
	21,077	
Less	− 7	Housing units converted to other uses
	21,070	
Plus	+ 4	Other units converted to residences
	21,074	
Plus	+ 38	Added units to existing structures
	21,112	
Plus	+ 393	New construction
	21,505	Existing stock, end of current year

Demolition and Destruction

In a changing community, any land use will eventually become the *wrong use* of the site at some future time. Changes in the community almost guarantee that this will happen. As a better use comes along, land values rise. The contribution of the existing building to the total property value decreases, as the land value increases. The building contribution also decreases in value as the building gets older, and decreases more if the existing use is affected by new buildings with better uses. At a certain point, it becomes economically profitable to tear down the old building, and build a new one to reflect the new highest and best use of the land. At this point the old structure has reached the end of its **economic life**. This economic life can end *long before* the building has reached the end of its physical life, depending on its location and the rate of change of the community. **Demolition** is a reality in every city!

Not all buildings are torn down because they have reached the end of their economic lives. Some are destroyed by fire, earthquakes, and other disasters. Some buildings are demolished in order to build public improvements, such as highways and schools, or for urban renewal. In some American communities, demolition for urban renewal and highway purposes noticeably reduces the existing housing stock.

Thus, in forecasting the total future housing supply, analysts do not assume that the existing stock will be there forever. Some of the units will not be kept up, and reach the end of their physical lives. Other units will be torn down at the end of their economic lives, for construction of nonresidential properties. The probable rate of demolition for various public purposes must also be taken into account. In some communities, the number of homes demolished to make way for new public improvements exceeds the number demolished because of a loss in economic life. Fortunately, public projects are planned relatively far in advance, and their impact on supply can be anticipated.

Conversion and Its Effects on Supply

In addition to demolition, the housing stock is changed by conversions. Conversions can increase the number of housing units, by converting houses or other structures into apartments or flats. On the other hand, some conversions may change a residential unit into an office, medical center, or other nonresidential use, and this reduces the housing supply. One must combine the additions and subtractions to determine what net effect conversions have on the local housing market.

In general, conversion is not a major force in the change of total housing supply. Data on past conversions are obtainable from the same building permit sources as demolition and construction data.

However, another type of conversion is important, even though the total number of units may not change. This is the change of rental apartment units to "for-sale" condominiums, or rental homes to owner-occupied. Sometimes, **rent controls** will block evictions of tenants to allow owner-occupancy. And some cities block **condo conversions**, leading to multiple buyers as tenants-in-common owners, each planning on occupying a specific unit. These *TIC conversions* bypass the need for a condo conversion, but are considered more risky for buyers and sellers than a condo.

The rental-to-owner occupancy change can also go in the opposite direction! Some condo units have been bought by investors, who rent them out. And, due to the big drop in starter home prices in 2008 and 2009, many homes (including a lot that were in foreclosure) have been bought by investors and rented out.

New Construction

New construction varies greatly from year to year (as we have seen in Figure 9.7) and, especially, from area to area. The city of Brentwood, in the San Francisco Bay Area, grew from 150 dwellings in 1970 to 20,000 units in 2010! For many places, new construction is the largest element in the yearly change in housing supply. New construction occurs only when the required resources are available. These are the classic four elements of land, labor, capital, and entrepreneurial skills. Similarly, the costs of obtaining these resources must be in balance with each other and with the housing prices found in the marketplace. Changes in the availability of these resources will change their prices and affect the ability to build for a profit. Past experience demonstrates that shortages in these resources do occur.

For example, land shortages can result from environmental restrictions or governmental attitudes toward the zoning of land. Labor shortages can result from attempts to increase housing construction beyond the limits of the available trained workforce. Capital shortages, or a so-called "credit crunch," consisting of a shrinking money supply and high interest rates, have sometimes restricted new housing construction. Shortages of capital also show up as shortages of raw materials, because the raw materials require plants, mines, wells, and the like to produce them. Entrepreneurial shortages are less common in this country, because the nature of house construction encourages people in the housing industry to learn development skills. Other countries with different social attitudes, however, have had difficulty in obtaining sufficient people with necessary development skills and knowledge.

Forecasts of new construction thus have to consider the availability of related resources. In fact, the major factors influencing recent variations in new construction (see California data in Table 9.2) have been changes in the cost and availability of capital and the current state of the local economy. Table 9.2 shows the peak single family year, 2005, and the dramatic drop since. Compare the number of permits in 2005 with the other years shown, to see how abnormal that time was. Notice, also, that multiple unit permits have varied much less than single family residence permits (at least until 2009)!

Future Supply Trends

Many observers say that increasing restrictions on new construction and lack of key resources will create a housing shortage in the future.

TABLE 9.2 New Housing Units Authorized in California (in thousands)

Year	Total	Multiple	Single
1980	144,987	58,355	86,832
1990	164,394	60,219	104,175
2000	167,682	42,945	105,595
2005	208,972	53,650	155,322
2007	113,034	44,635	68,409
2008	64,962	31,912	33,050
2009	36,209	11,163	25,046

Source: California Building Industry Association.

Increasing shortages have driven up the cost of land, capital, labor, and many of the raw materials that are needed by the construction industry. With rising costs, a developer will build new housing only when home prices are expected to go up as fast as or faster than costs. Some forecast that future housing costs and prices will continue to increase faster than buyer incomes, thereby causing a reduction in the demand for new housing construction. The renovation and remodeling of the existing housing stock may be a more significant factor for the future housing supply than has been true for the last several decades.

Some advocates say that the construction of second units (Granny units) is the best solution for a housing shortage. However, this idea has met with some resistance from local governments and residents.

Is the Housing Suitable?

At any given time, the housing supply consists of the existing dwelling units. You remember from Chapter 5 that two special features of real estate are its long life and fixed location. Thus, the suitability of existing housing becomes most important.

What About Housing Condition?

Because of the long life of housing structures, the condition of existing housing is an important issue. Few houses are built of materials that will last for a long period of time without maintenance. Thus, housing units are vulnerable to deterioration over their lifetimes. The extent to which this has happened is of major interest to the real estate economist. Many older homes are not receiving adequate maintenance and are gradually deteriorating. When this happens to an entire neighborhood, blight gradually sets in. The decaying condition of the neighborhood seems to deter people from further maintenance, so that the blighted area gets worse and bigger. This has led to the complete abandonment of whole blocks of buildings in areas of cities like New York, Detroit, and Cleveland. Such abandoned houses effectively reduce the supply of housing units, because people refuse to move into the area. This condition, which need not occur, is being carefully studied by urban policymakers and is a central issue for the future.

What About Housing Features?

Buyers and renters tend to seek amenities, which are the benefits of ownership or occupancy. These can include physical features such as space, age, condition, and appointments. Some features can be measured by objective scales or techniques. Other amenities, however, are not so objective. They depend on taste, status, and public opinion, discussed earlier in this chapter. These features are often subject to fads, as well as being hard to measure. Forecasting residential markets is thus complicated by the difficulty of forecasting the attitudes of buyers, sellers, renters, and landlords toward amenities. Buyers and sellers in the past have periodically changed their views on the importance of such amenities as the size of units, newness, unconventional architecture, and suburban versus central living. Future changes must be considered in forecasting the housing market.

One example is the issue of energy usage. More broadly, this is the issue of "green building." Is the building designed to use relatively low levels of energy and water? Are the materials selected to minimize impacts on scarce materials or endangered locations? Structures consume a major fraction of total U.S. energy use, and it is very clear that structure energy use can easily be reduced by quite a bit. Will codes require this, or will buyers demand it?

Another example is the preservation of older buildings. Tastes change, so older buildings can fall out of favor. Many cities now inventory older buildings, to identify those with historical significance, perhaps for the architectural style, or connection to past events. There are major legal, economic, and cultural issues with preserving such buildings. It is not at all clear how preservation disputes will be resolved.

A third example of this concept is the issue of the density of occupancy. The federal government has used an average household density of one person per room as a housing goal. Some segments of the housing market are seeking lower density, and others are choosing higher densities, to free income for other purposes. Over the last 20 years, the trend in new home construction has been to reduce average density, or increase the number of rooms relative to the number of occupants.

How will density be in the future? Will crushing home prices force extended families to stay together and share housing costs? Some new subdivisions in the Inland Empire of California were advertising "up to eleven bedrooms." With the recession of the late 2000s, new home sizes are shrinking again!

As buildings age, it becomes more likely that some aspect of the housing unit will not suit people's changing desires for amenity features. Major changes in the features, design, or equipment of houses occur surprisingly slowly. However, the lifetime of an average house is long enough that some elements of design become out of date, old-fashioned, unworkable, inefficient, or irreparable. As this happens, the housing unit becomes increasingly obsolete unless corrected by remodeling. Thus, a study of neighborhoods must consider the amount of obsolete features and the remodeling or renovation rate. Will there be buyers in 30 years for the very large homes in deep suburban locations that were featured in 2004?

What About Housing Location?

Remember that another unique characteristic of real estate is its fixed and location. Because of this, it is possible for changes in the community to make a certain use of the land no longer suitable, that is, *locationally obsolete*. Thus, a building that is nearly new, but at a changing location, could become so obsolete as to be torn down, causing a fair amount of economic waste. This waste can be reduced if the building has the flexibility to be converted to another profitable use.

The problem of fixed location is compounded by the long life of buildings, as compared with the rate of change of the community in which the buildings are located. This has been especially true of rapidly growing communities in the western United States. This type of obsolescence, which shortens the economic life of the building, has a noticeable influence on the rate of demolition in the affected community. Thus, over the years, as a community's population mix or demography changes, the housing supply must meet these demand changes to maintain equilibrium.

Suitable for Whom?

In general, the long life of residential real estate means that the building must have sufficient flexibility to meet the changing needs of a long-term occupant or the differing needs of a series of users. This need for flexibility is a major reason for the slow and cautious rate of change in building design. Only the rich can afford to risk large sums to build a radical design that others may not be willing to buy.

Long life also means that the product can be expected to be occupied by people of differing backgrounds and income. Because older units are generally in poorer condition, more obsolete, and less desirable than new ones, their values are generally less than new ones. Thus, housing units are typically occupied by lower-income users as the units get older. Most housing for lower-income occupants comes from this process, which is called filtering. This is also described as a "trickle-down" process.

Filtering

Filtering is a central pattern of the residential market, given the long life of dwellings and the changing needs and tastes of people. Problems that develop during the filtering process nearly always have to do with the condition or obsolescence of the unit. Housing units are clearly capable of periodic renovation and renewal, if social and economic circumstances so dictate. The American student of real estate should realize that housing units in many other countries are expected to last hundreds of years. In many European cities, it is common to live in a building that is more than 300 years old. These buildings are given repair and periodic remodeling, and provide good housing at costs less expensive than new construction. The existence of slums in the United States is *primarily* a breakdown in the ongoing repair and renovation process that dwelling units *must receive*, as they filter through a series of occupants and owners. This point deserves *much* more attention than we, as a society, have given it in the past!

Available Supply

The above discussion focused on the *total supply*: the numbers, age, condition, and location, and how these change over time. But this is not the only way of looking at supply! Equally important is to consider that fraction of total supply that is available at any one time.

We talked earlier about the *turnover rate*, the percent of all owner-occupied units that sell in a time period. It can also refer to the percent of rented units that change occupants in a time period, or else the percent of all housing units that change occupants. The turnover rate varies with the location, type of dwelling unit, form of ownership, etc. Some apartment buildings that are close to a college find some units turning over every semester. But some owner-occupied homes may have the same occupants for many decades! The turnover rate also varies over time. In deep recessions, as well as in boom times, the turnover rate often increases!

Because of turnovers, there are always some units that are vacant, either for rent or for sale. A vacant unit may stay vacant for a while, if it is being renovated, or if the owners are in a dispute of some sort. Sometimes, too, more units come on the market than there currently are buyers or renters. Brokers, appraisers, and lenders keep a close eye on the inventory of homes and condos for sale. Usually, they compare the number of homes for sale with the current *rate* of sales. If a particular neighborhood is currently seeing 17 house sales close escrow in the most recent month, but there are 78 homes for sale, then it would take 4.6 months to sell the remaining inventory (78 divided by 17).

This analysis is widely reported, because the number of properties listed on the local MLS is readily available, as is the number of recently closed sales. However, data on the total number of vacant rental units is less available, and most areas have no data at all on the number of units that were rented up in any recent time period.

FIGURE 9.8 Delinquency, foreclosure and REO rates, U.S.

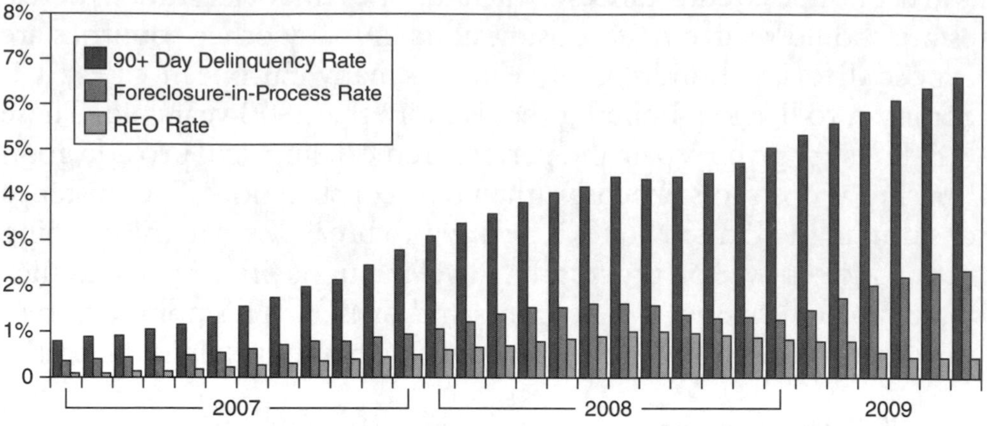

Source: First American CoreLogic.

Another problem is that the sales rate usually changes with the seasons, loan interest rates, and buyer confidence. So, after three months, the monthly sales rate might be cut in half, or double! Also, over the three months, no new sellers might list their homes, causing the number of listings to decline and buyers to start worrying. Or, there might be a huge number of new listings over the three months!

These issues have complicated housing market analysis, especially since the 2007 credit market crisis. Figure 9.8 shows monthly data from First American Core Logic for 2007–2009 (first six months) on three measures of how foreclosures might impact unsold home inventories. ("REO" refers to homes that have been foreclosed and are now bank "Real Estate Owned.") Particularly disturbing is the massive increase in the percent of loans that are over 90 days delinquent, contrasted to the low level of REO properties. There have been a series of foreclosure moratoriums, which caused lenders to delay the final foreclosure steps. And the government has encouraged lenders to modify loan terms, to reduce the rate of foreclosures.

The problem, of course, is shown by Figure 9.9, showing the Standard & Poors/Case-Shiller Home Price Index for 20 major cities and the San Francisco metro area. The huge increase in prices, from 2000 to the peak in mid-2006, means that many families have big loans. They either purchased at these high prices, or else they refinanced their loan and took cash out. But, the big drop in prices since then means that, by the end of 2009, many home owners owed more than their house was worth.

No one can reliably predict what homeowners who are "under water" (owing more than their home's value) will do. But it is clear that this is a major issue for future housing markets, and for appraisers, lenders, and brokers who try to analyze them! Figure 9.10 shows how this "shadow inventory" of possible homes for sale has increased since 2006.

FIGURE 9.9   Standard & Poors/Case-Shiller Home Price Index.

Standard & Poor's/Case-Shiller Home Price Index

The index tracks changes in home prices relative to prices in January 2000.*

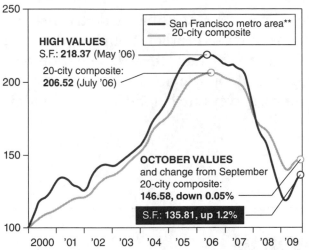

*The base value is 100. An index value of 150, for example, would mean that home prices increased 50 percent since January 2000.

**Defined as Alameda, contra Costa, Marin, San Francisco and San Mateo counties.

Source: San Francisco Chronicle, 12/30/09.

Around the nation
Index values for metro areas in the 20-city composite (percentage change from September to October)

Atlanta	−1.0%	▼
Boston	−0.6	▼
Charlotte	−0.7	▼
Chicago	−1.0	▼
Cleveland	−0.7	▼
Dallas	−0.6	▼
Denver	−0.4	▼
Detroit	−0.2	▲
Las Vegas	−0.1	▼
Los Angeles	−0.3	▲
Miami	−0.4	▼
Minneapolis	−0.5	▼
New York	0.0	▬
Phoenix	1.3	▲
Portland	0.1	▲
San Diego	0.4	▲
San Francisco	**1.2**	△
Seattle	0.2	▲
Tampa	−1.6	▼
Washington	−0.4	▼

FIGURE 9.10   Shadow housing inventory.

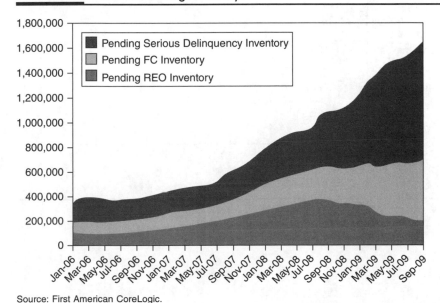

Source: First American CoreLogic.

The Future of Construction

Does all of this gloom mean that new construction is finished for years? Not at all! Remember that real estate markets are *always* strongly influenced by local factors. Average data are only averages! The past price increases shown in Figure 9.9 are averages of 20 locations. The increases varied around the country, by neighborhood and by price range. Locations that had a smaller increase generally have had smaller declines and fewer foreclosures.

Location is not the only issue. The housing market contains a range of different products, as discussed earlier. Some products are now stronger than others. Figure 9.11 rates the 2010 development prospects for different categories of for-sale housing, based on a survey of developers. Similar annual surveys are helpful in understanding future market trends!

FIGURE 9.11   Development prospects for for-sale housing in 2010.

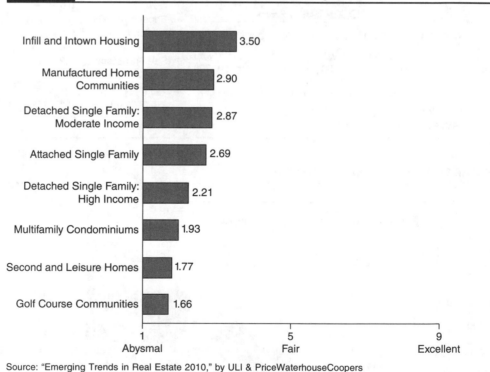

Source: "Emerging Trends in Real Estate 2010," by ULI & PriceWaterhouseCoopers

---

REVIEWING YOUR UNDERSTANDING

The Supply of Residential Housing

1. What are the two central issues or viewpoints of housing supply?
2. How important is demolition to housing supply?
3. What is the impact of new construction on housing supply and what causes the rate of new construction to vary?

9.3 THE GOVERNMENT AND HOUSING

Why is the government so deeply involved with housing? The reason frequently given for governmental intervention in the housing markets is to change some unsatisfactory aspects of the usual working of supply and demand. Examples cited to justify government involvement include the need for a disclosure requirement because of the buyer's inadequate knowledge, the need to prevent discrimination by sellers or brokers, and the need to provide housing for low-income people. Government intervention in the housing markets comes in the form of either *housing regulations* (usually restricting supply), *financial support* (increasing demand), or actions to *increase supply*. Some actions focus on owner-occupancy housing, while others address rental housing.

Regulating Housing Markets

One set of governmental actions *restricts or regulates the housing markets*. These policies are intended to halt some action that the market would otherwise allow. Zoning and planning ordinances are common examples, explored further in Chapter 13.

Subdivision laws are another type of government restriction. Local laws typically define street widths, utility standards, and the like. Most states have laws setting forth minimum requirements for the subdivision process itself. State and federal subdivision laws tend to focus on developer responsibilities for disclosures to buyers and for completion of any promised features. See Chapter 13, "Land-Use Controls," for more details.

Building and housing standards are also regulated by government codes. These codes specify *minimum* housing construction standards. There are codes covering electrical work, plumbing, grading, foundations, structural design, and nearly all details of construction and renovation.

The future will probably see even more government regulations. Most other industrialized countries have more restrictions on the housing market than the United States, and offer some specific clues to future changes that we are likely to see.

Encouraging Housing Production

The second group of governmental policies attempts to support or encourage housing production. Over the years, the numbers and types of programs have increased. Some programs stimulate demand, while others work to increase supply, or make it less expensive. And some programs essentially benefit *all* housing markets, while others are targeted at specific types of housing or groups of buyers. Originally, most programs were developed by the federal government. Now, there are also many state and local programs. It is important for brokers, appraisers, and lenders to try to be aware of all these programs, because they influence housing sale prices and rent levels.

Some government programs work to reduce the cost of supplying new housing units. These policies include programs to reduce shortages of land, labor, or capital. Examples are urban renewal programs to assemble large parcels of land, and organized apprenticeship programs for skilled labor training. On occasion, government programs have provided subsidies to reduce the cost of housing production. An example is the provision of federal or state income tax credits to developers of low-income housing, generating equity funds for the project. And some local governments have leased land at low rates to non-profit organizations, to be used for elder housing.

Programs to Stimulate Demand

There have been a large number of federal, state, and local programs. This can only be an overview of them all. The number grew rapidly during the boom years of the early 2000s. With the recession of 2007–2009, local programs were often scaled back. State and federal programs generally shifted to focus on foreclosure prevention. Generally, however, these programs either try to reduce downpayment needs, or else try to lower the cost of financing.

Obtaining the funds for a downpayment has always been a major barrier to home ownership. The early efforts were by the federal government in the 1930s. By insuring the loan, the government was able to convince lenders to make larger loans, originally at 70 percent of home value, and for longer terms, originally 20 years. These loans proved so successful that some were resold to investors by the end of the 1930s. The low rate of defaults led to loans at 80 percent of value (80 percent loan-to-value ratio, or LTV) and for terms of 30 years. By the 1980s, 80 percent LTV loans no longer required government guarantees at all. Ninety percent LTV loans, with government or private insurance on the top 10 percent, became common. Some 95 percent LTV loans became available from a government agency, the Federal Housing Administration (FHA), which insured and resold the loans.

There were also federal government low-downpayment programs oriented to specific groups. The largest was the veterans' loan program run by the U.S. Veterans Administration ("VA loans"). Another was the farm home loan program ("Farmers Home Administration") of the U.S. Department of Agriculture.

You can see how these federal programs acted to reduce the required downpayment. In the process, they also demonstrated to private investors the relative safety of mortgage loans. This, over time, led to the growth of a secondary market. The market provided an easy method for lenders and loan investors to buy and sell loans when desired. In turn, bundles of loans were turned into securities, like bonds, which were considered less risky than an investment in any one mortgage. And, of course, that led to the abuses of the early 2000s, and the collapse of 2007.

State and local programs were also established to assist with downpayments. State programs commonly benefit either veterans or low-income buyers, and were combined with features designed to lower monthly loan payments. Local programs, on the other hand, commonly benefit first-time home buyers (often low-income), or in a few cases local public school teachers or public safety (police or fire) workers, and even university faculty. The local programs also often combine lower downpayments with lower monthly payments.

Beyond a doubt, however, the most significant impact on demand has come from federal, state, and local programs that work to lower monthly loan payments. The basic idea is always to lower the lender's risk of borrower default. With less lender risk, the borrower is able to borrow at a lower interest rate, which reduces the payments. One concept is for the government to take title to the property, providing a very strong assurance to the lender against a borrower default. This is the case with *VA loans*. The veteran does not get formal title to the property until later, under the contract with the VA.

A second concept is for the government to guarantee the loan. This is the case with most FHA home loans. FHA charges a small premium (above the loan interest rate) on each loan. These premiums go into a reserve fund, and usually generate sufficient funds to cover losses in meeting the guarantees. However, in each major housing cycle downturn, the balance in the reserve fund declines. In a few instances, the reserve fund has had to borrow money from the general funds of the government. This was an issue on the table in 2010, for example.

The third concept is for the government to commit in advance to buy the loan from the originating lender. This is now the most common. It was originally developed by Fannie Mae (Federal National Mortgage Association, FNMA) when it was first set up as a government agency. The concept was so successful that FNMA was transformed, essentially "sold off," and converted to a "government-sponsored entity" or "GSE." It was followed by a second GSE, Freddie Mac (Federal Home Loan Mortgage Corporation, FHLMC) originally set up by the nation's savings and loans.

The process in this third concept is for the GSE to define the type of loans that they will buy, in great detail. They establish relationships with lenders who agree to comply with the rules. The lenders *originate* loans, and then sell these "conforming loans" to the GSE. The GSE raises the money to buy loans either by simple borrowing, or else by bundling loans into pools and selling securities that are secured by the pool of loans. In some cases, the GSE might also sell loans directly to investors. In the 2007 credit crisis, as home loan defaults rose, the value of loans held by Freddie and Fannie declined. The government was forced to step in and take them over, due to their tremendous size!

What About Rental Housing?

It is clear that many federal, state, and local programs have acted to encourage the production of rental housing of various types. For example, most senior housing rental projects are developed using either federal income tax credits, federally guaranteed or insured loans, or a combination. Some state and local programs have supplemented the federal support.

Low-income rental housing production has also heavily relied on federal or state loan programs. Commonly, local programs have focused on land assembly by urban renewal/redevelopment programs, or by inclusionary zoning programs. **Inclusionary zoning** refers to a requirement for developers to provide a certain percentage of the total housing units as subsidized low-income rental or for-sale housing. Many cities, and a few counties, have adopted inclusive zoning programs since, perhaps, 2000. However, there has been continued controversy regarding whether these requirements are constitutional, and/or good economic policy. These are important issues for land brokers, appraisers, and construction lenders to monitor!

Low-income housing has been a focus of many new programs over the years. At one time, government money was invested in building and owning low-income housing, usually called "public housing." Much still exists. However, there were major problems with graft, design, and construction flaws, and management corruption and failure. These have caused voters and politicians to turn away from this approach some years ago.

The next concept involved the voucher concept. Eligible people were given housing vouchers, in the federal Section 8 program. Private landlords applied to have rental units approved for Section 8 tenants. When approved, the landlord would select a tenant from those on the list, and be paid the authorized rent for that city and size of unit. The tenants would pay only a defined percent of their income, and the federal government would pay the rest. Section 8 has been a very popular program, with surprisingly few criticisms. However, there is much more demand for Section 8 than there is federal funding. And, when the economy is booming and housing demand is high, landlords are less willing to participate.

Regular rental groups have also benefitted from federal programs. FHA and Fannie Mae have both had programs funding loans to owners of apartment houses. By making credit more available, apartment construction is encouraged, the theory goes, and the increased supply will reduce the pressure for increased rents.

Special programs also made loans in support of college student housing, and for nursing homes. Essentially, just about every segment of housing has been supported in some way by government actions, especially at the federal level.

These federal, state, and local actions affecting financing have been an especially important (and changing) factor in the residential market.

Many of these government programs have not produced the desired results and have been dropped. Some, like FHA loan insurance, have been so successful that they have encouraged the market to pick up the idea, in the form of private loan insurance. When this happens, the need for governmental action is reduced, and the program, in some cases, may be discontinued.

In general, despite changes in the various programs, the overall degree of governmental involvement in the housing markets has been increasing. The most obvious examples have been the efforts to meet capital shortages and the subsidies for low-income and elderly housing.

Special Interest Topics

Rent Controls—Do They Make Economic Sense?

Rent control is a controversial topic, with strong emotions and misconceptions on both sides of the issue. From a purely economic point of view, long-term rent controls make little sense. The issue has been repeatedly studied by both liberal and conservative economists, and most agree that rent controls do not solve housing problems. The reality is that when rents are high it is because demand for rental housing is high and supply is inadequate. The solution is to either decrease demand for rental units or increase the supply.

Rent controls do neither. Rent controls artificially depress rent levels, which in turn increases the quantity demanded, instead of reducing it. Rent controls reduce returns and yields on apartment investments, thereby discouraging the construction of new units or the conversion of large homes into apartments. In short, rent controls tend to perpetuate the ill they are supposed to cure!

Condo Conversions—Good or Bad?

One of the most interesting developments has been the conversion of existing apartment buildings to condominiums. The conversion rate is spurred by:

1. An increase in demand for owner-occupied housing.
2. An opportunity to gain greater profits for apartment owners whose rents have not kept pace with costs and inflation, especially in areas hit by rent controls.
3. An inability to build new housing, because of environmental and other controls.

When apartments are converted to condominiums, the supply of housing for purchase increases, while the supply of housing for rent decreases.

Several local governments have enacted ordinances restricting the rate of conversions, because of the concern that lower-income people will be priced out of the rental market. When condo conversions are restricted, government is essentially declaring that the demand for rental units shall take precedence over the demand for owner-occupied housing—that is, renters shall have priority over owners.

Both programs are expected to continue to grow. It is clear, however, that the exact form of governmental action will change from year to year.

It is important to try to stay abreast of changes in government programs, in order to know which are likely to affect housing supply and demand. It is also important to remember that some programs fail to achieve their goals and in some cases may even be harmful to local real estate values. A real estate analyst should study all existing and proposed government housing programs, to estimate what impact they will have on local housing prices.

REVIEWING YOUR UNDERSTANDING

The Government and Housing

1. What are the two ways in which government intervenes in the housing market?
2. Give two examples of government actions that restrict the supply of housing and two ways government helps to increase the supply of housing.
3. In the future, will government increase or decrease its role in the housing market? Why?

CHAPTER SUMMARY

The residential market is predominantly made up of homes and apartments. The demand for housing is influenced by population and demography, income and credit terms, and consumer taste and lifestyles. However, housing demand really consists of groups of demand for units of differing ages, locations, sizes, features, and so forth. Housing supply is dominated by the existing stock of housing units. New construction, demolitions, and conversions will alter this supply, but relatively slowly. Repair and renovation of older units are important to maintain the quality of the supply of housing, in light of the long life and fixed location of real estate. The importance of house amenities was also stressed. Governmental programs were shown either to restrict or to help market behavior. An overriding concern is the lack of affordability in the housing market. The problem is especially acute in high-population, high-cost areas, such as the urban and coastal sections of California.

REVIEWING YOUR UNDERSTANDING

1. Which of the following is considered a demand variable in the housing market?
   A. construction rates
   B. population change
   C. government growth controls
   D. demolition rate

2. If the supply of housing units is fixed, and demand decreases, the price of homes should:
   A. increase
   B. remain the same
   C. decrease
   D. not react

3. The number of real estate listings by brokers has increased and the number of qualified buyers has decreased. This is called a(n):
   A. buyer's market
   B. seller's market
   C. unbalanced market
   D. underbuilt market

4. Which of the following is a supply factor that influences the housing market?
   A. cost of consumer credit
   B. taste and lifestyle
   C. population
   D. no-growth policies by local government

5. The median home price is $450,000, the monthly PITI for an 80 percent loan is $3,000, and the qualifying ratio is 30 percent. What household income is required to qualify for the median price home?
   A. $120,000
   B. $108,000
   C. $90,000
   D. none of these

6. When a homeowner trades up to a larger new home, this frees his or her smaller older home for a first-time home buyer. This process is called:
   A. trading down
   B. exchanging
   C. filtering
   D. leveling

7. In the past, the increased migration rate to the Sunbelt and West Coast states should increase the demand for:
   A. housing
   B. growth controls
   C. jobs
   D. all of the above

8. If housing costs rise beyond the income level of one household unit, two or more households may share a home. This process is called:
   A. cohabitating
   B. equity sharing
   C. time sharing
   D. doubling up

9. The study of a population by group-
ings such as sex, occupation, and
income levels is called:
   A. diminution
   B. demography
   C. demonstrats
   D. demostatistics

10. The number of people in ten years can
be estimated by taking the number
of the present population, then
adjusting for projected birth and
death rates and in-and-out migration.
    A. true
    B. false

11. Which of the following is a direct
influence on the turnover rate for
housing?
    A. labor supply
    B. construction cost
    C. divorce rate
    D. technological changes in home
       construction

12. If personal income increases faster
than the increase in home prices,
affordability will:
    A. increase
    B. decrease
    C. remain the same
    D. cause the demand curve for
       housing to shift to the left

13. Availability of mortgage credit has a
significant impact on the demand
for housing. Which of the following
should decrease mortgage interest
rates?
    A. increase in the U.S. budget deficit
    B. a tighter monetary policy by the
       Federal Reserve
    C. capital shortages
    D. increase in the U.S. savings rate

14. How people choose to spend their
household dollars influences the
demand for housing. This variable is
called:
    A. life style
    B. demography
    C. crowding out
    D. amenity

15. Which of the following *will not* add
to the housing supply?
    A. commercial to residential
       conversions
    B. new home construction
    C. demolition of housing units
    D. zoning changes that allow an
       increase in the number of homes
       per acre

16. The economic life of a building can
end before its physical life.
    A. true
    B. false

17. Occasionally, a home's value may be
below its outstanding mortgage
balance. Which of the following can
lead to this "upside-down"
situation?
    A. the housing supply exceeds
       demand
    B. the owners took out a 125-
       percent loan
    C. the local economy declined
    D. all of the above

18. When homes in a neighborhood
deteriorate, this is called:
    A. blight
    B. downsizing
    C. blockbusting
    D. filtering

19. Over the last 20 years, the average density level (people per square foot) for new home construction has:
    A. increased
    B. decreased

20. Which government actions tend to restrict or regulate the housing market?
    A. zoning
    B. subdivision laws
    C. building codes
    D. all of the above

21. Which government actions tend to expand the housing market?
    A. public housing
    B. FHA insurance
    C. income tax deductions for home interest and property taxes
    D. all of the above

22. Rent controls tend to increase the:
    A. quantity of apartment units demanded
    B. supply of apartment units
    C. rate of return on apartments
    D. upgrading of apartments

23. A local law prohibiting the conversion of apartments to condominiums is another way of stating that owners shall have a priority over renters.
    A. true
    B. false

The housing market you are studying is comprised of the following elements: sewer and water moratoriums have been in place for three years, and a large corporation has recently decided to move its headquarters and 500 employees to the city. Construction loan funds are difficult to obtain because of a crisis in the financial markets. A new slow-growth initiative has qualified for the ballot for the next local election. Citizens are complaining about local traffic congestion. Based on this information alone, answer Questions 24 and 25.

24. In the near future, the greatest percent increase in values should be in:
    A. unimproved land zoned residential
    B. unimproved land zoned commercial
    C. unimproved land zoned industrial
    D. new homes in a recently completed subdivision

25. In the short run, the value of existing homes should:
    A. increase
    B. decrease
    C. drop sharply
    D. stay the same

Gated Communities—American Apartheid?

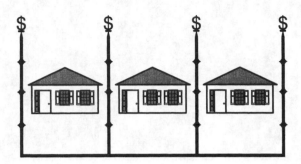

In some areas, because of the fear of crime, there has been a trend to develop high-priced homes in gated developments. In turn, gated communities became status symbols! In some cities, owners in existing ungated subdivisions have petitioned local government to abandon streets, in order to create gated communities. Within some gated communities, there are schools, parks, recreation facilities, and occasionally convenience stores. A few communities have their own security police force. In short, gated communities can be a sort of reverse prison, designed to keep so-called undesirables out, instead of a traditional prison that keeps undesirable people locked up.

Gated communities generate many questions:

1. If this trend continues, will the United States end up with housing patterns similar to many Third World countries, where well-to-do and professional people live in guarded homes, surrounded by squalor, poverty, and squatters?

2. If government planners deny the right to create gated communities, will this be an infringement of a person's constitutional right to select the housing of his or her choice?

3. Where does freedom of choice end and the need for an inclusive community begin?

4. If gated communities are denied in one city but allowed in a nearby city, will the former city end up with all poor people, while the latter city ends up with all affluent people?

This politically incorrect topic may ultimately need to be addressed.

Chapter 10

IMPORTANT TERMS AND CONCEPTS

Accessibility

big-box stores

Central business district (CBD)

Comparative advantage

Footloose industries

Industrial location theory

Industrial parks

Labor-oriented industries

Linear strips

Live-work housing

Linkage

Local community forces

Market-oriented industries

Shopping centers

Community centers

Neighborhood centers

Power centers

Regional centers

PREVIEW

This chapter discusses the major influences on the value and uses of commercial and industrial property. Section 10.1 and Section 10.2 examine the economic, social, and political forces that affect business real estate. Section 10.3 focuses on commercial properties, and industrial properties are the subject of Section 10.4. The Case & Point at the end of the chapter explores major changes in retailing and the impact on land use. When you have completed this chapter, you will be able to:

1. Explain how economic trends impact the value of business property.

2. List and define the four major forces that influence the selection of commercial sites.

3. Describe the signs of a change in a commercial real estate market.

Commercial and Industrial Markets

10.1 BUSINESS REAL ESTATE

Business real estate includes a broad range of property types. The major headings or categories include: *retail, service, wholesale, entertainment, hotel/motel, medical*, and *manufacturing*. These categories are not rigidly used. For example, *wholesale* and *manufacturing* uses are often located close together, and are often labeled *industrial*. *Medical* is often included in *service*, along with *hotel/motel*. And *entertainment* is often included in *retail*. Also, as noted earlier, many new buildings today, especially in larger cities, are mixed-use buildings. Figure 10.1 illustrates a mixed-use building, with residential over ground-floor retail uses.

To confuse things even more, these many headings are often combined into just two: *commercial* and *industrial*. In many older cities today, older industrial buildings, and sometimes vacant industrially zoned sites, are being converted or used for **live-work housing**. These are usually larger complexes, where a dwelling unit is combined with a ground-floor shop, store, or craft area. Usually, some code or density requirements are reduced, to lower costs, making these popular with young artists and craftspeople. Figure 10.2 shows an older industrial building that has been converted to live-work units.

And all of these labels exclude traditional multifamily residential properties or apartments. Condominium buildings often look the same as apartments, but their values are influenced by the same factors as detached homes. Apartment owners, on the other hand, usually are influenced by the same factors that influence buyers of other business properties as investments. We have discussed condominiums in Chapter 9. Similarly, we will discuss agricultural properties in Chapter 11, as buyer motivations are also different.

FIGURE 10.1   A mixed-use building.

FIGURE 10.2   Live-work industrial conversion.

Investors versus Users

Nearly any type of property can be purchased either as an investment, for its income or potential for value increase, or else to occupy and use. Even some hotels today sell individual rooms to people who want both the income and also the use of the room some of the time. The *motives* of investors and users can be very different. Sometimes, (with Small Business Administration—SBA—loans, for example), the available financing can be very different. As a result, prices can be different, in a sub-market where one or the other type of buyer dominates.

For example, small store, warehouse, manufacturing, and office buildings are usually occupied by small businesses. They may rent or buy, depending on the relative costs and their long-term plans. Often, when SBA loans are more favorable, users will outbid investors, dominating the market. However, many larger properties do not qualify for SBA financing due to their size. Other large buildings may be physically divided for multiple rental occupancies, and investors of various types will dominate markets and set prices. Notice, however, that the condominium concept is slowly emerging in the office, retail, and industrial markets!

The User Viewpoint

A business that buys business real estate in order to *occupy* it usually has clear reasons to do so. Among these reasons are the following:

Control the location, so that the owner cannot sell it to another user.

Reduce the monthly cost, due to the low interest rates of SBA loans.

Reduce future occupancy cost increases, since the loan payments often are fixed, and can increase much slower than rents.

Build an estate for retirement, by the loan principal payments and any value increases.

Gain greater flexibility and control, in case of any needed remodeling, or signage and use changes.

There are risks to the owner-user, however. The user becomes tied to this location and could run out of room if business grows. If the business or the location declines, it is likely to cost a user-owner much more to shut down and leave than it would a tenant, because of the loan and any downpayment and remodeling investments.

Another complication is this: When an owner-occupied building sells, does the sale include the business, or just the real estate? If it includes the business, the price will be influenced by any receivables, business fixtures, or furniture that are included in the sale, by the profitability of the business and its prospects, and by any liquor licenses or other special license or permit that the business has. Business brokerage and valuation are specialties, as the value of businesses can vary tremendously, depending on what is included, and the prospects of the business.

If the sale is only of the real estate, what is to happen to the business? Will it stay, sign a lease, and pay rent, or will the building be vacant? These questions are critical ones for lenders, agents, appraisers, and prospective buyers!

The Investor Viewpoint

The benefits to investors of ownership of business real estate differ from the benefits of owner-occupied homes or other user-occupied real estate. For the homeowner (and owner-users in general), in addition to any appreciation potential, the price paid for the home is influenced by the personal benefits of ownership. These include amenities such as status, security, pride of ownership, school district, and so on. These amenities are not directly related to the property's ability to produce rent. For investment business properties, these personal amenities are less important than the specific economic factors that influence the property's ability to generate rent and maintain value.

The business property road to value, for investment properties, runs as follows: Economic trends influence current business profits. Business profits in turn influence the business owner's ability to pay rent. Rents then help to determine the property's net operating income. Finally, net operating income establishes a business property's market value. Thus, changes in current economic trends can have a greater near-term impact on investment real estate values than on values of owner-user property, or can occur at a different time, earlier or later. Figure 10.3 illustrates this road to value for investment property.

FIGURE 10.3   Road to value.

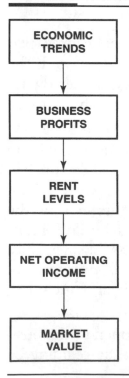

Because the value of investment property usually is closely tied to the anticipated income from the property, the nature of the income becomes very important. The three key issues about property income are often described as the *quantity, quality, and durability* of the income. It is important to consider any leases very carefully. If the tenant is paying a very low rent under a long-term lease, the value of the *owner's interest* in the real estate will be less!

REVIEWING YOUR UNDERSTANDING

Business Real Estate

1. What determines whether business real estate is purchased by a user or by an investor?

2. Give several reasons why a business might want to own its building, and several reasons why not.

3. Why does income usually matter to investors? Is it only the current income?

10.2 MAJOR VALUE INFLUENCES

There are a large number of issues or influences that can cause the value of business real estate to change. These can be grouped into two main headings: economic issues and government control issues.

The Economic Issues

Demand Is Tied to the Business Cycle

The demand for business real estate is tied to current economic activity. When the economy is booming, sales are up and the need for more commercial and industrial space increases. When business slows down, sales decline and most businesses put expansion plans on hold.

Supply Factors

Changes in the supply of business real estate primarily depend on the rate of new construction, with a minor influence from conversions and demolitions. Because construction takes so long, supply cannot immediately match increases in demand. Business property development projects take years to package. The work needed to meet government requirements is especially time consuming. Also, no-growth and environment groups frequently challenge major development projects in court, or by referendums at the polls. Then, once a project

FIGURE 10.4 Average vacancy rates by property type.

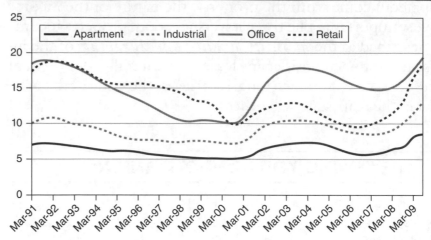

Source: Commercial Real Estate Multifamily Finance Data Book, 3rd Quarter, 2009, by Mortgage Banker Association. (www.mortgagebankers.org)

is finally started, the "pipeline effect" takes over. Even though a shift in the business cycle may reduce the demand for more business space, it is difficult to stop a project in mid-construction.

As a result, the business real estate market has a history of building booms, with a gradual buildup of too much new space. This, in turn, is followed by a period of slow construction activity, as the excess inventory is gradually rented up or sold to users. Figure 10.4 shows the effect of this cycle on vacancy rates. In turn, the increases in vacancy result in lower rents, which mean lower prices! Refer back to Figure 10.3, to see how the process results in lower values. And Figure 10.5 demonstrates the cyclical behavior of prices.

In many ways, there seem to be *two different real estate cycles*, one on top of the other. The shorter cycle seems to be tied to the general business cycle, taking perhaps four to six years from one peak to the next. The longer one is more focused on real estate. As noted in Part One, it used to be described as being about 18 years in length. The bottom of the long cycle always occurs around the same time as a bottom of the business, or short, cycle. For example, 2009–2010 was a recent bottom of the long cycle, following the bottom of the short cycle in 2007–2009. The prior bottom of the long cycle was about 1991, roughly 18 years earlier.

The long cycle affects all aspects of real estate, so there is usually a cycle of all three components of investment values: rents, rates, and values. The cycle of rates means that loan interest rates move up and down in a cyclical pattern. Increasingly, the cycle is also seen to include a cycle in *direct capitalization rates*—usually called "cap rates" on the street, and loosely defined as the property

FIGURE 10.5 Price indices. December 2000 = 100.

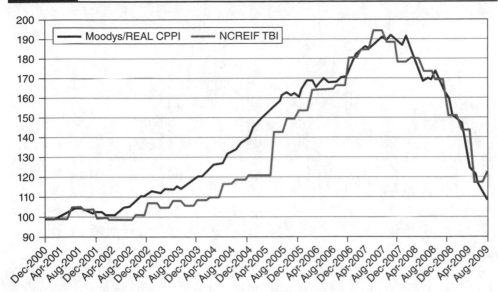

Source: Commercial Real Estate Multifamily Finance Data Book, 3rd Quarter, 2009, by Mortgage Banker Association. (www.mortgagebankers.org)

income, net of only operating expenses, divided by the sale price. These terms will be explored further in Chapter 16.

Some observers note that the several most recent long cycles have had larger swings, from peak to trough, than previous ones. Indeed, the 2009–2010 commercial real estate bottom looks to be the worst in many years. Is the economy becoming more cyclical or just commercial real estate, or is this a one-time severe dip?

Financing Is Critical

Because business real estate is often expensive, buyers usually borrow money to purchase property. Borrowing is also a standard investment tool when one seeks leverage and income tax advantages. Chapters 16 and 17 will explore these topics further. The availability and cost of financing affect the profitability and value of nearly all real estate investments. During severe credit crunches, many proposed developments never get off the drawing board, for lack of money.

Because the availability of mortgage money is so important, developers cater to the building preferences of lenders. For example, many lenders favor commercial property, occupied by national businesses with good credit ratings. As a result, projects aimed for local, smaller tenants must often wait until lender attitudes are most favorable.

Lenders may dictate building design, layout, or the wording in leases. In many ways, lenders hold veto power over proposed business buildings. This veto power, and a healthy skepticism, can be a

FIGURE 10.6   Commercial/multifamily mortgage bankers originations index. 2001 quarterly average—100.

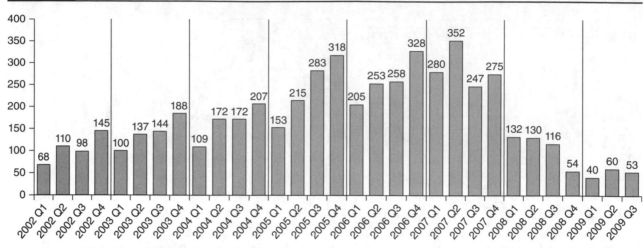

Source: Commercial Real Estate Multifamily Finance Data Book, 3rd Quarter, 2009, by Mortgage Banker Association. (www.mortgagebankers.org)

valuable check on the over-enthusiasm of some developers. On the other hand, the savings and loan fiasco of 25+ years ago and the resulting crisis illustrate how some lenders financed many ill-conceived business real estate projects. The same pattern was repeated in the boom of the early 2000s. Figure 10.6 shows quarterly data for loan originations (new loans). Notice the decline from the peak in Second Quarter 2007.

The Governmental Issues

Government Controls

In addition to the restraints imposed by lenders, the development and use of business real estate are subject to many government controls. Governmental land-use controls were developed many years ago, in response to problems with incompatible commercial uses in residential areas. Later, they were broadened to restrict use in commercial and industrial districts. Real estate economists, brokers, appraisers, lenders, and investors all study government requirements, because land-use patterns in many areas are dominated more by government controls than by economic forces. Community concern about business property development is more vocal than about any other land use, except for mines, heavy industry, landfills, and power plants. This topic is explored in Chapter 13.

Tax Impacts

It is an accepted fact that tax law changes affect investor/owner behavior. Changes in income tax laws have been used to either stimulate or suppress the rate of business real estate development. The Economic Recovery Act of 1981 gave business property owners accelerated depreciation deductions and income tax credits to stimulate construction, to help the economy recover from a major recession. Then, the Tax Reform Act of 1986 reversed the process, by eliminating accelerated depreciation, lengthening straight-line depreciation, and enacting passive loss rules. These were all designed to reduce the rate of business property construction, and they did. Changes in capital gains taxes have also been a major issue over the years. Any major tax changes in the 2010 decade must be watched, as they will also have an impact on the supply and demand for business property. See more on this topic in Chapter 17.

Income and capital gain taxes are not the only tax issues that impact commercial real estate use and value. Property taxes can also have a major impact, especially on property subject to long-term leases. And, in states like California, where property tax increases for existing owners generally can only increase a maximum of 2 percent per year, it is very important to understand what can happen to property taxes upon sale. Buyers, lenders, brokers, and appraisers all must consider carefully if the old pre-sale taxes will continue, or be replaced with new taxes, based (usually) on the sale price. More than one party has missed this issue! But even more important is the issue of change to property tax laws. Nearly every year, there is discussion about increasing the property tax revenue from commercial real estate. An increase in property tax is an increase in expenses, which usually reduces net income and reduces values. Even where the tenant pays the property taxes, the increase reduces the tenant's net income, and thus the ability to continue to pay as much rent. So, property tax change is an important issue to watch.

Special Issues

Buyers and Sellers Are Sophisticated

One of the important issues in commercial real estate markets is the real estate knowledge of many of the parties. Contrary to many in the home markets, buyers and sellers of business properties are often highly knowledgeable about the real estate market. Both buyers and sellers have access to attorneys, accountants, appraisers, and real estate specialists. Frequently, the buyer or seller is a financial institution, insurance company, or a real estate investment trust. Sophisticated foreign investors are also becoming a powerful force in the U.S. real estate market. These enlightened buyers and sellers frequently insist on using well-trained, investment-oriented real estate agents and appraisers. As noted in Chapter 5, investors in business properties create a more perfect market by being highly knowledgeable about the product—that is, real estate.

Using Leases

Another special issue in commercial real estate markets is the frequent use of leases. Many investor-owners rent out business properties on long-term leases, because the owner wants protection against vacancies and rent losses. The length of the lease and the tenant's credit (or other guarantees against default) are very important to investors. In short, a long-term lease is an important issue, in estimating the reliability of the property's future cash flow. Lenders, appraisers, and investors generally study the lease carefully. The key elements in the lease are the length of the lease, the rent, the risks, and any special lease insurance or guarantees.

In relying on a long-term lease, one major risk is that the tenant might default. Thus, the stability and credit rating of the tenant are important factors. Buyers usually review the lease to be sure that it is binding, but some leases contain loopholes. In case the tenant defaults on the lease, the prudent lender, appraiser, and investor *must study* what the value of the real estate would be *without the lease*, and also estimate the strength of any lease guarantees.

Default is not the lessor's only risk. A major concern to a landlord is the risk that inflation will reduce the purchasing power of the rent money collected on the lease. Therefore, many business leases call for rent increases, to match all or a portion of the rate of inflation. In addition, it is common to require the business tenant to pay the landlord's operating expenses, such as property taxes, building insurance, and maintenance. These are called "net leases." In other cases, the tenant agrees to pay any *increase* in expenses over the initial year.

In the past, problems caused by eminent domain takeovers of private property by government agencies have led many attorneys to insert eminent domain clauses in business leases. These clauses spell out the rights of the parties regarding trade fixtures (such as shelves and other items that were attached by the tenant), loss of business and relocation cost provisions, and other related items.

REVIEWING YOUR UNDERSTANDING

Major Value Influences

1. How do changes in economic trends influence business property values?
2. What are three types of risk in leased real estate and how can they be reduced?
3. Explain why financing is important to the sale of business real estate.

10.3 COMMERCIAL PROPERTY

Commercial property, as noted above, is a subcategory of business property. Commercial property is a broad term that includes various subcategories, such as retail, office, lodging, and multiuse buildings that combine both commercial and residential use. Although each subcategory has its own unique economic characteristics, for simplicity this section discusses general principles that apply to most commercial properties.

What Are the Major Forces?

There are four major forces that have an impact on commercial real estate markets: local community forces, comparative advantage forces, customer convenience forces, and the unique forces of a particular type of business.

Local Community Forces

Local community forces are important to the value of commercial properties, because these properties are used to provide goods and services to the local community. Local community forces include trends in population, demography, taste, effective income, and purchasing power. Review Chapters 6, 7, and 8 for an extended discussion of these topics.

Increases in local population or income produce additional demand for commercial goods and services. This in turn creates demand for more retail stores, offices, and the like, in proportion to the increased change in purchasing power and population. Increases in other variables, such as changes in consumer taste, have similar impacts.

Comparative Advantage Forces

Commercial space users want a location where they will have a *comparative advantage* over their competitors. **Comparative advantage** is created by favorable location characteristics, such as good transportation, positive government controls, the proper combination of stores, and natural land features.

Transportation influences retail store locations because customers (other than through catalog or Internet sales) must visit a store to purchase goods. Accessibility is critical! The easier it is to reach a store, the better the customers like it, and the more likely they will continue their patronage. Locations where people already congregate (e.g., at transportation hubs or nodes) are among the most convenient. Offices and warehouses also need good transportation, for easy access by their customers, employees, suppliers, and shippers.

Government controls also influence commercial locations. Some highly desirable locations may not be zoned for commercial use, which means that less-desirable locations must be used, because of their commercial zoning. Government controls can also affect the value of a particular location, by placing restrictions on lot sizes, yard and parking allowances, building height, setback, and other density issues.

A third category of comparative advantage is a *favorable combination of stores*. Simply put, some stores benefit from being near other stores in a proper mix. For example, several high-fashion stores can locate adjacent to one another, and have a greater combined sales volume than if they were separated. A famous example is Rodeo Drive, in Beverly Hills, California. Figure 10.7 shows a collection of retail users that feed customers to each other. People come to have coffee with friends, and then browse the shops, or vice-versa. Favorable combinations also exist for office buildings: Legal offices benefit from proximity to one another and to the courthouse. Medical offices usually seek proximity to a hospital.

Finally, *natural features* can be a comparative advantage. Some sites are more level, drawing uses that need level sites. In addition, climate can play a role if there are noticeable local differences in wind, fog, rain, or snow.

FIGURE 10.7 Good retail tenant mix.

Customer Convenience Forces

The differences in how customers shop for various goods and services influence the location needed. Stores that sell *convenience goods*, like razor blades, hosiery, and everyday groceries, must be located close to their customers. Some products (gasoline) should be convenient to the commuter, whereas others (cafeterias, florists) seek convenience to workers and shoppers. Most convenience stores, such as supermarkets that are oriented to homemakers, are located near residential areas.

Stores and offices that offer a specialized product or service have a different relationship to their customer. Specialty businesses find that customers will travel a much greater distance, but frequently desire to have numerous alternative choices at one location. Thus, similar *shopping goods* stores often benefit from clustering in favorable combinations, such as car dealers on an "auto row."

The nature of the contact between customers and vendors is always changing. In recent decades, it has changed considerably. Improvements in communication systems and financial procedures have increased the number and type of customer transactions that can occur without any face-to-face contact. This change occurred first in wholesaling. Improved truck transportation and standard product lines now allow wholesalers to be hundreds of miles away from the retailer, instead of the few city blocks that were customary 100 or so years ago. And increasing numbers of retailers market by Internet, catalogs, or TV ads, take orders by internet, email, or phone, and take payment by credit card. Where is the "store" located? Who cares!

Effects of the Type of Business

The type of business activity influences the choice of location. For example, businesses handling inexpensive, bulky products, such as sand and gravel, need such a large amount of land that location becomes less important than land cost. Retailers of unique products with strong brand loyalty, such as Harley Davidson motorcycles, find that customers will travel long distances to reach them. Service offices, such as accountants, appraisers, and consultants, may find that they also have flexibility in where they locate. On the other hand, businesses such as real estate brokers usually must locate close to their customers, to maintain visibility and loyalty. In general, the more common the business, the more its locations will be scattered through the community.

What Are the Patterns of Commercial Land Use?

Commercial land use is not uniformly spread throughout a city. Instead, as noted in Chapter 7, there are four general types of commercial neighborhoods or areas: the central business district, linear strips along main streets, local commercial clusters, and shopping and power centers, and they tend to be concentrated in set areas. All commercial real estate users are concerned with linkage and accessibility. **Linkage** refers to the interrelationship between one business and others. **Accessibility** is the degree of ease by which a store or business can be reached by employees, customers, and suppliers.

The Central Business District

The **central business district (CBD)** lies at the center of the community's transportation system, nearly always close to the physical origins of the community. In the smallest town, the CBD may consist of stores at the main crossroads. In a very large metropolis, the CBD is many miles in area, divided into specific commercial neighborhoods.

Commercial uses typically cluster at the major intersection or the frontage of the main streets. In small towns, offices locate over retail stores. As the CBD becomes larger, office buildings often cluster at locations a short distance from the main intersection.

Trends in the Central Business District

Even with advancements in telecommunications, the need to cluster near other businesses (*linkage*) is still an important issue to certain companies, which is why the downtown business area tends to maintain high land values. In the past several decades, the following trends have occurred in CBDs in most major cities:

1. A huge office building boom in the 1980s changed the skyline of many cities. Another boom occurred in the mid-2000s. In between and since, office construction in most CBDs was slow.

2. Major department stores have declined in both number and volume of sales. Many downtown stores have closed and either gone out of business or moved to suburban shopping malls.

3. Older movie theaters closed, new multiscreened theaters opened in the suburbs, and, more recently, downtown.

4. Attempts to create downtown malls, by closing off streets, have for the most part failed to produce good results.

5. Downtown hotels have suffered, as more business meetings are conducted at airport hotels. In convention and tourist cities like San Francisco and Chicago, downtown hotels are still enjoying a brisk business, but many other cities have experienced a decline in the downtown hotel business.

6. Current attempts to revive the CBD include adding or improving rapid transit systems from the suburbs to the central city, the creation of sport complexes and convention centers, and a push to

restore multiuse buildings to make it fashionable to live and work in the downtown area. One of the best examples is downtown San Diego. The past decade saw a large number of downtown housing units built, which is likely to have a major impact on the CBD over time.

Will CBDs return to the bustling round-the-clock activity of yesteryear? Or will they continue the past trend towards becoming strictly 8 A.M. to 5 P.M. cities that are abandoned at night? Only time and economics will tell.

Linear Strips

As people travel from the outlying districts to the downtown center, their movement usually concentrates on particular routes. This can result from the type of transportation system (buses and rapid transit) or from street widths and traffic controls. These avenues of heavy traffic attract commercial real estate uses. This exposure to the passing traffic can substitute for the more expensive downtown locations.

Many planners criticize these common linear *commercial strips*, because they prefer cluster development. Most of the commercial uses occupying **linear strips** fall between the convenience-store and the shopping-store categories. These businesses do not need the neighborhood convenience of a grocery store, but neither are they big enough to pay downtown rents. Some are commercial uses with marginal profits; others are simply easy access stores for those who travel on a particular road.

Local Commercial Clusters

The transportation pattern of the community often produces major crossroads away from the downtown area. These nodes become the focus of a local commercial cluster, similar to a small central business district. Usually these clusters are concentrated just off main streets. There has been a tremendous surge in retail store clusters. They are known as retail "power points" and are pulling sales from traditional shopping centers.

Shopping Centers

Detached suburban *shopping centers* date back to the 1920s. The modern central enclosed-mall shopping center, with surrounding parking, was first built in the 1950s. Shopping centers were traditionally divided into three categories: *neighborhood centers, community centers,* and *regional centers.*

Neighborhood centers are usually anchored by a supermarket, with a few other stores such as a drugstore, laundry, small restaurants, and so on. Most do not have an enclosed mall. These centers cater to the immediate neighborhood. People do not drive across town to shop at these centers.

Community centers have a department store, banks, variety stores, and some specialty stores, with restaurants clustered nearby. Some have enclosed malls. People will drive further to shop at community centers. However, few community centers have been built in recent decades.

Regional centers are large, planned projects containing several major "anchor" department stores. In addition, they include 50 or more national and regional specialty chain stores. Easy freeway access, plus acres of free parking, have made regional shopping malls a part of the American landscape. Nearly all older regional centers have enclosed malls. There is a trend toward clusters of large free-standing "big box" stores forming a regional center, as opposed to the traditional enclosed mall.

In the larger shopping centers, called *super regional*, traffic volumes are as great as or greater than in central business districts. In addition, these centers have multiple-story buildings, and often contain dental, medical, legal, and accounting offices, and other businesses. Hotels and restaurants are often nearby, as are apartment complexes. To get better land use, newer regional centers are putting in multilevel parking areas.

These regional centers in turn attract office building developers. In some cases, regional centers and the surrounding area became self-contained "cities." However, by the mid-2000s, the percentage of total retail sales by shopping centers was declining.

Most of the recent development has been of what are commonly called **power centers**. Typically, a power center is a cluster of separate retail buildings, with adjacent parking areas. There is no expensive indoor covered mall, and usually no department store. The major tenants are usually large specialty retailers, featuring product lines like office supplies, electronics, toys, pet food, or building supplies. Increasingly, they include large movie complexes and retailers like Costco, Wal-Mart, or Target. Figure 10.8 shows an older community center that was remodeled into a Power Center.

The growth of retailers with very large stand-alone stores has created a need for a label: These are often called **big-box stores**, due to the size of the building. Big-box stores were initially located on separate sites, often in locations with good visibility and accessibility, but low land prices. Most had no other retail uses adjacent. Gradually, however, the power center concept has emerged. Many new big-box stores today are in power centers.

FIGURE 10.8 Power center.

Another emerging issue, however, is how to reuse a big-box store when its original occupant is not successful. Often, another type of big-box store, or even a competitor, will take over the building. A few have become churches. As the number of big-box stores grows, this will be an important issue.

Interesting Changes

As we watch changes in the many factors that influence commercial property location, three of the more fascinating are changes in transportation, services, and consumer tastes. These changes have had interesting impacts on commercial real estate.

The Automobile City

The late 1820s to the early 1900s were the railroad era for travel, both cross-country and intercity, and the 1920s to the present has been the age of the automobile. The growth of shopping centers and suburban office buildings and the decline of the downtown area reflect the swing from streetcars to automobiles. Will the automobile continue to be king? Or will a shift to rapid transit systems, spurred by air pollution and congestion caused by automobiles, once again change the desirable location sites for commercial real estate users? Will the Internet and telecommunications become the ultimate "transportation system," eliminating the need to physical travel for business purposes?

The Service Sector Explosion

As the U.S. economy continues its long-term shift from producing goods to services, the need for service office space will continue to grow, while the need for manufacturing plants will decline. This process has been changing the face of American business centers. Office and service center building has expanded rapidly in the last two decades, especially office construction in downtown areas and along suburban freeways. In some areas, by the mid-2000s, the supply of office buildings far exceeded the demand, leaving a tremendous amount of unused office space to be worked off. At the same time, the past growth in demand for office space has slowed way down. Will the office building market ever balance out to the point where supply and demand are equal? Witness the massive office space vacancy in the San Francisco Bay area, after the dot-com collapse.

Shifts in Consumer Taste

Today's consumers are better informed and more knowledgeable. They seek better prices and a wider selection of goods and services. In the process, consumers have changed the methods used to deliver goods and services. This in turn has created a need for changes in commercial real estate use. Super regional shopping centers, with many stores, provided a wide array of merchandising and services, whereas clustered local power points provide convenience goods and services. But now many consumers are turning to warehouse clubs, or to "manufacturer outlet" complexes, seeking better prices. Huge automobile dealerships line freeways, with groups of large freestanding building-supply and discount stores nearby.

Any gains in consumer disposable income will cause changes in consumer tastes. For example, additional income has increased the purchase of prepared foods and the number of restaurants, especially fast-food places. Also, past increases in income have increased automobile and airline travel, and decreased rail and bus services. Income gains in the past have increased the construction of freeway and airport hotels and motels, while activity at downtown hotels, except for convention centers, has declined.

Is Your Local Commercial Area Changing?

Real estate is always changing. Everyone working in or interested in real estate needs to be able to conclude whether a particular commercial neighborhood is stagnant, stable, or improving.

Special Interest Topic
Shopping Center Trivia

According to the International Council of Shopping Centers (www.icsc.org), the five states with the largest number of shopping centers are, in ranking order:

- California
- Florida
- Illinois
- Texas
- New York

The five largest shopping malls, as measured by leasable space, are, in ranking order (area in millions of square feet):

- King of Prussia Mall, Pennsylvania (2.8 m)
- The Mall of America, Minnesota (2.8 m)
- South Coast Plaza/Crystal Court Retail Center, California (2.7 m)
- Millcreek Mall, Pennsylvania (2.6 m)
- Aventura Mall, Florida (2.4 m)

The Stagnant Commercial Neighborhood

At first glance, a stagnant commercial neighborhood might seem all right. Stores and office buildings have been established for years. Building sales or changes of tenants are rare. However, this apparent stability or lack of change is deceptive. Buildings need upkeep and remodeling, or else they become worn out and obsolete. A close look shows that the condition of properties in stagnant neighborhoods is usually deteriorating.

The lack of change in occupancy is also deceptive. Failure to make needed changes in the sizes or types of retail stores creates problems. The lack of new faces and stores in the neighborhood is a sign of stagnation, rather than stability.

The Stable Commercial Neighborhood

The stable neighborhood lacks these problems. Adequate maintenance and remodeling are occurring. Some new tenants move in, and new business owners buy out the old. The average age of the people in business stays relatively constant. The types of businesses and offices in the area slowly change. Occasionally, new buildings appear, along with additions to and remodeling of existing buildings.

The Rapidly Changing Commercial Neighborhood

Recently built commercial neighborhoods change rapidly. Business-people are younger, and there may be many failures of new businesses, as managers experiment and sort out the location factors and product mixes in the neighborhood. Sometimes, these rapid changes strike an older commercial neighborhood, but most often, rapid change is stimulated by a major change in a freeway or transit system, providing better access to the area. First signs are often an increase in property sales, as speculators respond to the early clues of the transportation change. Upon completion of the new transportation system, increasing rent levels cause a rapid tenant turnover, and an influx of new tenants or businesses.

Another rapid change occurs when the community's population sharply increases, following the establishment of a major new business. First come speculators, then construction, and then changes in rent levels, tenants, and types of establishments.

Finally, changes in smaller commercial neighborhoods can result from changes in the surrounding residential neighborhoods. Changes in the surrounding residential neighborhood are followed by changes in the number and type of customers on the street, in how much stores sell, and in what they sell. In California and a few other states, this is especially noticed when a neighborhood experiences a large influx of immigrants.

Making a Simple Market Survey

To make a simple commercial market survey, one must look for change. Elements of change on the local level often have the greatest economic effect. However, occasionally a decision made on a state or national level will be crucial to the local economy. An example is the closing of a military base.

Figure 10.9 is the table of contents for an actual market study of the retail market in Billings, Montana. The full study is available at www.downtownbillings.net. This is more detailed than many market studies, due to the study of each separate retail cluster of retail uses in the study area.

FIGURE 10.9 Downtown Billings retail market study.

TABLE OF CONTENTS

Source: Dr. Scott Rickard, Center for Applied Economic Research, Montana State University, Billings, Montana, 2002.

Community Economics

The economy of the community affects each commercial property in the area. Community economic changes can involve short-term local or national business cycles, or long-term trends of permanent change. Therefore, it is necessary to view the national economic picture, as well as what is happening to employment in the local community. Contact local planning agencies for recent forecasts of trends in a community's economic base.

Population Factors

Population changes in the community are related to community economic change. A growth in jobs usually means a growth in community population. Where there is a large nonworking population, such as retirees, population can increase without employment growth. Changes in demography are important to commercial property, because demographic groups vary in income, spending habits, and so forth.

People's tastes also change. Changes in consumer preferences are among the most subtle influences on commercial property. Sometimes, the analyst will find it advisable to "walk the street," asking business people what changes they see in their customers.

Institutional Factors

Transportation change is one of the most dynamic institutional factors that affect real estate value. Is the present transportation system adequate? What are the problems and proposed changes in transportation? Are these changes likely? How will these transportation changes alter travel patterns? Other institutional factors influencing property values include government controls, with zoning as the starting point. Is the community general plan achieving what people want? Are government changes pending? If so, what impact will they have on real estate values? Are pollution problems apparent?

Supply Characteristics

What is the total number of existing buildings? What are the ages and conditions of the buildings? How much and what kinds of new construction are present? Are there any apparent trends in renovation or remodeling?

Similarly, information about the business occupants is important. What is the vacancy factor? Has there been much tenant turnover? What are business occupants' average age and length of stay? What is the satisfaction level of occupants with their general business situation, their customers, and the location?

Economic data, if available, will sharpen your understanding. What is the number of commercial properties currently listed on the market? Are the numbers of sales increasing or decreasing? Are rent levels and values increasing? Are tenants renewing leases? What are the levels of retail sales in the area and how are they changing? If data are available, how are sales volumes changing for the various types of businesses? From this information, the direction of future change in a commercial neighborhood should become apparent.

As discussed in Chapter 8, after noting changes, the real estate analyst should try to judge what forces are causing the changes, their strength, and at what pace the changes are occurring. Finally, the analyst tries to estimate what effect the changes will have on commercial real estate needs and investment opportunities.

REVIEWING YOUR UNDERSTANDING

Commercial Property

1. What is meant by linkage? Accessibility?
2. What are four types of commercial neighborhoods? Give an example of each from your city.
3. What are the characteristic differences among stagnant, stable, and rapidly changing commercial neighborhoods?

10.4 INDUSTRIAL PROPERTY

As with commercial property, the demand for industrial property is tied to swings in the business cycle and the availability of mortgage funds. Linkage and accessibility, along with a good shipping system, are important for industrial site selection.

Theory of Industrial Location

A lot of effort has gone into studying *industrial location theory*. A truism in the study of **industrial location theory** is that a business seeks a location that reduces its costs and increases its profits. Obviously, no one location is ideal, so the choice involves compromises. Cost of land is a critical issue. However, land cost is only part of the picture. The availability and cost of skilled labor may also be essential. Transportation costs to move raw materials to the plant and finished goods to market must be considered. The location of markets and raw material sources thus become issues to consider.

Because of the importance of transportation costs, a plant that uses a bulky raw material to make a lightweight, non-bulky finished product would seek to locate near the raw material, in order to reduce shipping costs. Processing of tons of ore to recover gold would be the extreme example of this type of location. For any industry, one should consider what type of raw materials (or inputs) and what type of finished products (or outputs) are involved.

Melvin Greenhut found that new plant sites were selected for one of three main reasons, involving either the demand for the manufacturer's products, cost savings, or purely personal reasons. Greenhut called plant sites chosen for easy access to customers *demand plants*. Plants located for their nearness to raw materials and a plentiful labor supply were called *cost plants*.[1]

In addition to demand and cost factors, business owners' personal preferences may dictate industry location. For example, the original Boeing family's preference to locate its aircraft factories in Seattle was a personal as well as an economic decision. Table 10.1 lists factors companies study when selecting an industrial site.

Others have classified industries as *market oriented*, *material oriented*, *labor oriented*, or *footloose*. The Los Angeles fashion garment industry, packed within a few blocks' radius, is the classic **market-oriented industry**. Industries oriented to their raw materials include steel mills, sawmills, and fish processing plants. **Labor-oriented industries** can locate either for low-cost labor, as do automobile plants in the southern United States, or for specialized skills, as do the computer software companies around the San Jose, California, area.

Footloose industries are considered capable of locating in any number of locations, depending on personal factors. The number of footloose industries is increasing, because of relative declines in the

TABLE 10.1   Summary of Location Variables

Land cost	Energy, water, and sewage facilities
Transportation cost	Pollution and environmental requirements
Labor cost and skills	Climate
Nearness to materials and markets	Housing cost
Community attitudes	Education facilities
Tax levels	Personal, non-business reasons

[1] Melvin Greenhut, *Plant Location in Theory and Practice*, University of North Carolina Press, 1956.

costs of transportation. Many times, footloose industries locate midway between suppliers and customers.

The Changing Pattern of Industrial Locations

Early industrial communities were mostly in the eastern United States. Many had their origins in port towns, such as Norfolk or Baltimore, because of the access to inexpensive water transportation. Often, raw material access was important, especially for coal and timber. Most early manufacturing plants were located downtown, for easy worker access, and close to waterways or rail lines for raw materials transportation.

Some early plants were close to waterfalls, to use water power to run machinery. The New England textile mills, now all closed, were in this group.

Most of these past patterns are obsolete. Raw material transport is still important, but the orientation has shifted to a few expanded ports, like Oakland and San Pedro, California, and to airports and freeways. Ocean transport, trucking, and air freight have become more important, and rail has become less important. Outsourcing and exported manufacturing have changed locations for both manufacturing and warehousing.

Because of its high product-handling cost, the multiple-story plant has been replaced by one-story plants. When combined with the need for automobile parking lots for workers, the one-story plant makes cheap land a necessity. These pressures have led to **industrial parks**, which are large clusters of industrial uses, often located well away from existing conventional districts. They feature inexpensive land and ample space for isolation from competitive or troublesome land uses. Table 10.2 is a summary of industrial trends.

For the most part, the industrial market has not suffered the dramatic boom and bust syndrome of the commercial office market. However, the accelerating rate of change in manufacturing and warehousing has sharply increased the rate of turnover in this market. Larger corporations often are cutting back, whereas spinoffs and startups are everywhere. With the high price of housing, companies

---

TABLE 10.2   Summary of Industrial Trends

1. Development of industrial parks, with pleasant settings and employee parking lots.

2. Large, one-story buildings, instead of multistory buildings.

3. Locations near airports, freeways, and major shipping ports.

---

in certain California locations have a difficult time attracting employees. Many potential transferees from other states have refused to relocate in California.

The Industrial Market Study

For industrial market studies, key issues start with the degree of diversity of so-called export employment, and the economic health of the city's major industries. A city economically dependent upon a large single company or industry has a different industrial market situation than a city with a large diversified employment base.

Institutional factors are also important in making industrial market surveys. Are income and property tax rates reasonable? Are community attitudes receptive to industries of particular types? Is zoning appropriate? Are transportation systems for both workers and goods adequate? What are the environmental constraints? Are educational facilities desirable and adequate for the needs of workers involved? Are needed support facilities, such as suppliers and financial, technical, and consulting people, readily available? Housing cost and availability are growing issues.

Supply characteristics are essential, too. An industrial market survey must examine the age, condition, and vacancy of existing buildings. The rate of new construction and absorption of that construction should be verified. What is the turnover? What is happening to the rate of property sales and prices? Are rents stable or increasing? Are investors happy with their investment experience? Is there land available for additional construction at appropriate locations? Are pollution and noise controls realistic and enforced in a non-discriminatory manner?

In short, is the community going to be a successful location for a manufacturing operation, or are there factors (reasonable or unreasonable) that block the establishment or expansion of types of manufacturing processes? These factors then become important to the future of industrial land use in the community.

REVIEWING YOUR UNDERSTANDING

Industrial Property
1. List five things a company looks for when selecting a site.
2. What changes in industrial locations have occurred in your community in the past decade?

CHAPTER SUMMARY

Properties in commercial and industrial markets are diverse, but they share some common influences, especially the need for linkage and accessibility. Advancements in telecommunications has lessened, but not eliminated, this need. Many properties are leased, so that lease considerations are significant, especially in providing a landlord with security against risks such as default, vacancy, cost increases, inflation, and unforeseen economic changes.

The availability and costs of financing to purchase such properties are also important. The lender's requirements for design, lease language, tenant type, and the like also have significant effect.

Business properties are influenced by public requirements such as nuisance standards, environmental concerns, land-use controls, and others. The number and kinds of controls are increasing, and this crucial subject is discussed further in Chapter 13.

Some influences are especially important to commercial property. These are community economic forces, forces of comparative advantage, customer convenience forces, and the effects of the type of business. Because of these influences, commercial land uses occur in four different locations: the CBD linear strips, local commercial clusters, and shopping and big box centers. Shopping centers are typically classified as neighborhood, community, regional, and super regional. Forces that generate changes in commercial locations include transportation changes, the service sector explosion, shifts in taste, and increased disposable income.

A particular commercial neighborhood can be either stagnant, stable, or improving. A market survey is a careful study of a commercial neighborhood and all of the forces that influence the neighborhood, in order to get the best possible description of the current state of affairs.

Special factors in industrial markets determine industrial location. Transportation, labor, materials, community attitudes, and markets are significant factors. There is a recent trend toward large suburban industrial parks. Industrial market surveys also seek to understand what forces are at work, what changes have occurred, and what current trends are forming. The goal is to develop an image of the community's future employment, population change, and industrial future. This is then used to estimate the investment potential for business property.

REVIEWING YOUR UNDERSTANDING

1. Which of the following is least important for a business property investor?
   A. rent level
   B. noneconomic amenity
   C. credit rating of the tenant
   D. terms of the lease

2. Nearness to other compatible businesses is called:
   A. accessibility
   B. location
   C. linkage
   D. trading area

3. Which of the following regarding the commercial real estate market is generally false?
   A. Demand is tied to swings in the business cycle.
   B. Income tax law changes can influence the rate of construction.
   C. Lenders can have veto power over projects.
   D. Buyers and sellers are unsophisticated.

4. Once the building of a commercial or industrial project begins, it is difficult to stop even if it becomes apparent that the demand for the project has declined. This is known as the:
   A. gravity effect
   B. pipeline effect
   C. financial effect
   D. continuous effect

5. A thin line of commercial development along a city street is a:
   A. strip development
   B. power-point cluster
   C. neighborhood center
   D. community center

6. Small local clusters of trendy retail stores are called:
   A. power-point clusters
   B. regional centers
   C. megacenters
   D. super regional centers

7. Changes that have influenced the location of commercial properties include:
   A. the shift from emphasis on the production of goods to the providing of services
   B. increased use of the automobile
   C. changes in consumer tastes
   D. all of the above

8. Which of the following is a current trend in the industrial real estate market?
   A. large multiple-story buildings
   B. downtown locations
   C. industrial parks
   D. locating near upscale housing developments

9. A market-oriented industry tends to seek a location near its:
   A. raw materials
   B. customers
   C. lenders
   D. employees

10. Which of the following is considered a store selling "convenience" goods?
   A. minimarket
   B. jewelry store
   C. gun storc
   D. high-fashion retail outlet

11. The ability of business to pay rent is influenced by economic conditions, leading to changes in property net income and value.
   A. true
   B. false

12. Development of business property tends to:
   A. lead changes in demand
   B. result when rents are dropping
   C. lag changes in demand
   D. not involve market changes

13. Project design, layout, types of tenants, and the like are often influenced by the lender.
   A. true
   B. false

14. Government income tax changes have tended to stimulate or suppress the rate of business real estate development.
   A. true
   B. false

15. Good leases add important value to business property. Regarding a net lease, a potential investor is *least* concerned with the:
   A. length of the lease
   B. risk of default by the tenant
   C. protection in the lease against inflation
   D. age of the building

16. Which type of shopping center tends to cater only to people within a single city?
   A. neighborhood
   B. community
   C. regional
   D. super regional

17. Changes in consumer tastes and lifestyles will not change commercial real estate patterns.
   A. true
   B. false

18. Which of the following is an example of a market-oriented commercial use?
   A. gravel pit
   B. lumber mill
   C. garment district
   D. clothing mill

19. The telecommunication explosion has altered the need for some businesses to seek a location near their customers.
   A. true
   B. false

20. The number of large department stores in the downtown area of most major cities in the United States is at an all-time high.
   A. true
   B. false

21. Linear commercial strips are:
   A. favored by city planners
   B. often of marginal economic quality
   C. usually weakest at major crossroads and strongest in midblock
   D. usually dominated by national or regional chain tenants

22. Outlet malls and warehouse clubs are new examples of changes in commercial real estate arising from:
    A. new zoning categories
    B. changes in building design
    C. changes in consumer taste
    D. changes in climate

23. A very low turnover rate over a long period of time in a commercial neighborhood is:
    A. a good sign
    B. irrelevant
    C. a bad sign
    D. a bad sign if store sales volumes are increasing

24. Which of the following is a trend in retail sales?
    A. increase in T.V. home shopping networks
    B. decrease in catalog sales
    C. decrease in credit card purchases
    D. increase in downtown department stores

25. Footloose industries tend to locate:
    A. to be close to their customers
    B. to be close to their workers
    C. because of personal noneconomic reasons
    D. to be close to raw materials

CASE & POINT

The Revolution in Retailing

It is clear that retailing has changed much in the past 75 years. The typical retail district of 75 or so years ago was located in the CBD, and contained a few large department stores at key corners, plus small stores around it. The department stores were local or regional companies, and the small stores were nearly all locally owned and operated.

Over the years since, retailing moved out to major regional crossroads intersections, creating the modern shopping center. The driving force was the increased accessibility created by automobiles, arterial roads, and expressways. Department stores merged into national or regional chains. The small stores grew larger, and many became regional or national chains or franchises.

The impacts of these retailing changes were profound. Most downtown department stores closed, along with many of the stores selling better-quality merchandise, as consumer shopping trips shifted to the shopping centers. Downtowns of larger cities survived, because of the tremendous growth of office land use during this time. However, downtowns of smaller towns were hurt, as office growth was more limited. The culture of the community changed, as well. People were less likely to meet downtown (except for those that worked there), and "hanging out at the mall" emerged as entertainment. These locational shifts in retailing also shifted the patterns of land values, as the values of rural lands fortunately close to arterial intersections exploded, while downtown retail land values lagged.

In recent decades, however, two new retailing influences have emerged. The first has been *the movement toward low-margin retailing*. Examples include the discounters, the warehouse clubs, such low-margin retailers as Wal-Mart and Costco, the super drug and grocery stores, and the outlet store craze. Generally, these stores have avoided the expensive enclosed malls of modern shopping centers and the premium retail locations. Many have located in relatively low-cost industrial locations, with good freeway access. Most have featured self-service and minimal store finish. Selections often are limited and variable. These are most commonly labeled as "big box" stores.

CASE & POINT

The weaker department store chains have consolidated, in a shakeout that is far from over, and the remaining central city retailers have fallen further behind. In a few cases, the decline in central city retail values has been pronounced enough to allow assemblage of numerous parcels, to create a retail project with parking and a cluster of different retailers that appeal to customers.

Such clusters arise in response to the second major new retail influence of the past 20 years: *the return of retailing as entertainment.* Its early manifestation was in "hanging out" at malls. As mall developers became more aware of this trend, they added more eating areas, often in a restaurant commons, and expanded central seating areas. These were followed by movie theaters, skating rinks, and other amusement areas. The culmination of this trend currently is the Mall of America in Minnesota, which has an amusement park and extensive recreation areas, and is being promoted as a destination for excursion trips from hundreds of miles away! However, it is expensive to provide such an elaborate setting, and the result is likely to be higher rents to tenants and higher prices to customers.

Clearly, then, these two recent influences are somewhat in opposition. We should expect that the growth of low-margin retailing will involve convenience goods more than shopping goods. (The outlet store clusters manage to bridge both camps, as they offer somewhat lower prices for specialty shopping goods. The key, of course, is how low prices can be when more and more of the total sales are through outlet stores!) In addition, because of the economic strains of the 2000s, we can expect low-margin retailing to be the dominant influence in the near-term.

What of the next 20 years, then? It seems clear that central city retailing is likely to continue to weaken. And smaller malls will be trapped between the pressure for low prices and an entertaining environment. But other issues are emerging. Specialty catalog sales are growing, even though old-time catalog sellers are closing down. Internet and cable shopping channels are growing even faster, but from a lower base. Will these grow to become a significant distribution channel, or will they remain a smaller specialty channel? And if Internet sales continue to grow, what will be the impacts on "bricks and mortar" retail? It seems clear that there already is a distinct impact on retailers of books, music, videos, and electronics.

Chapter 11

IMPORTANT TERMS AND CONCEPTS

Crop markets

Environmentalism

Growing season

Local market

Minerals

Permits and quotas

Pollution controls

Price supports

Recreational subdivision

Resource processing plants

Soil banking

Soil productivity

Solar power

Time-sharing

Topography

Transportation

Water

Wind power

PREVIEW

This chapter, which concludes Part Two, "Understanding Real Estate Markets," emphasizes rural land uses. All of us depend on rural land uses, much more than we usually realize! Section 11.1 explores agricultural property. Section 11.2 examines rural homes, from farmsteads and retirement homes to second homes and recreation rentals. Section 11.3 studies timberland and similar resource properties. The Case & Point at the end of the chapter explores the issue of government subsidies for resource development. When you have completed this chapter, you will be able to:

1. List and understand the major factors influencing agricultural land values and trends.

2. Discuss the important differences between rural homes and urban housing.

3. Understand the special problems and features of resource land, and the trends in their uses and values.

Rural and Recreational Real Estate Markets

11.1 FARMLAND MARKETS

Agriculture is a major land use in the United States, producing a tremendous amount of food and fiber. The market value of all products sold in 2007 (the most recent agricultural census) was $297 billion, $134,807 per farm. Table 11.1 lists the major agricultural states. The order of the states changes each census, as crop prices change. For example, Texas was number four in 2003, but number two in 2007. California stayed number one, by a large margin. Figure 11.1 shows the average value per acre for farm land in 2009, and the percent change from 2008. Notice how much the average varies, from state to state. Also note how different the changes were, from 2008 to

TABLE 11.1 Leading Agricultural States and Counties

Top 10 States by Crop Value (2007)

1. California	6. Illinois
2. Texas	7. Minnesota
3. Iowa	8. North Carolina
4. Nebraska	9. Wisconsin
5. Kansas	10. Indiana

Top 5 Agricultural Counties in California (2007)

1. Fresno
2. Tulare
3. Kern
4. Monterey
5. Merced

Source: U.S. Department of Agriculture (www.usda.gov) and California Statistical Abstract, 2008 (www.dof.ca.gov).

FIGURE 11.1   Farm real estate value by state (2009).

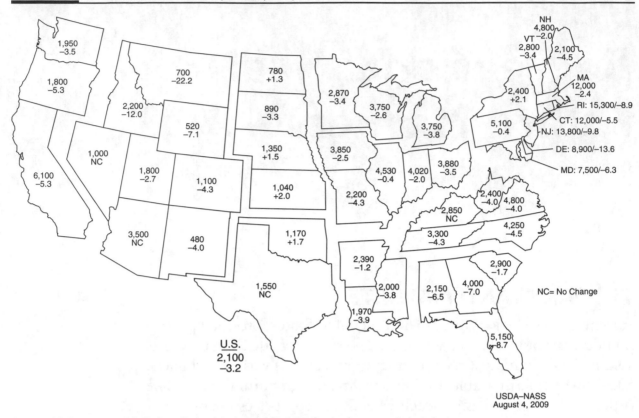

Source: U.S. Department of Agriculture, National Agricultural Statistics Service (www.nass.usda.gov).

2009. Major revenue categories, and their percentage of total farm revenue in 2007 are:

- Grains and oilseeds: 26%
- Cattle and calves: 21%
- Poultry and eggs: 12%
- Milk: 11%
- Fruits and nuts: 6%

The different farming uses (orchards, irrigated croplands, dry croplands, irrigated and dry pasture, and rangelands) vary in value. However, there are common factors at work, that influence how farmlands are used, and their values. This section explores these key factors, and discusses the major trends.

Key Factors

The use of a parcel of farmland is determined by a combination of factors. The main concerns are which crops can grow at that location, at what cost, and the estimated yields of each. The more profitable crops are planted and the less profitable ones ignored. The major factors are as follows:

Soil productivity   Topography
Rainfall   Shape, size, and layout
Growing season   Improvements
Water supplies   Access
Markets   Urban influences
Community facilities   Crop prices
Permits and quotas   Financing
Competition from other uses

Soil Productivity

Every location has different **soil productivity**. Soils differ in many ways. Soils are formed from the interaction between the underlying rocks, the local climate, and the influences of topography. Some soils (often on hillsides) are only a shallow layer on the rock, inches thick. Others (usually in valleys) are many tens or hundreds of feet deep. Some soils are so sandy (most deserts) that rainfall quickly drains out. Other soils have so much clay or silt that soils stay wet and rot the plant roots.

Farm soils are generally placed in one of eight major classes, depending on their productivity or richness. Rural soil mapping is so complete that most established agricultural areas have detailed maps available from the Agricultural Extension Office, County Farm Advisor, or comparable offices. Soil mapping often extends beyond the eight general classes to subcategories, and to suitability for various specific crops. Figure 11.2 is an example, showing the soil class, the slope and amount of erosion, and an overall productivity index.

Rainfall

The amount, timing, and nature of the available moisture are every bit as important as the soil. In fact, the moisture will have played a large part in developing the soil into its current form. Many marginal agricultural regions have everything except adequate natural rainwater, leaving low-value grazing as the only possible land use. Alternatives such as wells, irrigation projects, or cloud seeding can help change marginal soil into productive soil. However, most of the U.S. cropland relies on rainfall. As a result, much of the variation in farm production each year results from variations in when, where, and how much rain falls. Figure 11.3 shows this variation by location. However, rainfall also

FIGURE 11.2   Soil class, slope, and erosion. A map of the soil and its capability. The symbols pertain to various aspects of soil and topography. For example, 10B1 refers to the kind of soil; the number 10 refers to the soil type; the letter B to steepness of slope; and number 1 to degree of erosion. The symbol //e2 refers to the land capability unit; // designates the land capability class; e indicates the subclass; and 2 indicates the unit. Heavy lines on the map indicate boundaries of a capability unit.

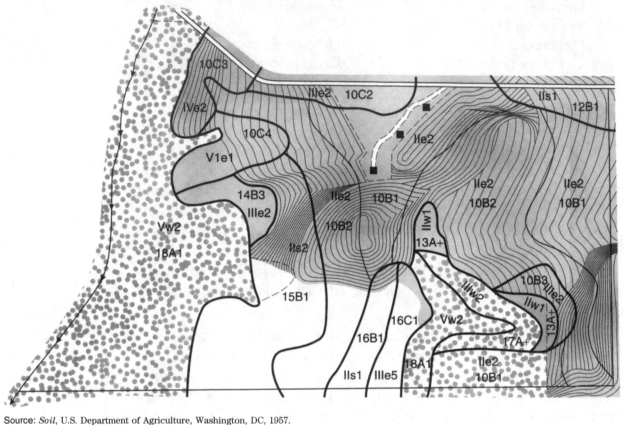

Source: *Soil*, U.S. Department of Agriculture, Washington, DC, 1957.

varies with the seasons, as well as from year to year. Rain at the wrong time (at harvest, for example) can be as bad as no rain at all!

Growing Season

The amount of sunlight influences a farm's **growing season**. The amount is generally the most at the equator, and declines towards the North or South Pole. In some areas, like Alaska, only one crop can be grown in a year. In sunny areas, such as the Imperial Valley of California and the homestead region of Florida, year-round agriculture is practical. However, some crops grow best in a particular climate and growing season. Oranges, for example, do not thrive in either a hot, tropical climate or a cool, temperate climate but grow best in a narrow subtropical belt that includes Florida, parts of Texas, and Southern California. Figure 11.4 maps the variation in the sun's energy across the United States.

FIGURE 11.3 How rainfall varies. The average annual precipitation over the United States, in inches.

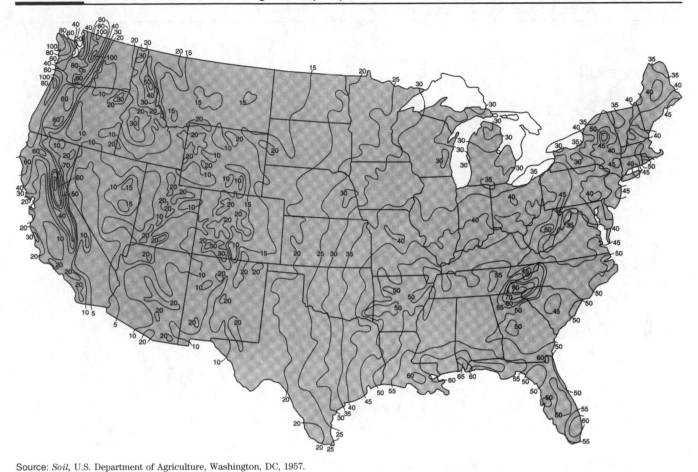

Source: *Soil*, U.S. Department of Agriculture, Washington, DC, 1957.

Water Supplies

No crop can grow without **water**. In addition to *rainfall*, other possible sources of water have become more important in recent years. Rainfall runoff in rivers has been used for irrigation in the past. Now, however, its use can be subject to complicated legal water rights. These can tie up the available water during the drier parts of the year, or divert it to storage reservoirs and urban water systems. The use of well water has been increasing for many decades. As more people pump, however, the underground water level goes down. To pull water from deeper wells requires larger, more expensive pumps, plus more electricity. These have reduced the numbers of new wells. In some areas, small irrigation projects of the past have been followed by immense water projects. These have been developed for both urban and agricultural purposes.

However, irrigation projects must be properly managed. There are many examples of failed ancient irrigation projects, as in

FIGURE 11.4   How sunshine varies. The distribution of solar energy over the United States, in BTU (British thermal units) per square foot of land on an average day.

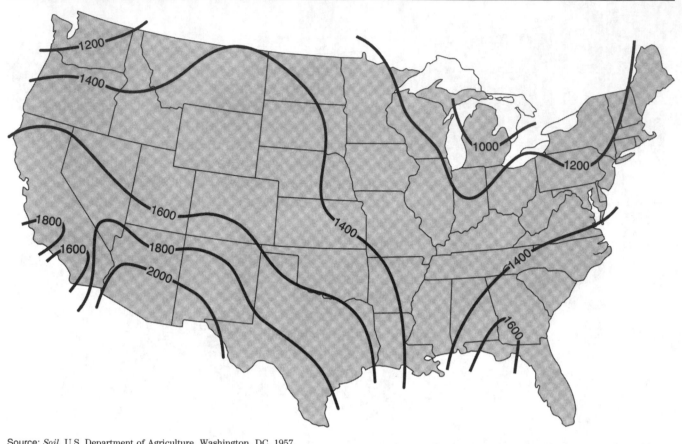

Source: *Soil*, U.S. Department of Agriculture, Washington, DC, 1957.

Mesopotamia and Jordan. More recent projects include parts of the Imperial Valley of California. The major problem is the gradual accumulation of various salts in the land, deposited from the water. The land can become so salty that it poisons most plants.

In many irrigated areas, growth in nearby urban areas leads to conflict over the limited water. In time, urban dwellers tend to bid up the prices for available water. As irrigation water gets more expensive, saltwater and wastewater reclamation become more feasible as possible farm water sources. Good water is especially important to agricultural land use in certain areas, as some well and groundwater is so salty or full of chemicals (e.g., boron) that it kills plants or slows their growth.

Topography

Topography plays a key role in soil productivity. The slope of the parcel, as well as gullies, rock outcrops, marshes, and the like, affect what the land can produce or how it can be farmed. Crops that are irrigated by flooding, such as rice, must be on level fields. Crops that are harvested by big machines, such as wheat, must be on fairly level land that is fairly dry at harvest time. The slope of a parcel is particularly important, because steeper slopes usually have thinner layers of soil, are harder to work with machinery, and are also much harder to irrigate without causing soil erosion.

Shape, Size, and Layout

The shape, size, and layout of fields all influence farm production, depending on the crops involved and the farming technology used. As a result of high prices, rice in Japan has been economically farmed with hand labor, in steep plots of a few acres. In California, on the other hand, mechanized rice farms on level terrain require hundreds of acres. Today, the Japanese small plot rice farmers depend totally on government willingness to restrict rice imports. This forces domestic rice prices well above world market levels.

Over the past several centuries, the average farm size has been increasing, and the number of farms declining. Today, there are still many small farms in the United States, but most are really rural residences with some part-time farming. The productive farms are now very large.

Improvements

This term covers a wide range of physical items that can be found on farms and ranches. A milking parlor is an expensive but necessary building on a dairy farm. Underground drain tile, to keep fields dry enough, may be an equally necessary improvement for the asparagus farmer. Almost all farms and ranches have a variety of outbuildings, for animals and equipment. The design and condition of these improvements must be appropriate, if they are to have a positive effect on value. Changing crop demands can occasionally make the existing improvements obsolete.

In addition to improvements on farms, rural areas often have specialized facilities to handle or process local agricultural products. These include stockyards, feed lots, seed or nut dryers, cotton gins, grain elevators, packing plants, canneries, and more. These specialized plants nearly always are fairly close to the areas where the particular product is grown or harvested. The values of these plants depend on both the supply of that product at that location, and on the demand for the processed product. Thus, values are quite variable, and call for specialized appraisal, broker, and lender skills.

Access

Some good farms sell for much less than others, because of their remoteness. Remoteness can be the distance to markets to sell the farm's products. Or it can be the distance to shops, stores, and services that farmers need. Remoteness can also be caused as much by the type of **transportation** as much as the distance. Isolated farms also have been less popular with farmers' families. In addition to the farmland price pressures caused by encroaching urban sprawl, the close-in farm will often be worth more than the remote one! This will occur solely because of the time and cost of travel to and from the remote farm. However, there is a market for smaller, isolated farms, for people seeking a more self-sufficient life away from cities.

Markets

Crop markets are key factors in agricultural land values. Farmers and ranchers sell many crops through specialized marketing channels, such as stockyards and the grain elevator. Some specialty crops are very difficult for farmers to sell, *except* in the places where most of the production for that crop is centered. An obscure California valley might be an excellent small lettuce-production area, but the extra cost of shipping to Salinas, California, where the regional wholesale market for lettuce is centered, strips isolated producers of their profit margin. On the other hand, isolated locations that have good access to major truck routes can sometimes economically justify agricultural production.

Community Facilities

Rural areas, just like cities, can vary in the amount, variety, and quality of public and private services available. However, most rural areas must settle for fewer services. Farmers are as interested as city dwellers in good schools, medical services, and adequate stores. Sad stories of inadequate rural health care and educational facilities have been highly publicized in the national media. Because of distance and low population, it is difficult to economically justify the cost of bringing topflight medical and educational facilities to rural areas. As noted above, farmer productivity has increased over the decades, the number of farms has fallen, and rural population has declined. Rural community facilities have suffered as a result.

Permits and Quotas

Permits and quotas are critical for several crops. Governmental permission is sometimes needed to grow some crops, including tobacco, cotton, and sugar beets, and to produce fresh milk. Forest Service grazing permits allow a rancher to graze cattle on government land during the summer, sometimes doubling the number of cattle that a rancher can handle. These permits and quotas can be very important to the value of private land. The ability to hold and sell the permit to use government land adds to the value of a particular privately held ranch.

Government **price supports** and crop payments exert a similar influence for farmers. When a support program changes, farm incomes can change drastically, thereby influencing the choice of crop or the value of farmland. Recent increases in the fees for cattle grazing permits are a case in point. Total government payments to farmers were $88 billion in 2007, or about 3.4 percent of total farm income. However, a few crops generate most of the revenue, so most farms get next to nothing, and a few get a lot.

Competition from Other Uses

A particular rural parcel may have limited agricultural value, but be of greater utility for other rural uses. Many of the rural recreational subdivisions created in the Sunbelt States in the 1960s were located in areas of poor farmland, where low land prices made such subdivisions more profitable and thus economically more feasible for the developer.

Similarly, some poorer farmlands, especially in the Northeast and Southeast regions of the United States, have potential value for tree farms that might equal their farmland values. Sand, gravel, and other resources may be mined, too, if the competing agricultural uses of the land are not as profitable.

Increasingly, some land is valuable as a site for **solar power** or **wind power** production. Often, these locations are where the land has very limited agricultural value. For solar facilities, flat desert areas are attractive. For wind turbines, tree-less foothills are common choices. Both uses may not interfere with some other agricultural uses, especially grazing. But lands suitable for solar use may not be in private ownership. Especially in the western states, many acres are owned by the U.S. Government, especially the Bureau of Land Management (www.blm.gov).

Urban Influences

Many states have farming areas that are close to urban areas. Rural land values in these locations have been driven up by speculators, anticipating future city expansion. The nature and expectations of urban expansion, general planning, zoning, utilities, and transportation systems cause speculative premiums to be paid for rural land. However, such speculative premiums rise *and* fall!

Farm lands that are close to urban areas are in a difficult spot. Land values increase, which is fine if the farmer wants to sell. But if the higher land values lead to higher property taxes, the farmer can't make a profit, and is forced to sell. In addition, urban residents build near existing farms, and then find the odors, flies, and equipment noises objectionable. Some states have moved to protect farms from property tax increases related to urban growth—California's Williamson Act was one of the first.

Crop Prices

The prices of the various farm crops rise and fall, with changes in supply and demand. Farmland prices tend to change as crop prices change. Soaring crop prices in the mid-1970s, coupled with wild inflation, generated record high farmland prices. Then the decline in crop prices in the 1980s, coupled with a drop in inflation, caused farmland prices to drop. They dropped to levels that were below the balances on many farm loans. The result was a wave of farm foreclosures. By the mid-1990s, crop prices stabilized and so did farmland prices. This cycle continues today.

Special Interest Topic

Agricultural Foreign Investment Disclosure Act

There is no law that prohibits foreigners from purchasing U.S. real estate. However, there has been a concern over foreign purchases of farm land. In 1978, Congress passed the Agricultural Foreign Investment Disclosure Act, which requires that a report be sent to the government (the Farm Service Agency, Department of Agriculture, www.fsa.usda.gov) within 90 days after the sale of farm or timberland to foreign investors. This law only covers parcels of ten acres or more, or one acre or more that produce $1,000 or more in output value per year. The purpose of the law was to monitor foreign purchases, to see if any further action was needed. The data developed as a result of this law suggest that such foreign purchases have not been very significant (1.6 percent of all privately owned agricultural land, as of February 29, 2008). Most is forest land. On the other hand, anecdotal evidence suggests that many foreign investors simply chose to invest elsewhere, after the law's passage.

Financing

Farms are usually purchased and also operated with some borrowed capital. Today's rapid changes in the availability and cost of all types of loans directly affect the profitability of farms. Higher loan interest rates increase the cost of operating a farm, and that reduces farmland values. On the other hand, the expectation of inflation in the economy, although it produces higher loan interest rates, tends to stabilize farmland values. Investors then seek land investments, to hedge against inflation. But investing in farmland, as a hedge against inflation, can produce land uses different from investing in farms for crop production, distorting the entire economic process.

Special Interest Topic
The Farm Problem

The so-called "farm problem" is a classic example of a supply that varies a lot with natural conditions, meeting a fairly constant demand, causing big swings in farm product prices and farm incomes. On the demand side, basic farm products, such as grains, have an *inelastic demand*, meaning that a large increase or decrease in price causes only a small change in the amount consumers are willing to buy. For example, if the price of wheat drops by 50 percent, people do not increase their consumption of wheat by 50 percent. You will not double the size of your meals if food prices drop, even by 100 percent! Meanwhile, on the supply side, technological advances in equipment, fertilizers, pesticides, water systems, land management skills, and so on, have greatly expanded the output from farms and ranches. Each decade, fewer and fewer farmers are needed to feed us. At the same time, changes in weather cause unexpected shifts in production.

The classical economic solution to the farm problem would be to allow farmers to fail when prices are low, thereby reducing supply. This would cause production of farm products to fall to a point where supply and demand are in balance, at a price that would support the remaining farmers at a reasonable income. But the unpredictable changes in the weather make it impossible to obtain stable prices.

As a result, for many years, the government has felt political pressure to protect farmers from wild price swings. The reasons are many, such as: the need to "preserve an American way of life"; "farmers have fed a growing nation at great personal cost"; farmers sell in a nearly pure competitive market, but must buy goods and services in monopolistic competitive markets; and so on.

Government's Solution—Farm Aid

The political solution to this economic problem has been to set up government programs to support farmers. The major government farm aid programs are:

1. *Price supports*, in which the government guarantees the farmer a certain minimum price for crops. If consumers will not buy up all the output, the government buys the surplus at the support price. In theory, the government plans to resell the surplus in years when production is lower than demand, because of droughts and the like.

2. *Set-aside programs*, in which the government pays the farmer for not planting an allotted number of acres, sometimes called **soil banking**. Because the land usually is instead planted with crops that are plowed in, to increase soil fertility, these programs are considered to be good for the land. Ideally, the land set aside should increase when crop yields are expected to be high. Set asides would then drop when yields are expected to be poor.

3. *Increasing the demand for farm output*: by paying for research on new uses for farm products, by creating food stamps and other government programs designed to give food to U.S. citizens who cannot afford to pay, and by promoting food exports to foreign countries.

The Results to Date

Have government programs solved the "farm problem"? Most economists agree the answer is no. What went wrong? The farm aid programs started with the goal of reducing the pressure from major price swings. Over time, however, the programs were altered, to focus on keeping farm incomes up. Another growing problem with government farm aid is that the greatest amount of aid now goes to the large corporate farmers, who need increased personal income the least. The final critique of the past government farm policy is the way these programs live forever, at tremendous cost to U.S. consumers and taxpayers. There is no better demonstration of this than the large sums spent to subsidize the growing of tobacco leaf, and keep the U.S. price of sugar well above world price levels.

Environmentalism

Any analysis of important factors in farmland markets must consider **environmentalism**. Although not a main factor until the 1970s, environmental protection and agricultural pollution controls are now an important factor affecting agricultural operations, and thus farmland prices. Early environmental actions focused on broad-span, long-life pesticides, such as DDT. Today, all pesticides are under government review. Agricultural burning of waste (such as rice stubble and orchard cuttings), once common in rural areas, is now tightly controlled, to reduce air pollution. Water pollution caused by chemical runoff from irrigation is a major concern. Environmental groups are lobbying heavily to restrict many insecticides and other chemicals currently used in farming.

If environmental and pollution constraints reduce the volume of crop production, the value of the farmland could be adversely affected. On the other hand, if environmental constraints reduce farm production, if demand increases or at least remains the same, the result could be higher unit market prices for the farmer. If this occurs, the price of farmland could rise or at least hold its present value. However, the net effect might be to encourage food imports from other countries with weaker controls. Only time will tell! In general, however, when there is a reduction in output of a given crop, prices rise *less* than the reduction in output, so that farmers' total receipts decline. This again illustrates *inelastic demand*.

Labor Relations

As farm operations have become larger and more specialized, they have needed more labor than any one farm family could supply. Seasonal labor crews have been necessary to handle key high-labor jobs, usually at harvest time. The scattered job locations and seasonal workload make it difficult for such crews to bargain effectively over wages and work conditions. In the 1970s, unionization, strikes, and jurisdictional fights affected some farm crops. Today, many farmers have successfully turned to mechanization and the use of smaller work crews, and more year-round labor. All of these changes have affected individual crop costs, profits, and land values, but in varying ways.

Major Trends

Studies of agriculture over the past two centuries document a *huge increase* in output per farmer. This increase has involved a sharp rise in the average farm size, in mechanization, and in the invested capital per farm. However, there have also been big increases in output per acre, in greater specialization of farmers in one or two crops, and in the greater use of petrochemical-based agricultural fertilizers and pesticides. A significant factor has been agricultural research, which has produced crops with higher yields and pest resistance. Research also improved the efficiency of use of water.

These trends have continued in recent years, but as mentioned before, concerns about the effects of agricultural fertilizers and pesticides may slow the future rate of growth of output per acre. There is increased experimentation with fertilizers and with weed and pest controls that have short lives, with less long-term impact. Increasingly, research is turning to *plant genetics*, to improve yields, drought tolerance, and resistance to bugs.

Crop exports to other nations have grown dramatically in recent decades. Exports are now over 20 percent of total farm production, but partially offset by imports, which are equal to just over 10 percent of sales. Imports are mostly fresh fruits and vegetables, while exports are much more varied. Exports are expected to increase, as world peace and trade treaties open up foreign markets that are not currently served by U.S. agricultural products. Improvements to world purchasing power and transportation have the potential to sharply increase demand for many agricultural products that were once luxuries.

Another trend is toward *contract production,* where the farm output is sold in advance. Often, the buyer also provides production financing, or supplies seed, fertilizer, or baby chicks, calves, or pigs. In 2007, only 2 percent of farms were involved with contract production, but these farms produced 16 percent of all agricultural products sold. Contract production increased 55 percent, from 2002 to 2007! The major advantage is that both farmer and buyer define what the price will be, sharply reducing the risk of a wild swing in the market, in either direction. It also assures the buyer of a fairly certain supply, and some control over the quality.

The farm crisis era of the 1980s involved a large number of farm foreclosures. Most were the result of rising farmland values in the 1970s and early 1980s. During these high-flying years, farmers and ranchers refinanced their land. These dollars were used to buy added equipment and land. And in some cases, the money was used to purchase luxury goods or to acquire investments. Then, when the price of agricultural products dropped, or production dropped as a result of a drought, farmers and ranchers could not meet their loan payments. The result was a highly publicized wave of farm foreclosures in the 1980s. By the mid-1990s to the mid-2000s, stability had returned. Many farmers learned a lesson, and did not expand as much, when interest rates were very low in the mid-2000s. As a result, agriculture seemed to have suffered much less than other areas of the economy, during the collapse in the late 2000 era. Farmers had trouble obtaining annual crop loans in 2007 and 2008, but the strains were *relatively* minor!

Another long-term trend is the growing split, between a relatively limited number of efficient big producers, and a large body of small, inefficient subsistence farmers. In 2007, 36 percent of all farmers held regular jobs and farmed on the side. Only 125,000 farms produced 75 percent of the total value of production! The large farms are also becoming more significant—in 2002, it took 144,000 farms to produce 75 percent of the total production. Intermediate-size farms appear to be dwindling. The total number of farms has been declining for centuries, but increased 4 percent from 2002 to 2007. It will take several decades to see if this is a lasting shift, or only a temporary uptick. Finally, only the future will tell if organic farming will be a fad or a long-term movement.

REVIEWING YOUR UNDERSTANDING

Farmland Markets
1. List at least five factors that influence farmland values.
2. Explain several ways that climate affects these factors.
3. List three current trends in farming operations.

11.2 RURAL HOMES

An increasing number of people are turning to the rural land market for housing, rather than farming. The reasons for the rural housing boom are many, but retirement and recreation are two of the more important factors. This section discusses new rural subdivisions and older homes separately, because of differences in how they are marketed, and in buyer motivations.

The New Subdivision

Most people have seen a newer rural subdivision, or have received promotional information about one. Key features in the sales literature generally are the area's recreational facilities. The subdivision often includes some facilities within its boundaries, such as a lake, lodge, golf course, or tennis courts.

Rural subdivisions have primarily been marketed as second home-sites or retirement areas for weary city dwellers. The subdivisions fall into several categories, generally based on the location of the site. Locations in the ski country have had strong demand, and most subdivisions in this category offer to sell homes, rather than just lots. Condominiums and cluster townhouses are also common. Occasionally, housing and recreation buildings may be restricted, in order to maximize the skiing area. Some coastal beach subdivisions have had similar strong demand, and regular building programs. Desert subdivisions have in some cases been successful, but others have been massive failures. The demand for these developments is tied to the ebb and flow of the general economy and the current demography of the population. In boom times, people tend to buy second homes; in recession times, they tend to back off.

"Buy a Lot at Lost Acres"

Some rural subdivisions are in remote areas, with very limited demand for new homes prior to the subdivision. (This discussion, of course, ignores some subdivisions that are within the commuting range of a larger urban area, and are essentially suburban.) Remote subdivisions have differed from ski condominiums in several ways, the *limited preexisting demand* being only one. Some of these remote rural developments have concentrated on lot sales, rather than sales of new homes. Indeed, even several years after the lots have sold, usually less than 5 percent, and often less than 1 percent, of the lots have been built upon. Thus, the buyer is simply purchasing a site, and the potential for future benefits. The seller often provides very generous financing, which makes the purchase easier.

The limited preexisting demand in the area means that such subdivisions must be sold by extensive marketing, often to people in urban areas. The low price to purchase only the land, coupled with a low down payment, have tended to attract buyers of limited economic means and experience. Their limited resources make second-home construction a future possibility, rather than a current one. As a result, sales discussions often emphasized the benefits of land ownership, and the profits to be made from the land investment. Unfortunately, this rosy future has not arrived for many buyers.

From your review of economic principles in Part One, as well as your experiences in the real world, you should be prepared to answer this question: Consider a subdivision in a remote area, with 1,000 lots developed and sold, but only 10 homes are started, in the first four years. If the remaining 990 lots were bought for speculative profit, in hopes of selling for building in five years at higher prices, what will happen to lot resale prices? The laws of supply and demand are hard to evade. In other words, there never was any real, permanent demand to use the lots; there was only a temporary, speculative fever, created by an "overactive" sales pitch.

There are recreational subdivision lots that are worth less today than when they were sold 10 or 20 years ago, or 50 or 75 years ago! Moral: Not all land values go up—some go down!

Trends in Ski Country

The more successful ski and coastal subdivisions differ sharply from the examples above, because they have a strong enough demand to support immediate housing construction. The success of many of the initial **recreational subdivisions** of this type led to a burst of favorable publicity, an increase in demand, and new imitators, who often had to pay higher prices for raw land. All of these factors produced rapid increases in values of the original subdivisions, which generated still more favorable publicity. It may take many years for the area prices to stabilize.

It is important to stress that the rate of second-home and recreational development is tied to movements in the economy and to the cost of ownership. When the economy is booming, many people are optimistic and spend their discretionary income. When the economy is weak, some find they have to sell. The strength of the second-home and recreational property market is closely tied to swings in discretionary income.

Another issue that strongly influences the market for second homes and recreational properties is price. Prices in many of these markets have risen rapidly. This resulted from high demand and increased new home sales prices, because of escalating land prices, expensive building components, and added cost to meet environmental requirements.

Over time, many families find that they use their second home too seldom to completely justify owning it. They then try to rent it out when they are not occupying it, for the weekend, the week, or the month. Experience with this growing supply of rentable buildings has led to sophisticated rural property-management firms, and the concept of **time-sharing**, or the ownership of a unit during a specified time block (e.g., the month of May). Unfortunately, some poorly conceived time-share projects, plus the growing volume of renters, the increasing vacancy ratios, and turnover of strangers, have tended to reduce the attractiveness of the rural features that were original attractions of the projects. As owner usage declines, the space may be filled with renters. Then, amenities to attract renters become more important. This switch from owner occupied to tenant occupied may cause the time share to decline in value. Prices may reflect tenant rent levels and occupancy rates, as investments.

The Future

The key factors of the newer rural subdivisions are their orientation to recreational attractions and the limited number of buyers in the market. Even in the stronger markets, rising prices have reduced user demand, and led to attempts to support ownership cost by part-time rental income. Investment motives have been a factor in a surprising number of rural purchases. This is often openly stated in vacant land subdivision transactions, but more subtly expressed in purchase of lots with houses and condominiums. The strength of demand to *buy and use* the property, as contrasted with *investment demand*, is the key issue, as it will have a major impact on future property values.

The Older Home

Older rural homes, as well as single rural lots or homesites, have entirely different market factors from the newer recreational subdivisions. Many recreational subdivision buyers are not aware of these differences, and of the numerous other buying choices they actually have.

The Local Marketplace

One of the major differences between new rural developments and older rural homes is that the older rural home is generally sold on the **local market**, through the local newspaper, brokers, or word of mouth. This does not mean that only local people are the buyers, for many newcomers also look for vacation housing using local information. However, this local market contrasts sharply with the mass advertising urban market where the new recreational subdivisions typically have been sold. Historically, small-town prices have been much lower than prices for comparable locations in larger cities, because population pressure forces land and home prices up in larger cities. When recreational properties are sold on the urban market, their prices seem bargains in comparison to urban prices and tend to get bid up closer to urban levels. Rural markets, meanwhile, continue on their own way, at their own price levels.

Local influences in each local rural market determine the price level for homes and lots. Some towns and rural areas are declining in population, as logging mills close or the numbers of farmers decline. Then, home prices tend to be low or declining. Other rural areas gain new employment or an influx of retirees, and the population increases, and home prices move higher. This increase is especially true for rural areas that are on the edge of urban growth, or within a half-day's drive of major metropolitan areas.

On the Other Hand...

The older rural home, although often quite inexpensive by urban standards, is not always a bargain. Some factors that are taken for granted in the city can be major problems in the country. For example, city sewer mains and sewage treatment plants are not common in the country, but septic tanks are. Problems with sewers backing up, polluted wells, and saturated septic tank drain fields are all too common.

Water availability is also a problem. The polluted well is one aspect, and the dry well another. Legal quarrels over water rights are occasionally a problem. Some residents have good water; others have water that is so salty, or contaminated by agricultural chemicals, that it is undrinkable or fatal to plants. Not all sites have water, but the only way to find out usually is to drill, which costs money.

Buyers of older rural properties may have trouble finding boundaries, obliging them to pay for a survey or risk later problems. They may also encounter problems with the condition of their dwellings. Older rural homes probably are more likely to have been built without building permits, or code inspector supervision! Or they may have had substantial owner alterations of varying quality. Even when new, the heating, wiring, and plumbing systems often do not meet the standards expected of most urban homes. Deferred maintenance of roofs, chimneys, windows, and sills is common. Foundations may be far more casually built, or even nonexistent. Damage from wood-destroying organisms (termites, fungus, and beetles) may be extensive.

Thus, the buyers of an older rural home must anticipate more problems, ask more questions, and look far more carefully than they would for an urban home purchase. The benefits of lower prices are there, but lower prices can be offset by high repair expense, if the buyer is not wary. Even with today's higher standards of seller and broker disclosure requirements, urban buyers of older rural homes need to be very careful.

Who Buys What?

Buyers of such older rural homes are often quite different from buyers of recreational subdivision homes. Many are older, either retired or nearing it. They are seeking a less expensive or more peaceful retirement home than their former urban location. Others are young families with children, unable to afford the prices in recreational subdivisions, but eager to obtain a rural recreational second home.

These contrast with the couples without children, or the well-to-do middle-aged families, who buy many newer recreation subdivision homes. However, all these groups can occasionally be enticed into buying the recreation subdivision lot, because of the lure of supposed profits on resale.

A final factor in the market for older rural homes is the relatively small job base in the area. This is particularly noticeable in areas that are dependent on one industry, such as logging, tourism, food processing, or a mine or other mineral operation. All too often, that industry will reach the end of its economic profitability, and close or move its local operation.

When it does, the local area will go into a severe economic depression, because of the loss of jobs. People will leave town looking for work, and real estate prices will fall. In time, people may return and prices may rise. But some towns never recover, and become stagnant or even ghost towns, abandoned and worthless. The rural town with one major employer is thus a special risk, and the buyer should be wary.

REVIEWING YOUR UNDERSTANDING

Rural Homes

1. What are the two main categories of rural homes, and what is the principal difference between them?
2. How would you describe the past, present, and future demand for lots in a new recreational subdivision in a remote scenic area, where the main sales pitch is the investment and resale potential?
3. Explain four problems that the older rural home buyer may encounter that generally cause few problems in urban homes.

11.3 TIMBER AND OTHER RESOURCE LANDS

There are a number of different resources that are found on rural lands. Some are often found on urban lands as well. These include timber, water power, oil, natural gas, coal, gravel or rock, geothermal power, salt mines or ponds, and numerous ores, either strip-mined or underground, including iron, uranium, gold, copper, salt, diatomaceous earth, and many others.

In California, for example, the major **minerals** produced in 2007, by value, were:

- Boron ($4.6 billion)
- Sand and gravel ($1.4 billion)
- Cement ($1.2 billion)
- Stone ($569 million)
- Gold ($413 million)

Oil ($2.6 billion) and natural gas ($3.3 billion) are in addition to the above minerals. Currently, there is little or no coal mining in California. Total mineral production in California has been increasing. Timber production, on the other hand, has declined, from 2.1 billion board feet (the standard measurement) in 1998, to 1.6 billion board feet in 2007.

The location and marketing factors of the many resources differ in many ways, making this subject far too complex for full coverage here. But this section will examine a series of related factors and trends that influence most resource lands. Each resource then brings its own market, processing, and locational characteristics to mix with these factors, to produce resource land prices and trends.

Key Factors

The most important fact about all resource lands is that *the demand for the resource*, and thus for the land, is usually *not connected to the local economy* or real estate market. Rather, the demand and supply of the resource in nationwide or regional resource markets dominate. This is the opposite, of course, of the usual locally influenced land markets. The map of coal fields in Figure 11.5 illustrates that the resource need not be located where the resource is used.

A second major factor is *transportation*. Most resource commodities are relatively bulky, low-valued materials. Their transportation cost *per dollar of value* is higher than most other transported goods. Most resource commodities also require some processing, at a timber sawmill or smelter, reduction plant or crushing mill. The processing usually reduces the bulk considerably, and increases the commodity's

FIGURE 11.5   Coal fields.

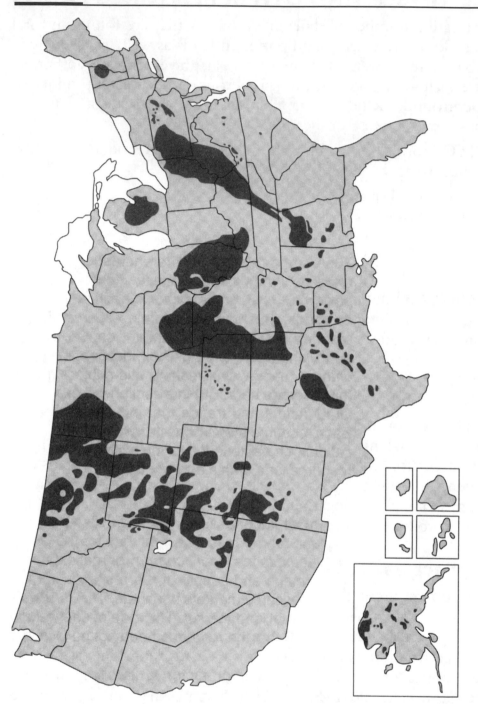

Source: Economic Research Service, *Our Land and Water Resources*. Washington, DC, Government Printing Office, 1974.

value per pound. Thus, a resource is more valuable if it is located close to an existing processing plant. The location of these **resource processing plants**, their transportation access, and their cost heavily influence the market value of resource lands.

A third major factor is the *characteristic of the resource parcel* itself. The *size* of the ore body or timber stand is important. A larger collection of the resource in one holding allows more potential revenue, to cover the original costs for exploration, roads, permits, and the possible huge development expense before the first sale occurs. The land parcel size may also be important in other ways. A big parcel may be needed to provide a buffer from other property owners who might be injured by the operation if it were close to them. Or space may be needed for various support, maintenance, and resource-processing facilities.

Parcel topography and shape may also influence value, as does the exact nature of the resource. Issues such as the chemical composition of ores, the species composition of timber stands, the thickness of ore bodies, the amount of dirt on top of the ore ("overburden"), the density and age of timber stands, and the amount of underbrush, all impact the cost to prepare the resource, extract it, and ship it to the nearest market. The lower the cost, the more valuable is the land.

Related to this, but a distinctly different fourth factor, is the limiting effect of *environmental* and **pollution controls**, which will vary for different resources and in different political jurisdictions. Their effect is primarily to increase the cost of producing the resource. They require the product to directly pay the full costs of resource development, rather than imposing some costs on the people, animals, or lands downstream or downwind from the resource.

Finally, the fifth key factor found in markets for these resource lands is the presence of *special income and property tax laws* and *title laws and procedures*. That is, resource lands are generally treated as a special category by many government agencies, often in a favorable or preferential way. Income tax treatment includes depletion allowances for underground resources and capital gains treatment for timber sales. Special property tax treatment in California, for example, is provided, primarily for timberlands, which have both potential for agricultural preserve taxation by contract, and also constitutional restrictions on taxation of immature timber. Many states give preferential property tax treatment for agricultural land, in exchange for the landowner's promise to keep the land in farming and ranching.

Major Trends

As with the other land uses surveyed, there are clear trends in resource land markets. The extent and importance of these trends will vary from location to location.

One of the longest established trends is the slow-paced, gradual *depletion of the richer resource concentrations*, and eventual development of what originally would have been inferior quality resources. Some firms today, in fact, are successfully reworking old oil wells and waste dumps of older mines. In part, this is a result of higher resource prices! But sometimes new processing techniques allow low-cost utilization of minerals that once were too expensive to process, or even impossible to extract.

A second long-term trend is the general *increase in resource market prices*. Although some resources, such as crude oil, have had ups and downs in prices over the last 20 years, the trend is generally up. In the long run, nearly all resource goods have increased in price, as a result of supply cost increases, growing scarcity of quality resource concentrations, and worldwide rising demand. The increase in market price for processed resources often circles back, to produce an increase in resource land prices, as, for example, for western timberlands. Notice, however, that resource prices are very cyclical. Figure 11.6 shows a well-known commodity price index, tracking 19 commodities. The cyclical pattern is very clear, as is the price bubble in the mid-2000s.

More recently, the search to locate these lower quality resources has emphasized *research in exploration techniques*. The concepts and tools now in use are increasingly complex and expensive to own and operate! The small prospector on a burro is not a major source of today's resource discoveries. Instead, the source may be equipment on an airplane, a helicopter, or a space satellite, owned or controlled by larger corporations, able to fund this type of study. With the end of the cold war, many eastern European countries opened up as a source of raw materials, a trend that could serve to increase worldwide supply.

A fourth trend is that growing amounts of resources are legally blocked from development. Sometimes, the barrier is federal, state, or local laws or regulations. Or some valuable resource lands have been purchased by land trusts. Common reasons include desirable

FIGURE 11.6 Price index by commodity.

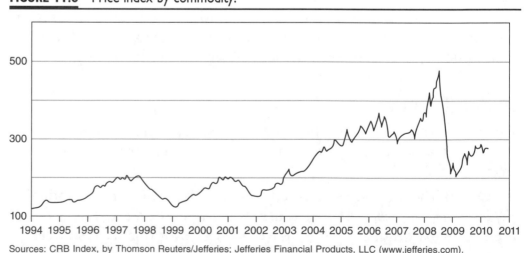

Sources: CRB Index, by Thomson Reuters/Jefferies; Jefferies Financial Products, LLC (www.jefferies.com).

habitat, species, or open space preservation. However, one effect is a reduction in supply and increased resource prices.

Finally, the rapid increase in the *environmental and pollution control costs* that are directly paid by the resource developer is a major recent trend. Many new resource programs are more influenced by this, than by any other factor. For some resource users, adequate pollution controls cost too much, relative to current resource market prices. New technology, lower costs, higher prices, or some combination of these three, will be necessary for continued resource production at lower pollution levels. Because nations differ in how strictly pollution controls are enforced, another result is international shifts in the production of various resources.

All of these major trends are interrelated to the key factors initially covered. As mentioned before, different resources are being influenced by these trends at different rates, as are different areas of the country. The interplay of factors will determine what happens to resource land values in each region and category.

REVIEWING YOUR UNDERSTANDING

Timber and Other Resource Lands
1. List five key factors influencing resource land use.
2. Give two examples of each and explain their effect on resource land use or value.
3. List four recent trends in resource land use.

CHAPTER SUMMARY

This chapter has emphasized the important influences on markets for rural land uses, stressing agricultural property, rural homes, and resource properties.

Key factors in determining the use and value of farmland include soil productivity, rainfall, length of growing season, water supplies, topography, the parcel size, shape and layout, and farm improvements. Other factors include access, markets, community facilities, permits and quotas, competition from other rural uses, urban influences, crop prices, financing, environmentalism, and labor relations.

Major trends include increases in output per farmer, in the average farm size, in specialization, and in export orientation. More recently, trends include a decrease in farm foreclosures, use of natural as opposed to chemical fertilizers and insecticides, and increasing environmental requirements.

The rural home market is really two markets—new recreational subdivisions and older rural homes. Each market attracts a different type of purchaser, and each has its own advantages and liabilities. Investors in new rural subdivisions must beware of buying into areas for which there is likely to be little or no resale demand. Buyers of old homes must carefully inspect their prospective properties for problems, and investigate the economic strength of the area they are considering.

Investors in rural lands for resource purposes should examine a series of key factors that relate to the cost of processing the resource. Recent trends in technology and the continued depletion of resource stocks have made the exploration and further exploitation of old resource areas attractive.

REVIEWING YOUR UNDERSTANDING

1. The U.S. "farm problem" is caused by:
   A. demand exceeding supply
   B. supply often exceeding demand
   C. technological change occurring more slowly in agriculture than in other industries
   D. worldwide hunger

2. A technique used by the government to reduce the supply of farm products is:
   A. favorable tax breaks for farmers
   B. price supports
   C. soil banking
   D. guaranteed farm loans

3. Which of the following would *not* have an impact on the price of farmland?
   A. soil productivity
   B. direction of urban growth patterns
   C. access
   D. all have impact

4. Which of the following is a demand factor (as opposed to a supply factor) that influences the value of farmland?
   A. increased output per acre
   B. better pesticides
   C. government quotas on crop output
   D. low interest rate farm loans

5. A rural residential homesite subdivision is considered misplaced if after several years:
   A. no building occurs
   B. the resale market for lots is active
   C. extensive building occurs
   D. commercial stores are constructed

6. The demand for recreational real estate is increased by all of the following, *except* an:
   A. upswing in the business cycle
   B. increase in the cost of building
   C. improved transportation access
   D. increase in discretionary income

7. Purchase of the use of real estate for a particular two-week period of the year is called:
   A. a condominium
   B. equity-sharing
   C. time-sharing
   D. periodic tenancy

8. Which of the following is typical of older rural homes?
   A. easier to finance than urban homes
   B. rarely suffer from deferred maintenance
   C. private water and sewer systems
   D. prices always rise over time

9. The value of timber and other resource land is tied to the demand for the resource itself. The market price of the resource is determined primarily by:
   A. supply and demand forces in the national and international market
   B. supply and demand forces in the local market
   C. government decree
   D. the health of the local economy

10. All of the following are trends in resource real estate markets, *except*:
    A. gradual depletion of resources
    B. less concern for environmental issues
    C. resource land prices shift with the market price of the resource
    D. improvements in resource extraction technology

11. Rainfall is very important to agricultural land value, especially if it occurs:
    A. in sufficient quantity
    B. at the right time, place, and amount
    C. during the growing season
    D. without too much erosion

12. The length of the growing season:
    A. does not influence the types of crops grown
    B. is determined by consumer preferences
    C. determines how many crops per year can be harvested
    D. has negligible effects on farmer incomes

13. Irrigation:
    A. is the only solution to food shortages
    B. does not have an impact on land value
    C. allows inexpensive farming of former mountain areas
    D. requires very careful land management

14. Topography refers to the:
    A. surface features of land
    B. placement of improvements on the land
    C. mineral content beneath the land
    D. support one piece of land gives to an adjoining parcel

15. A location close to crop-processing facilities:
    A. is a necessity for only a few specialty crops
    B. is more for farmer convenience than profitability
    C. is highly desirable for many crops
    D. is not influenced by transportation systems

16. Past long-term trends in U.S. agriculture include:
    A. a sharp rise in average farm size, mechanization, and invested capital per farm
    B. big increases in output per acre and in use of fertilizers and pesticides
    C. greater specialization by farmers in one or two crops
    D. all of the above

17. The government farm aid program that pays farmers for not planting an allocated number of acres of a specific crop is called set-asides or:
    A. price supports
    B. soil banking
    C. tariff guarantees
    D. inelastic supply

18. In terms of less successful rural homesite subdivisions or so-called "premature subdivisions," many original buyers were too motivated by investment potential and less motivated by the intent to use.
    A. true
    B. false

19. Vacation or second homes are often:
    A. available to rent
    B. very similar in size, design, features, and appearance to urban homes of similar size and age
    C. of significantly better quality than urban homes of similar size and age
    D. located in dense urban areas

20. The least common type of new vacation home is the:
    A. condominium
    B. time-share
    C. retirement home
    D. mansion

21. Units in new vacation home developments are almost always sold by established local real estate brokers.
    A. true
    B. false

22. Rural home prices:
    A. are influenced by local employment as well as demand from outsiders
    B. tend to be higher than comparable urban homes
    C. are easier to appraise than urban homes
    D. are not influenced by the ease of accessibility

23. Which of the following is normally *not* a major concern when buying a rural vacation home?

    A. square footage of the home or unit

    B. condition of sewage facilities

    C. quantity and quality of the water supply

    D. boundaries of the local school district

24. When buying an older rural home, a smart buyer should assume that maintenance problems exist, and the buyer should carefully investigate before purchasing.

    A. true

    B. false

25. The price of resource land is influenced by:

    A. access to processing facilities

    B. environmental requirements

    C. cost to develop the resource

    D. all of the above

CASE & POINT

Should the Government Subsidize Resource Development?

Historically, many governments, including the United States, have subsidized resource development. For example, people are encouraged to prospect for valuable ore on land owned by the U.S. government (excluding parks and military bases) and to file a mining claim if they find something of value. The law then allowed people to buy the land for a low fixed price, if they spend the required sum of money developing a proper mine.

Other government subsidies include preferential income and property tax incentives for resource extraction. Federal or state funds are sometimes spent to improve access to the area, to provide job training, or to provide flood control protection, if it will help with resource development. And sometimes the subsidy is more subtle, as when government agencies issue needed permits, without requiring the resource developer to eliminate all material pollution or other impacts on the adjoining properties. Finally, sometimes a government agency will step in and acquire property needed for the resource project, using its power of eminent domain. This can allow a private project to go ahead, despite the refusal of local property owners to sell land necessary to the project.

What economic reasons are given for these subsidies or assistance? Today, the foremost reasons are increased private jobs and the need to increase government revenue. Most government jurisdictions are very aware that they can help or hurt job growth and business survival. The economic recession of the late 2000s has made the creation of new jobs a major priority of government. In addition, resource developments are usually large enough to generate substantial amounts of new property taxes. In addition, spending by the resource company and its new employees increase sales tax revenues.

A particular benefit of most resource developments is that the new revenue generated is much greater than the cost of any required government services. Resource developments do not cause major increases in police, fire, and school costs, so local jurisdictions may consider resource projects to be profitable and to be encouraged.

CASE & POINT

But are resource extraction projects really profitable? The answer, of course, lies with how we measure profitability. Every resource project, no matter how well designed, will have impacts or "spillover" effects on a surrounding area. These are sometimes called *externalities*, because the impact is external to the project itself. Resource projects often have the potential for substantial air or water pollution. The degree of pollution abatement or mitigation that is required of the developer firm is critical to the financial feasibility of the project! This is heavily debated at public hearings. Clearly, then, resource projects are probably not as profitable to the government as they appear at first glance.

Every resource is always competing with other resources to be the most economic use. We can build homes with lumber cut from trees, or we can build homes with steel studs. We can use trees to make paper, or we can use other fibers like cotton (and papyrus) to make paper. Often, too, we can recycle or reuse existing resources.

The bottom line questions are: Should the government be subsidizing the development of resources, or should resource extraction costs be left to the private market? What if the project that the government is subsidizing generates waste that is hard to get rid of? Should the government only subsidize recycling, as opposed to any new resource development? Clearly, we are entering an era where we must look more closely at all of the subsidies for resource development, and modify those that no longer make economic sense.

PART 3

Major Influences on Real Estate Development

Chapter

12

PREVIEW

In an effort to raise needed revenue, governments levy various taxes. Many of these affect real estate. Income taxes (discussed in Chapter 17) and property taxes are particularly important. This chapter examines the impact that property taxes have on the use and value of private real estate. Section 12.1 reviews the general principles of taxation, with emphasis on what influences the selection of a particular type of tax. Section 12.2 outlines the effect of property taxes on real estate values. Section 12.3 deals with the problems of property tax reform. The Case & Point at the end of the chapter discusses tax terminology used by government officials, as opposed to economists. When you have completed this chapter, you will be able to:

1. List two basic taxing philosophies in the United States.
2. Describe why the property tax is used by local government.

The Economics of Real Property Taxation

3. Discuss why many economists believe that the property tax is regressive and a burden on lower-income people.

4. Give three examples of how property taxes can influence land usage.

5. Discuss current and proposed property tax reforms.

12.1 THE PRINCIPLES OF TAXATION

Why must the government collect taxes? What is the philosophy behind taxation? Why doesn't the government just print more money? Who bears the burden of taxes? This section answers these questions, thereby laying the foundation for understanding the impact property taxes have on real estate activity.

Taxes Can Be Used to Redistribute Wealth

The government must collect, or levy, taxes, in order to generate revenue. The tax revenue is used to buy resources, which the government then redistributes, in the form of governmental goods and services.

The economic impact of the taxing process can be viewed as follows: A tax (of any type) on consumers or businesses reduces their spendable income. With less spendable income, consumers and businesses buy less, causing a drop in demand. This drop in consumer and business demand releases resources—unsold resources are left on the seller's shelf. The government then uses tax money to acquire these released resources. In short, a tax diverts some resources from the private sector (consumers and businesses) to the government sector. Once acquired, these resources are redistributed by the government, according to the guidelines established by elected officials. Therefore, every tax has effects on when, where, and how people spend their money.

In addition to taxing, the government can obtain revenue by borrowing, by charging fees and issuing fines, and (for the national government only) by printing money. All states, counties, cities, and districts must legally adopt a balanced budget each year—the projected revenues must at least match the adopted spending. Only the federal government can adopt a *deficit* budget, where the projected revenues do not cover the authorized spending. Fees, fines, and borrowing all have an economic impact somewhat like taxes. Each reduces spending in the private sector, thereby releasing resources for governmental use. However, printing money is an entirely different matter. Printing money does not reduce spending. Instead, it stimulates spending. During periods of prosperity and full employment, printing money can cause excessive spending, and bring on massive inflation. Thus, the government cannot print money as its only source of revenue. Given all of the alternatives—taxes, fines and fees, or printing money— taxation is the primary method for generating government revenue.

Pay Now or Pay Later?

As noted in Chapter 3, there are times when the U.S. Government borrows money (or prints money) and spends more, in order to stimulate the economy. In times of war, borrowing also typically increases. In theory, when the country is at peace, and when the economy is strong, government borrowing declines, and past loans are paid off. It should be noted that in recent years, the U.S. Government has borrowed heavily, even during a strong economy, to fund current government spending. This avoids the politically troublesome need to raise current taxes. However, down the road when the borrowed funds are paid back, taxes will have to be spent on payments, instead of purchasing goods and services for government use, or else taxes will have to be raised. This technique, of borrow now and pay later, shifts the tax problem to future generations. The bottom line is that, as economists are fond of saying, there is no free lunch. Every new or increased government program that spends money must be funded. The funding choices are to pay for it now by increasing taxes, or borrow the funds, which will cause an increase in taxes at some future time. Another choice is to cut current spending to match the tax revenue on hand. This latter choice has not had a good track record! Another way of saying this is that the voting public has developed a taste for the benefits of government spending—but doesn't want to pay for them.

The Theory of Taxation

In *The Wealth of Nations*, Adam Smith stated that a tax should be:

1. Equitable, meaning that the tax burden should be spread equally among all citizens.

2. Certain, meaning that every taxpayer should know *how much tax is owed*, when it is due, and for what it is being used.

3. Economical, meaning that the cost of collecting the tax should be *small in relation to the amount of taxes collected*. In other words, it is uneconomical to institute a tax that costs $1,000 to administer but only brings in $2,000 in tax revenue.

Two Philosophical Principles

There are two major alternative philosophies regarding taxation. The first is that taxes should be based on a person's **ability to pay**. In other words, the rich should pay a higher percentage of their income for taxes than do the poor. The *federal income tax* is an example of a tax based on the ability-to-pay philosophy.

The second major philosophy is that taxes should be paid according to the benefits received from the government. A bridge toll is an example of a **benefits-received tax**. If a person uses the bridge, he or she pays the toll. If the bridge is not used, the toll is not paid. This is a so-called "user" tax. The gasoline tax to pay for roads is another example.

Both of these philosophies have their problems: Does taxing based on ability to pay stifle incentive? Economic studies indicate that business people are less willing to take risks, when a high tax rate reduces the potential rewards. Does it encourage people to seek tax loopholes? Or worse yet, does it provide an excuse for illegal tax evasion?

On the other hand, if taxation is based on the benefits received, the "user" philosophy, will only the middle- and upper-income citizens receive government services? Will the poor, who may need the

Special Interest Topic

Morton's Fork

John Morton was the Tax Collector for King Henry VII of England, in the late 1400s. He said that *all* must pay taxes: those living in luxury obviously had money to spare, and those living frugally must have accumulated savings they could use to pay. (The name is because common eating forks at that time had only two prongs.)

government's help the most, be denied this help because they cannot afford to pay? Would this increase conflicts between the rich and the poor? In general, there has been an increase in the use of taxing according to some measure of benefits received. For example, most assessment districts are set up to provide some specific government benefit. This might be to pay for the roads, sewer, and water for a new subdivision. Some provide street lighting. A few provide police or fire protection service. Most often, these districts generate their revenue by allocating the costs among the users on a benefit basis. Large home lots would pay more than small home lots, while apartments would pay less per unit, but more per parcel.

There is a third alternative. That is to tax each person (or perhaps each household) the same amount. Parcel taxes, where each home pays the same amount, are increasingly used to provide added income for schools or libraries. However, equal taxation is relatively rare.

Major Taxes and Expenditures

Each level of government—federal, state, and local—usually uses several different types of taxation in an effort to generate revenue. Table 12.1 shows the major tax and the largest single expenditure for each level of government in the United States.

The major source of revenue for the federal government is the **income tax**. The largest federal expenditure is for welfare, and the second largest expense is for national defense. Welfare refers to the various federal programs to assist the unemployed and the disabled and aid the children, the homeless, and so on. In times of war, defense expenditures can be larger than welfare expenditures.

For most state governments, the major sources of tax revenue are income taxes and the **sales tax**. The largest expenditures are for education and welfare. Corrections typically is third. Those states without a sales tax, such as Oregon, usually use a strong state income tax as a substitute. In California, the personal income tax produces almost twice as much revenue as the sales tax.

TABLE 12.1   Major Tax and Expenditure by Each Level of Government

Government Level	Major Revenue Source	Largest Expenditure
Federal	Personal income tax	Health and welfare
State	Personal income tax	Education and welfare
Counties	State and property tax	Public protection
Cities	Property and sales taxes	Public safety
Schools	Property tax and state	Education

For county governments, the **property tax** has historically been the major revenue source. However, California's Proposition 13 and similar actions in other states have reduced its importance. In 2007–2008, for example, California counties received 29 percent of their revenue from the state, 20 percent from property tax, and 17 percent from the federal government, usually through the state. That year, the three largest categories of expenditures were 28 percent on public protection, 26 percent on public assistance programs, and 15 percent on health and sanitation.

For cities, historically, property tax was also the major revenue source. Now, the pattern is much more complex. Cities have had property tax revenue drastically reduced. For California, in 2007–2008, property tax generated only 11 percent of revenue. Sales tax has been increasing, to 10 percent. Other taxes, especially **transfer tax** (collected when real estate is sold) have also increased, to 7 percent. Service charges (water, sewer, refuse) reached 39 percent. And revenue from state and federal sources reached 10 percent. Major city expenditure categories were public safety (26 percent), public utilities (19 percent), transportation (16 percent), and health (10 percent).

Schools now are usually separate from city and county governments. Funding in many states is a mixture of property tax and state and federal funds. In states with property tax limits, the state is the dominant source of funds.

Is the Tax Progressive, Proportional, or Regressive?

One way of evaluating a tax is to calculate how the cost of a tax relates to the taxpayer's ability to pay. To help analyze the impact or burden of a tax, economists describe taxes as progressive, proportional, or regressive.

A progressive tax increases in rate as the value of a taxable item, or a person's income, increases. Thus, if taxable value increases from $1,000 to $2,000, the tax rate—the amount taken as tax—will also increase, from perhaps 5 to 15 percent. A proportional tax retains the same rate as the value of the item being taxed increases. If the value of the taxable item increases from $1,000 to $2,000, the tax rate remains the same (5 percent at $1,000, and still 5 percent at $2,000). A regressive tax declines in rate, as the value of the item being taxed increases. If the value of the taxable item increases from $1,000 to $2,000, the tax decreases, perhaps from 5 to 2 percent.

When evaluating a tax based on a taxpayer's ability to pay, economists frequently modify the definition of progressive, proportional, and regressive by substituting the word *income* for the phrase *value of the item being taxed*. Thus, a **progressive tax** in this sense means that when income increases, the percentage of the tax also increases. A **proportional tax** means that when a taxpayer's income increases, the percentage of tax remains the same. A **regressive tax** means that when the income of the taxpayer increases, the percentage paid in taxes decreases.

There is another way to consider the impact of taxes. The discussion above looked at how the tax rate changed when the purchase price or income level changed. Another viewpoint is to consider how a particular tax impacts different groups of people, regardless of whether the tax rate changes with price or income change. Suppose that you had to pay $1,000.00 every time that you added any gas to a car. This is a proportional tax, the same for all, regardless of income level. But the *tax burden* would fall completely on auto users. Bus, rapid transit, bike or sidewalk users would pay nothing. If the revenue from this tax went to pay for schools, would that be a fair tax?

Evaluating Major Taxes—Who Bears the Burden?

The *personal income tax* is considered somewhat progressive, in that the tax rate usually rises as taxable income increases. This reflects the ability-to-pay philosophy. However, it should be noted that higher-income individuals tend to make more use of tax experts and tax loopholes to reduce their tax bite. So in the real world, the progressiveness of the income tax is not as steep as the tax charts indicate.

The *sales tax* appears to be proportional, in that the tax rate remains the same as the value of taxable items increases. But if one plots the amount of taxes paid against the income level of people paying the sales tax, the *impact* or *burden* of the sales tax turns out to be regressive. The poor end up paying a higher percentage of their income for sales taxes than do the wealthy. This is because lower-income individuals spend a greater percentage of their income on items that are subject to the sales tax than do wealthier individuals. Poor people must spend all their income to live. Wealthy people do not spend all their income on living expenses that are subject to the sales tax. They save a certain portion (savings are not subject to the sales tax) and spend some on nontaxable services. Assuming a sales tax rate of 7 percent, Table 12.2 illustrates a hypothetical example of the regressive impact of a sales tax when compared with personal income.

In an attempt to make the impact less regressive, many states have exempted food, rent, and utilities from the sales tax. Poor people tend

Special Interest Topic

Are State Lotteries a Form of Regressive Taxation?

During the 1980s, state governments were looking for additional sources of revenue. Many turned to state-operated lotteries. Groups opposed to lotteries warned that the source of this revenue would be from those citizens least able to pay. They noted that people who buy lottery tickets tend to come from low-income backgrounds. The money spent on lottery tickets would be better spent on food, health, clothing, and other essentials of life.

Groups in favor of a lottery argued that lotteries would raise money for education and other programs that benefit everyone, including low-income people. The alternative would be to cut education and other programs, because people would refuse to vote for the required tax increases to maintain these programs. However, people would vote for a lottery, and some of the lottery revenue would be targeted for education and other needed programs.

What have been the results? When presented to the people for a vote, in almost every case the state lottery law passed. Did the prediction come true that the lottery would be used primarily by low-income people? According to a study by the National Bureau of Economic Research (www.nber.org) in Cambridge, Massachusetts, approximately 50% of all money spent on lottery tickets comes from 5% of the lottery players. This group's profile is predominately middle-aged and/or minority, with a blue-collar background.

Win $20 Million (and Get a Lot Less!)

If you beat the odds and win a $20 million lottery, how much do you really get? Most state lotteries are exempt from state, but not federal, income tax. Further, the proceeds are not usually paid up front, but rather in 20 equal annual installments.

Example: Twenty million dollars less approximately 35 percent for federal income taxes, leaves a balance of approximately $13,000,000, which, divided by 20 years, equals $650,000 per year. This $650,000 per year, discounted for the time value of money, say, 6 percent, for the next 20 years, equals a present value of $7,455,450, and this is the current real value of your prize. Not shabby, but not $20 million!

TABLE 12.2 Example of the Regressive Impact of a Sales Tax

Income	Amount Spent Subject to Tax	Tax Rate	Sales Tax	Percent of Income
$10,000	$10,000	7%	$700	7
$100,000	$30,000	7%	$2,100	2.1

to spend a major portion of their income in these areas. By providing exemptions, low-income people gain some relief from the regressive nature of the impact of the sales tax.

Who Really Pays the Tax?

Ultimately, all taxes are paid by people. But the person who is *legally* responsible for the tax payment may be able to shift the tax cost to someone else. Example: Retail store owners may be required to pay sales taxes to state and local governments—the actual check for the tax is paid by the store owner. But the store owner collects the tax from the consumer at the point of sale. Therefore, although charged for the sales tax, the store owner does not end up out-of-pocket for the tax, the customer does! When studying what impact existing or proposed new taxes will have on society, economists trace who will actually end up with the tax burden.

Analyzing the tax burden is not easy. One problem is that each tax causes tax payers to change their behavior. For example, when the tax on gain from reselling an asset is high, people tend to postpone selling stocks and real estate. A high sales tax in one area may cause people to drive to another area to buy. If property taxes on land are relatively low, people will tend to invest a bit more in land for future development, and sometimes hold it for a long time, changing the development pattern of an area. The economic costs of postponed development may be high, but are hard to trace back to the taxing decision!

REVIEWING YOUR UNDERSTANDING

The Principles of Taxation

1. In addition to taxes, name three other sources of government revenue.
2. How does taxing according to ability to pay differ from taxing based on benefits received?
3. Describe the differences between progressive, proportional, and regressive taxes. What are some problems associated with a progressive tax? With a regressive tax?

12.2 EVALUATING THE PROPERTY TAX

What do we mean by the property tax? **Property tax** is a tax that is collected from the owner or user of each privately owned parcel of land. The typical property tax is based upon the *value* of the property, so it is often called an *ad valorem* tax, Latin for "from the value." Note that not only real property can be subject to property tax: In many places, machinery and equipment or even business inventories are subject to property tax. However, most of the revenue comes from taxes on real property. And the property tax on real property can be based on just the land value, or on the value of the land and buildings.

It is important to recognize that the property tax bill received by a property owner may cover more than just *ad valorem* taxes. Increasingly, agencies are using the existing bill as an efficient way to collect other taxes. These might include assessment district bond payments, parcel taxes, and even public utility charges. This becomes very important when estimating future taxes. In many jurisdictions, including California, the assessed value for *ad valorem* taxes will change when the property sells. The other charges on the tax bill will not!

Use of the property tax in the United States dates from the founding colonists, who brought to this country Britain's concept of taxing land. When the U.S. Constitution was written, the new federal government used excise (a tax on goods and commodities when produced), sales, and other forms of taxation. The power to tax property was left to the states and local governments. By 1900, state governments for the most part had also abandoned the property tax in favor of other forms of taxation. This left local governments as the sole collector of the property tax. This tradition has continued; property taxes are still a major source of revenue for city and county governments. At one time, cities, school districts, and other local government agencies each set, mailed, and collected their own property taxes. Now, the establishment of taxable value, called **assessed value**, is primarily by the county assessor, and all of the taxes for the various agencies are collected on one tax bill. This section examines what impact property taxes have on real estate use and value.

Local Government and the Property Tax

Why have local governments held on so firmly to the property tax? With so many people complaining about high real estate taxes, why do local governments continue to use this tax?

First, if the property tax is discontinued, a new tax would be needed to raise the money to replace it. The levying of any new tax runs into massive political and administrative problems. So, for better or worse, there is a tendency to stick with the existing tax system. Second, a tax on real estate has certain advantages that other taxes do not have. Real estate is visible and immobile—real estate cannot be hidden from the tax collector. Also, unlike the income tax or the sales tax, property tax revenue, historically, has not fluctuated widely with short-term swings in the business cycle. However, the major real estate cycles do indeed cause a revenue fluctuation! Also, people tend to pay their property taxes, because the penalty for not paying is loss of the property, and for most people, this is too high a price to pay.

Local governments like the property tax because it has historically provided a stable source of revenue. This in turn makes establishing annual local and county budgets an easier task.

Who Really Pays the Property Tax: Owners, Tenants, or Consumers?

Who actually pays the property tax? The property taxes paid on owner-occupied homes are usually not shifted to others—the owner pays. There are no tenants or customers to whom the tax can be passed. However, the situation for rental and business-owned property is entirely different. First, the owner of an office, retail, or industrial building often requires the tenant to pay the property tax bill. And in the long run, property taxes are just one of the costs of doing business. They are shifted to the customers—be they apartment tenants or business clients.

What about tax increases? Are they immediately shifted to consumers? If market conditions allow, landlords usually shift property tax increases to tenants, in the form of higher rents. It must be recognized that this shift will occur only if there is a "landlord's market"—a strong tenant demand and a limited rental supply. When this exists, property tax increases are easily shifted to tenants. On the other hand, in a "soft" rental market, with many vacancies, property tax increases tend to be absorbed by the landlord, for fear that higher rents would cause a loss of tenants.

What if the tenants are businesses? If landlords can shift property tax increases to business tenants, do these businesses then shift the taxes to their customers, in the form of higher prices? Do businesses that own their property shift the tax to their customers? The answer depends on the condition of the market in which the tenant-business operates. If the market is highly competitive, business can shift the tax to customers only to the extent that other business competitors pay the same taxes. If Business A pays a tax of $10 and competitor Business B pays $5, then in order to remain competitive, Business A must absorb the difference. If both Business A and Business B pay the same tax, they both can shift the full tax on to customers.

Special Interest Topic

The Dilemma of the City: Taxpayers Are Decreasing While Tax Users Are Increasing

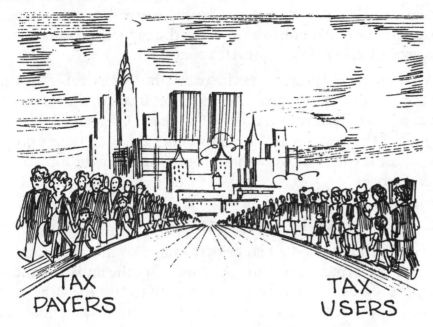

When city congestion drove upper- and middle-income people to the suburbs, their places were often taken by poor people seeking jobs. If the jobs failed to materialize, the poor went on welfare and drew upon other government services. Many major cities now have a dilemma: Taxpayers are decreasing while tax users are increasing.

How can this problem be solved? Should the city raise taxes to generate the needed revenue? Or would a tax increase just drive out additional taxpayers? Should the federal government increase its subsidies to the cities? Will suburban and rural people resent paying taxes to support cities where they do not reside?

We must also realize that some properties are rented on long-term leases, which may control whether the tenant or the landlord absorbs the property tax increase. Also, in some areas, governmental rent controls determine who shall pay any increase in property taxes.

Property Taxes and Capitalized Real Estate Values

We stated earlier that an increase in property taxes that cannot be shifted to others (e.g., tax increases on owner-occupied homes) can reduce the value of real estate. How much value will the property lose? Will the loss be equal to or greater than the tax increase? The answers to these questions depend on how the tax monies are spent.

If the government uses the increased revenue from property taxes for expenditures that benefit the taxpayer's home, such as street improvements, outdoor lighting, or neighborhood cleanup, the taxpayer's property values may remain stable or even increase. However, if the tax increases are spent in such a way that the taxpayer receives little or no perceived benefits, the taxpayer's property will lose sales value. The amount of the maximum loss would be the capitalized value of the tax increase. Table 12.3 illustrates this concept.

When there is a property tax increase, the loss in real estate value is not the amount of the annual tax increase. Instead, the loss is the tax increase capitalized over a number of years. Of course, this applies only if (1) the tax increase does not benefit the taxpayer's property, and (2) the tax increase is not shifted onto others, in the form of higher rents or prices.

Is the Property Tax Regressive?

Do poor people spend a higher percentage of their income on real property taxes than do wealthy persons? If so, the impact of the property tax is regressive. If real estate taxes tend to take the same percentage of income regardless of how much is earned, the impact of the property tax is proportional, not regressive.

Real property taxes are levied at a tax rate multiplied times a value. Thus, higher-valued properties are charged the same tax rate as lower-valued properties. But studies reveal that when one plots the dollar amount of real estate taxes paid against the income levels of the taxpayer, the impact of the real property tax is regressive. Lower-income people spend a higher percentage of their income on property taxes than do wealthy persons.[1]

TABLE 12.3   Capitalized Loss Caused by Property Tax Increase

	Before	After	Change
Taxes	$1,000/yr.	$1,100/yr.	$100 tax increase
Net Income *divided by the*	$10,000	$9,900	$100 reduction
Capitalization Rate *equals the*	10%	10%	none
Value Estimate	$100,000	$99,000	$1,000 value loss

$$\frac{\text{Net Income}}{\text{Capitalization Rate}} = \text{Value Estimate}$$

[1]D. Netzer, *Economics of the Property Tax*, Washington DC, Brookings Institute, 1966, pp. 46–56.

Special Interest Topic

How the Budget Process Works

Local government expense budgets are established, and sources of revenue are estimated. Often, there is not enough estimated revenue to fund the first draft budget. This leads to a political fight over whether to increase taxes or cut expenses, and which expenses to cut. Participants in the local tax procedure are:

- The *Board of Supervisors* or *City Council* members, who set the budget.
- The *auditor*, who verifies that taxes are collected according to the law and spent according to the adopted budget.
- The *assessor*, who appraises the property and maintains the tax rolls.
- The *tax collector*, who is responsible for actually collecting the tax.

Reasons for Regressiveness

Economists usually note two reasons why the property tax is regressive. One deals with the tax assessment procedure; the other looks at the percentage of consumer income spent on housing. First, assessors may assess high-priced properties more conservatively than low-priced properties because (1) there are more low-priced properties, (2) they tend to be alike, and (3) they are bought and sold frequently. This gives the tax assessor plenty of current market information for assessment purposes. On the other hand, high-priced properties are not as common, and they are exchanged less frequently. Therefore, the tax assessor has less information to work with. In addition, wealthy property owners are usually able to hire experts to challenge the assessor's value estimates. Not wanting to face the dilemma of a formal property tax appeal and hearing, the assessor might tend to assess the expensive property at a lower value. In essence, the assessment process could be regressive, and this in turn makes the tax regressive. However, property tax revolts, such as California's Proposition 13, have tended to even out the tax assessment process and defuse a portion of this argument.

The other main reason given for the regressive nature of the property tax is that lower-income people must spend a higher percentage of their income on housing than do wealthy individuals. Although people do trade up to better housing as income levels increase, spending on housing does not increase as fast as gains in personal income.[2] If their income doubles, people usually will not double the amount they spend for a home. Therefore, as income rises, housing costs (and property taxes paid) become a smaller percentage of income. This is a classic example of a regressive tax *impact*.

Property Taxes and Land Usage

Although the primary purpose of the property tax is to generate revenue for local government, it is also possible for government to influence land use by manipulating the property tax. This issue of the *property tax and land usage* effects is of growing importance. Some examples of how property taxes can influence land use are given below.

1. By exempting property owned by and used for religious, educational, and charitable institutions from property taxation, the government is, in effect, using taxes as an incentive to create more of these institutions.

2. Assessing rural land, based on its suburban residential potential, can force up property taxes to the point that rural owners must sell to developers. On the other hand, a low preferential tax treatment of rural property may create an incentive to keep the land rural, thereby maintaining open green space.

3. Taxing resources such as timber and minerals at full value may force owners to develop resources in the quickest manner possible, whereas special tax concessions during growing periods may encourage resource development and conservation.

4. Some communities have used artificially low property tax rates to attract industries and other new businesses to occupy city-owned industrial parks. Other cities may pursue a "no-growth" philosophy by raising taxes, in an effort to discourage commercial development.

5. High property taxes during economic depressions can cause private property to be converted to government ownership, as property owners default on their tax payments. Many cities and counties acquired large land holdings during the major depression of the 1930s.

6. Higher property taxes can cause greater density or intensity of land use, as property owners rent out spare rooms and garages, plow more acres, use more fertilizer, and so on, in an effort to offset tax increases with higher incomes.

---

[2]Ibid., p. 57.

7. Cities are tempted to encourage retail land use, which generates more local revenue by way of sales taxes, and discourage residential uses, which may need additional services that cost more than the property tax revenue generated

8. Cities are tempted to encourage luxury homes, which generate more property tax revenue than the cost of services provided, and discourage apartments, which may not be as "profitable," when comparing tax revenue with the cost of services.

9. The fear of increased property tax may cause some owners to do less property remodeling and maintenance, especially where tax assessors are quick to increase the assessed value when work is performed.

10. But the reverse is true, when specific work is exempted from property tax reappraisal. Examples include seismic retrofit (earthquake strengthening), solar hot water and electricity panels, or insulation.

These are but a few of the many ways in which government can influence how land is used through changes in property taxation. It should be stressed that any special concession to one type of property shifts the tax burden to some other property. In your community, who pays for church exemptions? Veteran's exemptions? Rural property exemptions? New business exemptions? Homeowner's exemptions? These issues are closely watched by real estate agents, appraisers, and investors.

REVIEWING YOUR UNDERSTANDING

Evaluating the Property Tax

1. What are some reasons that local officials give for continued use of the property tax? How much of your local government's revenue comes from property taxes? What is your largest local government expenditure?

2. What is meant by "shifting" the property tax? When is it difficult to shift the tax?

3. How does an increase in property taxes affect real estate values? How does it affect land use?

4. When people state, "Property taxes are regressive," what do they mean by regressive?

12.3 PROPERTY TAX REFORM

Property taxes are despised by property owners and tenants, labeled as regressive by economists, attacked by politicians up for election, and lobbied against by real estate trade organizations. Why does such an unloved tax still exist? If everybody hates it, why hasn't it been eliminated? This section examines property tax reform.

Political Realities

In spite of all its faults, the property tax, as mentioned earlier, does have a strong feature—it produces a fairly constant, predictable source of revenue that usually does not fluctuate widely with short-term movements in the business cycle. Local governments have experimented with other forms of taxation, including transfer taxes, sales tax, and income tax. However, most other taxes vary more than the property tax, and often are subject to more tax evasion. Another problem is that citizens resent new taxes. They approve the reduction or removal of existing taxes, but fight the introduction of a new, substitute tax. So it appears that until an acceptable substitute tax is devised, the property tax will remain. And there is also increasing political argument about what level of government services we as people want to provide. This in turn means arguments over whether to fund more services—increase taxes—or to reduce funding levels and decrease taxes.

Current Reforms

If people are stuck with the property tax, can it be modified to remove some of its inequities? Most criticism of the property tax concentrates on how regressive it can be. Thus, many reform proposals are aimed at aligning property taxes more closely with one's ability to pay. Several reforms are currently under way that can help to reduce the regressive features of the real property tax.

Exemptions for Low-Income People

Some communities have provided property tax exemptions for low-income people, especially the older, retired property owner. This exemption reduces the tax bite for people with low or fixed incomes, thereby shifting the property tax burden to those with higher incomes.

Exemptions for Homeowners

Some states have enacted laws exempting from taxation a flat dollar amount of the value of owner-occupied residential property. For example, the California **homeowner's exemption** provides a $7,000 value reduction, which works as follows:

Appraised Value	$500,000
Less: homeowner's exemption	−7,000
Assessed value for property tax purposes	$493,000

This gives some small degree of relief to homeowners, who arc usually unable to shift the property tax onto others.

Upgrading the Professional Skills of the Assessor's Office

Many states have established uniform assessment procedures to correct possible inequities in local assessors' offices. Statewide assessment rates, mandatory review procedures, and professional appraisal training are a few of the reforms. In most areas, the assessor is an elected official, and some reformers advocate changing this to a civil service appointment, to try to remove the possibility of political favoritism from the assessment procedure.

Placing a Limit on Property Taxes

A so-called "taxpayers revolt" began in California on June 6, 1978, when the voters passed Proposition 13, the Jarvis-Gann Initiative. Proposition 13 limits property taxes to 1 percent of the "full cash value" of the real property, plus an additional amount for local bonds (with limitations).

Beginning with a retroactive cutoff date of March 1975, property taxes can only be increased by a fixed amount, 2 percent per year or less, depending on the rate of inflation. However, the real estate is reassessed to full cash market value upon sale or other specified transfers of title. The effect is to limit property tax increases to 2 percent per year, measured from the time a property owner acquires title. Thus, two homeowners, side by side with identical homes, could have vastly different property tax bills, depending on how long each has owned the property. Several states have followed California's lead and enacted their own versions of Proposition 13.

Groups opposed to this property tax limitation concept have challenged the constitutionality of these laws, on grounds of unequal taxation. Some groups attack the concept based on the observation that owners of commercial and industrial properties get a better break than do homeowners. This argument points out that homes are bought and sold more often than commercial and industrial properties. Therefore, homes are reassessed and taxed at the new market price more often than business properties, and this shifts some of the property tax burden from business property owners to homeowners. In 1992, the U.S. Supreme Court declared Proposition 13 to be constitutional.

Henry George and The Single Tax

Library of Congress

Henry George (1839–1897) was a reformer, concerned about economic inequities. As a newspaperman in San Francisco, he wrote emotional articles about rising land values and profiteering. George outlined his philosophy in an 1880 book entitled *Progress and Poverty*.

George believed that land was a free commodity, like air and sunlight, and thus belonged to all the people. However, he did believe that individuals should be able to own all other types of property. He proposed that all rents for land were an unearned surplus, and should be taxed away and given to the government to help eliminate poverty. He envisioned that if landowners were charged 100% taxes on land value, they would still develop the land, because profits made from improvements would not be taxed. George argued that if all land were taxed as surplus value, enough revenue would be generated so that no other form of taxation would be required. This is called the **single tax theory**. It originated with Adam Smith, and was later advocated by Benjamin Franklin, Thomas Jefferson, and others. George became famous, and moved to New York. In 1886, he came close to being elected Mayor of New York.

The single tax was never widely adopted in the United States. Henry George had a tremendous impact on the idea of equity and taxing according to the ability to pay. Some current reform proposals regarding higher taxation on land and less on improvements have their roots in George's philosophy.

A number of cities in Pennsylvania, and several in Alabama, Delaware, and Maryland, use a two-rate system, with a higher land rate. Hong Kong gets 35% of its revenue from a land value tax. Taiwan, Singapore, Estonia, and some areas of Australia and Mexico also use a split rate.

Proposition 13, and similar property tax limits in other states, had several major effects on government financing. One was to shift more of the tax burden from property tax to sales tax, and to fees for government services. Another was to force cities, counties, and school districts to rely much more on state and federal funds, reducing their independence.

Possible Future Reforms

Other reform possibilities include increasing the tax burden assigned to land, and reducing the tax rate on improvements. If land is taxed at a higher rate than improvements, there would be an incentive to bring vacant land into use. Also, an incentive would exist for property owners to improve their properties, without the fear of a large increase in assessed value. However, there may be some practical problems in implementing this proposal, such as opposition from farmers and groups that wish to keep land as open space.

Another reform proposal suggests that inefficient, overlapping community services should be combined into larger regional units, to gain economies of scale. For example, instead of having individual city schools, water, sewer, road construction, and utility departments, there would be a combined regional system, thereby reducing overhead. However, others object that combinations such as this isolate government from the control of local citizens. To some degree, this type of consolidation has existed for some time. It is likely to increase, especially for utilities, police, and fire services.

Other Taxes Affecting Real Estate

People tend to forget that in addition to the property tax, there are many other taxes that affect real estate. Major examples include:

Capital gains tax	Transfer tax
Inheritance tax	Severance tax on
Gift tax	natural resources
Special assessments	Income tax

All of these taxes are controversial in their own right. Currently, the issue of the level of the real estate transfer tax is being hotly debated in many areas of the United States. In an effort to raise additional revenue, local governments are increasing the tax on the sale of real estate.

Often, a major change in the *level* of one of these taxes will cause a significant change in some type of real estate activity. The result will depend on who is affected and the nature of the effect. For example, the Savings and Loan Crisis of the late 1980s started with a real estate boom caused by a change to allow very favorable income tax depreciation rules.

REVIEWING YOUR UNDERSTANDING

Property Tax Reform

1. List four types of real property tax reforms.
2. List two types of real property tax exemptions. Who pays for these exemptions?
3. What was Henry George's idea?

CHAPTER SUMMARY

When government levies a tax, resources are diverted from the private sector to government, for redistribution according to the decisions of elected officials. Taxes are based on the ability to pay, the benefits received, or an equal split. Any tax can be analyzed to determine who bears the greatest burden relative to their ability to pay. A progressive tax, like the federal income tax, places a heavier burden on the wealthy. A regressive tax, like the sales tax and property tax, places a greater burden on the poor.

The property tax is used primarily by local governments and in most cases constitutes one of the largest source of total revenue received by schools, cities, and counties. The greatest criticism of the property tax is how regressive it is—the heaviest burden is placed on lower-income individuals. In spite of all its shortcomings, the property tax persists because it does have one saving grace: It generates a constant, steady, and predictable source of revenue that usually does not fluctuate widely with short-term movements in the business cycle.

Property taxes can reduce real estate income flows. If the taxes are not spent in a manner that enhances real estate, property values decline. The loss in value is the capitalized amount of the property tax. Property taxes can be used by local government to influence land usage. Preferential tax treatment will encourage certain kinds of development, whereas high taxes can discourage other development.

A number of property tax reforms have been used, including low-income exemptions, homeowner's exemptions, and upgrading the skills of tax assessment officials. However, reform does not mean elimination. In the immediate future, it appears that the property tax will remain as a major source of revenue for local governments.

REVIEWING YOUR UNDERSTANDING

1. All of the following sources of government revenue reduce private demand, *except*:
   A. taxes
   B. borrowing
   C. user fees
   D. printing money

2. Two major taxing philosophies are (1) ability to pay, and (2):
   A. redistribution
   B. regressive
   C. benefits received
   D. better distribution

3. As the taxpayer's income increases, the tax rate increases faster. This is an example of a:
   A. progressive tax
   B. proportional tax
   C. regressive tax
   D. reverse tax

4. Which of the following property owners is least able to shift a property tax increase to others?
   A. homeowner
   B. apartment landlord
   C. retail store owner
   D. office building owner

5. When measured against the income of the taxpayer, all of the following are considered by most economists to be regressive, *except*:
   A. property tax
   B. income tax
   C. sales tax
   D. lottery tickets

6. If the prevailing capitalization rate for real property is 10 percent, an increase in real estate taxes of $500 that cannot be shifted and is not beneficial to the subject property will cause a loss in value of approximately:
   A. $500
   B. $5,000
   C. $50,000
   D. $500,000

7. Taxes are used by governments to:
   A. raise revenue
   B. redistribute income
   C. encourage or discourage a private activity
   D. do all of the above

8. A charge levied by government to a developer for the cost of upgrading a city road, to accommodate the increased traffic caused by the proposed development, is a(n):
   A. ability-to-pay charge
   B. benefits-received charge
   C. progressive charge
   D. proportional charge

9. The main advantage of a property tax for local government is that it:
   A. is popular with voters
   B. swings quickly with changes in the local business cycle
   C. places a greater burden on the wealthy, as opposed to the modest landowner
   D. is easier to predict property tax revenue compared to other taxes

10. Regarding property tax limitations such as California's Proposition 13, which of the following is true?
    A. The tax is evenly spread across all homeowners
    B. Homeowners seem to get a better break than business property owners
    C. Tax expenditure decisions have shifted from local to state government
    D. All economists agree that the limitations are beneficial

11. Ultimately, all taxes are paid by:
    A. people
    B. government
    C. businesses
    D. corporations

12. When government borrows on a long-term basis to pay for current expenditures, this shifts the tax burden to future generations.
    A. true
    B. false

13. During peace time, the largest expenditure for the federal government is:
    A. defense
    B. education
    C. health and welfare
    D. employment costs

14. The largest expenditure for most city governments is:
    A. defense
    B. public safety
    C. education
    D. employment costs

15. The major tax for the federal government is:
    A. sales tax
    B. excise tax
    C. income tax
    D. property tax

16. The major tax for school districts is:
    A. sales tax
    B. inheritance tax
    C. income tax
    D. property tax

17. Which is considered a progressive tax?
    A. sales tax
    B. excise tax
    C. income tax
    D. property tax

18. The person legally obligated for a tax is always the same person who actually bears the burden for the tax.
    A. true
    B. false

19. Which item subject to taxation is the least apt to be hidden from the tax collector?
    A. income
    B. goods
    C. real estate
    D. profits

20. In a high demand market, if all businesses pay the same tax, there is a tendency to shift this tax to:
    A. stockholders
    B. customers
    C. other businesses
    D. employees

21. Lower-income people tend to spend a lower percentage of their income on housing costs.
    A. true
    B. false

22. Property tax exemptions for churches, veterans, and homeowners constitute a tax shift to owners of nonexempt properties.
    A. true
    B. false

23. The famous advocate of a 100 percent tax on land value as a substitute for all other taxes:
    A. Adam Smith
    B. Karl Marx
    C. John Maynard Keynes
    D. Henry George

24. Which of the following proposals would substitute one regressive tax for another?
    A. decrease property taxes and increase sales taxes
    B. decrease property taxes and increase income taxes
    C. decrease use of lottery revenue and increase income taxes
    D. decrease income taxes and increase sales taxes

25. Which of the following taxes can have an impact on real estate?
    A. transfer tax
    B. inheritance tax
    C. gift tax
    D. all of the above

CASE & POINT

Tax Talk ... Say What You Mean!

The so-called *T word* is considered politically dangerous for elected government officials! As a result, the language of taxation, in political circles, has changed from the standard economic definitions. Here are how some key tax phrases are used by economists and elected government officials.

Economists Say:	Elected Official Say:
"Tax"	"Revenue Enhancement" if they voted for the tax. If they voted against the tax, they call it a "tax."
"Tax Burden"	"Fair Share" if they voted for the tax. If they voted against the tax, they call it a "Tax Burden."
"Government Spending"	"Government Investment," unless they voted against the spending; then it is called "Pork."
"Tax Incentives"	"Tax Incentives," unless they voted against; then they call the incentives "Tax Loopholes."
"Tax Increase"	"Tax Reform," unless they voted against the increase; then they call it a "Tax Increase."
"Removing a Tax Exemption in Order to Raise Revenue"	"No New Taxes."
"A Need to Raise Taxes"	"Need for more government leadership," or "Need for public responsibility," or "The American people wish to increase their contribution."

CASE & POINT

The political reality is that many voters want to receive benefits from government programs, but are not willing to pay for them, or feel that someone else should pay for them. This presents a major problem for elected officials, who need to raise government revenue in order to fund programs that voters demand. If the politicians openly raise taxes, there is a good chance they may have problems at the polls at reelection time. Likewise, if they fail to deliver the government programs, they may not get reelected. To solve this dilemma, some elected government officials have resorted to the new language illustrated above.

Chapter

13

Affordable housing

Economic highest and best use

Eminent domain

Environmental controls

General plan

Inclusionary zoning

No-growth policy

Police power

Private deed restrictions

Property rights

Regional planning

Subdivision regulations

Urban planning

Zoning

PREVIEW

Land-use controls are controversial: Some people feel that land is a commodity, a useful thing, a staple to be bought and sold for personal advantage like any other product. They consider any type of land-use control an infringement on free enterprise. At the other extreme are those who believe land is a resource that belongs to all the people, the use of which should be completely controlled by public agencies. Somewhere in the middle is the view that land is both a commodity and a resource, which should be privately owned but used constructively to benefit society. At the heart of the controversy is the bundle of rights one has in property ownership.

Section 13.1 outlines the major forms of private and public land-use controls. Section 13.2 summarizes the principles of urban land-use planning. Section 13.3 examines recent land-use trends, noting nationwide emphasis on the environment, coastal zoning, and

Land-Use Controls

pollution regulations. The Case & Point at the end of the chapter presents two viewpoints regarding property rights. When you have completed this chapter, you will be able to:

1. List two reasons for the current controversy over land-use controls.
2. List two forms of private land-use controls and two forms of public land-use controls.
3. Describe the three major steps in creating a comprehensive plan for a community.
4. Describe recent trends in land-use controls.

13.1 TYPES OF LAND-USE CONTROLS

The current debate over public land-use controls has its roots in two economic concepts: (1) The supply of land at the right location is now scarce, and (2) many people view land as a resource, not just as a commodity.

In the frontier days, land was plentiful and inexpensive, and there was little concern over its use. Wastefulness was tolerated because of the seemingly inexhaustible supply. Land was treated as a commodity to be bought, sold, and speculated on, much like agricultural products.

With the settling of the West and the massive increase in urban population, land-use controls were deemed necessary to protect neighbors from each other and to protect and preserve the land. Governmental police powers affecting land use have increased. However, controls meant surrendering a degree of individual freedom and conflicted with the deep-rooted traditions of free enterprise and private property rights.

Today the land-use controversy centers on this question: To what extent can private land be controlled without destroying the principles of private property rights? There is no "right" answer to this question. Each person must make a decision based on his or her own interpretation of the issues. This section outlines private and public land-use controls.

Private Land-Use Controls

Private land-use controls refer to non-government regulation of land. Three major private controls are (1) economic highest and best use, and (2) private deed restrictions, and (3) easements.

Economic Highest and Best Use

In a pure capitalistic economy, the basic control over land use is market allocation: The interaction of supply and demand will eventually determine the highest and best use of land. Economic **highest and best use** is defined as that legal use that will produce the greatest net income attributable to the land at a specific location. In theory, if the market is left alone, competitive bidding would eventually determine what is the most profitable use of the land. Once this use has been established, it will continue until a more profitable use comes along. The private market controls land use through maximizing private profit.

In a pure capitalistic system, land control using the concept of economic highest and best use can work. But our capitalistic system is mixed, not pure, and the goal of private profit may not correspond with social goals. Under mixed capitalism, if private interests differ from social interests, private interests must frequently be modified to support social goals. In today's real estate market, the economic concept of highest and best use exerts a powerful influence on land use, but it is not the only one. Other private and public tools are used to modify land use in spite of profit considerations.

Private Deed Restrictions

Private land use can be controlled by the placing of restrictions in deeds. Private deed restrictions are commonly referred to as "covenants, conditions, and restrictions," or CC&Rs for short. The law of real property allows owners to limit the use of land by contract as long as the contract restrictions are not contrary to public policy. Although there are technical differences between a covenant, a condition, and a restriction, the basic concept is the same—they attempt to maintain property values by preventing land from being used in a manner that would hurt nearby properties. The importance of compatible nearby uses was stressed in Chapter 8.

Private deed restrictions are usually created in one of three ways:

(1) Existing property owners get together and agree to create restrictions mutually beneficial to all parties; (2) an owner of a large parcel of land sells off a portion or portions and inserts restrictions in the deed to protect his or her remaining parcels from adverse uses by the new neighbor(s); or (3) a land developer creates blanket tract restrictions for a new subdivision.

Recent inroads made by public controls have somewhat diminished the use of private deed restrictions. However, many questions not usually controlled by zoning or by codes can be handled by private restrictions. Examples include architectural uniformity, landscaping standards, light and air easements, maintenance agreements, and homeowner association controls. Some old deed restrictions even forbid the sale of alcohol forever.

Private deed restrictions for subdivisions created before the 1968 Civil Rights Act (also known as the Fair Housing Act) may forbid the sale of property to certain minority groups specifically identified in the private deed restrictions or CC&Rs. The 1968 Civil Rights Act expanded on previous civil rights acts and prohibited discrimination concerning the sale, rental, and financing of housing based on race, religion, and national origin. In 1974, gender was added. In 1988, the act protected the disabled and families with children. These discriminatory restrictions still exist in the recorded documents, but they are now legally void.

Easements

An **easement** is a document, a deed, that transfers a *limited* right of use to a defined property over to someone other than the owner. Usually, the easement is for the benefit of, or use with, another property. Some easements cover only a strip: a driveway or road easement, a pipeline or power line easement, or a water, sewer, storm drain, or drainage easement. Others might cover a larger area, even the whole property. Examples include an easement for low-flying planes close to an airport, or a height limit to protect someone else's view. And the easement might be an exclusive one, so no one else can use that driveway, or it might be non-exclusive, a road that can be used by everyone.

Because the easement deed gives some rights of use to someone else, it limits the uses left to the owner. Thus, easements are a form of private land-use control, and a common one.

Special Interest Topic

Land Use Control Through the Health Codes

Local Cities have attempted to restrict growth, maintain community culture and ambiance through various ingenious methods. The most common tool has been through the health codes. Communities have limited the number of water and sewer connections to developers through the high cost of connections or actually limiting the number of connections available. Limited water, sewer, and infrastructure resources are often cited in communities impacted by limited property tax revenue. Often the desire to keep a "small town" atmosphere, when people see their new town transformed by population growth.

Public Land-Use Controls

Industrialization and urban crowding have created a need for public controls to maintain order and promote social harmony. One way to maintain order is to control the use of the land. Government can use one or all of the following powers to control land use: (1) police power, (2) the power of eminent domain, (3) government spending power, and (4) the power of taxation. As taxation was discussed in Chapter 12, this section discusses only police power, eminent domain, and government spending.

Police Power

Police power refers to the constitutional right of the government to regulate private activity to promote the general health, welfare, and safety of society. Police power has often been used in the United States to direct land use. Some major examples of police power include zoning ordinances, building and health codes, setback requirements, pollution abatement, and rent controls. Of the many police power enactments, zoning and subdivision regulations emerge as the most influential methods of controlling land use.

Zoning

Zoning refers to the division of land into designated use districts. In zoning's simplest form, the land is divided into residential use, commercial use, industrial use, and rural use. Each use in turn can have several subclasses. For example, residential can be broken down into single-family, multifamily, and mobile home zones. Commercial zones are often divided into zones for retail, office, and wholesale space. Industrial zones can be divided into light industry and heavy industry, and rural zones into agricultural, resource, or recreational uses. In a large city, there can be several dozen different zones.

Often now, there are also combining districts, where the regular district might be combined with an added set of rules for one part of town. A common example is a hillside or slope combining district, applied just to those parts of the community that are sloping or hilly.

Zoning as a land control tool was not common in the United States until the 1920s. Prior to that time there was some doubt about the constitutionality of zoning, although early zoning laws can be traced to Colonial times. But in the 1926 landmark case of *Euclid v. Amber Realty Company*, the Supreme Court held that zoning was a reasonable exercise of government police power. Since this decision, every state has passed legislation allowing individual cities and counties to enact zoning ordinances.

Early zoning ordinances were aimed at safety and nuisance control. The idea was to use zoning to protect individual property values by prohibiting offensive use of surrounding land. The use of zoning has gradually been expanded, and now it is used to promote the general welfare of the entire community.

Subdivision Regulations

Another important use of the police power is **subdivision regulation**. Poorly conceived subdivisions, with inadequate streets and facilities, can become a burden to taxpayers in later years, when expensive redevelopment is needed to correct earlier oversights. Proponents of subdivision controls believe that the origin of some slums and urban blight can be traced to inadequate regulations. Opponents disagree, arguing that today's slums are the result of government ordinances that prevent land from rising to its economic highest and best use.

Today, subdivision regulations are used in most areas of the United States. Real estate developers are frequently required to provide water, sewer, storm drainage, paved streets, sidewalks, street lights, and school and park sites as a condition of being allowed to subdivide. The idea is to plan for the future at the inception and to require the purchaser of the subdivided lot, not the community as a whole, to pay the expense of added community facilities. Like all public controls, subdivision regulations are controversial in that they require the surrender of some individual rights in an attempt to promote the general welfare.

Eminent Domain

Police power allows government to regulate private land without the payment of compensation. The power of eminent domain is different in that it allows the government to acquire title to private land in

Special Interest Topic
Conflicts Between Police Power and Eminent Domain

POLICE POWER   EMINENT DOMAIN

Police power allows government to regulate private land without the payment of compensation, whereas eminent domain converts private property to public ownership and requires the payment of compensation. The question might be asked: How far can the government limit or interfere with the private use of land without taking the land for public use, which involves eminent domain and the payment of compensation? There is no clear answer. The line of distinction between the police power and eminent domain is fuzzy. Various courts have moved back and forth depending on the circumstances in each case.

exchange for the payment of just compensation. **Eminent domain** can be used for a variety of government land-use projects such as schools, parks, highways, public housing, and urban renewal.

Most levels of government may exercise power of eminent domain regardless of how unwilling the property owner may be. The main issue in most eminent domain cases is the amount of compensation. The courts have ruled that the property's fair market value is the usual basis for determining compensation. In addition, most federal and some state agencies must also pay for moving and other miscellaneous expenses incurred by any occupant being displaced, whether owner or tenant.

Special Interest Topic
Connecticut Eminent Domain Case Upheld by U.S. Supreme Court

The long-standing rules regarding the taking of private property for public good changed dramatically in 2005 as the U.S. Supreme Court upheld a taking of private, nonblighted property by a government municipality for private development.

The case of *Kelo v. City of New London, 545 U.S. 469 (2005)* was decided by the Supreme Court of the United States. It involved the use of eminent domain to transfer land from one private owner to another private owner to further economic development. The case arose from the condemnation by New London, Connecticut, of privately owned real property so that it could be used as part of a comprehensive redevelopment plan. The Court held in a 5–4 decision that the general benefits a community enjoyed from economic growth qualified such redevelopment plans as a permissible "public use" under the Takings Clause of the Fifth Amendment.

The new precedent changed the interpretation of Eminent Domain held since the *Berman v. Parker*, case 348 U.S. 26 (1954) was that property could be "taken" for private development only for public benefit.

Government Spending as an Influence on Land Use

Through its enormous spending power, the government can influence the use of land. The courts have held that the government can spend money for almost any purpose as long as it is for the benefit of the public. Government funds have been used to finance many types of real estate-oriented developments such as roads, dams, canals, and power facilities. In addition, governmental subsidies such as aid to farmers and FHA and VA (Veterans Administration) mortgage guarantees can influence land use. The spending power of the government is so great that it can direct some land use without the necessity of eminent domain, police power, or taxation.

REVIEWING YOUR UNDERSTANDING

Types of Land-Use Controls

1. List the two economic concepts that are at the root of the current land use control controversy.

2. List two private land-use controls and give one example of each.

3. List two public tools for controlling land use. Give two examples of each.

4. How does the power of eminent domain differ from the police power?

13.2 PRINCIPLES OF URBAN PLANNING

Since the early 1900s, the United States has shifted from a rural to an urban nation. In 1900, approximately 40 percent of the United States population lived in urban areas. By the mid-2000s, this percentage had increased to over 70 percent. Some states have even greater concentrations of population; well over 90 percent of Californians live in urban areas.

Most cities and suburbs were unprepared to handle this massive increase in urban growth. In some cases, the result has been overcrowding, slums, property tax problems, traffic congestion, and many other urban ills. Out of this confusion has risen the cry for better urban planning. This section describes the principles of urban planning.

Definition of Urban Planning

The dictionary defines planning as "thinking out acts and purposes beforehand." **Urban Planning** can be defined as anticipating and achieving community goals in light of social, economic, and physical needs. Urban planning requires that a community analyze its assets and liabilities, establish its goals, and then attempt to achieve these goals using land-use control as a primary tool.

The word planning causes apprehension among some people, because they fear planning will mean loss of economic and political freedom. Those who support the concept of urban planning believe that directing a community's growth presents no threat to personal freedom.

Creation and Implementation of Urban Planning

The establishment of a community plan requires three major steps:

(1) resource analysis, (2) formulation of community goals, and (3) implementation of the plan.

Resource Analysis

The first step in urban planning is to recognize the individual character of the community. What are its strong points? What are its weaknesses? To accomplish this, several substudies may be required, including an economic base study, a population trend study, a housing element study, a survey of existing land use, a city facilities study, and an analysis of the community's financial resources. Once a resource inventory has been taken, the next step is to formulate community goals in light of its resources.

Formulation of Community Goals

The formulation of community goals is the most difficult phase of urban planning because of the conflict among various special-interest groups, each trying to secure its own definitions of the community goal. However, citizen input should be encouraged, because a community plan must be based on the desires of community residents as a whole, not on the desires of staff planners alone.

Once the goals are established, a comprehensive plan to achieve these objectives must be formulated. The plan is frequently referred to as the **general plan**, and it should encompass all social, economic, and physical aspects of the desired growth. The plan should be long range but provide for short-range flexibility as the need for modification arises. Under no circumstances must the general plan be viewed as an inflexible, permanent fixture that will never require modification. A community's attitudes and resources can change, and the general plan must be modified to recognize these changes.

Implementation of the General Plan

The final step in urban planning is to implement the general plan. The implementation phase requires local government to use police power, eminent domain, taxation, and control over government spending to enact the plan. These powers have been discussed earlier, but it should again be stressed that the two most powerful tools for implementing a community plan are zoning and subdivision regulations.

Zoning can be used to separate incompatible land uses, promote health and safety standards, preserve property values, and minimize the cost of public improvements, whereas subdivision regulations can be used to chart the quality and quantity of future land division. When these two tools are used in conjunction with other public controls, the general plan has the best chance of being implemented.

If the general plan has been well conceived, and if it represents a consensus of the community, the implementation should proceed with a minimum of friction. On the other hand, if the community plan fails to represent citizen input, or if public agencies misuse the tools of implementation, the plan will meet with failure.

The Need for Regional Planning

Historically, planning has been a local matter. Each community developed its own plans within the confines of its own territorial limits. In the process, each community attempted to optimize its own

Special Interest Topic

Summary of Planning Terms

Planning commission—An appointed body of citizens charged with the responsibility of advising the elected board of supervisors or city council members in matters of land use.

Planning department—City or county staff employees who lend professional and technical assistance to elected officials.

Zone—An area defined on a map by a boundary line within which the land-use regulations are the same.

Rezoning—The process of changing the land-use regulations on specified property from one zone to another.

Variance—A deviation from the zoning regulations for a particular parcel.

Condition—A requirement imposed by the government in connection with the approval of a permit or a division of property.

Development plans—Plans showing the details of the proposed development. Normally includes a plot plan, architectural renderings, and factual information relative to acreage, building area, units, and parking.

Subdivision—A division of property into five or more parcels.

Lot split—A division of property into two, three, or four parcels.

Architectural review—Certain zoning areas in which a special citizen group approves or rejects the proposal based on its architectural compatibility with the surrounding area.

Appeal—The right to request review of a negative planning commission decision. The appellate process goes from the planning commission to the board of supervisors or city council to the courts.

LuLu—Stands for Local Undesirable Land Use, a slang phrase.

NIMBY—Stands for Not In My Back Yard, a slang phrase.

Host Community Benefits (Impact Fees)—Payments by a developer to local government in exchange for the right to proceed with the building project.

social and economic well-being, frequently at the expense of surrounding areas. For example, the placing of a smelly industrial plant on the border of one city has a spillover effect on the neighboring community downwind.

The growth of multicity metropolitan areas has underscored the need for more efficient **regional planning** for such projects as water and sewage systems, rapid transit, highway traffic patterns, airports, and pollution controls. Any attempt by individual cities to attack these problems can result in inefficient small-scale operations and needless duplication.

From an economic point of view, what might be needed is a regional government, with the power to tax and administer regional programs. However, from a political point of view, there is a widespread resistance to the creation of another layer of government. Moreover, local government officials are reluctant to surrender some of their power. What usually occurs is a compromise—a regional commission or district created to solve a single problem. Metropolitan rapid transit districts, regional park commissions, and regional water quality control boards are some examples.

William Penn (1644–1718)

THEORIES AND THEORETICIANS

Early American Planners

Library of Congress

Systematic land planning in the United States began with William Penn in 1682. Penn, an English Quaker and founder of the Commonwealth of Pennsylvania, began in 1682 to plan and design the city of Philadelphia. Using a checkerboard grid, he mapped out the city and a surrounding system of agricultural villages to help feed the city inhabitants. As a land promoter, Penn traveled throughout Europe selling land in an attempt to populate his colony. Penn died in 1718, deeply in debt.

THEORIES AND THEORETICIANS

Early American Planners

Pierre Charles L'enfant (1754–1825)

National Archives

L'Enfant was a French-born engineer and architect who fought for the colonies during the Revolutionary War. In 1791, L'Enfant was commissioned by George Washington to design a new federal city in the District of Columbia. Avoiding the grid street plan, L'Enfant designed a city of radiating streets with wide avenues and numerous parks. Two years later, a dispute with Congress led to L'Enfant's dismissal. Numerous disputes over compensation followed, and L'Enfant died in poverty in 1825, never seeing his dream city completed. However, many of his key ideas can be seen in the city today.

Regional planning is easiest to implement when the regional organization is given the power to tax and receive direct federal and state aid. If the regional commission depends wholly on annual grants from the treasury of individual cities within the geographic area, political infighting between cities tends to slow the implementation of regional planning.

Special Interest Topic

Special Purpose Districts at a Time of Limited Government Funding

The 500-Pound Canary "Where Can He Sing? Anywhere He Wants!"

A new actor in regional government has appeared at a time when most state, county, and city governments are laboring under limited tax revenues. The special purpose or regional parks and recreational district has become a new player in regional development. Special bond issues assessing small but regular per parcel taxes have provided enormous cash reserves for regional park growth while other government agencies struggle to maintain police and fire budgets.

This is the case with the East Bay Regional Park District, functioning in Alameda and Contra Costa Counties in California. The Park District was established in 1934 and is the largest regional park system in the United States. Measures AA, passed in 1988, and WW, passed in 2008, have raised over $500 million. Of this amount, $375 million (75%) of revenue will fund Regional Park acquisition and capital projects. The bond issue was passed by a 75% vote of the electorate. The large capital reserve was developed at a special tax rate of $10 per year per $100,000 of assessed valuation (i.e., the owner of a home assessed at $400,000 will pay $40 per year). Note that California property taxes are capped by Proposition 13 at 1% of market value at sale. The property owner in the aforementioned home assessed at $400,000 would pay $4,000 annually in property taxes. The special tax of only $40 per year seems a small amount but look at its impact.

The East Bay Regional Park District, at the time of this writing, is able to purchase just about any parcel it wishes while many local governments and school districts are contemplating insolvency. The Park District has an aggressive plan to acquire large parcels of land in compliance with its General Plan.

There seems to be a movement toward more planning on a regional basis. The impact of this planning will depend on the willingness to forgo some local control in favor of a regional commission. In some cases, local communities have little choice because national and state legislation may require regional controls. But, required or not, regional planning will work best if it can be proven to local citizens that the result will be better coordination and perhaps a savings of tax dollars. If the evidence is to the contrary, regional planning will meet tremendous resistance.

REVIEWING YOUR UNDERSTANDING

Principles of Urban Planning

1. What is the purpose of urban planning?
2. List three major steps needed to establish a community plan.
3. What are the two most powerful tools for implementing a community plan?
4. Why is regional planning being used?

13.3 RECENT TRENDS IN LAND-USE CONTROLS

As stated earlier, land-use controls are controversial. At the core of the controversy is the recognition that usable land is a scarce resource that needs some public controls. But how much control is needed? There are those who feel that recent land-use controls are too stringent, whereas others feel that more controls are needed.

Some recent and controversial land-use controls include: (1) control over premature subdivisions, (2) pollution and environmental regulations, (3) slow-growth or no-growth policies, (4) the creation of new towns, (5) state and federal intervention in land-use controls, and (6) inclusionary zoning. Many of these are interrelated and are a by-product of the environmental movement.

Preventing Premature Subdivisions

Public control over the subdividing of land has existed for decades, but there has recently been a concerted effort to control what is known as a premature subdivision. A subdivision is "premature" when home construction fails to take place after the subdivision lots are sold. Frequently, the developer has already dedicated the streets, sewers, and other off-site facilities to the local government. Local government then finds itself in the position of having to maintain the unused facilities. The lack of home construction fails to generate the needed property tax revenue, and the local government is put in a financial bind. For small, rural governments, this situation can be especially painful.

To reduce the risk of having premature subdivision, some planning agencies require would-be developers to show the likelihood of home construction as one of the conditions for obtaining a subdivision permit. This requirement, along with the difficulty in meeting environmental regulations, has caused subdivision activity to decline in many rural areas.

Pollution and Environmental Regulations

Beginning in the 1960s and continuing today, there has been a tremendous amount of federal legislation dealing with pollution and environmental issues, including water and air quality, waste disposal, resource recovery, endangered species, coastal preservation, and environmental impact report requirements, just to name a few. State efforts at pollution and environmental protection have produced similar laws. **Environmental controls** have greatly complicated the real estate development process.

Much of this legislation seeks to regulate land use to minimize environmental damage. Before a construction project is approved, the developer must show what impact the proposed project will have on the environment. The permit-issuing agency then decides, after first consulting with experts and holding public hearings, whether to issue the permit.

Like other controls, pollution and environmental regulations increase the cost of land development in terms of both time and money.

The contents of an environmental impact report will be discussed in more detail in Chapter 15.

Slow-Growth and No-Growth Policies

For many years, communities and local business groups spent large sums of money advertising the amenities of their area in an attempt to attract industry and people. Their goal was more growth. However, increased congestion and pollution have led some communities to reverse their positions, adopting slow-growth or no-growth policies.

Communities can discourage growth by making it difficult to build a home or by preventing the establishment of businesses that will create jobs. Land-use controls can be an effective tool in discouraging unwanted growth. For example, a community can keep additional people out by converting vacant land to public parks. Or it can allow only the affluent to move into a community by creating zones for expensive homes. Another common slow-growth policy tool is to only allow a limited number of building permits each year. Builders competing for permits are required to submit proposals that are rated on how "beneficial" each is to the community. A community can prevent business expansion by creating tough pollution standards, levying excessive taxes, or by preventing the construction of new transportation facilities.

A case can be made for slow- or no-growth policies by stressing the need to preserve open space, to avoid pollution, to maintain the community's way of life, and to keep from straining community fiscal budgets. However, equally good cases can be made against no-growth policies by pointing out that they can discriminate against lower-income persons who are attempting to improve their status. A **no-growth policy** can freeze low-income people at their present level by reducing economic opportunities, which in turn can prevent upward social mobility.

On a national basis, the only effective no-growth policy is a decrease in the rate of population growth. However, on a state or local basis, no-growth can be achieved by shifting the burden of population growth to another state or community. This naturally leads to infighting and dissension among states and communities. Several court cases are currently attempting to resolve the no-growth question by delineating the right of the government to control growth and the rights of individuals to live and work where they please. Once this question is resolved, the answer will have a significant impact on local real estate activity.

The Creation of New Towns

Among planners a debate exists about whether urban density can best be relieved by (1) creating new towns in rural areas; (2) shifting people to existing smaller cities; or (3) leaving the countryside as it is and redeveloping the major cities to accommodate more people.

Planners who favor the creation of new towns believe that, in the long run, it is more economical to build entire new cities to handle population increases than to attempt to redevelop existing major cities. The new cities would be self-contained, so that people could live, work, and shop with a minimum of commuting. Columbia, Maryland, and Reston, Virginia, although several decades old, are two examples of such "new" cities.

Others feel that instead of building entire new cities, the government should encourage the growth of existing small towns. Greatest emphasis would be placed on enlarging towns in economically depressed areas, where such action would help fight chronic unemployment. A key proposal is to use government contracts or subsidies to entice businesses to relocate to the depressed regions.

Some planners are critical both of the new town concept and of the idea of encouraging growth in existing smaller towns. They believe that the problems of urban America will not evaporate with the development of new cities. They also believe that it is improper to destroy the culture of existing rural areas by importing population from major cities. Instead, this group believes that the best solution is to redesign existing metropolitan areas to allow for living with a higher density. The planners note that by European standards our major cities are under-populated and that through good design we can increase the number of people per acre without an increase in their feeling of being crowded. This can be accomplished by converting our existing horizontal parking spaces, residential areas, and shopping centers to mid-rise or high-rise buildings, thus instantly generating more space without expanding the city limits. However, planners who favor new towns or the expansion of existing smaller cities rebut by stating that given the opportunity, people prefer low- as opposed to high-density living.

Although planners disagree on the best solution for urban congestion, most do agree that any solution is going to require massive government assistance in at least two forms: land assemblage, using the government's power of eminent domain; and financial assistance to build initial off-site improvements such as streets, sewers, water plants, and other basic facilities. However, the building of new towns or reconstruction of existing cities need not be totally a government project. After the initial planning, land acquisition, and off-site development financing have taken place, the project can be turned over to private enterprise for completion. The combination of urban dwellers seeking better surroundings and profit-motivated businesses willing to provide these surroundings could produce the economic setting needed to help defeat urban congestion.

State and Federal Intervention in Land-Use Controls

In the past, land-use controls were essentially a local matter. Cities and counties enacted land controls to achieve their own goals. However, recent urban pressures have increased the amount of land regulation at the state and federal level. There is a feeling that some problems are too large for a single city to handle, or that self-interest causes some communities to seek a solution that has a detrimental effect on a neighboring community.

Metropolitan problems have led to the creation of regional commissions charged with overseeing the activities of all regions within the state. An example of a regional-state relationship is the California Coastal Zone Conservation Act of 1972. This act recognizes that the coast of California "belongs to all the people and that it has a delicately balanced ecosystem that should be permanently protected." The act requires local regions and communities to incorporate coastal planning into their general plan. Each local entity is charged with controlling coastal development within its area, but the state commission established guidelines that local planners must follow. Further, the Coastal Commission not only establishes but also enforces the guidelines, and adjudicates the appeals. In this instance, the Commission embodies the legislative, executive, and judicial functions of government in one agency, sparking constitutional questions about its authority.

On a still higher level, there is considerable discussion whether the federal government should enact a comprehensive national land-use policy. The proposal would require each state to adopt a statewide environmental, recreational, and industrial land-use plan. The federal plan would require the establishment of industrial, conservation, and recreational sanctuaries. Federal grant-in-aid funds would be available to assist states in creating and maintaining the plan. To assure adoption, the federal government would use its power to withdraw federal aid and expenditures from any state that failed to comply with the regulations. This threatened loss of federal funds would assure state compliance.

People in favor of more state and federal land-use controls believe that an overall general plan for land use is needed. They note that many communities have general plans for development within local boundaries and that state and national governments should likewise have a general plan for land within their boundaries.

Opposition to state and national land-use controls comes from individuals who argue that the power of land regulation should be limited to local government. They fear that planning on a state or federal level would not be sensitive to local needs. Who is correct? Like most issues of land-use controls, the correct answer depends on one's value judgment.

Inclusionary Zoning

Inclusionary zoning is a type of regulation that requires a developer of new residential housing to set aside a designated number of units for low- and moderate-income people. If the project is an apartment complex, the developer must rent a percentage of the units to low-income people at specified below-market rent. If the project offers houses for sale, a certain percentage must be sold at below-market prices. To assure that the units will remain available to low-income families after the initial sale, restrictions are inserted in the deed.

If a developer does not provide units per the inclusionary ordinance, either the building permit is denied, or in some cases an in-lieu fee is paid to the government entity. To entice builders to cooperate, many inclusionary zoning ordinances provide for density bonuses, by which the builder is allowed to construct more units per acre.

Again, there is a financial cost. Inclusionary zoning does incur a cost. The price of other units in the development usually must be increased to offset the losses the builder incurs on the below-market priced units. In essence, the buyers of regular units subsidize the buyers of the below-market priced units. Thus, the burden for providing **affordable housing** units is shifted from the government sector to the private sector. Inclusionary zoning laws are highly controversial, and the issue is constantly under legal challenge.

Land-Use Controls and the Real Estate Industry

The trend seems to be set—more and more public control over private land use. Instead of being just a vehicle for the production of profit, land will more than likely also be viewed as a resource to be used to achieve social as well as economic well-being. As this attitude toward land use expands, the real estate industry must participate in the decision-making process to present its views. Both property owners and the real estate industry must see that land-use regulations consider the views of all the citizens, not just those of a select few. The key is to eliminate the undesirable aspects of poor land management while maintaining the good qualities of private real estate ownership.

Special Interest Topic

The National Affordable Housing Act (2007)

The National Affordable Housing Trust Fund is the largest expansion in federal housing programs in decades, with a goal of producing, rehabilitating, and preserving 1.5 million housing units over the next ten years. The bill initially allocated $1 billion annually directly to states and local communities. The program, administered by HUD, is designed to serve more subprime borrowers at affordable rates and terms, recapture borrowers that may have received risky loan products in recent years, and offer refinancing opportunities to borrowers currently struggling. The law allows Trust Fund monies for construction, rehabilitation, acquisition, preservation incentives (including for manufactured housing and community land trusts), and operating assistance to facilitate affordability. Funds may be used for both rental housing that is affordable and for down payment and closing cost assistance by first-time homebuyers.

This is a difficult task that will require cooperation and compromise from preservationists, conservationists, environmentalists, private real estate interests, government, and all other groups who are interested in real estate use.

REVIEWING YOUR UNDERSTANDING

Recent Trends in Land-Use Controls

1. List two examples of recent pollution and environmental regulations that have influenced land use in your area. Are they local, regional, state, or federal land-use controls?

2. Some economists state that no-growth policies are discriminatory against lower-income people. What reasons do they give to justify their statement?

3. Why have some recent land-use regulations been adopted by the state, as opposed to local, government?

CHAPTER SUMMARY

The current debate over public land-use controls has its roots in two economic concepts: (1) the supply of land at the right location is scarce, and (2) the public is viewing land as a resource, not just a commodity. Land-use controls can be divided into two broad categories: private controls and public controls. Private land-use controls include economic highest and best-use decisions, private deed restrictions, and easements. Public land-use controls include the use of government police power, eminent domain, government spending patterns, and taxation. Increased urban density has created a need for land planning. Planning can be defined as "anticipating and achieving community goals in light of the community's social, economic, and physical needs."

The establishment of a community plan requires three major steps: (1) resource analysis, (2) formulation of community goals, and (3) implementation of the plan. Zoning and subdivision regulations are the two most powerful tools for implementing a community's general plan. With the growth of multicity metropolitan areas, some planning power has shifted from the local community to regional commissions.

Recent trends in land-use controls include the prevention of premature subdivisions, pollution and environmental regulations, slow-growth or no-growth policies, the debate over the creation of new towns, and state and federal intervention. The trend seems to be toward more public control over private land uses. This has caused a polarization of the issue. There are those who feel present land controls are too stringent and are a threat to our economic system. Others believe that more controls are needed. Proper land-use control is a difficult issue that will require cooperation and compromise among all interested groups.

REVIEWING YOUR UNDERSTANDING

1. The land-use controversy is a debate over whether land should be viewed as a resource or:
   A. a commodity
   B. an asset
   C. an investment
   D. a possession

2. Critics of government use of land-use controls feel that it infringes on:
   A. zoning
   B. property rights
   C. eminent domain
   D. equal protection

3. A real estate example of government use of police power is:
   A. zoning
   B. property rights
   C. eminent domain
   D. equal protection

4. A real estate example of private land-use control is:
   A. zoning
   B. eminent domain
   C. deed restrictions
   D. inclusionary exceptions

5. Private deed restrictions are created in all of the following ways, except:
   A. mutual agreement among property owners
   B. deed reservations
   C. blanket tract restrictions
   D. government action

6. Government can control private land use by:
   A. tax incentives
   B. police power
   C. government spending patterns
   D. all of the above

7. Which of the following best describes the current philosophy behind government zoning ordinances? The purpose of zoning is to promote:
   A. property rights
   B. general welfare
   C. city development
   D. traffic flow

8. A community's general plan exerts more government control over private land use than does a community's health codes.
   A. true
   B. false

9. The creation of a community general plan requires resource analysis, formation of goals, and:
   A. federal guidelines
   B. urban analysis
   C. health codes
   D. implementation

10. A wrench is to a mechanic as _____ is to a planner.
    A. money
    B. escheat
    C. zoning
    D. a reference book

11. Which of the following is true?
    A. land-use controls reduce the cost of building homes
    B. environmental regulations reduce the cost of building homes
    C. it is usually easy and fast to obtain government permits for a new housing development
    D. government controls have probably increased the quality of homes

12. The legal use of land at a specific location that will produce the greatest net income is called:
    A. the right to use
    B. highest and best use
    C. intensified use
    D. economic use

13. Government taking of private land in exchange for just compensation is called:
    A. escheat
    B. police power
    C. forfeiture
    D. eminent domain

14. Government's design for the future of a community is called the:
    A. general plan
    B. economic base plan
    C. housing element plan
    D. demographic plan

15. The two most powerful tools for implementing a community's general plan are zoning and health codes.
    A. true
    B. false

16. When an individual parcel of land is given approval to deviate from a zoning regulation, it is called:
    A. rezoning
    B. CC&Rs
    C. variance
    D. restrictive use

17. A subdivision of vacant residential land is considered premature when:
    A. roads are paved prior to construction
    B. sewer and water improvements are put in before homes
    C. school sites are set aside for the future
    D. home construction fails to occur

18. Slow-growth policies that limit the number of annual homebuilding permits:
    A. are examples of supply and demand in balance
    B. tend to decrease local home prices
    C. tend to increase local home prices
    D. do not distort real estate market forces

19. A pro-growth government policy can bring more:
    A. jobs
    B. pollution and congestion
    C. housing construction
    D. all of the above

20. A no- or slow-growth government policy can bring reduced:
    A. jobs
    B. pollution and congestion
    C. housing construction
    D. all of the above

21. On a national basis, the only effective no-growth policy is a decrease in the rate of population growth. But on a state or local basis, no-growth can occur by shifting the population growth to another state or community.
    A. true
    B. false

22. A type of land-use control that requires a builder to set aside a certain number of units for low-to moderate-income people as a condition for obtaining a building permit is:
    A. inclusionary zoning
    B. fair housing law
    C. affordable domain
    D. equal housing rights

23. Debates regarding the solutions to urban density include:
    A. creating new towns in rural areas
    B. shifting urban dwellers to existing smaller cities
    C. redeveloping urban areas to accommodate more people
    D. all of the above

24. Which of the following is a trend in land-use controls?
    A. more state and regional control as opposed to local control
    B. more environmental regulations
    C. more shifting of costs from government to subdivision buyers
    D. all of the above are trends

25. The trend seems set: Land in the future will be viewed by government as a resource, not just a vehicle for the production of profit.
    A. true
    B. false

Property Rights: Two Viewpoints

Historically, the word property did not only refer to the thing owned but also included the right or interest that the owner had in the item possessed. Today, the word refers to both meanings.

The basic property rights are embodied in the "Bundle of Rights":

- The right to possess
- The right to use
- The right to encumber (borrow against)
- The right to dispose
- The right to exclude others

The current controversy over land-use controls centers around the extent to which these private property rights should be limited to promote the public welfare. Here are two viewpoints.

Viewpoint I

Government has gone too far. The U.S. Constitution bans the taking of private property without the payment of just compensation. All levels of government, whether federal, state, or local, in their desire to control private activity have come up with a sinister way of "taking" private land without paying for it. Government does this by placing excessive restrictive regulations on private landowners. Through zoning, building codes, health codes, and environmental laws, government has been able to box private landowners into a corner. The landowner cannot use the land, and government does not have to pay for it, because it is merely "regulating," not taking the land. Shame on the government for trampling on the rights of property owners! The reason government is taking this approach is simple: Citizens would not allow government to increase taxes to outright pay for the land, so government has come up with a sneaky way to circumvent basic property rights and the U.S. Constitution.

CASE & POINT

But at last, there appears to be some form of hope. In 1994, by a 5 to 4 decision, in the case of *Dolan v. City of Tigard*, the U.S. Supreme Court ruled that the City of Tigard, Oregon, could not require Florence Dolan to turn over 10 percent of her land for a storm drain and bicycle path in exchange for a building permit to enlarge her existing hardware and plumbing store. Perhaps this is the signal that will stop government from forcing private property owners to pay for public improvements.

Viewpoint 2

Get real! People do not "own" land; they are only the current caretakers. All of the land in the United States is owned by the government. If you don't believe it, don't pay your property taxes and see who gets the land! Government regulations over private land use are just another extension of laws needed to maintain an orderly society—no different from the need for traffic lights.

When you purchase real estate you are granted the right to occupy it until you sell, give it away, or die. You purchase this right with the full knowledge that your use is subject to an existing governmental control called zoning. The price you paid for this right was based on this knowledge. Along with most investments, land ownership carries risks. Although your land was zoned a certain way at acquisition, there is no guarantee things will stay the same. Change is a fact of life. If the land is currently zoned agricultural and you wish to enhance its value by attempting to rezone it commercial or residential, you have the right to apply for a rezoning. But you do not have any God-given right to the change. You knew what the zoning was when you purchased, and you took your chances.

CASE & POINT

Society is dynamic, not static. "Things happen." Therefore, if you wish to purchase the right to use real estate, you must recognize that as society changes, the allowed use of your land could also be changed by duly elected officials representing the wishes of a democratic society. Therefore, if your land is "down-zoned," you lose; if it is "up-zoned," you win. Welcome to the world of risk taking. If you don't like it, stay a renter!

Chapter 14

IMPORTANT TERMS AND CONCEPTS

Building
  construction

CPM®

Green building

Homebuilding
  industry

Impact fees

IREM®

Land development

LEED® certification

Nonresidential
  construction

Public works
  construction

Residential
  construction

Special assessment
  bonds

PREVIEW

This chapter outlines the principles of real estate development. Section 14.1 focuses on real estate construction activity, with special emphasis on the economic characteristics of the homebuilding industry. Section 14.2 deals with the development and building process and features flow charts that illustrate the steps in real estate development. The Case & Point at the end of the chapter explores the economic effects of the great wave of overbuilding in the 1980s. When you have completed this chapter, you will be able to:

1. List three categories of real estate construction.

2. List five economic characteristics of the homebuilding industry.

3. Differentiate between land development and construction.

4. Describe the six major phases of land development and construction.

Real Estate Development

14.1 REAL ESTATE CONSTRUCTION

Real estate construction is a major contributor to the economic expansion of the United States. Each year, new construction generates billions of dollars in income and directly or indirectly employs several million workers. This section outlines the various categories of real estate construction and then concentrates on the economic characteristics of the homebuilding industry.

Construction Activity

Real estate construction activity can be divided into three main categories: residential, nonresidential, and public works. **Residential construction** includes single-family dwellings, condominiums, and multifamily apartments. The volume of residential construction is closely tied to movements in the mortgage money market, employment, and personal income. When people are working and mortgage credit is available at reasonable interest rates, residential construction tends to accelerate. During periods of high unemployment or tight mortgage credit, residential construction and existing home prices decline. (See Tables 14.1 and 14.2.)

TABLE 14.1 Value of New California Construction

Type of Construction (Millions of dollars)	1997	2002	2007
Residential	$18,752	$33,305	$28,621
Nonresidential	$12,700	$14,529	$22,542

Source: Statistical Abstract of California 2010

TABLE 14.2   California Median Home Prices for the Period 1982–2009, By Region

Year	Statewide Average	Central Valley	High Desert	Los Angeles County	Monterey	Northern California	Northern Wine Country	Orange County
1982	$105,937	$72,200		$119,260	$113,890	$87,610	$91,697	$129,641
1983	107,393	73,210		118,540	112,585	85,650	94,723	131,456
1984	106,169	74,600		121,270	120,740	87,448		130,668
1985	109,063	75,600		124,790	129,119	89,661	98,077	132,758
1986	119,499	77,310		135,390	146,057	92,098	111,023	144,441
1987	128,048	82,410		146,630	161,787	93,672	119,128	163,218
1988	151,184	87,190		178,890	185,658	102,426	132,470	203,860
1989	177,009	97,370	92,700	214,830	232,191	115,075	160,802	241,708
1990	185,104	116,330	105,090	212,130	237,732	143,801	179,178	242,150
1991	185,174	118,730	112,250	218,580	233,660	135,020	185,740	239,680
1992	182,504	119,430	111,040	210,790	225,960	131,680	194,030	234,290
1993	177,928	115,890	108,440	195,430	224,150	138,430	190,640	222,280
1994	176,683	113,370	101,310	189,170	225,610	136,960	188,760	215,050
1995	172,394	108,410	97,340	179,900	226,810	136,830	189,250	209,660
1996	174,118	107,480	96,920	172,890	234,250	137,250	182,350	213,480
1997	186,118	109,140	96,380	176,520	259,000	134,880	191,340	229,960
1998	201,368	114,980	95,170	191,700	283,370	140,500	215,470	261,890
1999	221,019	120,600	84,340	198,980	333,650	150,100	245,600	280,900
2000	259,366	133,380	93,070	215,900	401,980	162,560	304,960	310,730
2001	284,898	157,250	111,660	241,370	425,140	176,340	344,800	350,810
2002	322,965	189,210	129,570	290,030	450,950	215,900	374,610	404,980
2003	370,799	225,210	157,300	355,340	490,460	264,520	425,490	483,240
2004	460,486	279,530	223,150	446,380	612,970	323,480	495,120	630,040
2005	540,087	347,200	291,830	529,010	703,740	382,600	621,170	693,280
2006	561,975	362,910	330,380	583,920	712,270	382,680	620,040	713,160
2007	561,122	324,590	296,380	593,610	727,870	358,760	589,050	709,540
2008	390,439		173,080	402,110	385,060	302,040	396,380	533,200
2009	324,077		115,410	333,920	275,330	260,820	346,350	477,240

Source: California Association of REALTORS®, Annual Historical Data Summary 2010. http://www.car.org/

Nonresidential construction consists of retail and office buildings, industrial plants, and institutional buildings such as schools and libraries. Nonresidential construction activity usually parallels changes in the business cycle. When real GDP is growing and the economy is experiencing prosperity, nonresidential construction increases. When there is a downturn in economic activity, nonresidential construction tapers off.

Public works construction refers to the building of streets, sewer systems, highways, bridges, and public projects other than buildings. Many public works projects are financed by federal grants supplemented by local matching funds. During periods of economic prosperity, tax revenues for local and state governments increase, thereby stimulating public works construction. In economic downturns local tax revenues decline, but at the same time government attempts to fight a recession by increasing its spending. This has been particularly evident as Congress passed the $787-billion American Recovery and Reinvestment Act of 2009, a.k.a. the 2009 Stimulus Package. The biggest effects will occur in 2010 as state and local government spend federal stimulus money on infrastructure such as roads, bridges, transit, and other projects. Private residential and commercial building starts are down, but bridges, repaving, new overpasses, bullet trains, and asphalt spreading are up. The unprecedented spending by Congress to take the country out of its recession surpasses even that of the Great Depression. The changes in public works construction normally do not fluctuate as widely as do changes in residential and nonresidential construction.

Table 14.3 shows the value of California new construction by categories as a percentage of total construction for select years. These figures show that residential construction tends to be 55–70 percent, and nonresidential 30–45 percent of non-government new construction. The "mortgage meltdown" and the lack of residential loan financing greatly affected the ratio of residential to nonresidential building.

Characteristics of the Homebuilding Industry

The **homebuilding industry** is noted for its booms and busts. Periods of high rates of construction are followed by hefty declines in buying and construction. Why does new residential construction fluctuate? Why isn't the rate of new home construction steady and predictable? The answer lies with the economic characteristics of the homebuilding industry, presented in the following list:

1. The industry is comprised of many small, independent builders and a few hundred large, corporate companies. This means that in some less-populated areas homebuilding is a local operation that cannot generate enough production to gain savings from large-scale building.

TABLE 14.3 Value of New California Nongovernment Construction as a Percentage of New Total

	1997	2002	2007
Residential construction	59.6	69.6	55.9
Nonresidential construction	40.4	30.4	44.1

Source: California Statistical Abstract 2010.

Special Interest Topic
Manufactured and Mobile Homes

Skyrocketing land values and construction costs have priced many people out of the conventional housing market. Older people living on fixed incomes and others who own large homes may wish to reduce expenses by selling their existing homes and moving into less-expensive quarters. For these people and many others, the answer has been manufactured and mobile home living.

Manufactured and mobile homes comprise 20–30% of all new single-family home sales in the United States. Mobile home dealers could probably increase their sales even more if a sufficient number of manufactured and mobile home sites could be located. In some areas, manufactured and mobile homes are allowed to occupy inferior locations only. This discrimination can be traced to the transient trailer-type camps of the 1930s. However, today's mobile homes are not trailers, nor are they very mobile. Studies have shown that four out of five manufactured and mobile homes are set on a site and never moved again. In fact, it is becoming more difficult to distinguish the better manufactured and mobile homes from conventional homes. Some units come with wood shingle siding, step-down living rooms, two baths, and three bedrooms. Some have second stories. They can be purchased using FHA, VA, or conventional financing.

Special Interest Topic

The Price of New Homes Sets a Ceiling on the Price of Existing Homes

Whenever the demand for homes is strong, prices for existing properties tend to rise. What stops them from rising dramatically, however, is that they get too close to the cost of building a comparable new home. Buyers generally refuse to pay a high amount for an older home when the same money can purchase a new home. Thus, the cost of new homes sets a ceiling on existing home prices. The cost of relatively new homes now in foreclosure depresses the prices of existing, nonforeclosed homes even further. The long-term price trend for older homes will follow along just under the cost trends for comparable new construction (including the impact of lot price trends).

2. It is relatively easy to enter the homebuilding industry. A skilled construction worker can usually start a small company with a limited amount of capital. This ease of entry, coupled with inadequate capital backing, can generate a high failure rate in the smaller-scale segment of the homebuilding industry.

3. As a result of a long physical and economic life, residential homes last for many years. In any given year, the supply of new homes rarely adds more than 2 percent to the total supply of homes in the United States. In short, a home does not wear out rapidly, and thus the replacement demand is low. A homebuilder, unlike an automobile manufacturer, cannot count on the replacement market to bolster activity.

4. Home construction is heavily influenced by the actions of government. The government can stimulate housing construction with

special financing programs such as the FHA, or it can retard housing construction through environmental controls or burdensome real property taxation, or, most important, increased interest rates.

5. The homebuilding industry depends on liberal mortgage credit terms, so that prospective homebuyers can finance the purchase of new homes.

From the preceding list, it is apparent that homebuilding can be a fragmented industry, comprised of many small-scale local builders who depend on the whims of others for their survival, counterbalanced by a few large-scale construction companies who can build thousands of homes in a single year. But in spite of handicaps, the homebuilding industry as a whole is making some innovative progress in green construction technology, building design, and cost controls. The standardization of parts, the creation of better tools, and the prefabrication of building components have helped to streamline the construction process. To continue this rate of innovation will require a positive attitude from lenders, government, construction workers, and homebuyers alike.

REVIEWING YOUR UNDERSTANDING

Real Estate Construction

1. List two other categories of construction besides residential.
2. List five economic characteristics of the homebuilding industry.
3. Explain why lending institutions and governmental agencies are important to homebuilders.

14.2 THE DEVELOPMENT AND BUILDING PROCESS

The creation of a new real estate project needs managerial talent to plan, coordinate, and control the factors of production discussed in Chapter 2 (land, labor, and capital). This managerial skill is provided by developer–investors, contractors, and architects, all of whom are instrumental in the creation of a successful real estate development. This section outlines the development and construction process.

Land Development and Construction

The production of urban real estate can be broken down into two major categories: land development and building construction. **Land development** refers to subdividing and preparing the land for building, and **building construction** refers to the actual erection of buildings and improvements. However, before private land development and building construction begin, at least four factors should be thoroughly investigated: market analysis, government approvals, adequate financing, and a reasonable profit margin.

Market Analysis

Prior to undertaking a real estate project, a developer should conduct an in-depth market analysis to estimate whether adequate buyer demand exists for the proposed project. Market analysis techniques vary according to whether the study is for residential, commercial, industrial, or rural purposes. But regardless of the nature of the proposed project, certain questions need to be answered: What is the present and future demand for this type of real estate, in numbers and price levels? Is the proposed site a good location? Are buyers ready to purchase? At what price? With what features? If not now, when? What is the current and future supply? Are there other sellers? What does the competition plan to do in the future? Is now the right time for this project? These questions form the heart of a market analysis and should be answered before any firm commitments are made. The time to be concerned with sales potential is before the project begins, not after!

Government Approvals

A real estate project is not possible unless proper government permits can be obtained. Meeting government regulations, such as zoning, building codes, density maximums, environmental reports, and utility requirements, is an essential step in any real estate development. A developer must be familiar with the relevant government requirements for this project and must assess the likelihood of obtaining government approval. The key factor is the time needed to obtain approval. Long delays because of government "red tape" can cause a project to fail, the victim of missed sales and increased cost for land, labor, materials, and capital. A careful review of the time needed and the penalties for delays is essential. Government reports and their time delays will be discussed in greater detail in the next chapter. In addition, it is critical to identify all costs that governments will require the project to pay. These could include road and utility line extensions, annexation fees for various districts, and impact fees to provide such facilities as a new school or park needed for the project's occupants.

Adequate Financing

Real estate developers and investors rarely pay cash for their projects. They are usually strong believers in the principle of leverage (using a minimum amount of equity funds and a maximum amount of borrowed funds to control a large investment). The funds needed for land acquisition can come from several sources. The seller can carry back a purchase money deed of trust, the developer can form a syndicate and raise the needed capital by selling ownership shares, or the funds may be borrowed from a financial institution or a private party. The common understanding in the development industry is that the eventual profit from the project is a function of how low the purchase price of the land is. Costs per square foot for the actual construction are relatively predictable and consistent regardless of construction location.

After land acquisition, the funds for construction usually come from traditional lenders, such as banks, thrift institutions, insurance companies, and mortgage companies. In addition to traditional sources, construction funds are occasionally available from pension funds, real estate investment trusts, and endowment funds. The importance of financing cannot be overemphasized. Without adequate funding, a real estate project, as developers put it, cannot "fly."

Adequate financing depends on two main variables: (1) the market potential of the project, and (2) the condition of the money market. If a developer can demonstrate to lenders that a strong market exists for the proposed project, and if lenders have funds available at reasonable interest rates, chances are the project will be funded. On the other hand, if the money market is tight and the supply of funds limited, a developer may find it impossible to borrow the needed capital, regardless of the market potential for the project. The project will have to be shelved because of the lack of mortgage credit.

Developers of larger projects increasingly consider the possible use of government-issued **special assessment bonds**, to pay for various needed road or utility work. At a time when local governments are unwilling or unable to construct roads, sewer systems, street lighting, and utility conduit, bonds become the only alternative. In California The Communities Facilities District Act in 1982, also known as the Mello-Roos Act, is often used to finance local infrastructure that benefit a specific community or development project. These bonds can be a specific amount assessed against the parcel, usually described as a *special assessment*, or they can be a general bond, to be paid off by a group of properties, a whole area, or the entire city. These bonds become a specific lien against the property in the same way as property taxes. These bonds exist outside of the California Proposition 13 property tax limitations (see Chapter 12), yet are usually income tax deductible for the property owner. Because these bonds are normally tax free to the investor who buys them, the interest rates are often cheaper than bank loans, despite the high costs of issuing them.

Profit Potential

After analyzing the market, estimating the cost and likelihood of government approval, and projecting the cost of financing, private developers can estimate the profit potential. If the profit return is too low relative to the costs and risks, the proposal is rejected as unfeasible. Unprofitable ventures often find the developer "land banking" the property in the hope of an opportunity for profitable future development. After all, the cheaper one acquires the land, the greater the future profits. Once the land is a purchased, that part of its cost is fixed. Future construction costs will undoubtedly increase. On the other hand, if the profit potential appears reasonable at the time, the project commences.

Figure 14.1 summarizes the four studies that should be conducted before real estate development and construction take place.

When This Process Is Ignored, Overbuilding Can Occur

The four steps listed previously are what should be done before ground is broken for a new project. However, during the 2000s, a tremendous amount of overbuilding occurred in the residential real estate market in most cities across the United States. This created an excess supply of homes for sale, not for rent. The reasons frequently given for this overbuilding include economic slowdown, income tax incentives, easy money from underregulated banks and investment bankers, tax base–hungry local governments, and massive foreign investment. Most of this overbuilding, and the resultant foreclosures, could have been prevented if realistic market studies had been conducted before the projects were developed. Instead, what occurred was analysis based on gut feelings, hopes, prayers, and a false reliance on perpetual increases in real estate values! From this perspective, then, the overbuilding was caused by (1) the collapse of old-time conservative banking, followed by (2) the failure of regulators to adopt and enforce meaningful restrictions to backstop mortgage lenders, and then, (3) the failure of legislators to recognize the folly of such a splurge and to require and fund adequate securities regulatory action.

By mid-2010 some sanity had returned to the residential real estate lending market. Traditional 20 percent down payments on

FIGURE 14.1 Feasibility study steps.

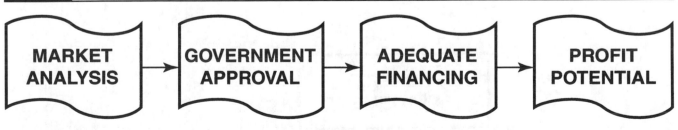

loans, and fully documented loan applications are once more the norm. However, commercial lenders have yet to see the full impact of the recession and foreclosure crisis on their investments.

Steps in Construction

Land development and construction take place in steps or phases. Figure 14.2 summarizes the major steps in land development and construction.

FIGURE 14.2   Major steps in land development and construction.

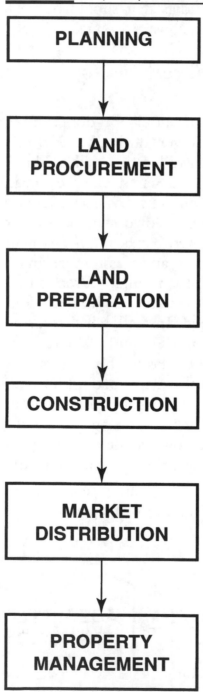

The *planning phase* encompasses market analysis, obtaining government approvals procedures, arranging financing, and profit analysis. *Land procurement* refers to the purchase of the property. In some cases, the purchase is just the acquisition of a single parcel. In other cases, however, land procurement may require the painstaking assemblage of several smaller parcels under different ownerships in order to create one larger parcel. Usually, the land is optioned, or contracted for, prior to the planning phase. Escrow then closes when government and lender approvals are obtained.

The *land preparation* phase is concerned with the clearing of the land and the installation of off-site improvements such as utilities, streets, and gutters to make way for on-site construction. *Off-site* means off of the individual building site, but not necessarily off of the larger parcel.

The *construction phase* begins as soon as land preparation activity permits access. In construction, timing is a critical factor. The actual building is usually done in phases, frequently by different subcontractors. Blending each phase to eliminate delays is one of the most difficult aspects of managing construction. Delays between construction phases can occur because of adverse weather, labor strikes, material shortages, and improperly estimated time requirements for various construction activities. Delays cost money, as interest accrues on construction loans and labor is paid for standby time.

The *market distribution* phase is concerned with the selling and transfer of property title. Frequently, the sale takes place before construction begins. These are called "build to suit" projects. If the project is not pre-sold but is built on speculation, ideally the property is sold before construction is completed. In other cases the property is not sold until after completion. In any case, the actual legal transfer of title usually does not occur until the property is completed and ready for occupancy.

The *property management phase* refers to the maintenance and servicing of the development after construction. If the property is owner-occupied, the service and upkeep rests with the owner. If the project is tenant-occupied, frequently a professional property manager is hired to supervise the servicing of the property. Professional membership in the **Institute for Real Estate Management (IREM®)** and education/certification as a **Certified Property Manager® (CPM®)** are the gold standard for the industry. Property management involves two major activities: physical upkeep and record keeping. Physical upkeep refers to maintenance and repairs; record keeping involves rent collection, ledger accounts, and the preparation of income and expense sheets for tax purposes.

Figure 14.3 is an expanded version of the construction process, outlining the individuals and institutions that are involved in each phase of construction.

Green Building

Green Building or "sustainable construction" or "green construction" has become the byword and darling of 21st century residential and commercial construction in both the private and government sectors. According to the U.S. Environmental Protection Agency, green construction is the practice of creating structures and using processes that are environmentally responsible and resource-efficient throughout a building's life cycle: from siting to design, construction, operation, maintenance, renovation, and deconstruction. This practice expands and complements the classical building design concerns of economy, utility, durability, and comfort. It is a philosophy of living, building, and sustaining dwellings, given limited early resources.

New technologies and modes of implementing reusable materials, energy efficiency, reducing waste, and minimizing the environmental footprint at every turn are part of green building. Sustainable design is incorporated in the siting and architecture of the building. Initially, purchase and installation of rated energy-efficient appliances met the market's expectations. Now, however, more is expected. Green technologies may be very expensive in an effort to keep material from the landfill or to reduce the carbon footprint of a project.

LEED® certification for contractors, builders, architects, and buildings is the recognized third-party certification for the building industry. The LEED green building rating system—developed and administered by the U.S. Green Building Council, a Washington D.C.-based nonprofit coalition of building industry leaders—is designed to promote design and construction practices that increase profitability while reducing the negative environmental impacts of buildings and improving occupant health and well-being. Individuals and buildings can achieve varying levels of certification. Often these certifications aid in marketing and obtaining government funding or obtaining aid in financing and expediting a project throughout the planning process.

The Cost of Construction Delays and Impact Fees

The old saying, "Time is money," is especially true in real estate development. Many real estate developers work on relatively thin profit margins, and any unforeseen delay can quickly erode profits. Construction delays can be caused by required government reports,

FIGURE 14.3   The housing process: major participants and influences.

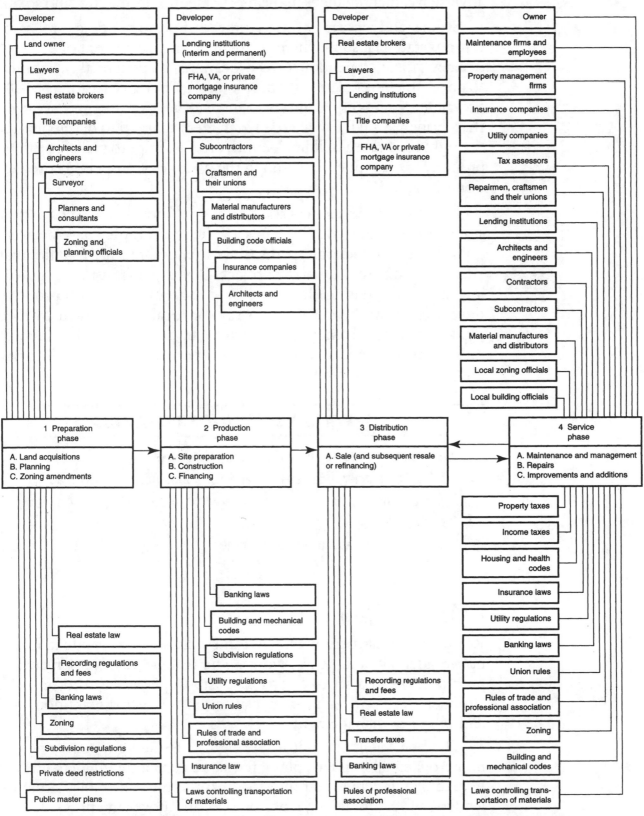

Source: The President's Committee on Urban Housing, A Decent Home. Washington, DC, Government Printing Office, December 1968, p.115.

mismanagement by developers, labor strikes, shortages of materials, adverse weather, changes in the mortgage money market, and so on.

Studies and reports by various universities and building trade associations state that somewhere between 20 and 40 percent of the price of a new home, depending on the location, can be directly attributed to government regulations. These high regulation costs are especially prevalent in states like California, where local governments have been sharply increasing fees (called **impact fees**) charged to developers for the right to obtain a building permit, in an attempt to make up for the property tax revenue lost through the passage of property tax reduction legislation.

Not only are developers asked to pay for direct costs, such as new streets, water, and sewer hookups for the project, they have been required to pay for schools, parks, and other community facilities that are not directly related to the project. Developers must recoup their impact fees by raising the prices they charge to the new property buyers. This can be viewed as a way for local government to raise money indirectly from property owners, to make up for the tax revenue lost by not being able to increase property taxes sufficiently to pay for these facilities directly.

REVIEWING YOUR UNDERSTANDING

The Development and Building Process
1. What is the difference between land development and construction?
2. List four things that should be considered before beginning a real estate project.
3. List six major steps in land development and construction.

CHAPTER SUMMARY

Real estate construction activity can be classified as residential, non-residential, and public works. The real estate development process flows in a series of phases or steps: planning, land procurement, land preparation, construction, market distribution, and property management.

The homebuilding industry is highly fragmented, consisting of numerous small builders, plus a few large corporate builders. Erratic homebuilding activity can be traced to the unpredictable nature of lenders, buyers, builders, labor unions, and government. Government impact fees have increased the cost of property ownership, as developers pass these costs on in the form of higher prices.

REVIEWING YOUR UNDERSTANDING

1. The three main categories of real estate construction are residential, nonresidential, and:
   A. mobile homes
   B. office buildings
   C. public works
   D. farms

2. The largest percentage of construction takes place in which sector?
   A. residential
   B. nonresidential
   C. public works
   D. farms

3. Fluctuation in the rate of new home construction is caused by:
   A. government actions
   B. availability of mortgage credit
   C. phases of the business cycle
   D. all of the above

4. Manufactured and mobile homes comprise approximately what percentage of new single-family home sales in the United States?
   A. 0–5
   B. 10–15
   C. 20–30
   D. 40–50

5. Regarding the prices of existing homes:
   A. prices are usually higher than comparable new homes
   B. prices are usually lower than comparable new homes
   C. prices are usually the same as comparable new homes
   D. prices are set by government actions

6. In terms of the factors of production (land, labor, capital, and entrepreneurship) the developer is the entrepreneur and therefore should earn:
   A. rent
   B. wages
   C. interest
   D. profit

7. Subdividing is considered:
   A. construction
   B. land development
   C. building
   D. assemblage

8. The first step in the real estate development process is to:
   A. do a market analysis
   B. obtain government approval
   C. line up the financing
   D. compute the return on investment

9. Impact fees are paid by developers to governments as a condition for issuing a building permit. In the final analysis, the cost for these fees is ultimately paid by:
   A. developers
   B. lenders
   C. taxpayers
   D. buyers

10. Real estate development takes place in a series of phases. The first phase is:
    A. planning
    B. procurement
    C. construction
    D. property management

11. Financing for land development does not involve:
    A. banks
    B. tax-exempt bonds
    C. FHA
    D. pension funds

12. To obtain government approvals, developers will need to do all of the following, except:
    A. study environmental impacts
    B. show compliance with the community general plan
    C. agree to provide needed utilities and roads
    D. provide a net worth statement

13. As the business cycle changes, public works construction is usually less affected than residential construction.
    A. true
    B. false

14. The rate of nonresidential construction is projected to decline throughout the 2010s, primarily because of:
    A. environmental conflicts
    B. overbuilding during boom
    C. shortages of materials
    D. shortages of labor

15. Manufactured and mobile homes today are:
    A. often moved
    B. more similar in appearance to regular homes
    C. found in all neighborhoods
    D. difficult to finance

16. The homebuilding industry:
    A. consists of many small, independent builders and several hundred large, corporate developers
    B. increases home construction output at a steady, even level each year
    C. is very difficult for newcomers to get into
    D. depends on tight mortgage credit terms to succeed

17. High impact fees and time delays caused by government "red tape" can increase construction costs by 20 percent or more.
    A. true
    B. false

18. Innovation in homebuilding requires a positive attitude from lenders, government, construction workers, and homebuyers.
    A. true
    B. false

19. Which of the following people at a homebuilding project would not be providing entrepreneurial (management) skills?
    A. carpenter
    B. architect
    C. developer
    D. construction superintendent

20. Land development and construction take place in a series of phases. Which of the following is the correct order?
    A. planning, land procurement, construction, land preparation
    B. land preparation, land procurement, planning, construction
    C. land procurement, planning, land preparation, construction
    D. planning, land procurement, land preparation, construction

21. Market analysis in real estate seeks to answer which basic question?
    A. Is there adequate demand for the project?
    B. Are there sufficient utilities?
    C. Will existing transportation systems provide access?
    D. Can financing be obtained?

22. In planning a real estate development, "government approvals" means reviewing:
    A. income tax requirements
    B. Federal Reserve standards
    C. the need for legislative approvals
    D. the government-imposed costs, as well as the needed approvals

23. Funding for construction of small projects is primarily by:
    A. traditional lenders
    B. government-issued bonds
    C. pension funds
    D. endowment funds

24. The construction of freeways and bridges comes under the category of:
    A. residential construction
    B. nonresidential construction
    C. public works construction
    D. on-site construction

25. In recent years, there has been a trend of using government bonds to finance off-site improvements and then levying special assessments against each lot in the development.
    A. true
    B. false

CASE & POINT

Real Estate Economic History: California in the 1980s: "The Build-and-They-Shall-Come Syndrome," Followed by a Decline in the 1990s–2000s

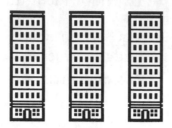

The 1980s represent an interesting decade for those who study real estate economics. From this period, real estate analysts gained a better understanding than ever before of how important the availability of money is to real estate development. In the 1980s, as money became available for almost any project, whether it made economic sense or not, more and more new projects lined up for funding.

A second lesson from the 1980s was the establishment of alternative ways for developers to profit from development. In the past, the developer's profit was gained only upon sale of the completed successful project. In the 1980s, however, most developers got income primarily by taking periodic payments from the loan funds toward "overhead costs." If the project failed, the developer started another project in another market, with a different lender, and repeated the cycle.

A third lesson from the 1980s was how much society had been relying on the concept of "lender's caution." Lender's caution disappeared when the inflation of the late 1970s led to high interest rates, which caused consumers to transfer funds from savings accounts to bonds and preferred stocks (disintermediation). Lenders, facing the very real danger that their institutions might go bankrupt, tossed caution out in the hope of earning enough profit from loan fees to save their jobs. But lender's caution had become the only lock on the door, because the politicians had eliminated the regulators, in the name of deregulation.

A fourth lesson from the 1980s is very sobering. Respected real estate commentators pointed out the folly of building such an excess of space as early as 1985. Yet the splurge continued on through 1986, 1987, 1990, and even, in some markets, 1992.

Clearly, lenders, developers, and the country lost the ability to see something inappropriate happening and act to correct it.

As significant as these lessons from the 1980s are, they are minor compared to the lessons of the 1990s and early 2000s. Foremost is the new encounter with supply and demand. Previously, when there was a temporary oversupply of some type of space, real estate economists and appraisers would look at the amount of available space, divide that number by the annual (or monthly) amount leased, and conclude that in six months or so the market would be back in equilibrium. Because the vacancy was fairly minor and the absorption period short, rents did not appear to decline. But in the 1990s and 2000s, the amount of vacant space has been very large. To make matters worse, in many markets new buildings have added to the supply, and tenants have downsized. As a result, the absorption period has stretched to two years, and then three years or more, and rents have started to soften: A tenant now, at a lower rent, is clearly preferable to a vacancy in the current market.

Along with the new focus on supply and demand, the market has discovered "negative absorption." As tenants have downsized, centralized, rationalized, gone broke, merged, or left town, the demand for office space has declined. Along with the available space in new buildings, the market has had to cope with growing amounts of available sublease space.

The drop in rents and demand has led inevitably to loan defaults and foreclosures, and then to the third major development of the 1990s and 2000s, the creation of systems to sell large amounts of troubled real estate efficiently. The motive, of course, is to sell off all of the failed real estate projects and other real estate accumulated by lenders. In the process, the real estate auction has emerged as a major vehicle for unloading unwanted real estate. In addition, sophisticated investors have combined to buy large groups of properties using purchasing pools. Moreover, at the start of the 1990s the primary form of real estate security sold on Wall Street was the bond backed by residential mortgages, available for some decades through FHA, then FNMA, GNMA, and FHLMC. But by the mid-1990s, bonds backed by commercial mortgages began expanding rapidly. Finally, the 2000s has marked the rebirth of the Real Estate Investment Trust, a concept almost abandoned in past years but now returning with great force.

CASE & POINT

Other lessons from the 1980s and 1990s are numerous. One is that excessive supply created in one period does have short-term favorable impacts, such as added jobs in banking, construction, materials manufacturing, and brokerage. The added jobs increased incomes and state and federal income tax revenues. Governments collected rezoning and building permit fees and property taxes on the new buildings.

But the negative economic impact of excess supply comes back to haunt the economy in later years. Because of the earlier oversupply, no new buildings are built, so the previous extra jobs are lost as well as some core jobs. Businesses that depend on new construction, from architects to contractors to equipment rental firms, are badly hurt. Some go out of business. The lost jobs reduce incomes and income tax receipts, and increase unemployment. Meanwhile, the oversupply has led to reduced market rents in all buildings, new and old. The declining rents lower owners' abilities to make loan payments, leading to foreclosures of fully occupied buildings.

The last lesson of the 1980s and 1990s is the consequences of over-building for property owners. Because of the high vacancies and declining rents of office buildings and some retail and industrial areas, many loans have been foreclosed, or net cash flow has all but disappeared. Contrary to popular belief, all commercial property owners are not rich insurance companies; some building owners were older, middle-class people, and the money lost was partly their retirement savings. As a result, surveys show a significant number of people have found it necessary to adjust to less income or reduced savings for the future. This has curtailed their spending, a silent secondary economic effect of overbuilding.

Chapter

15

IMPORTANT TERMS AND CONCEPTS

Environment

Environmental impact

Environmental Protection Agency (EPA)

Inflation costs

Negative declaration

Opportunity costs

Overhead costs

Private benefits

Private costs

Social benefits

Social costs

PREVIEW

This chapter briefly describes the reports that real estate developers must prepare to obtain government building permits. Section 15.1 discusses the types of reports required by federal, state, and local government agencies. Section 15.2 examines both the costs and the benefits of government reports. The Case & Point at the end of the chapter explores the Wetlands Controversy, an area of increasing regulation. When you have completed this chapter, you will be able to:

1. Explain the reasons given for requiring government reports before private real estate may be developed.

2. List the types of reports often required by federal, state, and local government agencies.

3. Describe both the costs and the benefits to real estate developers, property owners, and society of requiring government reports.

Required Government Reports

15.1 TYPES OF REQUIRED GOVERNMENT REPORTS

Government agencies need reports to see that proposed real estate projects conform to land-use laws. Reports and investigations provide the basis for government agencies to approve, deny, or modify proposed real estate development. This section summarizes major legislation with which real estate developers must comply in order to obtain governmental approval for their projects.

Federal Legislation

Although there are many federal laws and agencies that regulate the use of real estate, the two most important agencies are the United States Department of Housing and Urban Development (HUD) and the Environmental Protection Agency (EPA).

The United States Department of Housing and Urban Development (HUD)

The United States Department of Housing and Urban Development (HUD) is an umbrella department that oversees the activities of several federal agencies that influence real estate development. Some of the more important agencies are listed as follows:

1. The Federal Housing Administration insures real estate loans made by approved lenders. It is widely known as FHA.

2. The Public Housing Administration helps to fund and supervise administration of low-rent housing projects.

3. The Community Facilities Administration provides funds to cities, counties, and colleges to construct public buildings and public works projects.

4. The Urban Renewal Administration provides financial assistance to local governments for slum clearance and rehabilitation.

5. The Office of Interstate Land Sales Registration regulates the inter-state sales of subdivided land.

This is only a partial list of HUD's activities, but it is obvious that many real estate projects fall under the jurisdiction of one or more of these agencies. When this occurs, HUD requires extensive reports to see that its regulations are being followed. Some typical report topics include relocation plans for persons being displaced by the proposed project, a statement of fair employment practices, equal housing opportunities questionnaires, environmental impact statements, a complete economic base analysis, and a detailed market analysis.

Environmental Protection Agency (EPA)

The **Environmental Protection Agency (EPA)** was created in 1970 and, along with the Council on Environmental Quality, is responsible for seeing that federal pollution standards are enforced. Some of the federal environmental legislation acts of special interest to real estate users are given as follows:

1. *National Environmental Policy Act (NEPA)* requires the preparation of environmental impact statements on all federally assisted real estate projects.

2. *Federal Water Pollution Acts* regulate real estate development along waterways and underground water channels. These acts have been used to halt real estate construction until adequate antipollution protection devices are developed. They require the preparation of an extensive report outlining the water pollution impact before a developer is allowed to grade the land or erect a building.

3. *Clean Air Acts* control real estate development that could add to air pollution. These acts have been used to deny building permits for industrial and commercial real estate projects on the grounds that additional development will aggravate air pollution. They require a complete report regarding air pollution standards before construction is allowed to proceed.

Other federal acts that influence real estate development include the Noise Control Act; the National Coastal Zone Management Act; the Historic Preservation Act; the Flood Disaster Protection Act, which affects any real estate development in mapped flood plains;

and the very controversial Federal Wetlands Act. (See appendix.) All of these acts require the submission of reports before real estate development is allowed.

State Legislation

In addition to federal reports, real estate developers must also comply with state laws that may require reports. State regulations of special interest to real estate include: state housing and construction codes, state sanitation and health codes, subdivision requirements, statewide zoning controls, and state environmental regulations.

State Housing and Construction Codes

Most states have adopted minimum construction codes which require all new construction must meet state standards. As a condition for receiving a building permit, a developer must submit a plot map and detailed building plans with detailed specifications. After a complete examination of the plans, making revisions where necessary, the state agency usually approves them. In many states, the code is adopted and enforced at the county or city level for most buildings. However, schools, hospitals, mobile homes and manufactured housing (modular homes) are increasingly regulated by state codes rather than local codes.

State Health and Sanitation Codes

State health departments regulate statewide health measures. County or city health departments usually play a major role in enforcement, as discussed later. Drainage, plumbing, sewage disposal, hazardous waste materials, and water supply all come under the jurisdiction of health and sanitation codes. Each health officer has the authority to halt any proposed development that fails to meet the legal standards. As a condition for obtaining a building permit, a developer must submit a report showing that the proposed project meets all health requirements, or must get the approval of the health department for the project plans.

Subdivision Regulations

Subdivision regulation is one of the main tools used by state and local governments for controlling real estate development. Although subdivision laws are not new, amendments and changes are constantly being added by legislators. Usually, the primary law addresses the content and required approval process for any map that shows a division of an existing land parcel. In addition, some states like California require preparation of a public report, which must be prepared prior to the first sale of most subdivided parcels.

The State of California Department of Real Estate (DRE) oversees the Subdivision Map Act covering most developments and condominiums of five or more units. DRE reviews the preliminary and final public reports to ensure that sub-dividers deliver what was promised to the buyers. Local counties oversee the Subdivison Map Act as all subdivision maps are must be filed at the local county recorder's office.

State or local agencies usually require comprehensive subdivision reports, to ensure that a developer is complying with all subdivision laws before residential lots can be sold. A typical subdivision report must outline who holds title, any flood or drainage issues, details of any land filling, provision for roads and access, the nature of all utility hookups, complete plans for all off-site and on-site improvements, any major environmental impacts, any seller financing, proposed marketing techniques, and many other technical items.

Statewide Zoning Controls

Historically, zoning has been a local matter. Cities and counties enacted zoning ordinances to achieve their own individual goals, applicable only to property within their boundaries. However, urban growth pressures now create problems that overlap city and county boundaries. State governments have been enacting new forms of state-wide zoning. Much of the recent legislation has been environmentally oriented. States have assumed control over areas considered to have regional importance, such as coastlines, lake and river frontage, agricultural land, and desert areas. Statewide zoning also occurs in high hazard areas such as flood plains, earthquake faults, and landslide areas. Here again, real estate developers often must submit reports showing that their proposed project conforms to these state zoning laws.

State Environmental Regulation

Since the late 1960s, state legislatures have been enacting environmental laws, similar in nature to the federal legislation. Individual states have created special environmental agencies to ensure that the **environmental impact** of a real estate project is studied before a building permit is granted.

The typical procedure for the developer is to present the proposed real estate project to an environmental review board. In some cases, this will be the local planning commission. The review board then decides if the proposed project will have a significant impact on the environment. If the answer is negative, a **negative declaration** is issued, and the developer then proceeds with the project. If the review

Special Interest Topic

Zoning Codes and Their Purpose

Zoning codes have changed over the years. The various approaches to zoning can be divided into four major categories:

1. Zoning codes by area are the most extensively used in the United States, characterized by geographic districts; for example, "R" for Residential, "I" for Industrial, "A" for Agriculture, and "FR" for Forest Recreational to name a few.

2. Performance Zoning uses specific goals for development projects and is intended to better accommodate market principles and private property rights with environmental protection.

3. Incentive Zoning is intended to provide a reward-based system to encourage development that meets established urban development goals.

4. Design-based codes, which do not regulate the type of land use, but rather the form that structures may take (height, setbacks, materials, colors, windows, etc.).

board concludes that the project will have a significant impact, the developer must then prepare and submit a comprehensive environmental impact report.

For these reports, the **environment** is defined as all social, economic, biological, and physical surroundings. Thus, a typical environmental impact report contains a detailed analysis of how the proposed real estate project will affect each of these four areas. The report also requires that the developer outline the steps to be taken to counteract any environmental damage that might result from the real estate project. Usually, such reports must consider the proposed project and several alternatives, from no project at all, through a project version with fewer impacts, perhaps to a project version with greater impacts. In addition, alternate ways to mitigate the impacts must be presented.

Once the environmental impact report is completed, it is submitted to the environmental review board as a draft. The general public is usually invited to make comments on the draft report. The draft report is then amended and submitted for a final decision by the review board. All environmental review board decisions, either for or against the proposed project, can be challenged in the courts.

Special Interest Topic
New York City Sets the Standard

Completion in 1916 of the 36-story Equitable Life Assurance Society of the United States building in New York City cast a 7-acre shadow throughout the streets of Manhattan. Opponents of the building feared that subsequent buildings would turn the City into a series of dark, windy, canyons in which no sunlight could penetrate. In response, the city adopted the 1916 Zoning Resolution which limited the height and required setbacks for new buildings to allow the penetration of light to street level. This piece of legislation set the standard later adopted by most of the states, municipalities, and cities in the United States. Setbacks of skyscrapers are still the planning standard today almost 100 years later.

Local Legislation

In addition to meeting federal and state requirements, developers must conform with local real estate codes. City and county governments nearly always have local planning, public works, building, and sanitation agencies that require the submission of reports or review and approve the project plans before a local building permit is issued. Typically, local reports or review are needed in the following areas: grading, construction details, lot design, street and other off-site facilities, zoning and architectural conformity, environmental impact, and impact on traffic, schools, police and fire service, and property tax.

Who pays the cost of these government reviews and reports? What is the trade-off between costs and benefits? Is it worth the red tape? These topics will be covered in the next section, but before you proceed, check your understanding by answering the following questions.

REVIEWING YOUR UNDERSTANDING

Types of Required Government Reports
1. What is the reason for having government regulatory agencies?
2. Why does the EPA wish to regulate real estate development?
3. In addition to housing codes, list four other state codes or regulations that require the preparation of a report.

15.2 COSTS VERSUS BENEFITS

As mentioned in earlier chapters, "There is no such thing as a free lunch." Any use of resources, whether land, labor, or capital, incurs a cost that someone must pay. This section studies required government reports by comparing their costs with the benefits received.

Defining Costs and Benefits

To simplify their analysis, economists break costs and benefits into the following categories: private costs, social costs, private benefits, and social benefits.

Private costs are those expenses paid by a particular individual or business firm. They are the actual out-of-pocket money expenditures of that individual or business.

Social costs are the expenses paid by society as a whole rather than by an individual or business. For example, if a business pays for and constructs a $150-million factory, this is a private cost. But if the factory then pollutes the air, the pollution becomes a social cost paid by all, not just the factory owner or its customers.

Private benefits are rewards enjoyed by a particular individual or business and not by society as a whole. Private benefits are frequently stated in terms of money profits.

Social benefits are rewards that accrue to all of society, not just to an individual or business. For example, if a real estate developer builds a successful shopping center, the developer may reap private profit. In addition, if the project stimulates local business and increases employment and income, this could create a social benefit, a reward shared by all of society, not just the real estate developer.

Analyzing the Costs

The cost of required government reports can be broken down into private and social costs. Private costs include report preparation costs, government review fees, holding costs, inflation costs, and overhead costs. The cost of preparing government reports varies with the size and scope of the proposed project. But the consulting fees charged by attorneys, engineers, appraisers, economists, and environmental researchers can run to hundreds or thousands of dollars per day, and when all the required reports are completed, the cost can be quite high.

Most government agencies charge a fee to review the report or to review the plans for compliance. These fees are growing faster than general inflation. Many governments now are seeking to support planning or building department costs entirely from fees, rather than from general revenues.

The costs for holding unused land include expenses for property taxes, interest on land loans, minimum maintenance, and opportunity costs.

Opportunity costs refer to the unrealized, potential earnings that the money tied up in unimproved land might have earned if invested elsewhere.

Inflation costs refer to the increase in material prices and wages that occurs during construction delays. The longer construction is delayed, the greater the likelihood that inflation will drive up the cost of construction.

Overhead costs are the costs that continue whether a developer is working or not. Overhead costs include such items as rent on the developer's office, bank payments on equipment, equipment maintenance, and fixed salaries for office workers.

Preparation, review, holding, inflation, and overhead costs are all private costs that are either absorbed by the developer or, in most cases, passed on to the developer's customers in the form of higher real estate prices.

What are the social costs of required government reviews and reports? Does society also pay a price as a result of required reports or reviews? Yes, society as a whole may bear some costs, such as a loss or delay of jobs and income. Another social cost might be an increase in consumer prices because of the cost push inflation sparked by the increase in construction prices. At the higher selling prices, some consumers will not qualify, lowering the number of buyers.

Analyzing the Benefits

The benefits gained by requiring government reviews or reports on real estate projects can be broken down into social benefits and private benefits. Social benefits include less environmental damage, better land planning, consumer protection, and the fostering of social integration. Many of the recent land use regulations have been aimed at protecting the environment. By requiring environmental reports, society benefits by knowing that potential environmental damage will be studied, along with project alternatives and impact mitigations, before a real estate project is approved.

Another social benefit frequently cited is better land-use planning. By requiring reports, the government can see that private land is not used in a manner likely to harm surrounding landowners or the community. Thus, noisy industrial uses are usually separated from residential uses.

Consumer protection is one very common benefit of government review or reporting requirements. The consumer thus benefits from an expert review of health and safety issues that may be extremely complex and all but impossible for the consumer to evaluate.

Still another benefit from government regulation is that it can be used to promote social integration. By requiring real estate developers to submit reports on social goals, such as minority employment in construction trades, equal housing opportunities, and relocation assistance to persons being displaced by the real estate project, disadvantaged persons are given a better chance to become a part of the social mainstream.

Are there any private benefits that real estate developers or their customers gain from requiring detailed reports? Yes, in the long run, the private costs paid by requiring government reports may be offset by private benefits such as higher real estate values. For example, it is possible that by requiring a careful study of the environment, a completed real estate project may be so harmonious in its surroundings that its value rises rapidly. This enhances the image of the real estate developer and generates profitable resale potential for the initial buyer of the real estate projects.

The Trend

As you can see, there are certain costs associated with government laws and reports and there are certain benefits. Do the costs outweigh the benefits? Or do the benefits outweigh the costs? Obviously, there are no easy answers. Each case must be analyzed independently, but the trend appears to be set and more government reports will be required before a real estate project will be approved.

If this is the case, can the costs be reduced without sacrificing the benefits? The answer is a resounding YES. One area that real estate economists, environmentalists, conservationists, and developers agree on is that the duplication of work required by the various levels of government must be eliminated. In many cases, a real estate developer must prepare the same information in four or five different forms to conform to separate, overlapping guidelines of different government agencies. What is also needed is a simpler review system, where approval or denial is relayed more rapidly, thus saving both private and social costs.

Special Interest Topic
Saving the San Francisco Bay

Originally, much of the land around the edges of San Francisco Bay was marsh, wet at high tide and dry at low tide. Many of these marshes were surrounded by dikes and then drained, in the 1800s. Some were diked and converted to salt-producing ponds.

The commercial salt ponds once owned and managed by the Cargill and Leslie Salt Company are once more in the public eye. The company recently closed its 1,400-acre salt evaporation pond operation. A local developer wants to build a 30,000-person mixed use development consisting of over 12,000 residential and commercial units in the salt marsh. The Redwood City Planning Commission sees this as a much needed opportunity to build critical housing for Silicon Valley workers. Environmentalists, the Army Corp of Engineers, and elected officials from around the nation have entered the controversy.

The 1,400-acre parcel has been privately owned and commercially used for over 150 years. The wetland status and perhaps exempt status has rankled local wetlands advocates. Redwood City will soon start looking for a consultant to compile the environmental report, which is expected to be complete in 18 months to 2 years. The city plans to host dozens of public forums before making a final decision.

REVIEWING YOUR UNDERSTANDING

Costs versus Benefits

1. What is the difference between a social cost and a private cost and between a social benefit and a private benefit?
2. Define the following: preparation cost, review fees, holding cost, inflation cost, and overhead cost.
3. List three social benefits that result from government regulation of private real estate.

CHAPTER SUMMARY

Legislators pass land-use laws and then create government agencies to enforce these laws. As an enforcement tool, government agencies require real estate developers to submit reports verifying that public regulations are being met.

The cost of requiring government reports includes private costs such as preparation cost, holding cost, inflation cost, and overhead cost. Society also bears some costs, such as higher prices and loss of employment and income. The social benefits derived from requiring government reports in private real estate activities include less environmental damage, better land-use planning, consumer protection, and the fostering of social goals. Private benefits may include an increase in real estate values. The pattern indicates that more government reports will be required in the future. The key is to streamline the reporting system so that both private and social costs can be reduced without sacrificing the benefits.

REVIEWING YOUR UNDERSTANDING

1. The stated purpose of requiring government reviews or reports before a developer is issued a building permit is to:
   A. see that the project conforms to land-use laws
   B. allow environmentalists to delay or stop the development
   C. satisfy the lender's requirements for loan approval
   D. issue opinions as to the profitability of the project

2. Which law requires an environmental impact report on all major federal public works projects?
   A. Clean Air Act
   B. Hazardous Waste Materials Act
   C. National Environmental Policy Act
   D. Federal Projects Act

3. Environment includes:
   A. economic and social impact
   B. economic and biological impact
   C. economic, social, and biological impact
   D. economic, social, biological, and physical impact

4. Instead of a full environmental impact report, a small project with little if any impact on the environment can be approved using a:
   A. negative declaration
   B. payment of a waiver fee
   C. federal district attorney
   D. small claims court order

5. The final approval for the actual design and layout of a housing subdivision usually rests with the:
   A. federal government
   B. state government
   C. local government
   D. developer

6. The pollution of the air by an unregulated factory is what type of cost?
   A. private
   B. social
   C. customer
   D. abstract

7. The profit generated by owning a real estate building is what type of benefit?
   A. private
   B. social
   C. community
   D. environmental

8. The private costs incurred because of the delays of required government reviews and reports are called:
   A. holding costs
   B. environmental costs
   C. oversight costs
   D. impact fees

9. The benefits of requiring government approval before a real estate project can be built may include:
   A. higher property values
   B. reduced social costs
   C. less environmental damage
   D. all of the above

10. Economists, real estate developers, and environmentalists tend to agree that:
    A. the duplication of work required by various government agencies is wasteful
    B. real estate is a commodity to be bought and sold like corn
    C. environmental concerns will decrease as time goes on
    D. in the future, government will have a smaller voice in real estate development projects

11. The Federal Housing Administration:
    A. loans money for housing construction or purchase
    B. insures real estate loans made by approved lenders
    C. coordinates all federal efforts to increase housing production
    D. is responsible for environmental review of all housing developments

12. The Urban Renewal Administration:
    A. provides financial assistance to local governments for slum clearance and rehabilitation
    B. is responsible for assembling land parcels for new housing construction in rural areas
    C. is responsible for environmental review of all housing developments
    D. is a division of the Environmental Protection Agency

13. When federal funds are being used to buy property for a city or county project:
    A. the local agency is exempt from any need to prepare an environmental impact report
    B. the project ownership cannot be transferred to a private party
    C. no state regulations need be followed
    D. a relocation plan will be required, to assist people being displaced

14. EPA is a federal agency charged with:
    A. providing funds to local agencies to construct public buildings
    B. insuring real estate loans made by approved lenders
    C. enforcing federal pollution standards
    D. monitoring subdivision lot sales

15. The National Environmental Policy Act:
    A. requires preparation of environmental impact statements
    B. is the primary law affecting water pollution
    C. focuses primarily on wildlife protection
    D. has little or no effect on any local real estate activity

16. The Flood Disaster Protection Act:
    A. applies only to federal flood control projects
    B. affects development of property in mapped flood plains
    C. is the basis for water pollution control
    D. established the requirement for environmental impact reports

17. State health codes:
    A. often are enforced by county or city health workers
    B. regulate traffic patterns
    C. apply only to residential, not commercial, real estate projects
    D. cannot exceed federal health codes

18. The subdivision laws generally:
    A. apply when a single large building is to be occupied by more than one tenant
    B. set standards for approving and mapping any division of a parcel of land
    C. are enforced by federal, not state government
    D. define the required education and experience for residential developers

19. The potential earnings that money tied up in unimproved land could have earned if invested elsewhere are called:
    A. direct cost
    B. social cost
    C. opportunity cost
    D. preparation cost

20. A negative declaration is a:
    A. finding that a proposed project does not have a significant environmental impact
    B. finding that a proposed project is not located in an earth-quake zone
    C. statement that a proposed project is exempt from federal air pollution regulations
    D. statement that a proposed project meets all regulatory requirements

21. The trend is toward more and more government reports in order to undertake a large development project.
    A. true
    B. false

22. Mitigation means:
   A. ways to reduce the environmental impacts of a project
   B. the alternative projects that the typical environmental impact report need not study
   C. steps necessary to obtain permission to build in a flood plain
   D. the process of review that a proposed subdivision must go through

23. Environmental impact reports (EIRs) require a developer to list not doing the project as one alternative to reducing environmental damage.
   A. true
   B. false

24. Social costs of required government reviews and reports include:
   A. preparation costs and review fees
   B. overhead and holding costs
   C. better land-use planning
   D. higher prices to consumers

25. Social benefits of required government reviews and reports include:
   A. reduced demand
   B. greater profits for developers
   C. lower price appreciation
   D. better land-use planning

How Wet Is Wet?

In terms of required government permits, one of the most controversial is the U.S. Army Corps of Engineers 404 permit, which is an application to allow real estate development on designated wetlands. The Federal Wetlands Act was enacted in 1972 as part of the Federal Waters Pollution Control Act. This act requires the issuance of a permit by the Corps prior to allowing any land work or building in designated wetland areas, unless specifically exempt. The exempt activities include "discharges" for normal farming, forestry, and ranching operations. Another exemption from a permit is Exemption 26, which allows a landowner or developer to fill certain wetlands without a permit if no more than one acre of wetland is lost. Only one Exemption 26 is allowed for an entire project.

The original Federal Wetlands Act did not define wetlands, and each federal agency is allowed, to define in its own regulations what is meant by wetlands. Thus, the definition of wetlands can differ among the Army Corps of Engineers, the Environmental Protection Agency, the Fish and Wild Life Service, and the Soil Conservation Service.

Now the problem begins: Any application for a 404 permit to develop on wetlands as defined by the Corps must be submitted for review to other federal agencies, which may have a different definition of wetlands.

These other federal agencies have the power to deny the permit or impose mitigation requirements, which can be expensive. This in turn could make the proposed real estate project unfeasible.

Just what is meant by the term wetlands? The definition as used by the Corps and EPA is "areas that are inundated or saturated by surface or groundwater at a frequency and duration sufficient to support, and that under normal circumstances do support, a prevalence of vegetation typically adapted for life in saturated soil conditions." The definition then describes the character of wetlands as including: hydrology (presence of

CASE & POINT

water), the presence of aquatic vegetation, and the presence of saturated soil. Corps and EPA guidelines then state that if land is inundated or saturated seven or more days per year, and aquatic vegetation is present, the area is considered wetlands. By these guidelines it appears that the definition of wetlands can change each year depending on seasonal rainfall.

How far can the definition of wetlands be stretched? In one case the U.S. Army Corps of Engineers argued that an isolated mud hole that could be used by migratory birds as a rest stop should be declared a wetland and come under the Corps' jurisdiction.

The actual 404 permit process consists of the following steps:

1. Pre-application consultation with the Corps.
2. Formal application submission for a permit.
3. Posting of public hearing notice by the Corps.
4. Public hearing for the public and interested parties.
5. A public interest review by the Corps.
6. A review by other related federal and state agencies.
7. A decision by the Corps.

In the process, the landowner or developer will probably be required to prepare an environmental impact report and a cultural resource survey, to determine what impact the project may have on the environment and if any culturally sensitive lands are involved. If approval is granted, it may require the developer to mitigate the damage by creating new wetlands significantly larger than the wetlands affected.

The message is clear: Prior to purchasing any land for real estate development a prudent investor should hire a competent wetlands consultant and a qualified attorney to inspect the land and conduct an inquiry with the appropriate federal and state agencies regarding the status of the land. Failure to do so could become very expensive in the long run.

PART 4

Real Estate Investment
The Economics of the Parcel

Chapter

16

PREVIEW

This chapter looks at the economics of individual properties. Section 16.1 discusses basic investment principles. Section 16.2 presents real estate cash flow analysis. Section 16.3 shows how cash

Summary of Real Estate Investment Principles

flows are used to estimate offering prices and compute rates of return. The Case & Point at the end of the chapter contains a case study. When you have completed this chapter, you will be able to:

1. Define investment and list the five essential elements to consider when selecting an investment.
2. Complete a first-year real estate cash flow analysis.
3. Explain how real estate offering prices are determined.
4. Discuss how real estate returns are calculated.

16.1 BASIC INVESTMENT PRINCIPLES

Investing can be defined in several ways. One definition is to place money for profitable purposes, or to extend capital in exchange for perceived profits. Another definition of investing, favored by many economists, is this: **Investing** is defined as giving up present consumption in exchange for future benefits. This definition focuses on the idea that investing is the opposite of consumption.

In one way or another, most people can generate or earn money. Money can be used only in two ways: (1) spent, or (2) invested. Every dollar spent is a dollar that cannot be invested; every dollar invested is a dollar that cannot be spent. Therefore, one must decide how much money to use for present consumption (and taxes) and how much to invest. Any money not used for consumption is *automatically* invested. The money invested may be in savings, stocks, gold, real estate, or idle cash. These are all forms of investment!

Obviously, some people invest very little. This may be because they need every dollar to simply live. Or, if they are more affluent, they simply choose to consume now and not worry about the future. On the other hand, some people are active investors, giving up some current consumption, in order to build a nest egg for the future. This section concentrates on real estate as an investment.

The Key Investment Factors

The five major economic variables or characteristics of an investment are *return, management, taxability, liquidity,* and *risk.*

Return

Most investments involve putting up an initial cash outlay. If the investment is successful, it can generate income over a period of time. Or, there might be no income, but an increase in value. Either way, the investor eventually wants to get the original investment back (**return of investment**), along with some profit or benefit (**return on investment**). This profit or benefit is the economic reason for making the investment. The profit can be in the form of money, such as rents from a building, or less tangible benefits (amenities), such as occupancy of a home. The profits can also vary in their timing: now or later, and can come as one payment, a series of even payments, or as irregular payments. Common patterns include:

1. A series of payments over a period of time
2. A series of payments plus a large single end payment
3. A large single payment only

The higher the profit or benefits, the greater is the value of the investment. However, money received two years from now or at some other distant time is worth less than money received today. Thus, in comparing investments, both the amount of profits and the timing of their payment are all–important.

Management

Different investments require different types and amounts of management. **Management** is defined as the supervision needed to oversee an investment. A savings account needs almost no management, whereas an apartment building calls for a considerable amount. Sometimes, management is hired, so the investor need not do much. Various investments should be compared on the basis of the amount and skill of owner management time each requires. As "time is money," an investment that requires more management should produce a higher return, to pay for the time and effort.

Taxability

Investments differ in how their earnings are subject to *income tax.* Some investment earnings, like the interest from certain municipal bonds, can be free of income taxes. Others, like the dividends on corporate common stock, are subject to personal income tax. Investors are interested in the return received *after* income taxes. The taxability of the investment income is important in evaluating investment alternatives. *Taxability* of real estate investments is so important (and complex) that all of Chapter 17 is devoted to the topic.

Liquidity

Liquidity refers to the speed, cost, and ease of converting the investment into cash. Investments differ in their liquidity. Blue-chip stocks that are listed on the New York Stock Exchange are highly liquid—you can sell them on any business day, for a small brokerage fee, and receive your money in a day or so. Savings can be withdrawn in cash on the spot from a bank and therefore are very liquid. However, other investments, such as a loan to a new business, are *illiquid* (*not* liquid)—you might need to wait for years to recoup your money.

Real estate is considered an illiquid investment. It is difficult to convert an investment in real estate to cash quickly. To convert a real estate investment to cash, there are two choices: (1) sell the property or (2) borrow against the property. Both of these take time, and also cost money, in the form of seller closing costs or borrower loan costs. Therefore, it is frequently stated that one should invest in real estate only *after* seeing that personal future liquidity needs have been met with other forms of investment.

Risk

Investments vary in the amount of risk. **Risk** is defined as the danger of loss in the value of the investment. There are different types of risk. These include financial risk, interest rate, purchasing power, social change, and legal change risk.

For many investments, **financial risk**—the loss of the investment or earnings through failure to receive payments when due—is the greatest hazard. The financial risk of each investment varies, depending on the actual stability of the investment, the reliability (or uncertainty) of the investor's estimate of stability, and the margin or allowance that the particular investment has, before little problems become big ones! Financial risk is particularly important to real estate investments, because of the large up-front investment, the slow returns, and the frequent use of borrowed funds.

Interest rate risk refers to the possible loss in value of an investment, as a result of increases in market interest rates. This risk is usually associated with the market for corporate or government bonds. The basic rule is as follows: A decrease in market interest rates will increase the resale prices of existing bonds; or the opposite: An increase in market interest rates will decrease the resale prices of existing bonds.

For example, assume that in 2005 an investor bought a new bond, which was to pay 10 percent, interest only, for 10 years, and the purchase price and the face amount is $10,000. Thus, the annual income is scheduled to be $10,000 × 10% = $1,000 per year for 10 years, then a full payoff of $10,000. Suppose the investor needs money and attempts to sell the bond in 2010 and finds that market interest rates have risen to 20 percent on this type of bond. This means that a buyer of this bond will only pay the investor $5,000 for the $10,000 bond! Why? If the existing bond pays interest at $1,000 per year ($10,000 × 10%), in order to earn 20 percent, the new buyer will invest $5,000 × 20% to generate the $1,000 interest paid on the existing bond. Thus, the market value of the bond has dropped from $10,000 to $5,000 because of changes in market interest rates.

Are there interest rate risks for real estate investments? Yes, the wide swings of market interest rates do produce price changes. For example, assume that an investor purchased a leased warehouse for cash in 2005 on the basis of an 8 percent return. The investor attempts to sell the warehouse in 2010 and discovers that buyers now demand a 10 percent return because of changes in market interest rates. This situation will reduce the selling price of the warehouse 20 percent below the investor's purchase price. This is an example of how a change in market interest rates can reduce the value of an otherwise secure investment.

Purchasing power risk refers to the possibility of loss attributable to inflation. The investor can receive the same dollars from the investment, but with inflation the dollars purchase less! Investments that pay a fixed dollar return, such as certain bonds, are vulnerable to purchasing power risk. However, investments such as common stocks or real estate can provide protection from inflation and purchasing power risk, if the net earnings increase with inflation. Since inflation eats away at investment dollars, many investors insist upon a higher rate of return when inflation increases. Thus, if there is fear of continued inflation, the market will demand higher rates of return.

Risk of social change arises because every investment is vulnerable to social changes that can influence supply or demand and in turn can affect the earnings of an investment. Real estate investments are especially vulnerable because real estate is tied to a fixed location. For example, if urban dwellers leave a congested city for the suburbs, real estate values at the urban locations could decline in value.

Risk of legal change means that new laws may have an impact on an investment's ability to produce income. Changes in laws regarding wetlands, taxes, pollution, zoning, and landlord-tenant relations have had a significant past impact on real estate returns and values.

Other Risk Variables: Visibility and Specialization

Visibility means that the investment, the building, the occupants, or the co-owners are visible, or likely to be noticed. This affects the risk of social or legal change. A building occupied by a controversial tenant is more visible than one occupied by low-key tenants. The lease of an office building to the state government is more visible than a lease to an insurance company. An investment with a city council member as a partner is more visible than one with someone less well known. However, visibility can also help an investment, as when a central corner location gets a prestigious tenant, or when having a big-name tenant gets the landlord better loan terms or attracts buyers.

Specialization refers to the degree of uniqueness of a building. Often, this means the cost of converting the building to other uses. A highly specialized building, such as a medical office building or a fast-food franchise restaurant, is more expensive to convert to other uses than a standard building and is therefore riskier.

The Investment Decision

Each investor approaches an investment decision in his or her own manner. Some are careful and analytic, whereas others just plunge in. The economic approach to decision making consists of balancing the characteristics and risks of investments against the requirements or needs of the investor. In this fashion, an investor can analyze an investment in terms of returns, risks, liquidity, and so on, to see if it meets his or her needs.

The next section describes how to calculate the owner's cash flow from an income-producing property. Before you proceed, answer the review questions to test your understanding of the material in this section.

REVIEWING YOUR UNDERSTANDING

Basic Investment Principles
1. Define investing.
2. List and describe the five economic characteristics that affect an investment.
3. How would you rank real estate, high or low, in terms of each of these five economic characteristics?

16.2 REAL ESTATE CASH FLOW ANALYSIS

It should be stressed that real estate is an investment that normally produces a slow recovery of profit and the initial investment over a period of many years. The process of estimating the amount of money to be received each year, including the year of resale, is called **cash flow analysis**.

The cash flow analysis for each year can be viewed as a series of steps. These steps are outlined in common cash flow forms. Cash flow forms vary in steps and terminology, but a typical example of an annual cash flow analysis is shown in Figure 16.1.

The Steps in Annual Cash Flow Analysis

To illustrate the steps in an annual cash flow analysis, look at the following case study:

Case Study

An older 20-unit apartment, with an asking price of $1,700,000, requires $500,000 cash down, plus a new loan of $1,200,000. Each unit rents for $800 per month (which is at market); other

FIGURE 16.1 A cash flow analysis.

Annual Cash Flow Analysis

1. Gross Scheduled Income ($800 × 20 units × 12 mos.)	$192,000
2. Plus: Other Income ($300 × 12 mos.)	+ 3,600
3. Equals: Total Gross Income	$195,600
4. Less: Vacancy/Credit Loss (5%)	− 9,780
5. Equals: Gross Operating Income	$185,820
6. Less: Annual Operating Expenses	− 43,100
7. Equals: Net Operating Income	$142,720
8. Less: Annual Debt Service	−126,370
9. Equals: Before-Tax Cash Flow	$16,350

Tax Benefit Analysis

10. Net Operating Income (Line 7)	$142,720
11. Less: Interest (Loan 1)	−119,700
12. Less: Interest (Loan 2)	0
13. Less: Cost Recovery (Depreciation)	− 38,760
14. Equals: Real Estate Taxable Income (If Profit), or	$ 0
15. Equals: Estimated Allowable Loss (If Loss)	$<15,740>
16. Times: Tax Bracket (times Line 14 or 15)	× .38
17. Equals: Taxes Saved or Paid	$ 5,981

Net Spendable Income

18. Before-Tax Cash Flow (Line 9)	$ 16,350
19. Plus/Less Taxes Saved or Paid (Line 17)	+ 5,981
20. Equals: Net Spendable Income (After-Tax Cash Flow)	$ 22,331

income is $300 per month; and the vacancy/credit loss factor in this market currently is 5 percent. Annual verified operating expenses are $43,100, and the annual fixed debt service for the $1,200,000 loan is $126,370.

The first year's interest payment on the loan totals $119,700, and the annual estimated depreciation for income tax purposes is $38,760. The potential investor is in a combined federal and state income tax bracket at the marginal rate of 38 percent. According to the investor's accountant, all passive losses can be used each year. No passive losses will be carried forward to reduce gain in the year of resale. (Passive losses are explained in detail in Chapter 17.)

Based on this information, a cash flow analysis for the first full year of ownership is developed and is presented in Figure 16.1.

Before-Tax Cash Flow

The first series of steps in a cash flow analysis computes what is commonly called Before-Tax Cash Flow. It is also known as the Economic Cash Flow. (See Figure 16.1.)

Total Gross Income

The first figure is **Gross Scheduled Income**, and it is defined as the maximum amount of rents if the building is 100 percent occupied at either current rents or market rents. **Current rents** refer to rent levels set by lease or contract, and **market rents** refer to what the space or units would rent for if new tenants were sought. Whether current or market rents are being used should be noted by the analyst on the form. In the case study, the current rents are also the market rents; therefore, $800 × 20 units × 12 months = $192,000 Gross Scheduled Income. This is also referred to as *Gross Rent Roll.*

Next, Other Income, if any, is added. **Other Income** refers to items other than rent, such as vending machine income, storage or parking space income, and so on. In the case study, the Other Income is $300 per month. Thus, $300 ×12 months = $3,600 Other Income. The combination of Gross Scheduled Income ($192,000) and Other Income ($3,600) equals *Total Gross Income* of $195,600 (Figure 16.1, Line 3).

Vacancy/Credit Loss

Now, a dollar amount for *Vacancy and Credit Loss* (uncollected rents) is subtracted from the Total Gross Income to arrive at *Gross Operating Income* (or *Gross Receipts*). Usually, the loss is estimated as a percentage, based on recent experience in the market. In the case study, a 5%

Vacancy/Credit loss factor results in $195,600 × 5% = $9,780, which is subtracted from $195,600 to equal $185,820 Gross Operating Income (Figure 16.1, Line 5).

Annual Operating Expenses

The next item deals with the property's annual operating expense estimate. In some properties, like leased commercial and industrial buildings, it is common for the tenants to pay some or all of the operating expenses, under what is known as a *net lease*. In other properties, such as residential rentals, the owner usually pays these operating expenses. The expense analysis usually starts with an examination of the property's past expenses, as shown by property management records or the owner's income tax statements. It is important to note that *operating expenses* do not include loan payments or the depreciation write-off. Annual operating expenses are the actual cost incurred to run the property, such as property tax and insurance, maintenance, repairs, management fees, utilities, and supplies. But loan payments are not a cost to run the property, they are a financial cost to an owner who chooses to borrow, rather than pay cash. Depreciation is a noncash income tax deduction, and it is not related to the property's physical operation. Depreciation is a paper write-off for tax purposes and therefore is not an actual out-of-pocket expense. Loan payments and depreciation are dealt with in cash flow analysis, but not as operating expenses.

Once the past operating expenses have been verified, the expenses must be adjusted to reflect current information and the management policies of the new investor. When the adjustments have been made, they can be compared to expense data for other comparable properties to estimate reasonableness. In some cases, funds will be set aside as reserves for replacement of major repairable items, such as a new roof or carpets. This will be reflected in the annual operating expense deduction.

Net Operating Income

In the case study, the annual Operating Expense was given as $43,100, and is subtracted from the Gross Operating Income of $185,820 to give a *Net Operating Income* of $142,720 (Figure 16.1, Line 7). Net Operating Income (often abbreviated as NOI) is a key figure in cash flow analysis. First, it is the amount of money the property is estimated to produce to help cover the Annual Debt Service (loan payments for the year). Second, as shown later, the NOI is used by investors and appraisers to estimate the price or value of the property.

Annual Debt Service

The *Annual Debt Service* is simply the total of the monthly loan payments (principal and interest), if any, times 12 months. Obviously, the size of the annual debt service is a function of the amount of cash down payment and the size and terms of the mortgage(s). In the case study, the $1,200,000 loan, based on a certain interest rate and term, was estimated to produce a monthly loan payment of $10,530.83. When multiplied by 12 months this produces an annual debt service of $126,370 (Figure 16.1, Line 8).

Before-Tax Cash Flows

In the case study, the NOI of $142,720, less the Annual Debt Service of $126,370 = $16,350 positive Before-Tax Cash Flow (Figure 16.1, Line 9). If the Annual Debt Service is larger than the NOI, the property will produce a *negative* Before-Tax Cash Flow.

Before-Tax Cash Flow is what the investor is estimated to keep, after covering all costs, including loan payments, but before the payment of income taxes, if any, on the collected rents. It is widely used in analyzing investments. It is also used in estimating property value. In some circles, this is known as the "Economic" Cash Flow. It is also described as "cash on cash," the investor's annual pretax cash return on the cash invested. Some texts call it the "equity dividend."

Tax Benefit Analysis

In addition to the Economic Cash Flow, there are income tax aspects to owning and operating rental real estate. The income tax aspects could be positive and add to Before-Tax Cash Flow, or they could be negative and reduce the Before-Tax Cash Flow. A tax benefit analysis computes the positive or negative impact that income taxes are estimated to have on cash flow.

Taxable Income or Loss for the Rental Year

To compute the taxable income or loss for the rental year, the NOI is listed, and then the allowable *interest deductions* on the mortgage(s) are subtracted. It should be noted that only the interest portion of the loan payments, not the principal, is deductible for tax purposes.

The interest portion is computed using a financial calculator, or amortization tables. In our case study, the deductible interest is given as $119,700. There is no second loan, so the next step is to deduct the depreciation write-off, which is called Cost Recovery. (The depreciation rules will be explained in Chapter 17.) The figure of $38,760 given as depreciation in the case study is subtracted as indicated.

Thus, NOI $142,720, less $119,700 interest, less $38,760 depreciation = <$15,740> tax loss for the year (Figure 16.1, Line 15).

Note that after deducting interest and depreciation from the NOI, you could have net income left over, which would be taxable income. However, in the case study, the interest and depreciation deductions exceeded the NOI, thereby generating a *tax loss* for the year. The loss of <$15,740> is a paper loss, not a real out-of-pocket cash loss! How is this so? The depreciation deduction of $38,760 was a noncash deduction for income tax purposes, and this deduction created the <$15,740> tax loss, but with no current out-of-pocket expense to the potential investor.

Taxes Saved or Paid for the Year

If an investor has a taxable income or taxable loss for the year, a set of rules called the passive income and loss rules apply. The passive rules will be discussed in Chapter 17. Assuming that the ability to use the income or loss applies for the current year, a real estate investor then calculates the taxes saved or paid by multiplying the taxable income or loss by the marginal tax bracket for the year.

In the case study, the investor's marginal tax bracket is 38 percent. Therefore, the <$15,740> usable tax loss × 38% = a positive $5,981 tax savings (Figure 16.1, Line 17). How can a loss turn into a positive tax savings? First, remember the loss is paper, not real! Then, this paper tax loss of <$15,740> is used, dollar for dollar, to offset other income the investor has outside of the property. When $15,740 of other outside income is offset by the paper loss generated from the property, an investor would save $5,981 in taxes that he or she otherwise would need to pay on that outside income. This $5,981, in the form of tax savings, increases the investor's current spending power.

Net Spendable Income

Net Spendable Income, also known as **After-Tax Cash Flow**, is the Before-Tax Cash Flow plus or minus the taxes saved or paid. This is the so-called net bottom line. In the case study, the Before-Tax Cash Flow is $16,350, and the taxes saved are $5,981. Therefore, $16,350 + $5,981 = $22,331 Net Spendable Income (Figure 16.1, Line 20).

Multi-year Analysis

The cash flow steps given in Figure 16.1 reflect the first year's estimate. Although many small-investment properties are purchased using just a one-year analysis, investors in larger properties usually insist upon a multiyear analysis, in which the cash flow is projected for each year of the investor's estimated **holding period**. Typical multi-year analysis periods are for 5, 10, 15, or 20 years.

Given a set of assumptions regarding future rent, vacancy, expenses, loan payments, and tax aspect changes, the real estate analyst can estimate the cash flow for each subsequent year of the investor's projected holding period. The result is a Net Spendable Income estimate for each future year. In some situations multiyear analysis is completed using before-tax, instead of after-tax, cash flow numbers.

Net Sale Proceeds

When the Net Spendable Income has been estimated for each year of the investor's projected holding period, the cash flow analysis is still not complete. One step remains: calculation of the Net Sale Proceeds. Remember that the investor wants the return of the investment, plus return on the investment. Only when the investment is resold will these both be known. Therefore, a multiyear analysis not only looks at each year's income, it also estimates what price the property will resell at.

Net Sale Proceeds, often called the **reversion** by appraisers, is the amount of money the investor is estimated to net, after close of escrow and payment of income taxes on the sale, when the property is sold at the end of the holding period. In some situations, sales proceeds are calculated omitting the income tax aspects. If this is the case, the result is called net from escrow or net from sale, excluding income tax aspects.

To calculate the Net Sale Proceeds, the analyst estimates what the property can be sold for at the end of the investor's holding period, 5, 10, 15, or 20 years later. This is done using an estimate of the average annual change in value (an annual compound appreciation rate), or else by capitalizing the net income, based on the last holding year's NOI. (Capitalization of NOI will be discussed in the next section of this chapter.) Once the resale price is estimated, the seller closing costs, old loan balances, and capital gain taxes are subtracted, to produce the Net Sale Proceeds.

Referring to the previous case study, if the original price of the 20-unit apartment property is $1,700,000 and the annual appreciation rate is estimated to be 6 percent, the projected resale price in five years would be approximately $2,275,000 ($1,700,000 × 1.06, repeated five times). Then the seller's closing cost for the sale of a $2,275,000 property is estimated, say at 8 percent. The result would be a seller closing cost of $182,000 ($2,275,000 × 8%).

Next, the outstanding balance, after five years, on the original loan of $1,200,000 would be estimated, using a financial calculator or a remaining loan balance table. In our case study, assume the remaining loan balance on the original loan amount of $1,200,000 after five years is down to $1,158,000. The next step would be to estimate what the capital gain tax would be on the profit, when the property is resold for $2,275,000. This involves a series of substeps, illustrated in Chapter 17. Let us assume here that the capital gain tax came to an estimated $250,000. Then the net sale proceeds would be computed as follows:

$$
\begin{array}{rl}
\$2,275,000 & \text{estimated resale price} \\
-\quad 182,000 & \text{seller closing cost (8\%)} \\
-1,158,000 & \text{outstanding balance owed on the loan} \\
-\quad 250,000 & \text{capital gain tax on resale profit} \\
\hline
\$\quad 685,000 & \text{Net Sale Proceeds (net to seller upon resale)}
\end{array}
$$

Note that the analysis usually assumes that the property resale closes escrow at the end of the year. But the owner will also receive the income from that year. Thus, the total receipts for that year will include both net income and resale proceeds. Both must be calculated either before-tax or after-tax.

Garbage In, Garbage Out

When doing a multiyear projection, a real estate analyst is required to estimate future changes in the subject property's rents, operating expenses, and value. Obviously, there are no guarantees as to what will happen to a property in the future. For example, who in the mid-1980s would have predicted the collapse of the Soviet Union and the subsequent impact it would have on real estate values inregions dependent on the defense industry, such as Southern California! Or the dot-com bust in the early 2000s and its negative impact on the commercial real estate market in the San Francisco Bay area!

When estimating future changes in rents, expenses, and values, bitter lessons have taught real estate analysts to use conservative figures, and require potential investors to sign a statement that these figures are only estimates and not guaranteed.

Summing Up Cash Flow Analysis

Cash flow analysis consists of three major steps:

1. Estimate the first year's Net Spendable Income (After-Tax Cash Flow).

2. Using a set of conservative assumptions, estimate each subsequent year's Net Spendable Income, for the length of the investor's holding period.

3. Estimate the Net Sale Proceeds when the investor sells the property at the end of the holding period.

When these three steps are completed, the analyst has all the cash flow numbers—the amount of investment it takes to get into the property and the property's net bottom line estimates for each year of ownership, plus the Net Sales Proceeds in the year of resale. The next section discusses the various methods used to arrive at an offering price and several techniques used to compute rates of return on investment once cash flow numbers are generated. Before moving on, review your understanding of cash flow analysis.

REVIEWING YOUR UNDERSTANDING

Real Estate Cash Flow Analysis

1. Recite the steps to arrive at Before-Tax Cash Flow.
2. Under the concept of tax benefit analysis, starting with Net Operating Income, list the steps to arrive at income taxes saved or paid for the year.
3. If Before-Tax Cash Flow is a negative <$1,000>, and the amount of taxes that are saved is a positive $3,000, what is Net Spendable Income?

16.3 ESTIMATING PRICE AND RATES OF RETURN

Once an investor decides to seriously consider making an offer on a particular property, the three key economic issues are: (1) the offering price, (2) the amount of the cash investment, and (3) the rate of return on the cash investment.

The Offering Price

Some investors make an offer to buy that is contingent upon a favorable appraisal made by a qualified appraiser. The issue here is not how appraisers arrive at value; that is the subject of a course in real estate appraisal. The issue is: What rules of thumb do investors use to arrive at an initial offering price? Investors' rules of thumb are as many and varied as are investors, but three common techniques are: Gross Rent Multiplier, Capitalization Rate, and Price per Square Foot.

Gross Rent Multiplier

The formula for the gross rent multiplier (also known as the gross income multiplier) is:

$$\frac{\text{Asking Price}}{\text{Gross Scheduled Income}} = \text{Gross Rent Multiplier}$$

The investment property's Asking Price is divided by its Gross Scheduled Income to arrive at the property's **Gross Rent Multiplier**, often abbreviated as *GRM*, or *GIM*. In other words, "How many times does the potential rent go into the asking price?" Referring to our case study, the asking price for the 20-unit apartment property is $1,700,000, and the Gross Scheduled Income from Figure 16.1 is $192,000. Therefore, the GRM is:

$$\frac{\text{Asking Price } \$1,700,000}{\text{Gross Scheduled Income } \$\,192,000} = 8.85 \text{ Gross Rent Multiplier}$$

The 8.85 GRM itself is meaningless, until it can be compared to the market GRM from sales of comparable properties. Investors and their real estate agents are usually aware of prevailing GRMs and apply the following rule of thumb:

The lower the property's multiplier is, compared to the market multiplier, the better is the asking price. The higher the property's multiplier is, relative to the market multiplier, the worse (more overpriced) is the asking price.

If the prevailing market multiplier for comparable 20-unit apartments is 10, the 8.85 GRM from the case study indicates a good buy. If the prevailing market multiplier is 7, then the case study's asking price of $1,700,000 seems too high. If in fact the market multiplier is 7, an investor would compute the maximum offering price as follows:

Gross Scheduled Income × Market Multiplier = Maximum Offering Price

Thus, $192,000 × 7 = $1,344,000 Offering Price.

The GRM approach, because it uses the gross income instead of the net income, ignores the impact that vacancies, expenses, and financing have on price. It is possible that two properties could have the same gross income, but because of various factors could have very different net operating incomes. Because of this shortcoming, the GRM is most often used for apartments and other residential properties. It is rarely used for commercial and industrial properties.

Investors in commercial and industrial real estate generally prefer the Net Operating Income approach, using the **Capitalization Rate**, sometimes called the *Cap Rate*. Appraisers refer to this as *Direct Capitalization*, because it is direct. Another term is *Ratio Capitalization*, because the Cap Rate is a ratio or percent of the price.

Capitalization Rate

The Capitalization Rate is calculated from the offering price, by using the following formula:

$$\frac{\text{Net Operating Income}}{\text{Asking Price}} = \text{Capitalization Rate (Cap Rate)}$$

Notice in the formula that the property's *net operating income*, not its gross income, is used, and it is divided by the asking price. The answer is expressed as a percentage. In essence, the question is: "what percentage of the asking price is the NOI?" Assuming an investor paid all cash and therefore had no loan payments, the Cap Rate would be the same as the first-year before-tax rate of return on investment, if the investor paid the full asking price. The investor is asking, "If I paid cash for the property, does the net income produce an adequate rate of return for my money?"

Using the 20-unit apartment case study in Figure 16.1, the NOI is $142,720, and the asking price is $1,700,000. Therefore, the Capitalization Rate is:

$$\frac{\text{Net Operating Income } \$142,720}{\text{Asking Price } \$1,700,000} = 8.4\% \text{ Capitalization Rate}$$

The 8.4 percent Capitalization Rate is meaningless, until the prevailing market Capitalization Rate for comparable properties is known. Most investors and their agents and consultants know the range of prevailing Cap Rates in the market for comparable properties. Once the market Cap Rate is estimated, the following rule of thumb is usually applied:

The higher the property's Cap Rate above the market Cap Rate, the better the asking price. The lower the property's Cap Rate below the market Cap Rate, the worse (more overpriced) the asking price.

If the prevailing market Capitalization Rate is 7.5 percent, while the property's Capitalization Rate at the asking price is 8.4 percent, this would indicate that the asking price is below market and on the surface appears to be a good buy. If, on the other hand, the prevailing market Capitalization Rate is 9.5 percent, the case study's rate of 8.4 percent is too low! This means that the asking price of $1,700,000 appears to be too high. If in fact, the market Cap Rate is 9.5 percent, the investor figures the maximum offering price for the property as follows:

$$\frac{\text{Net Operating Income } \$142,720}{\text{Market Capitalization Rate } 9.5\%} = \$1,502,316 \text{ Maximum Price}$$

This Capitalization Rate technique is preferred by many investors, because it closely parallels a more sophisticated capitalization approach commonly used by appraisers to estimate the market value of an income property.

Price per Square Foot

As a backup to the GRM and Capitalization Rate approach to estimate an offering price, many investors use the *price per square foot* technique. Here, the offering price is divided by the square footage of the building, to calculate the price per square foot. Then the price per square foot is compared to the price per square foot of other, similar properties, to see if the offering price per square foot is in the market range.

Cash Flow Revisited

Once an investor establishes a price he or she is willing to offer (frequently below the asking price), another cash flow analysis is conducted. This new cash flow analysis looks at what the numbers will be if the lower offered price is accepted. A lower price usually means less money borrowed, and a lower annual debt service. This results in less deductible interest and, because of a lower price, less annual depreciation write-off. All of this will have an impact on net spendable income and net sale proceeds upon resale. This will then have an impact on the investor's rate of return.

Amount of the Cash Investment

One of the major economic issues is the amount of cash needed to acquire the real estate investment. Obviously, the amount of cash required varies with the terms and conditions of the sale, as well as the current requirements of real estate lenders. Some investors prefer to pay all cash, whereas some investors attempt to buy without putting any personal money down. There are numerous seminars, some questionable, on how to buy real estate with no money down, but for the most part, these seminars apply only to small residential rental properties.

In most cases, investors are required to put a 20 to 30 percent cash *down payment*, with lenders willing to finance the difference, if the borrower and property meet the lenders' standards. The terms of the financing will depend on four major items: (1) the current state of the real estate market, (2) the current state of the financial markets, (3) the current state of the occupancy and cash flow of the property, and (4) the credit rating and financial strength of the investor. Once these issues are settled, the amount of cash that is invested (for the purpose of computing rates of return on investment) is considered to be the cash down payment, plus all of the buyer's closing costs.

Computing Rates of Return

Formulas for computing rates of return on the cash invested can be broken down into two general categories: (1) rates of return for the first year, and (2) rates of return for the entire holding period.

Rates of Return for the First Year

The two common calculations to arrive at the first-year rate of return are the *before-tax cash on cash rate* and the *after-tax cash on cash rate*. The first-year before-tax cash on cash rate formula is:

$$\frac{\text{First-Year Before-Tax Cash Flow}}{\text{Cash Invested}} = \frac{\text{First-Year Before-Tax}}{\text{Cash on Cash Rate}}$$

Referring to the 20-unit apartment case study shown in Figure 16.1, the Before-Tax Cash Flow is $16,350, and the cash invested is $500,000; thus:

$$\frac{\$16,350 \text{ Before-Tax Cash Flow}}{\$500,000 \text{ Cash Invested}} = \frac{3.27\% \text{ Before-Tax}}{\text{Cash on Cash Rate}}$$

The before-tax cash on cash rate ignores any impact that income taxes may have on the rate of return. The before-tax cash rate is also called the "economic" cash on cash rate, or dividend rate.

Another common first-year calculation is the after-tax cash on cash rate. This formula is as follows:

$$\frac{\text{First-Year Net Spendable Income}}{\text{Cash Invested}} = \begin{array}{l}\text{First-Year After-Tax}\\\text{Cash on Cash Rate}\end{array}$$

Referring to the 20-unit apartment case study, the Net Spendable Income is $22,331, and the cash invested is still $500,000; therefore, the after-tax cash on cash rate is:

$$\frac{\text{Net Spendable Income } \$22,331}{\text{Cash Invested } \$500,000} = \begin{array}{l}4.47\% \text{ After-Tax}\\\text{Cash on Cash Rate}\end{array}$$

In both examples, at the asking price of $1,700,000, the first-year rates are relatively low, indicating that the asking price is probably too high. If the investor offers a lower price that results in better cash flow numbers, the rates of return, both before and after taxes, should increase to an acceptable rate.

Occasionally, some people factor in the first year's principal payments on the loan and the first year's estimated appreciation to compute a first-year rate of return. This is the so-called equity yield rate for the year. (Note that this is not an accurate *yield rate*.) More sophisticated real estate analysts reject this concept, pointing out that a rate of return should be on a cash-equivalent basis. They note that principal payments and appreciation are only on paper, until the property is refinanced or sold. They are not received as cash each year. They also point out that when a property is refinanced or sold, closing costs greatly reduce the actual cash received. Therefore, any equity yield computed in this manner, prior to liquidating the investment, will be overstated and might be a form of misrepresentation.

Multiyear Rates of Return

There are basically two types of calculations of multiyear rates of return used by real estate investors. They are the (1) *Internal Rate of Return* (IRR) and (2) *Financial Management Rate of Return* (FMRR). Both of these rates recognize the time value of money and use a discount system that reduces the future cash flows to a present value.

Multiyear rates are preferred over first-year rates, because they reflect performance over a period of years, as opposed to a single year, and they recognize the time value of money. Simply put, the **time value of money** states that a dollar today is worth more than a dollar tomorrow. The idea is that the faster you get your money, the quicker you can put it to work to earn even more money. Conversely, the longer you wait to receive your dollar back, the less the future dollar is worth to you today, because of the opportunities missed by your money not being reinvested to earn even more money.

Real estate investments are influenced by the time value of money. Investors place cash up front as the down payment (present-valued dollars), and, over time, receive back annual cash flows, plus net sale proceeds upon resale (future-valued dollars). Therefore, the concept of performing a **discounted cash flow analysis**, to adjust for the time value of money, is appropriate when computing rates of return for real estate investments.

Internal Rate of Return

The **Internal Rate of Return (IRR)** is defined as the discount rate, (yield rate, interest rate, or rate of return on investment), that reduces the future cash flows to just equal the amount of money invested. It takes the total cash returns and separates them into the *return of* the original investment, and the *return on* the investment, as a percent. The calculation is done on certain financial calculators or computers. The steps are as follows:

1. Once the IRR program is ready to run, the analyst enters the initial cash invested and the after-tax cash flows for each year in the order received, including the Net Sale Proceeds in the year of resale.

2. Then the calculator/computer discounts each year's cash flow, to solve for a rate that will discount all the future cash flows to a present value that equals the amount of the cash invested. Once the discount rate is calculated, this is the Internal Rate of Return— the amount each dollar is earning while in the investment. The IRR evolved from the field of corporate finance and is a generally accepted standard measurement of performance among more sophisticated real estate investors and brokers.

Financial Management Rate of Return

There is one shortcoming in the calculation process of finding the IRR. This major problem is known as the "IRR reinvestment assumption." The IRR calculation assumes that as an investor receives each cash flow each year from the investment, these cash flows are immediately reinvested and they continue to earn a yield *equal to the IRR* until the investment terminates. This can be unrealistic if the annual cash flows are modest and the IRR is higher than normal money market rates. Under these circumstances, the IRR overstates what actually will be earned on a portfolio.

The **Financial Management Rate of Return (FMRR)** attempts to overcome this problem, by readjusting each year's cash flows, in light of a "safe" rate: a reinvestment rate that is a reflection of the real world. Once the adjustments are made, a new discount rate is computed, and this is known as the Financial Management Rate of Return. In today's investment world, the FMRR is generally considered a better reflection of the actual performance of a portfolio than the IRR. However, most analysts consider the IRR to be better for comparing any one investment against another investment.

The concepts of the IRR and the FMRR presented here have been simplified. Readers who wish a more in-depth explanation of discounted cash flow analysis are encouraged to seek additional information, by researching these terms on the Internet, reading textbooks on corporate finance, or by contacting the National Association of REALTORS or the Appraisal Institute, for their trade publications on discounted cash flow analysis.

REVIEWING YOUR UNDERSTANDING

Estimating Price and Rates of Return

1. Write down the formulas for the first-year before-tax cash on cash rate and the first-year after-tax cash on cash rate.

2. What is the definition of the Internal Rate of Return (IRR), and how does it differ from the Financial Management Rate of Return (FMRR)?

CHAPTER SUMMARY

Investing is defined as giving up present consumption in exchange for future benefits. Some people invest using hunches; others use an investment analysis procedure. When selecting an investment, the five economic characteristics to check are return, management, taxability, liquidity, and risk.

Real estate cash flow analysis is the process of estimating the amount of money an investor might receive in each year of ownership, including the year of resale. When the cash flow process is completed, the Before-Tax Cash Flow, taxes saved or paid, and the Net Spendable Income for each year of ownership are estimated. Then, the resale price of the property at the end of the investor's holding period is estimated and the Net Sale Proceeds are calculated. Offering prices and rate of return estimates can be computed based on these cash flow numbers.

Offering prices are frequently based on the Gross Rent Multiplier approach and the Capitalization Rate approach and are double-checked by the price per square foot approach. Rates of return can be computed for the first year only, or can be based on a multiyear analysis of the investor's entire estimated holding period.

The most common first-year rates of return on investment are the before-tax cash on cash rate and the after-tax cash on cash rate. Multiyear rates of return should take into consideration the time value of money and use a discounted cash flow approach. The two most common multiyear rates are the Internal Rate of Return (IRR) and the Financial Management Rate of Return (FMRR). The FMRR attempts to overcome the reinvestment assumption shortcoming of the IRR.

REVIEWING YOUR UNDERSTANDING

1. The ability to convert an asset to cash quickly and inexpensively is called:
   A. management
   B. risk
   C. yield
   D. liquidity

2. The risk of loss because of an increase in inflation is:
   A. financial risk
   B. interest rate risk
   C. purchasing power risk
   D. social change risk

3. The decline in real estate values caused by a population shift from urban centers to the suburbs is an example of which risk?
   A. purchase power risk
   B. legal change risk
   C. social change risk
   D. financial risk

4. The maximum amount of rent assuming 100 percent occupancy is:
   A. gross scheduled income
   B. gross operating income
   C. gross rent multiplier
   D. gross domestic income

5. A contract in which the tenant agrees to pay all the operating expenses is a:
   A. gross lease
   B. net lease
   C. percentage lease
   D. residual lease

6. Which of the following is not considered a real estate operating expense?
   A. maintenance
   B. utilities
   C. management
   D. loan payments

7. In cash flow analysis, depreciation is:
   A. called cost recovery
   B. a noncash deduction
   C. an income tax concept
   D. all of the above

8. Before-tax cash flow is computed when:
   A. operating expenses are subtracted from gross operating income
   B. annual debt service is subtracted from net operating income
   C. taxes saved or paid are subtracted from net operating income
   D. vacancies are subtracted from gross scheduled income

9. According to the cash flow formula, a useable tax loss times a marginal tax bracket equals taxes saved.
   A. true
   B. false

10. Taxes saved or paid, plus before-tax cash flow, equals:
    A. net spendable income
    B. net rate of return
    C. net sale proceeds
    D. net operating income

11. Before-tax cash flow is $10,000, useable tax loss is <$5,000>, and the marginal tax bracket is 30 percent; therefore, the after-tax cash flow is:
    A. $ 1,500
    B. $ 4,500
    C. $11,500
    D. $15,000

12. Resale price, less outstanding loan balances, less seller closing costs, less capital gain taxes, equals:
    A. net spendable income
    B. net rate of return
    C. net sale proceeds
    D. net operating income

13. $$\frac{\text{Asking Price}}{\text{Net Operating Income}} = \text{Gross Rent Multiplier}$$
    A. true
    B. false

14. All things being equal, the higher the subject property's gross rent multiplier (GRM) above the market multiplier, the better the buy.
    A. true
    B. false

15. Comparable Property 1 sold for $500,000, with a gross scheduled income of $62,500. Comparable Property 2 sold for $450,000, with a gross scheduled income of $56,250. The subject property's gross scheduled income is $57,100. Based only on this information, the estimated market price of the subject property is:
    A. $456,800
    B. $420,500
    C. $357,200
    D. $318,750

16. The gross rent multiplier approach is most often used to estimate the probable resale price of:
    A. single-family homes
    B. apartment properties
    C. commercial properties
    D. industrial properties

17. $$\frac{\text{Net Operating Income}}{\text{Price}} = \text{Capitalization Rate}$$
    A. true
    B. false

18. All things being equal, the higher the subject property's capitalization rate over the prevailing market capitalization rate, the worse the buy.
    A. true
    B. false

19. The discount rate that reduces the future cash flows to a present value just equal to the amount of money invested is called the:
    A. cash on cash rate of return
    B. equity cap rate
    C. internal rate of return
    D. accounting rate of return

Answer questions 20–25 based on the following case study:

Small rental in a semi-rural college area requires 30 percent down. The small two bedroom home is listed for $300,000, and requires $90,000 down (30%), and a new loan of $210,000 (70%) @ 7% fixed, 30 years, payable $1,397 per month. The rent paid by four students totals $1,900 per month, vacancy factor 5 percent, and there is no other income. Annual operating expenses are $5,800. Interest deduction is $14,632 for the year, and the annual depreciation on improvements is $7,636. Per the accountant, all passive losses can be used in the current year. Potential investor has a combined federal and state tax bracket of 36 percent. **Based on the listed price, answer the following questions.**

First-Year Cash Flow

20. What is the net operating income?

    $_____

21. What is the before-tax cash flow?

    $_____

22. What is the net spendable income?

    $_____

23. What is the annual gross rent multiplier?

    $_____

24. What is the capitalization rate?

    $_____

25. What is the after-tax cash on cash rate?

    $_____

CASE & POINT

Case Study—Older 10-Unit Apartment Building

The following is a practice case study and the answers can be found in the **Answers to Reviewing Your Understanding Questions** section toward the end of the book.

The asking price for a 10-unit apartment property is $1,200,000.

Income and Expense Data

Each unit rents for $1,000 per month, and vending machines and other income net $700 per month. The vacancy factor is 5%. Annual operating expenses (property taxes, insurance, repairs, and management) are estimated to run 30 percent of the gross scheduled income (Line 1).

Financing Data

Lenders will only grant a 75 percent loan, thus the $1.2 million asking price × 75% = $900,000 loan. At 8% fixed interest for 30 years = approximately $6,600 monthly loan payment. The down payment would be $300,000 (asking price $1.2 million × 25%).

Income Tax Information

Based on the loan above, the first-year interest deduction is approximately $71,700. The first-year depreciation estimate is $28,400. The potential investor's combined federal and state tax bracket is 36 percent. Per the investor's accountant, all passive losses are useable in the current year.

Complete the problem below. Round all figures to the nearest dollar. Take all percentages two places past the decimal point.

First-Year Cash Flow Analysis

1.	Gross Scheduled Income	$
2.	Plus: Other Income	+
3.	Equals: Total Gross Income	$
4.	Less: Vacancy/Credit Loss	−
5.	Equals: Gross Operating Income	$
6.	Less: Annual Operating Expenses	−
7.	Equals: Net Operating Income	$
8.	Less: Annual Debt Service	−
9.	Equals: Before-Tax Cash Flow	$

CASE & POINT

Tax Benefit Analysis

10. Net Operating Income	$
11. Less: Interest (Loan 1)	—
12. Less: Interest (Loan 2)	—
13. Less: Cost Recovery (Depreciation)	—
14. Equals: Real Estate Taxable Income or	$
15. Equals: Estimated Allowable Loss (if loss)	$
16. Times Tax Bracket (times Line 14 or 15)	
17. Equals: Taxes Saved or Paid	$

Net Spendable Income

18. Before-Tax Cash Flow (Line 9)	$
19. Plus/Less: Taxes Saved or Paid (Line 17)	
20. Equals: Net Spendable Income (After-Tax Cash Flow)	$

As the investor's adviser, you are asked to answer the following questions:

1. What is the Before-Tax Cash Flow?	$
2. What are the taxes saved/paid?	$
3. What is Net Spendable Income?	$
4. What is the Gross Rent Multiplier?	_____
5. What is the Capitalization Rate?	_____ %
6. What is the before-tax cash on cash rate?	_____ %
7. What is the after-tax cash on cash rate?	_____ %
8. If the prevailing cap rate in the market is 8 percent, what is the maximum that should be paid for this 10-unit apartment?	$ _____

Assume the investor purchases the property for the price computed in Question 8, and the new loan amount is for $806,063 at 8% for 30 years, payable $5,915 per month. Due to the lower price, assume that Annual Operating Expenses will now be reduced to $34,000 per year, the annual interest deduction will be $64,242, and the depreciation write-off will drop to $27,000 per year. All other figures remain as before.

9. What will be the new net spendable income?

10. With an investment of $268,687, what will be the new after-tax cash on cash rate of return?

Chapter

17

IMPORTANT TERMS AND CONCEPTS

Basis   Installment sales $25,000 exception
Boot   Investor   to the passive loss
                                             rules
Depreciation   Passive loss rules
Dealer

PREVIEW

This chapter discusses the impact of the basic principles of federal income taxes on income-producing real estate, not tax aspects of primary residence or vacation homes. For homeowners, some income tax aspects are summarized as a special interest topic and are not stressed in this chapter. Section 17.1 of this chapter outlines the major income tax advantages of owning investment real estate. Section 17.2 discusses basis and depreciation rules. Section 17.3 briefly describes the passive loss rules. Section 17.4 illustrates how gain upon disposition is calculated and how gain and taxes can be deferred by installment sales and real estate exchanges. The appendix presents two views regarding the income tax deductibility of mortgage interest for homeowners.

The material in this chapter is basic and limited to federal, not state, income tax rules. This chapter is intended to illustrate how income taxes affect real estate investment decisions. Readers must recognize that income tax rules are subject to changes after the printing of this textbook. This textbook is not intended to be an aid for tax planning,

Income Tax Aspects of Investment Real Estate

for which all readers are encouraged to seek tax counsel. When you have completed this chapter, you should be able to:

1. List the major income tax advantages of owning investment real estate.
2. Describe how basis is established and why basis is important to real estate.
3. Outline how operating expenses, interest, depreciation, and the passive loss rules affect a property's cash flow.
4. Discuss how gain or loss is measured upon resale and how installment sale reporting and Internal Revenue Code Section 1031 exchanges can spread or defer gain and taxes into future years.

17.1 MAJOR INCOME TAX ADVANTAGES

There are six major income tax advantages for owning income-producing real estate:

1. Interest on loans used to purchase or improve rental real estate is fully deductible against the rental income produced by the property. In some cases any leftover interest, according to the passive loss rules, might also be deductible against an investor's other income. However, interest paid on other types of loans, such as consumer loans, certain raw land loans, and even some aspects of home loans, may not be fully deductible for income tax purposes.

2. For income property owners, repairs, maintenance, management, property taxes, insurance, and other operating expenses are deductible. In contrast, homeowners can currently deduct only property taxes.

3. Income property owners can take depreciation (cost recovery) deductions to shelter rental income. Depreciation is a non-cash deduction that has the same deduction impact as interest and operating expenses, which do require a cash outlay. Homeowners are not allowed to take depreciation.

4. Upon resale, if a property was held by an investor for the statutory time, it may qualify for favorable capital gain treatment if allowed at that time.

5. A real estate investor is allowed installment sale reporting when the property is sold and the seller carries financing (paper). This may save the seller income taxes by pushing a part of the taxable gain into a lower tax bracket in future years.

6. If the investor follows the rules of Internal Revenue Code Section 1031, a real estate exchange can be used to defer all gain and related taxes into another like-kind property.

Investor versus Dealer

An **investor** is a person who holds property for a personal investment portfolio. A **dealer** is a person who acquires real estate as inventory to be resold to customers in the course of business. A property developer constructing subdivision homes for sale to the public is an example of a dealer. Each house in a subdivision is an item of inventory available for sale as a unit. Conversely, an investor acquires property for productive use in business, later capital appreciation, or monthly rental income. Why the distinction? The federal tax code treats investors and dealers differently. For example, real estate investors get all of the six major tax advantages listed in the preceding paragraph. On the other hand, real estate dealers are not allowed depreciation, capital gains, installment sales, and Internal Revenue Code Section 1031 exchanges.

The length of time the property is held is not a determining factor in whether the property is held for investment or resale. More importantly the burden of proof has been the intent of the party. For this reason, dealers have found it difficult to convert their properties from resale to investment holdings. The current downturn in the new home market has forced many real estate developers to abandon their completed subdivisions and those still under construction, due to the lack of prospective buyers or financing.

Obviously, when analyzing a particular property it will make a significant difference, in terms of cash flow analysis, yield, and disposition strategy, whether the buyer is a dealer or an investor. There are no absolute, clear guidelines as to what behavior makes one a dealer or an investor. There are many gray areas that require the advice of tax experts based on individual circumstances. Factors to consider include the number of sales, length of holding period, sales after subdividing, and the like. For the remainder of this chapter it will be assumed that an investor position applies.

REVIEWING YOUR UNDERSTANDING

1. List six major income tax advantages of owning income real estate.
2. In terms of cash outlay, how do depreciation deductions differ from operating expenses and mortgage interest?
3. Compare the income tax differences between a real estate investor and a real estate dealer.

17.2 BASIS AND DEPRECIATION

In addition to deductions for out-of-pocket operating expenses and interest paid on mortgages, an income tax deduction is allowed for depreciation, formally known as cost recovery.

Depreciation is an annual bookkeeping deduction, allowed by the tax code as a cost recovery for the theoretical loss in value of the property over time. In reality, the property could be appreciating in real value, but an investor is still allowed to take a depreciation loss deduction for income tax purposes. This reduces the taxable income, without reducing the net cash flow.

The depreciation deduction is allowed only on the improvements, not on the land. First ascertain the cost of new construction or the market value of the improvements if purchased. This can and often does include any improvements apparent to the land including: outbuildings, barns, storage sheds, garages, cottages, and trade fixtures. Appurtenances such as grape vines, trees, and other perennial crops are also valued separate from the land and depreciated at their own schedules. Please remember that this usage of the word *depreciation* is different from the use of the word in appraisals.

How Much Is Deductible?

The dollar amount of depreciation allowed each year is a function of the taxpayer's basis in the real estate, the allocation between improvements and land, and the straight-line write-off period. **Basis** refers to the property owner's cost for income tax purposes. The allocation between improvements and land is determined by an appraisal or a set of guidelines. The straight-line write-off period for each category of improvement is established by Congress.

How Does It Work?

First, the property owner's basis must be determined. Basis is important for two reasons: (1) Basis is the starting point for computing depreciation while the property is owned, and (2) basis is used in calculating the gain or loss for income tax purposes when the property is disposed of.

The owner's initial basis in a property is determined by the method of acquisition, not by the value of the property. A $2 million property can be acquired one way and have a basis of $2 million. But the same property could be acquired another way and have a basis that is considerably lower. An investor must depreciate using basis, not value! The most common method to acquire title is to purchase the real estate. Basis upon purchase is usually the purchase price, plus a certain portion of the buyer's closing cost, called capitalized cost. During the investor's ownership, the basis will be increased by the cost of any capital improvements added and will decrease by the amount of allowed depreciation deductions. Depreciation expense is required by the tax code on investment property. It is taken either over the life of the property or upon sale. Owners cannot avoid the depreciation expense for income tax purposes.

Once the purchase price and capitalized closing cost have been determined, the next step is to allocate the basis between the non-depreciable land and the depreciable improvements. This allocation is done by use of an appraisal, comparable sales data, or sometimes the ratio established by the county tax assessor on the property tax bill. This allocation process is tricky and is subject to IRS challenge if the allocation does not reflect current market reality. Once the basis has been allocated between land and improvements, there is frequently further subdivision between real property and personal property, such as carpets, draperies, appliances, and so on, because of the different write-off rules for each.

The time periods for depreciating investments are set by law and have been subject to frequent changes. The depreciation periods for real estate were changed in 2006 to 27½ years for residential rental property and 39 years for nonresidential rental property (IRS Code Section 1250). Real estate must use straight-line depreciation. However, the first and last year straight-line system must be modified by what is called the mid-month convention. Accelerated systems that allowed more than straight-line depreciation were

Special Interest Topic

Initial Basis of Real Estate

The following are various methods of acquiring title to real estate and how basis is initially determined:

1. If real property is acquired by purchase, the initial basis is the purchase price plus capitalized buyer's closing cost.

2. If real property is acquired by gift, the initial basis is the donor's adjusted cost basis, or market value at the date of gift, whichever is less.

3. If real property is acquired by inheritance, the initial basis is market value at the date of death of the decedent. Seek a professional appraisal soon after death of the decedent to establish the new basis.

4. If real property is acquired by exchange, the initial basis is the market value of the new property, less the deferred gain from the old property.

The basis of a principal residence converted to a rental is the adjusted basis of the home or the home's market value on date of conversion, whichever is less. Seek a professional appraisal to establish the property market value on the date of conversion.

abolished for all real estate acquired after December 31, 1986. Personal property depreciation has various time periods, with five to seven years being the most common. Personal property is allowed accelerated write-off using the 200 percent declining balance system. This 200 percent system must be modified using the mid-year convention. Both mid-month and mid-year conventions require slight modifications to the straight-line and 200 percent declining balance systems when calculating the precise dollar amount of depreciation. The details are beyond the scope of this text. For specific information, readers are referred to IRS Publication 946 "How to Depreciate Property" at www.irs.gov, and encouraged to consult a tax professional.

Example

An investor purchased an apartment property for $1 million, plus $5,000 in capitalized buyer closing costs. According to an appraisal, the allocation is 20 percent to land and 80 percent to building, with no personal property items. The first 12 months' depreciation could be estimated as follows:

$1,000,000	Purchase price
+ 5,000	Plus: capitalized buyer closing costs
$1,005,000	Equals: Initial basis
× .80	Times: Percent building ratio
$ 804,000	Equals: Depreciable building

Then

$$\frac{\$804,000 \text{ depreciable building}}{27\frac{1}{2} \text{ years residential rental}} = \$29,236 \text{ estimated depreciation}$$

(actual amount will be slightly less because of mid-month convention—i.e., first year only 11½ months)

REVIEWING YOUR UNDERSTANDING

1. Discuss how initial basis is determined for real estate owners.

2. How is basis allocated between land and improvements? What is the length of depreciation allowed for residential and nonresidential rental real estate?

3. Purchase price for a small commercial property is $500,000, plus $3,000 capitalized buyer's closing cost. Land is 20 percent, building 80 percent, with no personal property. What is the approximate depreciation for the first 12 months?

17.3 PASSIVE LOSS RULES

The Tax Reform Act of 1986 was a major overhaul of the federal income tax system. One of the act's many features was an attack on real estate tax shelters. The main purpose of a real estate tax shelter is to produce a paper tax loss (as opposed to an out-of-pocket cash loss) that can be applied against the investor's other personal income. The paper tax loss was because of the allowable non-cash depreciation deductions. In short, paper tax losses offset other real income, resulting in a decrease in taxes owed and an increase in after-tax spendable dollars. In the meantime, the investment may appreciate, resulting in a capital gain upon resale. The purpose of the passive loss section of the Tax Reform Act of 1986 was to reduce the practice of using paper real estate losses to reduce otherwise taxable personal income.

Prior to the Tax Reform Act of 1986 any annual loss (rents, lower operating expenses, mortgage interest, and depreciation) could be used in the current year to offset any other current income of the investor. However, the general **passive loss rules** now state that real estate losses can only offset what is known as passive income. Understanding the passive loss rules and their impact on real estate cash flow analysis requires an explanation of income classifications.

According to the Tax Reform Act of 1986, income is broken into the following three classifications:

1. *Active Income.* Income generated when the taxpayer materially participates in an activity that produces income. Examples include wages, commissions, profits from owner-managed business, and other similar activities.

2. *Portfolio Income.* Income from paper types of investments, such as interest on savings, dividends on stocks, and coupons on bonds.

3. *Passive Income.* Income generated when the taxpayer does not materially participate in an activity that produces income. Examples include limited partnership income, business ventures in which the taxpayer has no active role, and rents from rental real estate. The Tax Reform Act of 1986 states that rental real estate is considered a passive activity, even if the property owner actively manages the rental real estate. This provision was a deliberate attempt to keep rental real estate in the passive income category.

Passive Income/Loss Offset Rules

The general rule is that a passive loss can offset only passive income. Passive losses cannot normally be used to offset active or portfolio income. If passive real estate losses cannot be used in the current year because of a lack of passive income, then the passive loss must be carried forward to offset passive income that might arise in a future tax year. If future tax years do not produce suitable passive income, the carry-forward passive loss can be used to offset gain when the subject property is sold.

This change was a dramatic shift from the earlier law, where a real estate loss could be used to offset any current income. By restricting the offset of annual real estate losses to passive income, if a real estate investor does not have passive income, the normal tax savings will not be realized in the current year. This reduces the investor's current cash flow, which in turn reduces the investor's current rate of return and lowers the interest in and willingness to invest in rental real estate.

$25,000 Exception to the Passive Loss Rules

The passive loss rules provide an exception to the general rule that passive losses can offset only passive income. This exception is known as the **$25,000 real estate exception is to the passive loss rules.** It allows a qualified rental property owner to use up to $25,000 of passive real estate rental losses to offset active or portfolio income each year, after first offsetting passive income. To qualify for this $25,000 exception, a taxpayer must meet the following tests:

1. The taxpayer must own 10 percent or more direct interest in rental real estate and not hold title as either a corporation, or a tax-reporting limited partnership which must file Internal Revenue Service Form 1065.

2. The owner must be active in the management of the rental real estate. "Active in management" means that the owner must deal directly with the tenants and make all management decisions or hire a property manager to deal with the tenants. If the owner hires a property manager, the two should confer periodically, and the management contract should specify that the owner is the decision maker regarding the operations of the property. If a property owner leaves all management decisions to a property manager and merely receives a check and accounting statements, the property owner will probably fail the active-in-management test and lose the use of the $25,000 rule.

3. For the tax year in question, the rental real estate owner's modified adjusted gross income must be $100,000 or less. If the owner's modified adjusted gross income for the year is more than $100,000, then the otherwise usable $25,000 is reduced $1 for every $2 the modified adjusted gross income exceeds $100,000. Thus, the $25,000 rule will be phased out entirely when a rental real estate owner's modified adjusted gross income reaches $150,000. Keeping with the spirit of the Tax Reform Act of 1986, this effectively reserves the $25,000 rule for moderate-income real estate investors.

For the real estate investors who meet this series of tests, up to $25,000 of passive losses can be used in the current tax year to offset active and portfolio income, reducing taxes owed. This in turn will increase the after-tax spendable income for the year and raise the current year's rate of return.

Professional Real Estate Exception

Qualified real estate professionals who spend at least 750 hours and more than one-half of all business time per year in real estate activities can use real estate losses to offset any business or personal income. In short, unlike other real estate investors, a qualified real estate professional does not need to follow the passive loss rules. Possession of a real estate license docs not exempt the individual from these rules if not supported by professional activity. Activities do not have to be specific to the individual investment or dealer property.

A qualified real estate professional can acquire income real estate and use any paper losses created by depreciation to offset ordinary income, not just passive income. This gives a qualified real estate professional a decided investment advantage over a regular investor.

To determine who is a qualified real estate professional, one must turn to ever-changing IRS interpretations. Examples of qualified real estate professionals include appraisers, property managers, loan brokers, real estate salespersons, and real estate brokers, who meet the hours and percentage of business rules and have been cleared by IRS interpretations.

Can a licensed real estate agent be an investor, dealer, and a real estate agent at the same time? Yes. An individual can hold property as an investment as well as hold an interest in property held for sale. That same individual may act as an agent bringing together a buyer and seller of property for a commission *(Williford v. Comm., TC Memo 1992–430)*. When in doubt, the ethical agent will always disclose.

Several other rules from the Tax Reform Act of 1986 have an impact on real estate investments but are beyond the scope of this chapter. Once again, readers are encouraged to seek competent tax counsel before entering into a real estate transaction.

REVIEWING YOUR UNDERSTANDING

1. What is a tax shelter?
2. What is the general passive loss rule?
3. What are the three tests to determine if the $25,000 exception to the general passive loss rule can be used?
4. What is the qualified real estate professional exception to the passive loss rules?

17.4 CALCULATING AND DEFERRING GAIN

Once owners decide to market their properties, they have a series of choices regarding how to handle the gain upon sale. A real estate investor has three basic choices:

1. sell for cash and pay the tax on the gain.

2. sell and carry some equity in a promissory note combined with a deed of trust, and report some gain as an installment sale.

3. do not sell and do a like-kind Internal Revenue Code Section 1031 exchange and defer the gain and tax into the new property.

Note that dealers do not have the option of a like-kind exchange, only investors qualify for this favorable tax treatment. Property is "inventory" to the dealer and not used for productive use in business, investment, or capital appreciation.

This section outlines the basic principles of each choice.

A. Calculating Gain and Taxes Owed on Income Property

Step 1: Calculate Adjusted Cost Basis

Initial (original) basis	$500,000
Plus: buyer's capitalized closing cost	10,000
Plus: capital improvements, if any	10,000
Minus: depreciation for term of ownership	(70,000)
Equals: adjusted cost basis on date of resale	450,000

Step 2: Calculate Gain

Resale price	$750,000
Less: seller closing cost	(8,500)
Less: adjusted cost basis from Step 1	(450,000)
Less: carry-forward passive losses, if any	00
Equals: gain on sale	$291,500

Step 3: Apply current capital gain treatment to the gain on sale to calculate the tax owed. Assume held for more than 1 year at 35% marginal income tax rate. (See the capital gains tax rate schedule provided later.)

Capital Gains Tax Rate to use	15%
Total Capital Gains tax due	$43,725

Capital gains tax rates are exceedingly favorable compared to individual income tax rates. Investors holding property for one year or longer see only a 15% tax on their gain. Qualified married homeowners residing in their property for two of the past five years are able to exclude $500,000 from their gain before applying capital gains tax rates. Real estate is a wonderful way to build equity and your estate.

Capital Gains Tax Rate Schedule							
January 1, 2008–December 31, 2010							
If Seller Had Owned the Sold Asset for	*and*	Seller's Marginal Income Tax Rate the Year of Sale Is					
		10%	15%	25%	28%	33%	35%
	then	the Tax Rate on the Capital Gain Is					
Less Than 1 Year		10%	15%	25%	28%	33%	35%
1 Year or More		0%	0%	15%	15%	15%	15%

Note: The rate remains 28% for long-term gains from sales of art works and other collectibles.

The Capital Gains rules are almost certain to change dramatically as of January 1, 2011. The new IRS rules that have been in place since 2003 will expire, unless Congress acts to extend them. The "new" rules will then revert to the old rules. The following maximum capital gains taxation rates will apply to capital asset sales occurring after January 1, 2011.

A. Capital assets held for more than 12 months:
1. If in 10% or 15% tax bracket, the rate is 10%.
2. If in 28% or 31% tax bracket, the rate is 20%.
3. If in the 36% tax bracket or above, the rate is:
   a. If held less than 5 years: 20%
   b. If held more than 5 years: 23.8%
B. Collectibles held more than 12 months:
1. If in 10% or 15% tax bracket, the rate is 15%.
2. If in 28% tax bracket or higher, the rate is 28%.

B. Use of an Installment Sale to Spread Out Taxable Gain

Section 453 of the Internal Revenue Code provides a way to spread over a number of years the gain and tax on the profit from a sale of an asset. This avoids paying the entire tax on the entire gain in the year of sale.

A note and deed of trust, a mortgage, a contract of sale, or other similar instruments. The seller "carry loan" must call for a due date in some year other than the same year as the sale. The seller carry loan can be either a senior or junior loan. Whenever the seller carries back debt, the installment method for reporting gain is automatic, unless the seller formally elects to take the entire tax in the year of sale. Installment sale reporting is allowed for real estate investors and homeowners. Real estate dealers are normally denied the use of installment sales. Once again, dealers sell their inventory of homes or property and acknowledge their sales income in the year in which the transaction occurred. Some advantages and disadvantages of an installment sale follow. **Installment sales** are often also called sales contracts or land contracts. Capital Gains tax rates apply once more.

Advantages

1. It is a way to sell a property in a tight real estate market.
2. An installment sale can lower the tax owed on the sale by throwing all or part of the gain into a more favorable, low tax bracket year in the future.
3. Interest can be earned from the buyer on gain not yet reported.
4. The tax can be paid in the future with inflated (cheaper) dollars.
5. Title of the property does not transfer until the last payment on the contract is made.
6. Seller may retain all buyer contract payments if the buyer defaults.

Disadvantages

1. Seller does not receive all of his or her equity in up-front cash, thereby incurring opportunity costs on reinvestment possibilities.
2. Seller may be in a higher tax bracket when money is collected from the buyer in a future year and thus may actually pay more in taxes than would have been the case in the year of sale.
3. Buyer could pay off the loan early and thereby force the seller to take gain in an unplanned, unfavorable tax year.
4. Buyer could default on the loan, and the seller could be forced to proceed with a foreclosure.

There are many other aspects to installment sales not covered in this brief summary. The installment sale technique for spreading out

Special Interest Topic
Application of 1997 & 1998 Tax Law Changes to the
Sale of a Principal Residence

1. The law now states that there will be no tax on a gain up to $250,000 for single home sellers and $500,000 for married home sellers who file a joint return. To qualify,  the home must have been the principal residence for at least two out of the last five years. The residence requirement need not be contiguous time. Only one spouse needs to have been the owner, but both spouses must have lived there for a two year period, and filed joint returns, to get the $500,000 maximum exemption. All age limits and requirements to buy another home have been eliminated. You can do this every 5 years! This is a tax-free event – no income tax – no capital gain tax!

2. This full exclusion can only be used once every 2 years. If a home is sold for a gain before the two year holding period, the gain will be fully taxable, UNLESS the sale is due to a job change, major illness, or unforeseen circumstances. Then a pro rata formula will be used to separate tax exempt from taxable gain.

Example: Assume the owner lived in the home for only 18 months, then due to a job change, the home was sold for a gain. The formula will work as follows:

$$\frac{18 \text{ months}}{24 \text{ months}} = 75\%$$

If homeowner is single, he or she would get $250,000 × 75% or $187,500 maximum exemption.

If homeowners are married, they would get $500,000 × 75% or $375,000 maximum exemption.

gain may or may not be a good tax move for a real estate seller. A real estate licensee should not give tax advice; however, a licensee should recognize that an installment sale is one of several choices a seller should discuss with a tax adviser.

C. Use of a Like-Kind, Section 1031 Exchange to Defer Gain

Section 1031 of the Internal Revenue Code provides a way to move ownership from one income or investment property to another and not recognize taxable gain. Although the rules are complicated, the basic concept states that real estate held for income or investment can be exchanged, tax deferred, for any other real estate to be held for income or investment. Section 1031 real estate exchanges can only be used by investors. Real estate dealers are not allowed to do tax-deferred exchanges. Homeowners cannot do 1031 exchanges, but rather have a different system regarding gain. (See Special Interest Topic discussed later for details.) U.S. property cannot be 1031 exchanged for foreign properties.

Key to a properly structured Section 1031 exchange is to ensure that the taxpayer does not directly or indirectly, through an agent or an accommodation, actually or constructively receive money or other cash equivalent ("boot"). Receipt of cash or cash equivalent triggers a taxable event which undermines the entire purpose of a Section 1031 exchange. To that end, use of safe-harbor rules go far to ensure a tax-free exchange. Depositing funds directly into a qualified escrow account is one such method. Seek professional tax assistance when contemplating a tax-free exchange.

Under a properly structured 1031 real estate exchange, no tax is paid on the realized gain at the time of the transfer. Rather, the gain is carried over to the new property, to be taxed when the new property is sold. Often the process is repeated, property after property, deferring gain until ultimately the owner dies. Since 2005, the decedent's heirs would receive the final property at a basis equal to market value at the date of death, and all previous deferred gains would be excused. Thus, a tax-deferred exchange can become a tax-free exchange upon death. You can "take it with you" after all.

When structuring a 1031 exchange, the different properties may have unequal equities. To balance the difference in equities, one party must give some additional items to the other. If the difference in equities is balanced using items other than qualified like-kind real estate, the party who receives the unlike property is said to have received "boot." **Boot** is defined as any unlike property received in the exchange. Examples of "boot" include not only cash but also cash equivalents. The market value of works of art, luxury or antique vehicles, jewelry and other personal property at the time of sale have consequences. Receipt of boot can trigger some tax in a real estate exchange. Thus, to have a completely tax-deferred exchange, a person must avoid receiving boot.

Computation of boot and other details of 1031 tax-deferred exchanges are beyond the scope of this textbook. Readers are invited to discuss this subject with tax experts and knowledgeable real estate investment agents. The purpose here is to offer 1031 like-kind exchanges as another alternative to a regular real estate sale and payment of tax on the resulting gain.

REVIEWING YOUR UNDERSTANDING

1. List the steps needed to compute gain upon sale of income real estate.
2. What are the advantages and disadvantages of an installment sale?
3. Who can and who cannot do a 1031 tax-deferred real estate exchange?

CHAPTER SUMMARY

The major income tax advantages of owning income real estate include: the deductibility of mortgage interest, operating expenses, and depreciation while you own the property; capital gain treatment; use of installment sale reporting; and the ability to use a 1031 tax-deferred exchange. These advantages are available to real estate investors. Real estate dealers cannot take depreciation and capital gains and are usually not allowed installment sale and 1031 exchange treatment.

Cost for income tax purposes is called basis. The amount of basis is determined by how title is acquired. Basis is used to determine the amount of depreciation allowed each year and to measure gain or loss upon resale. Once basis is established, it is allocated between land and improvements, after which the real estate improvements are depreciated for the time period allowed by law. Current rules allow 27½ years for residential rental and 39 years for nonresidential, using the straight-line method.

The Tax Reform Act of 1986 created the passive loss rules, which state that rental real estate is a passive activity and any passive real estate loss can offset only passive income. Passive losses can no longer offset active or portfolio income unless the $25,000 exception can be applied. The passive loss rules have had the impact of discouraging some people from investing in rental real estate. Some real estate professionals are exempt from these passive loss rules.

Once real estate owners decide to market their income properties, they basically have three choices for how to handle taxable gain. They could sell for cash, declare the gain, and pay the tax. They could carry some financing on behalf of the buyer and treat the gain in the seller carry note as an installment sale. Or, finally, the owners could decide to structure a like-kind 1031 tax-deferred exchange and transfer the gain into another income or investment property.

REVIEWING YOUR UNDERSTANDING

1. Which of the following is a non-cash income tax deduction?
   A. mortgage interest
   B. property taxes
   C. repairs
   D. depreciation

2. Which tax treatment does an investor receive that a dealer does not?
   A. mortgage interest deduction
   B. property tax deduction
   C. repair deduction
   D. depreciation

3. The initial basis to an owner who acquired title to real estate by gift is:
   A. donor's adjusted basis or market value, whichever is less
   B. market value at the date of gift
   C. purchase price, plus capitalized closing costs
   D. market value of new property less gain deferred from old property

4. The minimum depreciation write-off period for residential rental property is:
   A. 39 years
   B. 27½ years
   C. 7 years
   D. 5 years

5. For rental real estate investors, all of the following are depreciable except:
   A. carpets
   B. buildings
   C. land
   D. carport

6. Income or losses from rental real estate are considered to be:
   A. active
   B. portfolio
   C. passive
   D. tax sheltered

7. To use the full $25,000 exception to the passive loss rules, the rental property owner's modified adjusted gross income must not exceed:
   A. $125,000
   B. $100,000
   C. $75,000
   D. $25,000

8. When the seller of an income property carries financing for the buyer, the income tax reporting of the sale is known as:
   A. an installment sale
   B. a tax-deferred exchange (1031)
   C. an excluded gain
   D. a once-in-a-lifetime exemption

9. To qualify for a 1031 tax-deferred exchange, an investor must exchange:
   A. income or investment real estate for income or investment real estate
   B. real property for personal property
   C. a principal residence for a principal residence
   D. foreign rental property for U.S. rental property

10. The receipt of unlike taxable property in a 1031 exchange is called:
    A. leverage
    B. equity balance
    C. boot
    D. basis

11. Depreciation for income tax purposes is technically called:
    A. write-off
    B. cost recovery
    C. cash flow deduction
    D. tax loophole

12. The initial basis of real property acquired by purchase is best described as:
    A. basis of the seller, less closing costs
    B. market value at date of purchase
    C. purchase price, plus capitalized buyer's closing costs
    D. loan amount, plus closing costs

13. Purchase price, including capitalized buyer closing cost, of a commercial property is $1 million, with land 40 percent and real estate improvements 60 percent. Ignoring the mid-month convention, what will be the total depreciation for 12 months?
    A. $15,385
    B. $36,364
    C. $21,819
    D. $25,641

14. Which of the following is considered passive income?
    A. wages
    B. profits from an owner-managed business
    C. dividends from stocks
    D. rents from investor-owned real estate

15. The general passive loss rule states that passive losses can only offset:
    A. passive income
    B. active income
    C. portfolio income
    D. all of the above

16. To use the $25,000 exception to the general passive loss rule, an investor must own at least what percent of the property?
    A. 1 percent
    B. 5 percent
    C. 10 percent
    D. 20 percent

17. Real estate passive losses that cannot be used in the current year:
    A. are lost forever
    B. can be carried forward to be used in future years
    C. can always be used when the investor's income drops below $25,000
    D. are carried back to offset income earned the previous year

18. Qualified real estate professionals are exempt from the passive loss rules on their rental properties.
    A. true
    B. false

19. Purchase price of income property is $300,000; buyer's capitalized closing cost, $3,000; capital improvements added, $15,000; and depreciation accumulated during term of ownership, $20,000. Based only on this information, what is the adjusted cost basis?
    A. $338,000
    B. $318,000
    C. $298,000
    D. $262,000

20. The property in Question 19 is resold for $400,000, seller's closing costs come to 8 percent, and carry forward passive losses are $10,000. What is the gain or loss on the sale?
    A. $8,000 loss
    B. $100,000 gain
    C. $85,000 gain
    D. $60,000 gain

21. To qualify as an installment sale, the seller must carry back a junior lien or second, not a first, deed of trust.
    A. true
    B. false

22. For the seller who carries a loan, one disadvantage of an installment sale is that:
    A. it could lower tax on gain in year of payoff
    B. in the event of default, seller may need to foreclose
    C. if inflation continues, the seller will pay the tax using cheaper dollar
    D. the seller will earn interest on gain and tax not yet reported

23. 1031 real estate exchanges cannot be used by:
    A. homeowners
    B. investors who own land
    C. investors who own commercial property
    D. investors who own farms

24. Foreign properties can be exchanged 1031 tax deferred for U.S. properties.
    A. true
    B. false

25. For a married couple to exclude up to $500,000 in gain upon the sale of their owner-occupied principal residence, they must:
    A. both be on title
    B. earn no more than $100,000 per year
    C. occupy the home for a minimum of one year
    D. file a joint income tax return for two years

CASE & POINTS

Why Should Interest on Home Loans Be Deductible?

Whether homeowners should be allowed to deduct the interest they pay on their mortgages is currently under debate. After reading the following two viewpoints, see if you can separate the logical economic points from the emotional non-economic points.

Viewpoint 1

Allowing homeowners to deduct mortgage interest is an economic rip-off. An income tax deduction should only be allowed for business, not personal expenses. A business expense deduction can be justified as a fair revenue neutral concept. When a company pays someone for a legitimate business expense it should be deductible to arrive at true taxable profit. Owning a home is not a business; it is a personal consumer item no different from owning a personal car or a television set. In the U.S. tax code, interest paid on money borrowed to purchase consumer products is not deductible, except for homeowner interest!

When homeowners are allowed to deduct mortgage interest, this lowers their income taxes. To make up for this lost revenue, the government increases other people's taxes. Not only is this tax shift unfair, but it discriminates against home renters, who cannot deduct their rental payments from their income. Renters tend to be lower-income people; thus, the home interest deductions of middle- and upper-income people are extracted at the expense of lower-income people.

To add insult to injury, homeowners can refinance their homes and pull out money to purchase consumer products, then turn around and deduct the interest on the refinance loan. In short, the homeowner borrows to acquire consumer goods, thereby shifting the nondeductible consumer interest into deductible homeowner interest. A renter cannot do this and therefore pays the full cost of consumer borrowing.

The argument that we need homeowner interest deductions to encourage people to purchase a home is bunk! Many other developed Western nations do not allow homeowners to deduct mortgage interest, and they have an equal or even greater percentage of home ownership than does the United States. Don't fool yourself: The only justification for an interest deduction for a home mortgage is to appease a special interest voting bloc consisting of homeowners and their PAC fund fat cats and allied real estate industries.

Viewpoint 2

The facts speak for themselves: Countries with a high percentage of private real estate ownership have a stable, law-abiding society. Citizens tend not to revolt and destroy a country if they own a piece of the land. For its own preservation, a country and its government should use all tools available, including the tax code, to make home ownership affordable to as many people as possible.

It is a basic economic principle that incentives change behavior. Giving tax incentives to own a home encourages more people to seek home ownership Mortgage interest deductions for homeowners reduce the effective cost of owning a home. By reducing the cost of home ownership, a home becomes more affordable to more people. As homeowners pay off their mortgages, their equity increases and their interest deductions decrease. This increase in equity increases net worth, which in turn creates financial security and peace of mind. An increase in net worth reduces the need for government aid, which then diminishes the need to increase taxes.

Opponents of home interest deductions often state that they constitute discrimination against renters. One can counter by stating that by allowing interest deductions for homeowners, more renters can afford to become homeowners. If home interest deductions were abolished, fewer people could afford a home. This would result in less net worth and an increase in government aid, which would require an increase in everyone's taxes. If some renters cannot afford to purchase a home, the answer is to provide government loans so they can buy homes. The answer should not be to make everyone a renter!

It is slippery logic to state that home interest deductions are not needed to obtain a high percentage of home ownership and to cite the high ownership in other countries that do not allow home interest deductions. A comparison of the percentage of

CASE & POINT

U.S. home ownership with other countries is not "apples with apples" but "apples with apricots." Different countries have different social security and welfare programs, cultural values, and tax structures. Any comparison just by percentage of home ownership is dishonest economics.

The concept of home ownership transcends a mere listing of who pays what tax. It goes to the greater issues of private property, the ability to accumulate a personal net worth, and the commitment to one's country and its social values.

Chapter 18

PREVIEW

A complete investigation of a possible real estate investment includes a study of the general economic trends in the real estate market and the status of economic cycles, together with a detailed study of the value and investment return potential of the individual parcel. This chapter brings together these two elements to outline the real estate decision-making process. Section 18.1 explores the variables that a real estate investor should consider before making an investment decision. Section 18.2 uses flow charts to illustrate the steps in making a real estate investment decision. The Case & Point at the end of the chapter examines how to identify at what stage a real estate cycle is in. When you have completed this chapter, you will be able to:

1. Describe why real estate investing involves multiple choices.

2. List the five steps in the scientific method of analysis.

3. Summarize the steps in analyzing a parcel of improved real estate.

4. Summarize the steps in analyzing the alternatives for developing an unimproved parcel of land.

Applied Real Estate Economics

18.1 REAL ESTATE INVESTMENT VARIABLES

There are key factors that investors usually consider before making an investment decision. This section focuses on the two most important factors. One is the investor's future *expectation* for the investment. The second is the importance of selecting from *multiple choices!*

Expectations

As mentioned earlier, real estate is an expensive asset that is locked into a fixed location. The large initial investment frequently takes years to recoup. Appraisers often say that value is the present worth of future benefits. Because of these factors, real estate investments are heavily influenced by future changes. Therefore, real estate prices today are based on an investor's future **expectation**, or projection of earnings tomorrow and beyond.

The investor could simply assume that future earnings will be similar to the earnings today. But this is not a reasonable assumption, because of both trends and cycles at work. In fact, the key element of the investment process is the *study of how possible changes may affect future earnings.*

What are the future changes that will influence real estate values? By definition, they are all based on economic, social, physical, or political cycles or trends. Future real estate values, as always, will be influenced by changing economic events, changes in social attitudes, changes in physical conditions, and by the future political actions of governments.

Cycles and Trends

When investors seek to estimate future changes in earnings, they must remember that all **change** involves either a **cycle**—change that

479

repeats regularly—or a **trend**—a long-term shift in one direction. Therefore, to estimate future earnings, one must try to forecast the economic, social, physical, and political changes, the combination of cyclical and trend changes, and their influence on earnings. Because all future cycles and trends start in the past, this forecast must try to predict the movement of past cycles and trends into the future. Indeed, it is critical to understand, at the time of making an investment decision, where the major cycles are in their pattern! Much of the material in Parts One and Two of this book is intended to discuss the major influences on such movements, so that investors can understand them and better estimate their future direction and size.

"What If"

At any one time, there are numerous cycles and trends, perhaps millions. Investors should not be concerned with every change! Only those that most influence a particular real estate market need be of interest. To locate these important changes, analysts must play a game that is called **sensitivity analysis**. This means asking what would be the effect, if any, of each perceived change. A sample group of questions follows.

What if:

- the tenant went bankrupt?
- the seller could not meet a promise of 90 percent occupancy?
- the largest industry in town closed its doors?
- the country went into a recession?
- the cost of gas and electricity increased by 30 percent?
- zoning were changed to a land use of lower value?
- many lenders had problems with bad loans at the same time?
- auto gasoline was rationed, or the price doubled?
- depreciation deductions were eliminated?
- Congress removed all real estate tax advantages?
- the city ordered a mandatory building code inspection?
- there was a major natural disaster?
- the most liberal (*or* the most conservative) local political group received a smashing majority vote at the next election?

The purpose of asking "what if" questions is *not* based on any particular expectation that any one question will come true. Rather, it is to explore *how sensitive an investment is to change*, and which changes it is more sensitive to. No investment is completely protected! What an investor wants is an idea of what risks exist, so that he or she can more accurately judge a property's future profit potential.

Multiple Choices

Real estate investment analysis involves more than just assessing the likelihood of future benefits. It is also a process of selecting among a number of alternative investments. **Investment choices** are a key issue. There are several reasons why this is very important. First, different investors have different objectives and need different **investment characteristics**. A salaried person with a high income may seek some form of tax shelter. An elderly person with a limited pension and no other investments needs to avoid risk of loss. A young person investing for retirement may seek a hedge against inflation. It is critical for every investor to consider his or her own objectives.

Here is the second reason why selecting among multiple choices is so important. It is that the best investment is not the one with the best characteristics! Rather, it is the one with *the best characteristics for the price*. Let us imagine that a real estate analyst had the information needed to make a foolproof estimate of all future investment returns. The analyst might conclude that a particular property will have the best future of all! Should the investor rush out and buy this property immediately? Not necessarily, because the market may have already bid this property up to an unreasonably *high price level relative to its expected future returns*. In the real world, an investor should search for a property that is expected to do well, relative to its current price in the market!

Still another aspect of multiple choices is that vacant land might potentially be developed to many different uses. The legal use that develops the highest value for the land is known as the highest and best use. Thus, the investor faces a choice between possible uses for vacant land, often with different values for each use. (Sometimes, buildings also could be put to different uses, creating different values for each use.)

Investing Involves Outthinking the Market

At any given moment, any number of investment properties may be for sale. They may have similar list prices, GRMs, Cap Rates, or Price per Square Foot. Every potential buyer makes some sort of analysis, either consciously or unconsciously, regarding risks, returns, and the price he or she would be willing to pay. Years later, some of the investments will turn out to have provided much more in returns than their original prediction, whereas others will have become investment disasters.

The purpose of investment analysis, and of choosing, is *to select investments that contain opportunities for future profits that the market is missing,* or to avoid future problems that the market is ignoring. The goal of the average investor should be to do as well as or better than the market in general. This requires enough awareness of cycles, trends, and issues to buy or sell before prices have completely changed in response to the new market awareness. Obviously, the earlier the awareness, the better off the investor will be.

The investor must recognize that he or she *is in competition with all other investors* to obtain profitable returns, be they investment dollars or amenities of home ownership. The competitive market gives greater returns to those who see advantages or problems and act on them! This could involve when and how to develop a vacant land parcel, or a possible change of use or alteration to a building. Often, really successful real estate investing involves buying when the cycle is low and/or selling when the cycle is high!

Determining Investment Characteristics

Individual investments differ in location, type, size, rights, and financing. They also differ in how these characteristics affect the investment's future returns. Real estate investment textbooks contain many excellent discussions of the characteristics of the various investment types such as apartments, retail stores, and commercial office buildings.

Instead of describing the current investment characteristics for each type of real estate, this book has tried to focus attention on the future. Indeed, with the current revolutionary changes in the areas of energy, pollution, and work, it is certain that real estate investors in today's market had better carefully consider change.

Limits on Choice in a Normal Market

There is a major limit on the investor's choice of properties. These **limits on choice** affect buying strategy. In normal markets, there are only a few properties for sale at any given time. As some of these may be "losers," only a very few "good" properties may be left from which to choose. And these so-called good properties may have such high list prices as to discourage serious study.

Investment needs also limit the investor's choice. As noted earlier, different types of property differ in tax shelter, risk, and management. The investor's limited funds may restrict investments further and may require borrowing and pooling funds with other investors. Of course, in certain abnormal markets, there may be a flood of available properties! In a buyer's market, there will be plenty of cherry-picking by hard-driving buyers!

Fancy Footwork

Even a simple real estate investment can seem complicated enough. From time to time, however, experts discover investment techniques that appear to increase investors' returns greatly. These usually involve income tax deductions, to increase the tax shelter that the property offers. Past examples include rapid depreciation write-offs, prepaid interest, depreciation of separate building components, shortened economic life, and vineyard and orchard development cost deductions.

Some of the ideas that are suggested from time to time are perfectly legal; others may not be. There is a danger that the investor will allow these special tax benefits to override a careful study of the property itself. In addition, every gimmick or new technique carries new risks (of legal error, an adverse court decision, a change of law, etc.) until the idea is widely used and politically accepted. These risks should be understood by the buyer and evaluated in the purchase decision.

This overview leads into Section 18.2, which concentrates on the steps in arriving at a real estate investment decision. Before you proceed, answer the following questions.

REVIEWING YOUR UNDERSTANDING

Real Estate Investment Variables

1. Explain the concept, "the present value of future benefits."
2. Why should an investor ask "what if?" questions before making a firm real estate decision?
3. What is the significance to real estate investors of having multiple choices?

18.2 STEPS IN REAL ESTATE DECISION MAKING[1]

Real estate decision making can be viewed as a series of steps that gather real estate information, analyze the information, and then arrive at a decision based on the analysis. Everyone has to make

---

[1]Dennis J. McKenzie, Instructor's Guide for Real Estate Economics, Sacramento: California Community Colleges, 2000.

decisions! People who study the process of making decisions have developed clear outlines of the steps. The most formal process is called the **scientific method**. The scientific method involves five steps which are noted here. These same steps are helpful in organizing our approach to investing.

1. *Clearly identify and define the problem, or the purpose of the investigation.* This step is not as simple as it may sound. Unless a real estate investor knows exactly what he or she is attempting to decide, the investor will not acquire the information needed to make a sound decision. One clearly defined purpose might be to decide if now is the time to purchase a particular real estate property, which we shall call Property X.

2. *Collect relevant data.* With the problem or purpose clearly defined, the investor then gathers information that will be useful in arriving at a decision. It is equally important to avoid material that is extraneous, and irrelevant to the problem at hand. An investor would attempt to gather as much economic, social, physical, and political data relevant to Property X as time and money allow. Information on the state of the market, the position of key cycles, and the major trends will be critical.

3. *Analyze the data collected.* With the problem clearly defined and the relevant data collected, an investor must then correlate, classify, and analyze the data and arrive at a preliminary decision, often called a hypothesis. After analyzing the information, an investor may tentatively decide that Property X is the right property and that now is the time to buy.

4. Formulate and test the tentative decision (hypothesis). At this point in most scientific investigations, experiments are conducted to see if the tentative decision or hypothesis is correct. For real estate, it is difficult to experiment without having to make a firm commitment in advance. In other words, few sellers let an investor try the property before buying, to see if the property produces the desired results. However, there are two types of tests investors must do. The first is to research how other similar parcels with similar owners are doing in the marketplace. What are their vacancy levels and recent rent changes? The second set of tests is to evaluate alternative price offers, financing levels or types, added information from the seller, or even seller guarantees. Remember the need to ask "What if" questions, and see what the consequences are for the investment. Perhaps a larger down payment is necessary to protect the investment during the next recession!

5. *Arrive at a final decision or conclusion.* Taking into consideration steps 1, 2, 3, and 4, an investor now makes a final decision, by either accepting or rejecting the tentative decision (hypothesis). If an investor accepts the tentative decision (to buy Property X now), there is a possibility that the investor is making a mistake. In other words, there is a chance that this is not the time to buy, or this is not the right property, price, or financing. So an investor should then consider the possibility of being wrong, and decide if he or she is willing to take the risk. If it is decided that the property and purchase, as structured, is an acceptable risk, the purchase takes place.

The scientific method is the rational way to approach real estate decisions. Unfortunately, too many people make real estate decisions based on emotions. The role of the real estate specialist is to bring rational behavior to a very emotional business. Figure 18.1 illustrates the steps in the scientific method.

FIGURE 18.1   Steps in the scientific method.

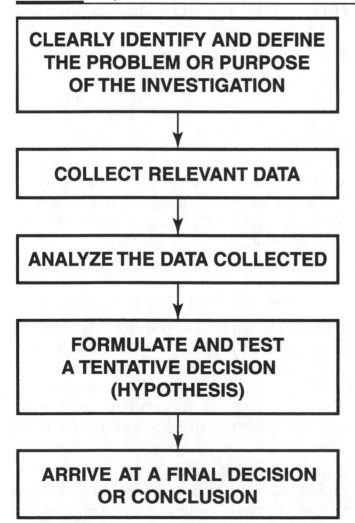

Steps in Analyzing an Improved Property

Using the scientific method as a foundation, an outline of the steps in analyzing an improved parcel of real estate follows. Because of the high purchase price, the first step for a real estate investor is to consider the available investment cash. If financing will be used, is adequate financing available? In some cases, investors decide to pay all cash, but usually financing is needed. However good a particular real estate investment might be, an investor may have to abandon the project, if adequate financing is not available.

After estimating whether financing is available, the next step is to analyze *national* cycles and trends. Questions that should be asked include: What is the state of the national economy? Where are we in the business cycle and the interest rate cycle? Does there appear to be a major real estate cycle to consider? What is government doing with fiscal and monetary policy? What is likely to happen over the next few years? How will this influence national real estate activity? How will these national changes affect the property being analyzed?

Once national cycles and trends have been studied, an investor should look at *regional* economic changes. Important questions here include: Does the region follow national changes? Is the region insulated against national changes? Is it growing? Declining? Why? What are the regional strengths and problems? What influence will this have on the property being studied?

After regional cycles and trends have been studied, the next step is to look at local changes in the city or county where the property is located. Is the city following regional changes? To what degree? Does the city appear to be growing economically? Why? What are the local strengths and problems? What are the directions of growth? What major transportation or development projects are pending? How will these factors influence the subject property?

Following the study of city or county changes, an investor should analyze the neighborhood where the property is located. Is it a growing, stagnant, or declining neighborhood? Why? Again, what are its strengths and problems? What new development has occurred and where? What are the urban renewal plans? Are any changes in transportation routes planned? What influence does this have on the subject property?

Once national, regional, local community, and neighborhood changes have been studied, an investor is in a position to analyze the individual subject property. This step has two phases: appraisal and investment analysis. The purpose of an appraisal is to estimate the market value of the property under consideration. The process of estimating market value is covered in appraisal courses.[2] Basically, an appraisal seeks to estimate what the property would sell for, if openly listed. Most often, the appraisal compares the property with indications of market price levels. This might be sale prices of similar property, rent levels and capitalization (cap) rates, or costs to construct similar buildings. The purpose of an investment analysis is to estimate if the property is "right" for the specific investor. The final step is to make a decision either to purchase or not. Figure 18.2 illustrates the steps in analyzing an improved property.

Steps in Analyzing Alternatives for Unimproved Real Estate Parcels

An in-depth analysis of the profitability of either a specific use or alternative uses for a parcel of land is frequently referred to as a **feasibility study**. The purpose of a feasibility study is to estimate if a proposed real estate project is economically sound. In other words, will it produce an acceptable profit? And, sometimes, which of several alternatives will produce the better profit? Although a complete feasibility study contains numerous other substeps, Figure 18.3 summarizes the steps in determining whether a particular real estate parcel has an economically feasible use.

From Figure 18.3, it can be seen that, when analyzing the alternatives for unimproved parcels, one of the first steps is to check what are currently the government-approved uses and/or the prospect of obtaining a use permit or a rezoning to allow a higher and better (more valuable) use.

After the government-approved uses have been established, an investor checks (for each use) the availability and cost of short-term construction financing, and also the long-term take-out financing (to pay off the construction loan).

After being assured of adequate financing, the next step is to estimate the physical barriers to the various alternative land uses, (such as residential, commercial, industrial, or rural-recreational). In some cases, there may be more than one land use allowed by zoning, and the site must be studied to estimate its physical suitability for each legally possible use. When this is completed, a market

---

[2] See also *Basic Real Estate Appraisal*, by Betts and Ely, published by Cengage Learning.

FIGURE 18.2   Steps in analyzing an improved property.

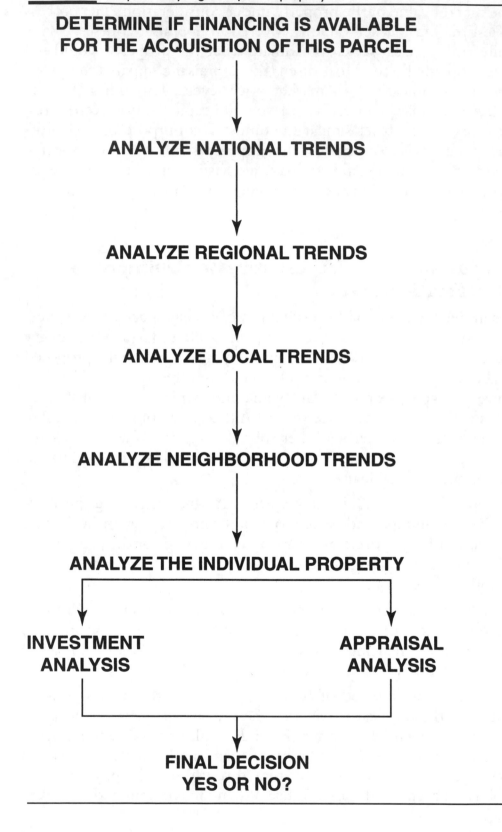

DETERMINE IF FINANCING IS AVAILABLE
FOR THE ACQUISITION OF THIS PARCEL

ANALYZE NATIONAL TRENDS

ANALYZE REGIONAL TRENDS

ANALYZE LOCAL TRENDS

ANALYZE NEIGHBORHOOD TRENDS

ANALYZE THE INDIVIDUAL PROPERTY

INVESTMENT
ANALYSIS

APPRAISAL
ANALYSIS

FINAL DECISION
YES OR NO?

FIGURE 18.3   Steps in analyzing an unimproved property.

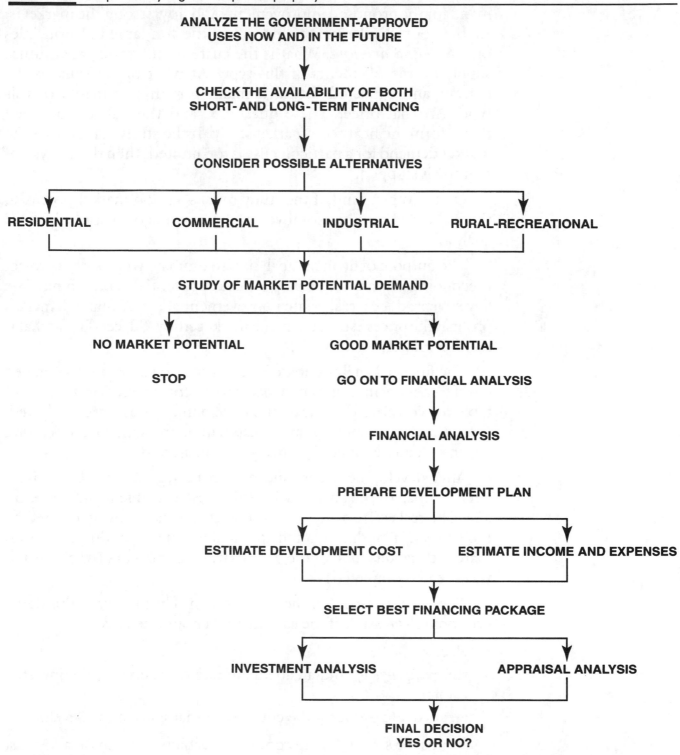

study is conducted for each use, to estimate if there is a market demand for the proposed improvements and how strong the market is. At the root of all market studies are the fundamental principles of *supply and demand.* What is the current and anticipated future supply of improvements of this type? At what price? What is the current and expected future demand for improvements of this type? At what price? These questions, and the balance between them, form the heart of a market study. If the study reveals that the market demand for a particular use is too limited, then the analysis of that use is stopped.

On the other hand, if the study reveals a good market potential, the real estate economist moves to the next major phase—financial analysis.

The purpose of financial analysis is to estimate whether the project is economically sound. Having a market potential is one thing. The key is to produce a real estate improvement at a cost that will make a profit at the prices estimated in the market study. Succeeding at that is another matter.

The financial analysis phase requires the preparation of a detailed development plan, outlining what is to be constructed and the timetable for construction. Next, the development costs are estimated. Once the development costs are estimated, gross income, operating expenses, and net operating income are projected.

After development cost and net operating income (NOI) have been estimated, the analyst selects the best available financing package. The real estate analyst then projects the cash flow generated by the project. In addition, a full appraisal is usually conducted to estimate the market value of the project when completed (or else as if it was already completed).

The last step is to make the final decision. The project is considered economically feasible if the earnings are enough to cover:

- all costs.
- the *recapture of*, and an adequate rate of *return on*, the invested capital.
- an adequate profit for the entrepreneurial skills of the developer.

It must be stressed that economic feasibility is based on a forecast of future earnings, which in turn is based on the projected income and expenses. Thus, the entire forecast depends on *realistic projections* of future income and expenses.

REVIEWING YOUR UNDERSTANDING

Steps in Real Estate Decision Making

1. What are the five steps in the scientific method?
2. In analyzing an improved property, does the analyst study regional changes? Why?
3. Why does the analysis include both an appraisal and an investment analysis?
4. How does the analysis of an improved property differ from a feasibility study?

CHAPTER SUMMARY

Future net earnings are the key element in investment profits, and estimating future earnings is the focus of investment analysis. The analyst seeks to understand past and present social, political, physical, and economic cycles and trends in order to anticipate possible future changes to earnings. Not every future change will be important to the property being analyzed! The investor must consider the effect of *each possible change* on the particular property.

Investment analysis involves not only estimating future benefits but also selecting among alternative investments. The investor must choose an investment that meets the desired investment characteristics (yield, tax aspects, risk, and so on). In addition, the investor must seek to find the investment that offers the best future returns for the current price. In practice, only a limited number of properties are for sale at any one time in a normal market. Therefore, the analyst is trying to outthink the market, or at least not do worse!

Real estate decision making should involve careful study. The five steps of the scientific method provide a convenient outline for such study. In analyzing improved property, key factors include financing availability; the impact of possible national, regional, local, and neighborhood trends or cycles; an appraisal of market value; and an analysis of the specific investment characteristics and investment value.

For unimproved properties, added steps are the review of legally allowable uses, estimation of physically possible uses, estimation of market potentials, and preparation of a development plan.

REVIEWING YOUR UNDERSTANDING

1. The city council's unanticipated re-zoning of an area to a lower density reduces the value of a property. This is an example of a(n):
   A. social force
   B. political force
   C. economic force
   D. physical force

2. A "what if" approach that anticipates the impact of various changes on an investment is a(n):
   A. sensitivity analysis
   B. cash flow analysis
   C. economic analysis
   D. fail-safe analysis

3. The first step in the scientific method is to:
   A. collect the data
   B. form the hypothesis
   C. analyze the data
   D. define the problem

4. A formal study of the profitability of various alternative uses for a vacant parcel of land is called a:
   A. "what if" analysis
   B. sensitivity analysis
   C. feasibility study
   D. critical path study

5. A real estate project is considered to be economically feasible only when:
   A. all operating costs are covered
   B. invested capital is not at risk
   C. one hundred percent occupancy is anticipated
   D. there is an adequate rate of return for investors and adequate profit for the entrepreneur

6. The main reason that an investor should study real estate trends and cycles is to help estimate a property's:
   A. potential for bankruptcy
   B. demographic characteristics
   C. physical feasibility
   D. future earnings

7. Sensitivity analysis refers to a property's:
   A. reaction to possible change
   B. expense ratio
   C. position on the real estate cycles
   D. future earnings

8. A *cycle* differs from a *trend* in that a cycle:
   A. is a projection of the past into the future
   B. consists of recurring regular changes
   C. involves long-term shifts in the same direction
   D. cannot be forecast

9. Changing economic events, social attitudes, physical events, and political actions are important considerations for real estate analysts.
   A. true
   B. false

10. The real estate analyst studies past cycles and trends because history always repeats itself.
    A. true
    B. false

11. The investor asks "what if" questions in order to:
    A. explore how sensitive an investment is to change
    B. identify issues that should be studied
    C. identify which issues can be ignored
    D. all of the above

12. An appraisal estimates the market value of a property, whereas an investment analysis estimates if the property is "right" for the particular investor.
    A. true
    B. false

13. The best investment is the one with the:
    A. lowest price
    B. best location
    C. best building
    D. most profit potential for the price

14. Highest and best use refers to:
    A. the use with the least sensitivity to change
    B. the allowable use with the greatest physical density
    C. the legal use that generates the most land value
    D. the use with the strongest market demand

15. The scientific method:
    A. is a formal process for decision making
    B. depends on the availability of statistically valid data
    C. is the same as cash flow analysis for real estate investors
    D. shows how to examine the emotional aspects of real estate investing

CASE & POINT

Where Are We in the Real Estate Cycle?

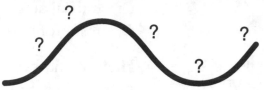

A difficult aspect of real estate investing has been interpreting where we are in the real estate cycle. This interpretation is critical! Investment articles often urge you to "Buy low and sell high!" And when you buy at the top of the market price cycle, and sell at the low, it is very hard to make a profit! It is a truism that "value is the present worth of future benefits." And the estimate of those future benefits will depend on the estimate of future cyclical influences.

Note that the term used is *cyclical influences*, rather than the *business cycle*. First, every region or city has its own version of the business cycle, and is at its own stage in that cycle. Each industry or occupation also has its own business cycle variation. Thus, each *user* of real estate, in each location, has a slightly different position in the business cycle. In addition, the supply and demand balance for each type of real estate in each location also has a distinctive cycle, only loosely related to the local business cycle. In real estate investment analysis, then, what counts is the combination of these various cycles, and how this combination influences the particular property being studied.

The massive overconstruction of commercial building in the 1980s produced some major supply and demand imbalances. The dot-com collapse in the early 2000s produced massive commercial property vacancies in high-tech locations such as the San Francisco Bay Area.

The peaceful defeat of the former Soviet Union in the early 1990s produced sharp declines in areas that were dependent upon the aero and defense industries. From 1990 through 1996, housing prices in the defense-industry dependent Southern California area dropped, in many cases 25 percent or more. During this same period, housing prices in Northern California dropped, but not as much as in defense-economy based Southern California. By the mid-2000s, housing prices in all areas of California (and many other areas) were up by record amounts.

CASE & POINT

This was followed by the staggering collapse of home prices in 2006–2008, financial markets in 2007, and income property prices in 2009–2010. This was the worst real estate recession since the Great Depression of the 1930s.

As with all cyclical markets, the main problem is in identifying *turning points* in the real estate market. In an "up market," the questions become: Will the escalation continue? If so, for how long? Or has the real estate market reached its top, with a decline imminent? Or will it bounce along at this high level, with only minor ups and downs? In a "down market," the questions become: Has the bottom been reached? If so, when will it start to turn up? Or will it continue to decline? If so, how far, and for how long? As always, it is easy to state what should have been done, after the game has been played, as opposed to making the tough calls during the game.

It is clear that many experts warned, as early as 2003, of the coming real estate collapse. They were not listened to. So, there are some signs when a boom moves toward collapse. However, estimating recovery timing in advance remains quite difficult.

Chapter

19

PREVIEW

We have stressed how important future change is to the success of any real estate investment, and to the evaluation of *any economic choice* or decision. This chapter points out areas of possible future change that, we believe, should be watched. In the process, we hope that readers will think about other possible changes. Section 19.1 examines the more important economic issues. Section 19.2 explores demographic, political, and legal challenges we may face. Section 19.3 considers the most unpredictable changes. As this is not

Anticipating Change

a book *about* the future, the coverage of these possible changes is brief. When you have completed this chapter, you will be able to:

1. List at least ten potential areas of change.
2. Describe the nature of possible changes.
3. Show how each potential change can be monitored.

19.1 THE MAJOR ECONOMIC ISSUES

As we begin the 2010s, we must look back at the economic turmoil of the 2000 decade. Clearly, the economic issues that were created then will be central problems for the years ahead. One part of this involves the short-term view: the recovery from the economic recession of 2007–2008. But a second part is the longer-term view: the long-run consequences of the financial crash of 2007.

Recovery from the Financial Collapse of 2007

The financial collapse of 2007, explored in earlier chapters, was no ordinary minor crisis. And the recession of 2007–2008, which it caused, was by most accounts, the most severe since the Great Depression of 1929. The next step in the economic cycle, after a recession, is the recovery (see Chapter 3). How will the **economic recovery** from this recession proceed?

Will This Be a Typical Recovery?

We know that the business cycle repeats itself, perhaps every four years. Is there a *typical recovery phase*? And will this recovery be typical?

Economists who study business cycles often describe or classify the recovery period by the speed of the recovery. Some recessions and recoveries are described as *V-shaped*, because the recovery is fast. And some are described as U-shaped, because the recovery is slower. Less common are *W-shaped* recoveries, where one decline and partial recovery is followed by another decline. So, the question is, how slow or fast will the recovery be, and also will it be steady or interrupted?

When we look at the recoveries of the past 50 years, we see that the usual pattern starts with drops in interest rates, as the Fed lowers rates to stimulate the economy. The low rates, in turn, increase sales of existing real estate and of automobiles. These recover well before the rest of the economy, and lead to increases in employment, followed by increases in retail sales, as consumer income grows again.

Therefore, the important question often is which segment of the economy recovers first, and provides the fuel for the recovery. How does the recovery from this recession compare with others? Clearly, *this will not be a typical recovery*. Interest rates have been low since 2008, but the recovery in housing is very weak, even with unusual buyer tax credits never tried before. And sales of autos and other "consumer durable goods" remain low. The employment figures have remained low for much longer than normal. So, we have to conclude that this is not a V-shaped recovery.

Will it be U-shaped or W-shaped? The federal government has applied never-before-seen levels of economic stimulus. This has included the cash-for-clunkers auto stimulus, the home-buyer tax credits, massive government support of home loan programs, increased unemployment insurance, and much more. This economic stimulus has helped the economy—things would have been worse without it! But the federal government has to borrow the money to spend on stimulus programs. There are limits, even for the federal government! What happens as the stimulus programs expire? Will the economy have enough strength to continue growing on its own, or will there be a W-shaped second dip?

The Housing Recovery

We have explored the home price collapse of the late 2000s earlier, in Chapter 9. There have been several major home price declines in recent decades, most notably in 1989. We know, from studying those prior price declines, that it could take ten years for prices to recover to their previous peaks. How will this **housing recovery** develop?

What aspects of the housing market cause it to be listed in this chapter's gallery of wild-card risks? One issue is the *shadow inventory*—the increasing number of houses which are in default, or even in the foreclosure process, but not yet showing up as listings on the MLS. Some clearly are tied up in loan modification proceedings, which may or may not succeed. But many experts are concerned that this large inventory of homes could come on the market, potentially reducing prices further.

A second issue is the increase in what are being labeled as *strategic foreclosures*—people who can afford to continue making loan payments, but choose to stop doing so, due to a loan balance that is well over the value of the home. Historically, people held on to their home, even if they owed 5 or 10 percent too much. Now, some owe 30 percent or more over their home's value. State law usually determines whether the lender can foreclose and still sue to collect the balance, by a *deficiency judgment*. Where none is legally possible, walking away becomes a good choice to some people. How big will this become?

A third issue is whether truly workable *loan modification programs* will emerge. The initial results were very disappointing, given the number of homes at risk of foreclosure.

A fourth issue is *whether housing markets can sustain* current price levels, when the massive federal economic stimulus and interest-rate lowering programs are ended. Some take a pessimistic view, believing that the combination of the above issues will cause home prices to drop further, increasing strategic foreclosures and driving buyers to wait for new signs of a firm market. Others are more optimistic, pointing to increasing consumer income, some employment improvement, and better retail sales.

It is important to recognize that the home price collapse had many different consequences. Agents have had to learn how to handle *short sales, bank-owed homes* (REO), a wave of investor buyers, listings with no offers, and more. Loan brokers all but disappeared. Appraisers struggled to appraise in markets with no sales, with how to handle REO sales as comparables, with the shift to appraisal management companies (AMC) as their major clients, and with sharply increased oversight and review. There were other impacts on society generally, which are explored later.

The Recovery of Commercial Real Estate

In hindsight, the increase in commercial property prices in the early 2000s was as much an asset bubble as home prices were. Abnormally low market rates for money came at the same time as a major easing of loan standards. And the general economy was bubbling as well, so office occupancy was strong, which increased rents.

But the bubble collapsed with the financial market collapse in 2007. Prices did not fall like home prices, at first. But the number of sales dropped sharply, as buyers turned cautious and lenders stopped lending. Soon, vacancies increased, as auto companies, financial firms, mortgage brokers, and transaction attorneys downsized or closed. Commercial real estate markets declined sharply in 2009 and 2010. How will the **commercial real estate recovery** proceed?

By 2010, vacancies were up, rents and revenue were down, and expenses continued to slowly increase with inflation. The net income of most commercial property, of all types, went down. Some were cut in half. Future prospects don't look as rosy as they once did. Meanwhile, the cost of money—both loans and equity investment funds—increased. As interest rates go up, values go down, everything else being equal. So in 2010, we faced a "perfect storm": falling net income and increasing rates, leading to a collapse in values.

Remember that most commercial property loans are due in relatively short terms—often five years. The huge numbers of sales in 2004 through 2007 nearly all were made with loans that are coming due. But the values have dropped, and lender loan standards have increased. So, a new loan from a different lender usually is not possible. As a result, most of these loans do not qualify for a new loan when they come due. An increasing number of property owners are not able to make monthly loan payments. Now, lenders have the highest percent of commercial property loans in default in decades. For small-to-medium banks, it was 33% in 2010!

What does this mean to the lenders, or to the owners? Some lenders are simply extending the due date on the loan, as long as the payments are kept current. Others are selling the loan to speculative investors, at a discount. And some properties are going into foreclosure, and then being sold.

Apartments are not under quite as much pressure. Rents have fallen and vacancies increased, but not as much as hotels, offices, and some other commercial properties. More importantly, the federal government has encouraged both FHA and Fannie Mae to refinance apartment loans that are due, whenever owners are having trouble finding a willing lender. However, note that this is increasing the risk of further loss to the government, if rents should fall further. Basically, the government is pushing the problem into the future, in the hope that conditions will improve.

For other property types, however, the increasing default rate means more foreclosures, more loan write-offs, more bank losses, and more bank failures. No one in 2010 is able to predict the bottom of the market downturn. And in 2010, the bottom for commercial real estate was still in the future.

Financial System Recovery

It is all too easy to see the impact of the 2007 financial crisis on Wall Street and on big banks. But as the bubble burst, the impacts spread to home prices and then to commercial real estate. Small banks and credit unions have also been hurt, especially over smaller construction loans and small business loans. By 2010, 10% of all banks in the United States were on the regulators' watch list, and the number of bank failures was growing.

Where will this end? What will be the nature, and especially *the* timing of the **financial recovery**? It is hard to say: as noted earlier, it is very hard to predict the bottom of an economic cycle. The collapse in trust between economic partners was the dominant issue in 2007 and 2008. Unprecedented federal government guarantees of many financial instruments gradually restored trust between U.S. financial institutions. However, the 2010 problems with European government debt demonstrate that the damage is not completely repaired. As the U.S. commercial real estate loan problem forces more small banks down, it is clear that the recovery of the U.S. financial system still faces challenges.

The Consequences of the Financial Collapse of 2007

There are a number of short-term results of the collapse. Job losses, real estate price drops and foreclosures, personal and company bankruptcies, and bank failures are among them. To some degree, these happen with every recession. However, some experts point out that this particular recession not only is the most severe since 1929, it also seems to be a turning point on a number of issues. The long-term future consequences may make this a very different recession. These are our next topics.

Trust in U.S. Financial Instruments

For many decades now, the world has considered the United States the safest place to invest. Our legal system was strong and relatively very honest. Our financial institutions were well-regulated. Our past accounting systems have led the world in honesty, accuracy, and full reporting. **Investor trust** was very high! As a result, investors all over the world purchased U.S. stocks, bonds, and other investment securities.

Now, however, that reputation is at risk. Our regulators allowed interest rates to remain so low and for so long that a massive asset bubble developed. And regulators at the same time allowed some financial companies to sharply increase their leverage, allowed issuance of new types of extremely risky mortgage loans, and allowed unwarranted ratings for loan securities. Financial companies in turn generated huge numbers of high-risk loans, bundled them into securities, obtained very unrealistic favorable ratings on the securities, and sold them to investors *all over the world*. There were individual retirement funds, credit unions, and banks who invested in these secure investments. Cities, counties, states, and companies all invested reserve cash in these secure investments.

Now, everyone in the room points the blame finger at someone else. But the consequences are real. No investor or advisor who went through this, worldwide, will ever have the same confidence in any investment rating by a U.S. rating company. And their confidence in bond insurers is also gone. Their trust in the reliability of asset and liability balance sheets of U.S. corporations is materially affected by the disclosures of major off-balance-sheet funding vehicles.

Commentators point out that the United States is a smaller nation, in population. And U.S. manufacturing as a percent of the world total has been declining for many decades. Our role as a center of financial strength and safety has become increasingly important. Now, it is being challenged. Can we recover that trust?

Increase in Regulation

A second consequence of the collapse is the general recognition that the Reagan deregulatory movement had gone too far. Most people surely view regulations as no more than a necessary evil, and would be delighted to see less. However, deregulation works only when there is some other force or influence that keeps things in line. Sometimes, it is simply a strong individual moral code, or a fear of disgrace or jail.

The financial collapse clearly occurred in part because of weak regulatory control on mortgage production, loan securitization, financial instrument rating, security insurance, and more. Part of this was the result of congressional actions to reduce and underfund regulators. Part of it was the result of Executive branch philosophical pressure on regulators. And part of it simply was a failure of the regulators.

As a result, newspaper articles and congressional hearings debate what went wrong and often point the finger at the regulatory agencies. Numerous proposals to reform, improve, or strengthen the process are proposed. **Regulatory change** is in the air! The resulting legislation will result in the most sweeping change to financial regulation in many decades. Clearly, the financial system and its regulators will be changed. The long-term economic changes may be substantial. Experience also tells us that most attempts to correct a problem also introduce new problems!

The Future of Real Estate Finance

In the early 2000s, the great majority of home loans were originated by small local mortgage brokers. In 2009, the majority were originated by a small number of very large national banks. That is a major change, and over a very short time. Something like 90% of all home loans in 2009 were immediately sold to a government agency, either FHA, Fannie Mae, or Freddie Mac. In turn, the agencies sold securities to investors almost all over the world backed by the mortgages *and by a full U.S. government guarantee.*

Contrast this with 50 years ago, where the majority of home loans were originated by a savings and loan company or a credit union, using funds obtained from individual depositors. The institutions were all fairly small, locally based, working with local borrowers. Clearly, then, home loan finance has changed.

Is the present situation a stable one? Probably not, because it will only work as long as the U.S. government stands ready to buy and guarantee such a large volume of loans. Political winds tend to change. There are those who say that the quantity and quality of loans being purchased is only setting the stage for a new wave of problems in the future. Republicans suggest turning Freddie and Fannie into private companies, and letting them sink or swim.

Another aspect of the problem is that these three agencies all handle only smaller loans. Larger, so-called *jumbo loans* are available, but with high down payments and higher interest rates. As a result, much of the home price weakness after 2009 has been in the higher-priced brackets!

Clearly, then, the current system of home finance is only a temporary one, driven by the government's attempt to slow down or stop the collapse in home prices. It is not clear what will happen next, or when!

Deleveraging

The term **deleveraging** refers to reducing the amount or level of debt that a person or company (or nation) owes. Sometimes, this can be done by selling assets. Other times, it might involve spending less, saving more, and using the added savings to pay down loan balances.

Why would one want to deleverage? There are many reasons. Most often, it is because total loan payments—principal and interest—are a burden, given the available income. Perhaps the income is declining. Or the interest rate on the loan might be variable, and an increasing rate is driving up the payments. Sometimes, it is because the loan is due, or is *called early* because of a decline in the value of the asset that is the security for the loan.

In the early 2000s, interest rates were low. It was easy to get credit, and the economy was strong worldwide. Not surprisingly, people, companies, and governments borrowed. Today, credit standards are very high, and incomes and asset values have fallen. The levels of debt that seemed reasonable in 2005 now are a problem. Loan payments are hard to meet. Many loans had lower initial interest rates and are now moving much higher. Many loans become due if property values or income drops a certain amount. And many loans were for a short term, on the assumption that they would simply be refinanced by the due date.

As a result, there is a *worldwide movement* to deleverage. People, companies, and governments are all struggling to meet debt payments, trying to increase incomes, and trying to cut spending, in the hope of paying down their loans. Those who cannot do so face foreclosure and bankruptcy.

In hindsight, the relative amount of debt in use is also something that changes in a cyclical manner. It went up, too high and too fast, and now it is contracting. According to the Federal Reserve, the ratio of total household debt to disposable income is shrinking, from 132% in 2007, to 122% by the end of 2009. And the personal savings rate increased from just above 1%, during the boom, to as high as 5% during part of 2009.

The favorite saying for economists is: *"There is no free lunch."* Every economic action, or even inaction, will cost something —an impact somewhere else in the economy. When people, companies, and governments save more, and use income to pay down loan balances, what are the economic consequences? The answer is that they *spend less* buying goods and services, which reduces retail sales and business activity! The funds sent to pay off lenders do not disappear, of course! Today, however, lenders may hold on to the funds to improve their own balance sheets. So the net effect of the worldwide move to pay down loans almost certainly is to slow down the business recovery slightly! However, when the deleveraging is complete, freeing up income for spending, the economy will get a boost.

Managing the Economy and Asset Bubbles

The whole reason for the Federal Reserve, and our entire complex system of financial regulation, is to try to avoid the serious financial panics of the 1700s, 1800s, and first third of the 1900s. By 1960, many economists might have argued that problems with financial panics were mostly behind us. Then came the Savings and Loan crash of the late 1980s, the Tech Stock Crash of the early 2000s, and the Financial Crash of 2007. The last one, especially, indicated to many people that something has gone wrong with our financial regulatory system. What went wrong will be heavily debated for years.

One common characteristic of all three of these financial collapses is that each was preceded by several years (or more) of strong general prosperity, with relatively rapid increases in the prices of many assets. With each, when the collapse occurred, asset prices also collapsed, and there was general awareness that the previous increases in asset prices were out of line.

This is the definition of what economists call an **asset bubble**. Prices rise relatively rapidly, often for several years. People will exclaim that prices are ridiculous, but the climb continues. The increase slows down, and then begins to fall. The decline is slow at first, and then faster and then it gradually slows down.

Sometimes, the asset bubble will involve only one asset. The most famous is the Dutch tulip bulb mania, from 1634 to 1637. This was an era when some of the first tulip hybrids were developed. As new tulip varieties were developed, prices for the new bulbs rose. Speculators began investing, then hoarding and reselling. Unusual colors brought extraordinary prices, with a single tulip bulb even being traded for land or jewels!

More commonly, however, asset bubbles involve a number of assets, occurring at a time of increasing general prosperity. There is a long history of asset bubbles, and a lot of research on why they occur. (See the article in *Scientific American* magazine, July 2009, "The Science of Bubbles and Bursts" for more.) There are also growing discussions about what, if anything, to do about asset bubbles.

Clearly, if the asset bubble only involves pet rocks, or beanie babies, the risk to society from a runaway bubble is small. The Tech Stock bubble, and crash, from the late 1980s on, is a more challenging question. A lot of funds were invested. People were hired, equipment purchased, and new space rented. After the crash, the people were jobless, the equipment sold for pennies, and the new space became vacant. From an economic viewpoint, this was a waste of valuable resources, and therefore, a drain on the economy.

For years, as discussed in Chapters 3 and 4, the federal regulators have defined their role as resisting inflation, and protecting from bank failure and widening panic. In recent decades, stabilizing employment has been proposed as a third key goal. Even as home prices soared in the mid-2000s, the Federal Reserve stated that resisting asset bubbles was not its responsibility.

It should be clear now that major asset bubbles, especially of an asset class as economically significant as real estate, have the potential to be very destructive to economic stability and employment. What, then, should be done about asset bubbles? Who should do it? Do they have the skills to do so?

The economic knowledge is there. Among the leading economic thinkers on asset bubbles are Ludwig von Mises (early 1900s), Arthur Pigou (early 1900s), and Hyman Minsky (late 1900s). And Janet Yellen, former Professor of Economics, University of California, Berkeley, and new Vice-Chair of the Federal Reserve Board, is considered quite knowledgeable as well!

Can we—will we—act to reduce the risk of dangerous asset bubbles? What will be the consequences to the economy? To major real estate markets? These are major future issues!

The Past and Future Role of Politicians

It is one thing to have economists agree what the regulators should do, in a given situation. First, however, Congress has to pass, and the president signs, legislation that gives the regulators the authority to act. Second, whatever the law says the regulators could do, they may or may not do it. They may in their professional judgment believe they should not do it, or perhaps should not do it just yet. Or they may believe that politicians, in the Congress and/or the Executive Branch, don't want them to do it.

Recall, too, that the Federal Reserve Board is not completely independent—the all-powerful chairman is appointed by the president! The president, as a practical matter, cannot remove the chairman! Recall, however, the grilling of the chairman at congressional hearings in 2010. When the Board acts, they want to be relatively sure that they are making the right decision, both economically and politically.

Because the Senate and presidential elections occur every four years, regulators tend to face worried politicians every four years. A weak economy at election time is usually a political problem for incumbents! So regulators seem to be more cautious in the nine months leading up to an election, postponing any major moves (especially to slow down the economy) until after the election. Some commentators suggest that it is no coincidence that the usual business cycle is roughly four years from one peak to the next!

In hindsight, a major portion of the blame for the crash of 2007 rests with the politicians. (The regulators also receive a big chunk of the blame!) The Savings and Loan Crash of the late 1980s also probably was primarily caused by major legislative errors.

How, then, can we hope to get rid of destructive economic crashes? Can economists speak loudly enough to be heard? Will the selfish interests of a minority continue to lead to such serious consequences? These problems have been particularly bad in recent decades: Is this a trend?

Interest and Inflation Rates

As part of what the government does to improve the economy, the Federal Reserve in 2010 is very actively working to keep short- and long-term interest rates low. As long as the economy continues to be weak, most economists would consider that to be appropriate. As part of that push, the Treasury is buying Treasury and Agency (Freddie and Fannie) debt, plus mortgage-backed securities and other financial assets.

To fund these purchases, the Treasury is borrowing. The total impact is measured by the *monetary base*. The monetary base, narrowly defined, consists of the coins and paper money in circulation, plus the commercial bank reserves on deposit with the Federal Reserve. A broader definition included checking accounts.

Figure 19.1 shows the monetary base, from 1910 through May 2010. The increase since 2007 is different from anything ever seen

FIGURE 19.1   Adjusted monetary base

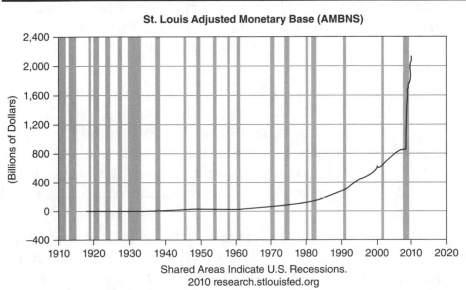

Source: Federal Reserve Bank of St. Louis.

TABLE 19.1   The Increase in the Monetary Base

Date	Amount (billion)	Percent Increase	Annual Increase (%)
5-1-00	604	—	—
5-1-08	858	42	12.5
5-1-10	2,033	137	118.3

before. Table 19.1 shows how rapid the recent increase is, as an annual percentage increase (without allowing for compounding).

Very few books about the future that were written during the 1960s listed **inflation** as a potential serious problem in the United States. By the 1970s, inflation was considered a serious problem. Then, in the 1980s, the rate of inflation in the United States dropped drastically. By the mid-2000s, inflation was reduced to exceptionally low rates.

What causes inflation? You will recall from earlier chapters that inflation is the result of too much demand relative to supply. Put another way, it is the result of too much money chasing too few goods. The buyers then "bid up" the prices.

When the Fed lowers interest rates too far or for too long, or pumps too much money into the economy, the result is to increase inflationary pressure. In May 2010, the economy is too weak for prices to increase. As the economy improves, however, the Fed and the Treasury must gradually unwind the stimulus. If it is too slow, inflation will return. If it is too fast, the economic recovery will stop.

In addition, economists believe that such an unprecedented increase in the monetary base could take a long time to unwind. Referring to the earlier discussion in this chapter on deleveraging, the U.S. government must also *at some point* begin deleveraging.

But the situation is complicated by the U.S. budget deficit, which seems likely to increase, rather than decrease, over the next five or ten years. The government must borrow to fund the annual deficit, but that just increases the amount to be paid off in the future. And the deficit potentially could grow in the future, when reserves will no longer be enough to fund annual Medicare and (later) Social Security costs.

What will happen to inflation in the 2010 and 2020 decades? If it remains moderate, price levels will be determined by basic supply and demand interactions. But if rapid inflation occurs again, the dislocations of the 1970s could once more hit the U.S. economy. High interest rates would reoccur, with a destabilizing impact on real estate markets. There is strong concern in financial circles about the future potential for inflation. This creates a political force against inflation. But in the past, federal, state, and local governments seem drawn, like a moth to a flame. The attraction of offering benefits to voters, without taxing them to pay for the benefits, pays off for politicians. Has government learned its lesson? Have voters wised up? Will pay-as-you-go become a permanent government philosophy? Does deficit reduction really matter?

REVIEWING YOUR UNDERSTANDING

The Major Economic Issues

1. Why do economists study the nature of economic recoveries?
2. What are four areas of uncertainty about housing market recoveries?
3. What are examples in your area of the results of a commercial real estate recession?
4. Why does the financial system recovery matter to real estate?
5. What might happen if foreign investors stopped buying U. S. stocks, bonds, and other financial instruments?
6. How important are Fannie Mae and Freddie Mac to residential real estate markets?
7. What happens to the economy when people and companies deleverage?
8. Should the Federal Reserve act to slow down major asset bubbles? Why?
9. Where will interest rates go, over the next ten years, and why?

19.2 NATIONAL CHANGES

National changes are those that involve many areas of the general U.S. economy, beyond the real estate industry. People outside real estate might not even consider these changes as affecting real estate, but they do! The issues mentioned here include a number of concerns involving demography, and several legal or political issues.

Demographic Issues

As you will recall from Chapter 9, *demography* is the study of the characteristics of population, such as birth and death rates and migration. The most important demographic statistic for real estate is the rate of net population increase, or births in excess of deaths, plus net immigration. These two are what drive changes in the number of household formations. World trends, as well as trends in a particular area, are important because of immigration (in-migration), the effect on demand for agricultural and other exports, and competition for world resources.

An increasing population means a greater demand for food and all other resources. To the degree that real estate is fixed in quantity, an increase in population means an increase in demand and in land prices.

Population Composition

Demographers also study how many people there are in each category of age, sex, race, education, and occupation. Income categories, and their changes, get special attention. Income, of course, is critical for *effective demand*. Demographers study the composition of the population, in part because of the obvious changes that occur as people get older. A population forecast for any area can be prepared by starting with the age, sex, and household characteristics of the current population, adding the expected births, subtracting the anticipated deaths, and forecasting the net migration. Analysis of *current populations* is commonly done by all levels of government, and many states and countries develop projections of future population. For California, for example, most reports come from the Demographic Research Unit of the State Department of Finance, at www.dof.ca.gov/research/demographic.

The population of every city, state, and nation is changing, because of changes in composition and number as the people age. These changes in composition can be projected in detail. Such projections would draw conclusions about the projected future mix of household sizes, incomes, occupations, and ages, which would be very relevant to real estate. Housing markets, for example, often go through cycles of demand for larger versus small housing units. This cycle is related to swings in the proportion of younger households to middle-aged ones. Because of the unusually large number of Americans born between 1945 and 1965, the period of the so-called baby boom, there will be a major effect on housing demand as this group retires during the 2010 decade. It is clear, therefore, that a number of *major future changes in housing demand* have already been set in motion by these expected changes in population composition.

Poverty

The U.S. economy is able to provide a minimum standard of living. Yet we still have some who are living in real **poverty**—too little money for safe and sanitary housing and a nutritious diet. The problem cannot simply be cured by increasing the incomes of the poor, because custom, behavior, attitudes, and failure in education can block the effective use of money. There is an obvious frustration that is created by living in poverty, but seeing televised and advertised luxuries. Avenues of advancement for the talented and motivated are needed as much as ever. However, what is needed, even more, are incentives to motivate people away from addictions and other self-destructive behaviors that often lead to poverty.

In addition to those living in long-term poverty, our society must also deal with people for whom poverty is new. This includes people who lose their jobs; become disabled or ill; lose their housing to foreclosure; or get affected by fire, tornado, or earthquake. In recent decades, many people have saved less than in the past, and spent more. Some are not prudent in purchases, or in the degree of debt that they agree to be responsible for. What do we as a society do about this growing problem, and its housing impacts?

Current housing programs for the poor have been criticized as much as earlier ones. Newer proposals range from direct rent supplements via vouchers to guaranteed minimum incomes. The growing frustration of voters complicates the already confused situation. When analyzing a particular real estate market, the real estate economist should consider the effects of current housing programs, the impact of any curtailment, and the various major proposals for change.

Because housing is a major expense for people with limited income, many programs have been tried to support low-income housing, especially for larger families (the most difficult group to house). Past ideas have included:

1. Relatively unsuccessful experiments with publicly owned housing for poverty-level households.

2. Experiments with subsidized loans to developers of low-income housing (the former Section 221(d)(3) loans, for example).

3. Vouchers, given to the poor to allow them to find their own housing in the private market ("Section 8").

4. Use of inclusionary zoning, as noted in Chapter 13, "Land-Use Controls."

The typical poverty-level household (especially if very large or very poor) is probably housed little better than it was ten years ago. Further changes in poverty housing programs seem likely.

As noted in Chapter 9, the *trickle-down* concept indicates that most poor people live in older buildings. To a major degree, providing decent housing for poorer people really depends on maintaining the existing stock of homes, despite the wear and tear of the years. The foreclosure wave of 2009–2010 is likely to lead to an increase in under-maintained housing.

Many ideas are being tried across the country, and the Housing and Urban Development Department and other federal agencies are seeking new concepts. Suggestions include rezoning, special rehabilitation loans and grants, and the formation of neighborhood groups.

Homeownership

Another important issue is **homeownership**. Many years ago, the federal government adopted the goal of increasing the percentage of households who own their own home, rather than rent. The income tax deduction for home property tax and loan interest payments are the major economic incentives. And federal efforts to lower interest rates and reduce down payment amounts are part of that effort. Table 19.2 shows the increase in homeownership over the years.

But Table 19.2 *does not show* how much it has cost the U. S. government, in lost income tax receipts, to produce this increase in homeownership. And this lost revenue had to be replaced by other taxes! There is an increasing level of concern by economists. Are the benefits of increased homeownership worth the costs? And can we afford these costs, given the growing budget deficits and government debt levels? The homeownership level is dropping now, due to the high foreclosure rate. Should we resist this drop? These are important unanswered questions.

The Elderly

As noted earlier, the birth rate was unusually high, from 1946 until about 1955, as people turned from World War II to raising a family. This created a huge group of people, called the *baby boomers*. As they have grown up, gone to school, gotten jobs, and then bought or rented a home of their own, they have had a major impact. Now, they are starting to reach age 65, and their impact is changing again.

TABLE 19.2 Homeownership in Percent

1910 to 1940	Less than 50%
1950	55%
1970	63%
2009	70%

Source: *Wall Street Journal*, August 15, 2009.

TABLE 19.3   World Population Over Age 60

1950	8%
2009	11%
2050	22%

Source: United Nations

The elderly will outnumber children, worldwide, for the first time in 2045. Table 19.3 shows the rapid increase in the percentage of the world's population over 60 years old. The impact on medical costs, housing, and the tax burden on workers are all issues of major importance.

As they age, like most older people, they have more medical problems. Therefore, we can safely predict that demand for medical services will increase noticeably, over the next several decades. And the new 2010 federal medical insurance bill will increase demand, as uninsured people gain coverage. But we know that an increase in demand leads to an increase in price (unless supply also increases). This increase in costs will be a major issue. Some clearly will seek medical care where it is cheaper.

The second major issue generated by the coming retirement of the baby boomers will be housing. A growing number of elderly prefer to stay where they are. Many, however, move to specialized **elder housing**.

There continue to be problems in providing specialized housing, suitable for the elderly, especially those with low incomes. Ideas that have been tried have included:

1. Federally subsidized elderly housing projects.
2. Property tax credits for elderly people.
3. Renovation grants or low-interest loans to elderly.
4. A voucher system, where the elderly are given vouchers to find their own housing in the private market.

The housing needs of the elderly have been better handled in recent years. The tremendous projected growth in the number of elderly, over the next few decades, will strain the existing facilities. Major growth in this specialized housing market is expected.

Lifestyles

How people choose to live (within the limits set by their incomes) determines how they allocate their resources and how they create the demand for goods and services that they bring to the economy. In the distant past, many people had to work hard just to survive.

In modern America, for most people, our society can provide an adequate *minimum standard of living*, with far less time spent on "work" than was true in the past.

To date, however, relatively few people reduce their workday. Instead, many work relatively long hours and use the added income to buy a standard of living that, in this country, goes well above the minimum level. The effects on real estate are substantial. Examples include second homes, recreation resorts, bed and breakfast inns, expensive restaurants, acreage home sites, and new luxury homes. **Lifestyle** is a major element in real estate demand!

There is now open discussion of alternatives to traditional full-time employment. One sees increasing desire for time for non-income-producing pursuits, despite possibly lower incomes. And some clearly have scaled back their life style, and increased their savings rate, as a result of the 2007 financial crash. It is too early to tell how widespread this movement toward nontraditional work patterns is, or whether these lifestyle changes will continue as people get older. Indeed, this trend is countered by the heightened emphasis on national and business competitiveness. However this plays out, the ultimate effect on the demand for various categories of real estate could be substantial.

Another aspect of lifestyles is the decision of *where to live*! The 1950s began the great move to the suburbs, and the era of the automobile. That continued through the 1960s, 1970s, and 1980s. Public transit systems grew, often primarily to serve suburban-downtown commuters. By the 1980s, the central cities had lost most of their retail dominance, and suburban offices and industrial parks were everywhere. Many central cities were in financial trouble, with escalating social problems. But the 2000 era shows signs of change. Central city infill housing grew at a very rapid rate (until the 2007 collapse). The new occupants have drawn new convenience retail stores. Central cities have also sharpened their focus on their continuing role as civic centers, and as entertainment centers. Most importantly, some central cities have become important as incubators of new ideas and companies, due to inexpensive older space and a hub of young creative people.

The 2007 housing collapse generally hit suburbs, especially deep suburbs, the hardest. And the areas with the noticeable new job growth since 2007 have often been central city areas. Where will this go, in the 2010 decade and beyond?

Labor Force Issues

The *quality of our daily life* depends in part on the quantity of goods and services that are available to us. In turn, *the quantity* depends in part on (1) what percentage of the population works and (2) their productivity as they work. In order for the quality of our life to improve, these two issues play a big role. The percentage of the population that works is called the **labor force participation rate**. For more than five decades, the participation rate has been increasing, due to the growing numbers of baby boom workers, and especially the increase in the percentage of women working outside the home. The Federal Reserve Bank of San Francisco estimates that these two factors added as much as 1.7 percent per year to the gross domestic product of the United States for the past several decades!

The positive effect of the baby boomers on the workforce participation rate is now pretty much over and the percentage of women in the workforce has stabilized. As a result, the Congressional Budget Office expects labor force growth to add only 0.5 percent per year to GDP from 2013 to 2017. (This may change upward, slightly, as baby boomers delay retirement, to rebuild nest eggs damaged by the recent economic crash.)

Productivity growth means that the same labor force produces more, for the same effort and hours, over the years. This can happen due to improved skills, improved equipment, better use of workers, and other factors. The long-term average growth in productivity has been about 2 percent per year since 1947. But it was unusually strong from 1996 to 2008, running about 2.7 percent per year, according to the S. F. Fed. Many economists believe that this productivity increase was the result of the benefits of improved computers and communications equipment, software, and the Internet. Indications are that annual productivity increases may well be less, over the next several decades.

Still another growing labor force issue is **unemployment**. First, unemployment is quite high, as a result of the recession (at least 9.5 percent in April 2010). Total payroll jobs in January 2010 were 129 million and falling, down from a peak in early 2008 of just under 140 million. Because of the slow economy, many are having trouble finding a new job. Figure 19.2 shows the average number of weeks that a worker was unemployed, from 1980 through March 2010. It is clear that this recession is different, because the average length of unemployment has increased so dramatically.

But Figure 19.3 shows a different aspect of the unemployment numbers—the unemployment rate by education level. (The data is as of January 2010, and unemployment has continued to deteriorate for some months more.) The lesson is clear: Unemployment is not as much a *jobs issue* as it is a *skills/education issue*. (It is also an issue of the sexes, a the unemployment rate for men is noticeably higher than for women.)

FIGURE 19.2   Mean duration unemployment

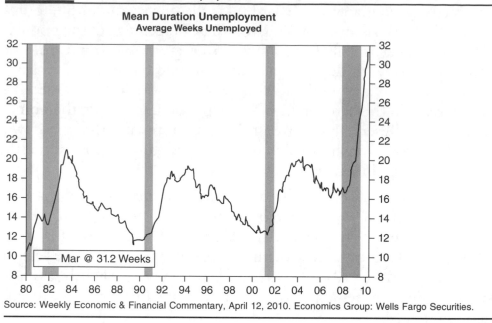

Source: Weekly Economic & Financial Commentary, April 12, 2010. Economics Group: Wells Fargo Securities.

FIGURE 19.3   Unemployment rate by education level

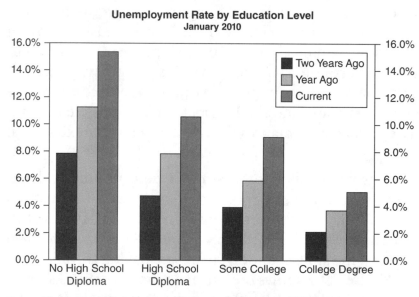

Source: Weekly Economic & Financial Commentary, February 12, 2010. Economics Group: Wells Fargo Securities.

So one concern is the lingering high unemployment rate itself, which is projected to decline very slowly. This concern grows with the realization that the unemployment problem is with low-skilled workers. Next, we must recognize that the baby boomers will indeed retire at some point, the only question is when! As that happens, over the next several decades, we will loose very large numbers of experienced and well-educated workers. The issue is: How will we fill those vacancies? Given the available pool of workers, what will that do to productivity, and to the annual increase in GDP per capita? And how do we improve all of our education institutions, to bring worker skills into line with the needs of the available jobs?

Political/Legal Issues

Today, it is clear that future real estate use and values depend in part on what happens in several areas of political and legal conflict.

Land-Use Controls

Land-use controls change over time as society's perception of ideal land use evolves. The most important land-use issue of the moment appears to be the environment, especially pollution. *Pollution control regulations* by local, state, and federal governments are likely to have considerable influence on public and private land use in the next decade. Continuing serious air pollution in some urban areas is likely to lead to shifts in transportation methods, which have a direct impact on industrial, commercial, and residential land uses. This in turn will have an impact on the market value of each property. And past regulation of land use to minimize water pollution is a pattern that is expected to continue throughout the nation.

After pollution controls, a second environmental issue of growing importance in studying property values is *wildlife protection*. Habitat protection is of growing importance in development planning. Future battles over water conservation to protect wildlife may sharply affect land use, water cost, and land values in some areas.

Finally, the *extent of government control* over private land will continue to be controversial. Where does legal land-use control under the police power end and public purchase under the eminent domain power start? In recent years, courts have ruled that certain government land-use controls were illegal and were used to avoid the outright purchase of private land under the power of eminent domain. The continuing debate over the limits of government controls has the potential to significantly affect the value and future use of private parcels of real estate.

Consumerism

Newspaper headlines feature consumer rebellions, boycotts, class-action lawsuits, and mass appearances at regulatory or congressional hearings. People now are more willing to express their objections to some of the goods and services they buy. So far, this has not been quite as noticeable with real estate as with cars, for example. Such a lag is to be expected, because people do not buy and sell real estate very often and find it complex and hard to understand. As consumers become more confident at expressing objections, however, their focus probably will include more real estate complaints.

Visible signs of this change can be seen in the increasing number of lawsuits against builders or sellers over structural and soil problems or contaminated drywall board. The spread of real estate sale disclosure laws is another sign of this change. Another sign is the increasing use of broker errors and omissions insurance, and home warranty insurance to cover house and equipment repairs in the year after sale. The increase in landlord-tenant conflict and changes in landlord-tenant law are added evidence of growing **consumerism**.

Political Conflict

The United States has had **political conflict** since it was founded. The Civil War was the worst political conflict that the country has faced. Nothing today remotely matches it. But there really is no effective gauge, or measure, of the relative intensity of political conflict, and how it changes over time.

However, this era does seem to feature more heated political dialogue than, say, 25 or 50 years ago. Is this a cycle or a trend? If it is a cycle, how much longer will it be until it starts to moderate? If a trend, what does that mean for the future ability of our society to resolve the problems that always come up from time to time?

The Infrastructure Question

The value of any parcel of real estate is totally dependant on all of the public improvements that support it. These include utilities, transportation networks, education systems, police and fire, and more. These are sometimes called **infrastructure**. All of it needs to be maintained, modernized when needed, managed and staffed, and expanded when the need increases. And all this takes a lot of money! Much of government spending goes to support infrastructure.

As noted in Chapter 12, the voter tax rebellions of recent decades have tended to reduce the revenues of most levels of government. In turn, funding for infrastructure has been impacted. Roads in many areas are not being maintained or modernized as would have happened in the past. Delays in funding needed expansion are causing increasing traffic congestion. Public transit budgets are under pressure, often resulting in service cuts.

Education has been particularly impacted, at all levels. Per capita public school spending in California, for example, is among the lowest in the country. But living costs are high, leading to growing teacher shortages and turnover. And the higher-education system in the state, once the model for the entire country, is eliminating classes and reducing enrollment. This is at a time when workforce changes, discussed earlier in this section, require increased education effort.

The significance of this is that it takes many years and a lot of money to develop a city's entire infrastructure. When we cut the money we spend on upkeep, the impact is not immediately apparent. For this reason, it is usually politically safer to cut infrastructure funding than funding for welfare or public safety. Over time, however, the deferred maintenance grows. The facilities become more out-of-date. And overuse and crowding become more apparent.

Many have suggested that the United States has not been spending enough on infrastructure upkeep for decades. Bridges, roads, mass transit, schools, and higher education are most often mentioned. Water supplies and hospitals are also a concern. It is not clear how bad the situation is. And, so far, the voters seem reluctant to pay for what they use!

REVIEWING YOUR UNDERSTANDING

National Changes

1. What is meant by population composition, and how does it affect real estate? Give an example from your community.

2. Can you give four reasons why poverty affects real estate?

3. What four problems of housing are listed? How does each apply to your community?

4. Show how attitudes toward the importance of work or leisure influence real estate use and value.

5. How do labor force issues affect real estate?

6. What appear to be the two major land-use problems? Give examples of each from your community.

7. Why is infrastructure important to real estate values?

8. What changes in consumer attitudes toward real estate have you noticed? List those that are favorable and those that are unfavorable.

19.3 THE UNCERTAIN FUTURE

The potential problems noted in the first two parts of Section 19.3 are ones that penetrate to the core of American culture and society. Although these issues may seem only remotely connected to real estate, they have a great long-range impact on land use and values. These will be among the major issues of the next generation. We end up exploring where the real estate industry itself is heading.

Telemobility

The medium, or process, of our time—electronic technology—is reshaping and restructuring patterns of social interdependence and every aspect of our national and personal life.

> Everything is changing—you, your family, your neighborhood, your education, your job, your government, your relation to "the others." And they're changing dramatically.[1]

We don't really know whether the world will ultimately become a "global village"—the thesis of this author—or whether the impact of electronic media will make us a world of isolated individuals, held together by a surface network of communication. But it is clear that the impact of electronics, and of digital technology on communications, has changed the fundamental nature of our lives. Many things that our ancestors could only do face-to-face, including talking and shopping, can now be done by us from a distance. Instead of traveling in person, we can travel electronically; that is, we have **telemobility**.

According to John Diebold, "It would be difficult to overstate the magnitude of change that will take place in the lives of all of us, in human history, as a result of the information revolution that has so unobtrusively taken place in our day."[2] Alvin Toffler, who created the expression "future shock" in 1965, describes the change that confronted us from 1970 on as a firestorm: "Change sweeps through the highly industrialized countries with waves of ever accelerating speed and unprecedented impact. It spawns in its wake all sorts of curious social flora—from psychedelic churches and 'free universities' to science cities in the Arctic and wife-swap clubs in California."[3]

Seventy years ago, futurologists predicted a world of video telephones, computers and faxes in the home, and executives working from desks in their homes, perhaps meeting with colleagues once a week or so. They foresaw people shopping by catalog and television, paying bills by electronics means, participating politically by cable TV, and entertaining themselves by video-recorders. Such a world—a world without office buildings, without massive customer facilities, without face-to-face contact—would have a *great impact* on real estate. Many of the futurologists' predictions have come true. What will the

---

[1] Marshall McLuhan and Quentin Fiore, *The Medium Is the Message*. New York, Bantam Books, 1967, p. 8.
[2] John Diebold, *Beyond Automation*. New York, McGraw Hill, 1964.
[3] Alvin Toffler, *Future Shock*. New York, Bantam Books, 1971, p. 9.

rest of the 21st century bring? Will working at home continue to grow, as it has in the past several decades? What does this say about home design? About central office rents? About downtown retail sales?

As one example, consider video conferencing, which is starting to come into common use. Each major past improvement in communications—from the telegraph to the phone, and then to email and the Web—has noticeably reduced the need for face-to-face contact. Will video phones have an added big impact?

Telemobility is not just an issue in our daily lives. It also has international impacts. Because of the size, wealth in raw materials, and location of the United States, the role of foreign trade in the economy of this country historically was rather small, when compared to the economies of other industrialized countries. As a result, the American economy in the past was able to resist the international economic fluctuations that have rocked other nations. This has been changing as a result of telemobility. It has allowed companies to purchase more goods and services from other countries, but still be in close contact. And the 2007 crash marked the end of this protected position. It was excellent communication that allowed Wall Street to sell mortgage-backed securities (and other types) worldwide, sending the necessary documentation by fax or email.

The eroding position of America's balance of payments was an added key. Our historic surplus of exports over imports has been gone for some decades. A growing lack of confidence in the strength of the dollar has caused the value of the dollar to drop over the past decade. And the massive changes in petroleum prices have added another dimension of insecurity to an already shaken international financial picture.

Now, the world economic picture is like a huge bowl of jelly. Every economy is so closely linked, with very high-speed connections. The smallest "plunk" on one side of the jelly sends quivers throughout. And very high-speed computers are watching every economic measure, shifting funds thousands of times a minute, in pursuit of a penny here and a penny (or peso) there. In the meantime, third world countries increasingly agitate for better export opportunities for their farm products, often blocked by protectionist policies in the developed countries. *All of these are consequences* of the electronic revolution!

Population Growth

Population growth, although it varies for each nation, has long been recognized as one of the world's most pressing problems.

Nearly always, this growth is "exponential," which means that population is growing by a certain percent each year, a *constant percentage increase*, rather than by a *constant number* like, say, 2 million people each year. The problem with exponential growth is that it compounds, so that the increase *in numbers* grows larger each year. If it compounds long enough, the growth clearly becomes insupportably large, as the following 1967 quotation indicates.

> At the present time, starting someplace about 1946, the average annual rate of increase in the world's population is about 2 percent. Using the 1962 population as a base, and applying this rate of growth to it, shows that in 650 years—somewhat less than the time backwards to the Renaissance—there would be, in our world, one person standing on each square foot of land.[4]

Table 19.4 demonstrates the power of compounding. There are many examples in nature of such exponential growth, but they all end with the collapse of growth, and a sharp drop in total numbers. The world obviously cannot physically hold enough people to accept a 2% yearly growth in population for the next 650 years! Some form of natural breakdown will reduce it. It seems clear that there really is an upper limit to population growth.

And there can be no question that this time limit is much shorter than 650 years. We will be in trouble long before there is one person per square foot of land! Early on, the world will face growing food shortages, which can be postponed only at great expense. Some experts point to the congestion of modern cities and other problems. They ask if human population may have other types of limits than just food, such as the chaos that may result from excessive social pressures. Population growth is also tied to limits in resources, pollution, and energy use. The population growth problem raises some fundamental questions about our future.

TABLE 19.4   A Familiar Form of Compound Growth

If we could place $1,000 in a savings certificate at 5 percent interest, with instructions to reinvest the interest, it will grow to:

1 year	$1,050
10 years	$1,629
50 years	$11,467
100 years	$131,501

[4]Don Fabun, *The Dynamics of Change*. New Jersey, Prentice Hall, Englewood Cliffs, 1967, pp. 1–10.

Population Control

The problems that exponential population growth creates can be delayed or resolved through population control. For religious and social reasons, population control is quite controversial. Yet more people appear involved with personal, social, or legal population control than ever before. It is obvious that this issue will be examined even more intensely in the future. The changes that could occur, whether legal or social, would undoubtedly affect general economic conditions; the relative growth of different countries, cultures, or groups; trends in particular industries; the economic base of cities; and real estate values, as well as the fundamental question of future world population levels.

Resources

Exponential population growth increases the need for agricultural products, petroleum, ores, timber, and every other commodity used by people. What makes it worse is that the worldwide *per-person* use of many commodities is also increasing exponentially. This means that production must increase even faster than population. An additional complication is that the better ores, fields, and wells are usually the ones already in production. Thus, the increased production must come either from new technologies or else from more marginal areas, at higher costs.

Much of the world's population in the 20th century lived a subsistence lifestyle. Much of their food was grown by the family, relatives, or people in the same or nearby villages. They used little or no outside energy, resources, or products. Over the past 50 years, this has been changing. Many countries have made truly dramatic economic growth. The result is that a huge number of people are moving out of a subsistence lifestyle, and into more of a *consumer* lifestyle! Some preliminary projections for resource use 50 years from now are, as a result, quite startling. The growth in **resource use** is a key long-term issue.

Many believe that there are limits to future increases of resource or commodity production. They state that the limits arise from increased costs, rather than from actually running out of the resources. As prices rise, it becomes more feasible economically to recapture or recycle the used resource, rather than to just hunt for new resources. Gold and platinum have long been in this category, more recently joined by silver, aluminum, and water. However, maximum recycling may only *postpone* the inevitable result of exponential growth, because some resources always are lost in ways that cannot be recovered by recycling.

But resource production now occurs all over the world, often far removed from where the resource is used. Thus, world trade is deeply involved with these resources that will become quite scarce. Interest rates, capital availability, import costs, and export jobs are all closely tied to international finance and trade issues.

And the increasing international movement of key resources makes world economics more vulnerable to various forms of pressure. For example, Germany gets most of its natural gas from Russia. Supplies were shut off in 2009, when Russia and Ukraine disputed issues with movement of natural gas across Ukraine. A conflict between Russia and Ukraine, or some kind of terrorist act, would have serious repercussions on the German economy (and Europe)!

Another issue is that resources are not evenly distributed around the world, or necessarily where they are used. Japan, for example, must import nearly all of its petroleum, while Saudi Arabia exports huge amounts. Consider Table 19.5, which lists the seven largest petroleum companies, by the size of the reserves that each controls. Note that all seven are now government controlled—a major shift from even 30 years ago!

Pollution and Global Warming

All human activities produce some air, water, and noise **pollution**. As population doubles, and production per person doubles again, pollution grows. Often the growth of pollutants is hidden for a while, because the natural system can partly purify the water and air, and muffle sounds. Sometimes, quite suddenly, a pollution problem can appear, when the natural cleansing system is overcome. Our society is now more aware of this and has begun to clean up the polluting by-products of centuries of past production.

Global warming is a form of pollution, resulting from the release of various gases into the air. The most common is apparently carbon dioxide (CO_2), which is released whenever fuels (coal, oil, and other

TABLE 19.5   Largest Petroleum Companies

Company	Country
Saudi Aramco	Saudi Arabia
Gazprom	Russia
China National Petroleum Co.	China
National Iranian Oil Co.	Iran
Petroleos de Venezuela	Venezuela
Petrobras	Brazil
Petronas	Malaysia

Source: *Wall Street Journal*, May 22, 2010.

petroleum products; flammable gasses) are burned. CO_2 is believed to trap more of the Sun's energy, so that it warms up the Earth, instead of being reflected or reradiated back into space. The science behind global warming is reported to be extremely complex. Most scientists in the field are convinced that it is a real problem, while some deny it completely. As economists, we don't know who is right. We only ask: "What if…?"

It is clear that energy sources with less effect on global warming are *currently* more expensive. To change to a non-petroleum-based energy system will take time and massive capital costs. For both reasons, then, global warming is a long-range issue with major economic consequences!

The cost of correcting pollution, or global warming, adds to the cost of operating plants and cities. It affects the demand for the plant's products, or for various locations in the cities. Correcting for past pollution shifts the production cost characteristics of nearly all products, and nearly all locations, but not by the same amount for each. This causes a great sorting out, or readjustment, among competing locations and products. In this process, some locations and products will gain and some will lose.

Transportation is a major source of pollution, as well as a major user of the nation's total energy. In addition, the different methods of transportation differ substantially in their impact on city shape and density, as discussed in Chapter 7.

The automobile currently dominates American transportation, but it is clearly a major source of petroleum consumption as well as pollution. The problems of automobile pollution, petroleum price increases, and possible petroleum shortages suggest that, over the long term, the present auto will be altered, or its part in our society will be changed. The impact on real estate will be significant, because of the impact the automobile has had in developing suburban areas. In some regions, the increased availability of public transit over the past several decades has unquestionably changed where people live and work. Will transportation problems be partially solved by the telecommunications revolution? Will this affect real estate trends and values?

The Los Angeles air basin was one of the first areas in the country to become troubled by automobile-created air pollution. The research and experience of Los Angeles has produced a wealth of information for everyone. Unfortunately, the L.A. region seems to be in a race. The population continues to grow, and the increasing rate of auto ownership raises auto growth even faster. As long as the exponential growth in the number of automobiles continues, sharper and sharper cuts in the rate of pollution per automobile are necessary, *just to stay even*! Because pollution control gets harder and more expensive the further you go; it must be concluded that either pollution will go up or the number of autos must not grow so fast. Every other polluting human activity is a similar problem, as long as the numbers continue to grow.

Energy

The United States is the world's predominant energy-driven society, substituting other energy sources in place of human labor. As a result, **energy use** per person has had its own exponential growth, on top of the growth of population and the growth of goods and services.

Unfortunately, the exponential increases in energy currently consume fuels, such as oil, natural gas, and coal, which cannot be renewed or recycled. The original solution pioneered in the 1950s and 1960s was nuclear energy. However, because of serious disasters worldwide, the development of nuclear plants in the United States came to a halt. Other alternatives—breeder reactors, fusion, geothermal energy, tides, winds, solar energy—require immense effort to be significant energy sources during our lifetimes. It is clear that energy demands of the next decade or so are likely to be borne mostly by oil, natural gas, and coal. However, energy conservation has had a significant initial impact. Best estimates indicate that a major push for energy conservation would have a big future impact. Heating, cooling, and lighting buildings consume a significant fraction of total U. S. energy use. This makes *building energy conservation* a big issue. Every aspect of economic production, resource allocation, and land-use determination is heavily influenced by energy availability and cost. The oil shortages that emerged with conflicts in the Middle East had major effects on real estate, as have increases in oil and natural gas prices.

Most countries of the world use much less energy per person than the United States does, but the growth rate of their use of energy per person is rising much faster. This means that worldwide competition for oil, gas, and coal is increasing rapidly. The result should be continued price increases, as well as pressure to develop new energy sources and reduce energy use.

From these changes in energy prices and use will come changes in real estate. Examples include additional emphasis on building insulation and other aspects of energy conservation. Energy change will affect many businesses; local economies will then feel the effects, and, of course, real estate will be affected by these changes, possibly heavily.

Where Does This Situation Leave The Real Estate Industry?

We all recognize that the era we live in is one of amazing change. Technology is a major force for change. Every area of our society is changing! As any product or industry changes, the people who handle the product or are a part of the industry must also change. The most obvious changes throughout the real estate industry are: (1) increased use of various forms of technology, (2) increased knowledge (via education or training), (3) increased specialization, or a narrowing of the area of activity, and (4) an increase in the average size of a real estate firm or organization. The size of the typical real estate brokerage company has expanded by growth and merger, and by joining franchise chains. Increased cooperation among real estate brokers also seems to be a trend.

Future potential changes include a need for greater specialized knowledge on the part of individual brokers. For example, those who broker homes now usually do not handle commercial property. And commercial property brokers rarely handle home sales. Some residential agents now primarily list property, separating themselves from those who represent home buyers. One specialization, already evident, separates brokerage for a commission from consulting for a fee. Further specialization could go so far as to produce separate broker's licenses for home sales, investment property, and so forth. With the increase in multiculturalism, there has been a trend for individual licensees, and in some cases entire real estate offices, to specialize along cultural lines. The increased use of clerical or semiprofessional assistants appears to be another trend.

The mechanisms for connecting properties with buyers may be the area for the most dramatic changes. The formation of regional, super regional, statewide, national, and worldwide multiple listing services can expose properties to previously unheard-of numbers of potential buyers. The entry of for-profit corporate-run listing services, competing directly with traditional, real estate association controlled, multiple listing services, will allow sellers to directly list their properties for sale, bypassing real estate agents. Finally, the possibility of "virtual" real estate companies on the Web could greatly reduce the need for "brick and mortar" buildings. In effect, a real estate company can have an "office" in every city, by having an agent in each town, working out of his or her home, and doing all broker-to-salesperson communications electronically.

The increased use of the Internet is rapidly changing real estate marketing. Many buyers make their initial search for properties online. Agents are exploring new ways of reaching them. Investors, appraisers, and lenders now often rely on Internet data sources. The use of the Internet to house records, as well as analysis programs, is growing. Clearly, technology can be expected to be a major future force for change throughout the real estate industry.

REVIEWING YOUR UNDERSTANDING

The Uncertain Future

1. Define the concept *Telemobility*. What is its significance to real estate? Can you give an actual example from your community?
2. Explain why the rate of net population increase is so important.
3. What is exponential growth?
4. How many examples can you give of connections between pollution and land use?
5. How do international issues affect local real estate? Give four examples from your community. Is your region affected by trade agreements such as NAFTA and WTO?
6. How does transportation change affect the value of real estate? Why is future transportation change likely? What is the most recent transportation change in your community, and what are its real estate effects?

CHAPTER SUMMARY

There cannot be a real summary of this chapter because no one can write a summary of the future! Others might see very different potential strengths and weaknesses. What is *your* view?

Answers to the *Reviewing Your Understanding* Questions

Chapter 2

1. b	6. a	11. b	16. c	21. b
2. d	7. c	12. a	17. d	22. b
3. b	8. a	13. d	18. a	23. d
4. c	9. d	14. b	19. a	24. a
5. a	10. b	15. a	20. c	25. d

Chapter 3

1. b	6. a	11. b	16. b	21. c
2. d	7. b	12. a	17. c	22. d
3. a	8. c	13. b	18. c	23. a
4. c	9. d	14. d	19. a	24. c
5. d	10. d	15. c	20. d	25. b

Chapter 4

1. d	6. b	11. c	16. d	21. a
2. a	7. a	12. a	17. c	22. a
3. c	8. b	13. b	18. b	23. b
4. c	9. c	14. b	19. d	24. d
5. c	10. a	15. a	20. b	25. d

Chapter 5

1. d	6. c	11. a	16. d	21. a
2. c	7. a	12. b	17. d	22. b
3. a	8. c	13. a	18. b	23. a
4. c	9. a	14. d	19. c	24. c
5. c	10. d	15. b	20. b	25. a

Chapter 6

1. b	6. d	11. b	16. c	21. a
2. c	7. d	12. b	17. b	22. b
3. a	8. a	13. c	18. a	23. b
4. d	9. d	14. b	19. b	24. a
5. a	10. d	15. a	20. b	25. c

Chapter 7

1. b	6. b	11. b	16. b	21. d
2. d	7. d	12. c	17. a	22. a
3. a	8. d	13. d	18. b	23. d
4. c	9. a	14. b	19. d	24. b
5. b	10. d	15. d	20. b	25. c

Chapter 8

1. a	6. c	11. b	16. b	21. b
2. d	7. b	12. b	17. b	22. b
3. c	8. c	13. b	18. c	23. b
4. d	9. c	14. b	19. a	24. d
5. d	10. d	15. a	20. c	25. a

Chapter 9

1. b	6. c	11. c	16. a	21. d
2. c	7. d	12. a	17. d	22. a
3. a	8. d	13. d	18. a	23. b
4. d	9. b	14. a	19. b	24. d
5. a	10. a	15. c	20. d	25. a

Chapter 10

1. b	6. a	11. a	16. b	21. b
2. c	7. d	12. c	17. b	22. c
3. d	8. c	13. a	18. c	23. c
4. b	9. b	14. a	19. a	24. a
5. a	10. a	15. d	20. b	25. c

Chapter 11

1. b	6. b	11. b	16. d	21. b
2. c	7. c	12. c	17. b	22. a
3. d	8. c	13. d	18. a	23. d
4. d	9. a	14. a	19. a	24. a
5. a	10. b	15. c	20. d	25. d

Chapter 12

1. d	6. b	11. a	16. d	21. b
2. c	7. d	12. a	17. c	22. a
3. a	8. b	13. c	18. b	23. d
4. a	9. d	14. b	19. c	24. a
5. b	10. c	15. c	20. b	25. d

Chapter 13

1. a	6. d	11. d	16. c	21. a
2. b	7. b	12. b	17. d	22. a
3. a	8. a	13. d	18. c	23. d
4. c	9. d	14. a	19. d	24. d
5. d	10. c	15. b	20. d	25. a

Chapter 14

1. c	6. d	11. c	16. a	21. a
2. a	7. b	12. d	17. a	22. d
3. d	8. a	13. a	18. a	23. a
4. c	9. d	14. b	19. a	24. c
5. b	10. a	15. b	20. d	25. a

Chapter 15

1. a	6. b	11. b	16. b	21. a
2. c	7. a	12. a	17. a	22. a
3. d	8. a	13. d	18. b	23. a
4. a	9. d	14. c	19. c	24. d
5. c	10. a	15. a	20. a	25. d

Chapter 16

1. d	6. d	11. c	16. b
2. c	7. d	12. c	17. a
3. c	8. b	13. b	18. b
4. a	9. a	14. b	19. c
5. b	10. a	15. a	

20. $15,860 Net Operating Income
21. Negative [$904] Before-Tax Cash Flow
22. $1,403 Net Spendable Income (After-Tax Cash Flow)
23. $$\frac{\text{Price } \$300,000}{\text{Gross Scheduled Income } \$22,800} = \begin{array}{c} 13.16 \text{ Gross Rent} \\ \text{Multiplier} \end{array}$$
24. $$\frac{\text{Net Operating Income } \$15,860}{\text{Price } \$300,000} = \begin{array}{c} 5.29\% \text{ Capitalization} \\ \text{Rate} \end{array}$$
25. $$\frac{\text{After-Tax Cash Flow } \$1,403}{\begin{array}{c} \text{Cash Invested } \$90,000 \\ \text{(down payment)} \end{array}} = \begin{array}{c} 1.56\% \text{ After-Tax} \\ \text{Cash on Cash Rate} \end{array}$$

Case & Point for Chapter 16

1. $6,780 Before-Tax Cash Flow
2. $5,083 Taxes Saved
3. $11,863 Net Spendable Income (After-Tax Cash Flow)
4. $$\frac{\text{Price } \$1,200,000}{\text{Gross Scheduled Income } \$120,000} = 10 \text{ Gross Rent Multiplier}$$
5. $$\frac{\text{Net Operating Income } \$85,980}{\text{Price } \$1,200,000} = 7.17\% \text{ Capitalization Rate}$$
6. $$\frac{\text{Before-Tax Cash Flow } \$6,780}{\text{Cash Invested } \$300,000} = \begin{array}{c} 2.26\% \text{ Before-Tax Cash} \\ \text{on Cash Rate} \end{array}$$
7. $$\frac{\text{After-Tax Cash Flow } \$11,863}{\text{Cash Invested } \$300,000} = \begin{array}{c} 3.95\% \text{ After-Tax Cash} \\ \text{on Cash Rate} \end{array}$$
8. $$\frac{\text{Net Operating Income } \$85,980}{\text{Market Capitalization Rate } 8\%} = \$1,074,750 \text{ Market Price}$$
9. $18,174 Net Spendable Income (After-Tax Cash Flow)
10. $$\frac{\text{Net Spendable Income } \$18,174}{\text{Cash Invested } \$268,687} = \begin{array}{c} 6.76\% \text{ After-Tax Cash} \\ \text{on Cash Rate} \end{array}$$

Chapter 17

1. d	7. b	13. a ($1 mill. × 60% ÷ 39 years = $15,385)
2. d	8. a	14. d
3. a	9. a	15. a
4. b	10. c	16. c
5. c	11. b	17. b
6. c	12. c	18. a

19. c $300,000 Price + 3,000 Costs + 15,000 Imp. Less
$20,000 Deposit = $298,000

20. d
$400,000
–32,000   Seller Closing Costs
–10,000   Carry-Forward Passive Loss
–298,000   Adjusted Cost Basis
$ 60,000   Gain

21. b
22. b
23. a
24. b
25. d

Chapter 18

1. b	6. d	11. d
2. a	7. a	12. a
3. d	8. b	13. d
4. c	9. a	14. c
5. d	10. b	15. a

Glossary

Ability to pay A measure of effective demand, more than just an unrealizable wish.

Accessibility Degree of ease by which a store or business can be reached by employees, customers, and suppliers.

Affordable housing Housing that rents for less than 30% of the occupants' annual income; housing for low-income families.

Affordability index A measure of the financial ability of U.S. families to buy a house.

After-Tax Cash Flow The Before-Tax Cash Flow from an investment, plus or minus the taxes saved or paid as a result of that income.

Asset bubble When prices of assets are over-inflated due to excess demand. It usually occurs when investors all flock to a particular asset class, such as real estate or commodities such as oil.

Assessed value Value placed on real estate or personal property by government assessors for determining ad valorem taxes.

Automatic stabilizers Policies or institutions that automatically tend to dampen economic cycle fluctuations in income, employment, etc., without direct government intervention.

Balance of payments A record of all transactions of the citizens of one nation with another, or with all other countries.

Balance of trade A record of the merchandise (goods, but not services) transferred between one nation and another, or with all other nations.

Basic employment Local companies that produce goods and services to be shipped outside the community or region that is being studied.

Basis refers to the property owner's cost for income tax purposes.

Before-Tax Cash Flow Net operating income from an investment (net of all operating expenses) less loan payments, but before the payment of income taxes, if any, on the income.

Benefits received tax A tax that is imposed on those who benefit from the service that the tax funds. A bridge toll is an example.

Big-box stores Very large stand-alone retail stores, either specializing in a single line of merchandise, or else a low-price general merchandiser.

Boot Any unlike property received in an exchange of properties, under the IRS Code Section 1031.

Break-cargo point A place where a shift in the transportation system or route, or an obstacle, requires the unloading and reloading of cargo.

Building construction One of the steps in the property development process; the construction of buildings.

Business cycles The reoccurring expansions and contractions in general business activity that take place over a period ranging from three to six years.

Capital A factor of production: any manufactured thing, instrument, or device that is used to increase production, such as machinery, tools, and buildings.

Cash flow analysis The process of estimating the amount of money to be received from an investment each year, including the year of resale.

Central business district (CBD) The center of the community's and its retail center, nearly always close to the physical origins of the community.

Central town A community that performs a variety of commercial, social, religious, and governmental services for a surrounding area.

Certified Property Manager® (CPM®) A professional designation awarded to real estate managers by the Institute of Real Estate Management an affiliate of the National Association of Realtors®.

Change in demand An increase or decrease in the number of available buyers, or in the quantity of goods and/or services they seek to obtain.

Change in supply An increase or decrease in the number of available suppliers, or in the quantity of goods and/or services they are prepared to sell.

Change in use A sign of neighborhood change, often noticed first at one side of the neighborhood.

Change: cycle and trend The two types of change: one repeats regularly and the other is a long-term shift in one direction.

Command economy An economic system in which a central authority plans and controls prices, production levels, and distribution.

Communism A form of economic or social structure, typically characterized by the abolition of classes and a community control over all property.

Community centers A retail shopping center with a department store, banks, variety stores, and some specialty stores, with restaurants clustered nearby.

Comparative advantage The benefit of a particular location for a specific business (retail, wholesale, office, etc.), created by favorable location characteristics for that business, such as good transportation, positive government controls, the proper combination of stores, and natural land features.

Concentric growth A town that grows by gradually expanding, in all directions, with older buildings being converted to a new use, or demolished.

Consumerism A modern social movement to protect consumers from inferior or dangerous products and deceptive advertising. Shown in real estate by the increase in landlord-tenant conflict and changes in landlord-tenant law.

Condo conversions The conversion of an existing multifamily rental dwelling (an "apartment") to individually-owned condominiums.

Counter-party risk The risk that a party to an agreement will not perform as agreed; specifically, that an organization does not pay out on a credit derivative, credit default swap, credit insurance contract, or other trade or transaction when it is supposed to.

Credit availability The amount of money that can be borrowed at a given time.

Crop markets Markets where farmers and ranchers sell crops, often specialized marketing channels, such as stockyards and grain elevators.

Current rent Rent levels that are already established, often by lease or contract.

Cyclical unemployment Unemployment caused when the economy slips into a recession and jobs are lost because of this slowdown.

Dealer A person who acquires real estate as inventory, with the intent of reselling it to customers in the regular course of business.

Deflation When prices and wages are declining.

Demand The total quantity that buyers are willing to buy, at a given time and location, at certain prices.

Demand composition The mix of types, ages and sizes of housing (or other types of real estate) that are in demand.

Demand deposits Funds on deposit at a commercial bank; checking accounts; part of the money supply.

Demography Breakdown of the population according to age, sex, occupation, income level, and other variables.

Demolition Tearing down a building.

Density of use A measure of how property is used; often a good indicator of neighborhood change.

Depository institution Bank, credit union, or other financial institution that solicits and accepts savings of the general public as demand deposits or time deposits, and pays a fixed or variable rate of interest.

Depreciation An annual bookkeeping deduction, or paper expense, allowed by the tax code as a cost recovery for the theoretical loss in value of the property over time.

Depression A period during which business activity drops significantly, a serious recession. High unemployment rates and deflation often accompany a depression.

Deterioration or decay The effects of weather and use as buildings get older, absent maintenance and renovation.

Deleveraging Reducing the amount or level of debt that a person or company (or nation) owes.

Discounted cash flow analysis An analysis of the value of estimated future money receipts, allowing for the time value of money, when computing rates of return for real estate investments.

Discount rate The interest rate charged when a bank borrows from The Fed.

Discretionary income A measure of personal income: gross income, less income taxes, and less necessary expenses.

Disintermediation The historical outflow of funds from depository institutions into corporate and government notes or other investments.

Disposable income A measure of personal income: gross income, less all income taxes.

Doubling up The tendency during recessions for people to share housing accommodations with their parents or other people, thus reducing demand for housing.

Easy-money policy Attempting to head off a recession, or reduce its severity, by easing the money supply.

Economic base study A study of a community or region. It forecasts population growth by forecasting basic employment.

Economic highest and best use The legal use of a property that will produce the greatest net income attributable to the land.

Economic life The time period over which a building contributes to the market value of the improved property, after which the improvements are likely to be demolished, and a new one built, to reflect the new highest and best use of the land.

Economic succession The process of change of use of a site, from its prior use to a new use. If there is a building on the site, it will be demolished only when a new use is profitable enough to pay for the site, the old building, the demolition cost, and the cost of the new building.

Economics A social science that is concerned with how individuals and societies choose to allocate scarce resources in order to produce, distribute, and consume goods and services.

Effective demand The quantity that consumers are able and willing to purchase at each conceivable price.

Elder housing Residential units designed for seniors. There are different types, both as to price level, and as to the degree of assistance needed by the resident.

Eminent domain The right of the community to buy, for full value, any site that the community needs to use, regardless of the owner's willingness to sell.

Employment data Data collected on workers, including wage levels, hours worked, breakdowns by job title, industry, and location, those who are working less hours than desired, and those who want work but have at the time stopped looking.

Energy use The amount of energy used by a home or a business.

Entrepreneurship A factor of production. The skill of assembling or organizing of the other factors of production, (land, labor, and capital), in a systematic manner, to produce goods or services.

Environment All social, economic, biological, and physical surroundings of a place.

Environmental controls Government regulations that are imposed in order to reduce or prevent damage to the environment.

Environmental Protection Agency (EPA) A federal agency, created in 1970 and responsible for seeing that federal pollution standards are enforced.

Environmental impact The long-range direct and indirect impacts of a proposed land use upon the environment.

Environmentalism A broad philosophy and social movement, focused on environmental conservation and improvement of the state of the environment.

Equilibrium point The price point where the quantity that buyers are willing to purchase equals the quantity that sellers are willing to sell.

Expectation A key issue in investment analysis: the projection of earnings tomorrow and beyond by investors.

Feasibility study An in-depth analysis of the profitability of either a specific use or alternative uses for a parcel of land, or improved real estate.

Federal funds rate The rate of interest that one bank charges another, for the overnight use of excess reserves on deposit with the Federal Reserve System.

Federal Open Market Committee of the Federal Reserve Makes most policy decisions regarding monetary policy.

Federal Reserve System Regulates the supply of money and credit, in order to achieve economic growth without inflation and unemployment.

Filtering The pattern of most residential units having a number of occupants, given the long life of dwellings and the changing needs and tastes of people. Typically, as units become older, they are occupied by people of lower incomes.

Financial Management Rate of Return (FMRR) A measure of the return on invested funds. Adjusts each year's cash flows, using a "safe" rate: a reinvestment rate, to try to more closely model actual investor reinvestment practice than does the discount rate.

Financial risk The risk of failure to receive income when or in the amount that is expected.

Fiscal policy The government's use of its taxing and spending power to help counteract recession, unemployment, and inflation.

Fixed land supply The land surface is fixed, and cannot be increased or decreased according to the whims of demand. However, the intensity of use can be changed.

Fixed short-term land use In the short run, land use and land supply are fixed, as a change in land use generally is a slow process, requiring many studies and approvals.

Footloose industries Those considered capable of locating in any number of locations, depending on personal factors.

Fractional reserve banking A system of banking where member banks in the Federal Reserve System must maintain a specified percentage of depositors' balances as reserves, some in cash and some on deposit with the regional Federal Reserve Bank.

Free trade When many or all restrictions, quotas, and tariffs are removed, and all goods and services can flow between countries without restriction, in an open competitive market.

General plan A comprehensive long-range plan created by a community or region, to include all social, economic and physical aspects of the desired growth.

Gentrification The cultural changes in a less prosperous community, resulting from a demographic shift to wealthier people buying housing.

Global warming A form of pollution, believed to be occurring due to the release of various gases into the air.

Green Building The practice of using materials and processes that are environmentally responsible and resource-efficient, both during a building's construction and throughout its life-cycle.

Gross domestic product (GDP) A measure of the economy of a country or area. For the U.S., compiled by the U.S. Department of Commerce and its reported on a monthly and annual basis.

Gross Rent Multiplier (GRM) A rule of thumb, or measure, commonly used to estimate the value of income-producing properties.

Gross Scheduled Income The maximum potential amount of rents for a building when it is 100 percent occupied at either current rents or market rents.

Growing season The time of the year, or season, in a given location, when farmers grow most of their crops.

Highest and best use See Economic highest and best use.

Historical preservation A social movement, seeking to identify and preserve buildings which are significant, due to their architecture or the history associated with the building.

Holding period The actual or expected period of time during which an investment is owned by a particular investor.

Home building industry The segment of the construction industry that is involved with home construction.

Homeownership The state of living in a housing unit that one owns, as opposed to rents; a person who owns a residence.

Homeowner's exemption A credit given to homeowners, to reduce their property tax.

Housing composition The mix of unit size, age, location, and condition, and whether the units are intended for owner occupancy or for rent.

Impact fees Fees charged by local governments to developers for a development application or building permit, to help pay for the offsite capital costs that the development will generate, such as schools, parks, roads, and water or sewer system expansions.

Imperfect markets A market where a group of buyers or sellers is able to directly influence the price or output of a good or service.

Inclusionary zoning A legal requirement for developers to provide a percentage of the total housing units as subsidized low-income rental or for sale housing.

Income Money received by a person or organization because of effort (work) or from return on investments.

Income tax Major source of revenue for the federal government and many states.

Industrial location theory The study of how industries choose site locations. Often, the business seeks a location that reduces its costs and increases its profits.

Industrial parks Modern clusters of industrial uses, often located well away from historical industrial districts.

Inflation An increase in the level of consumer prices or a persistent decline in the purchasing power of money, caused by an increase in money beyond the available goods and services.

Inflation costs The increase in material prices and wages that can occur during construction delays.

Infrastructure The basic physical, legal, and social elements around a parcel that make it useful. These include utilities, transportation networks, education systems, police and fire, and more. The value of any parcel of real estate is totally dependant on it.

Input-output study A study of a community or region, which examines the resources that go into the economic activity of the community.

Installment sales The sale of a property where the seller does not receive all of the sales proceeds at the time of closing the sale, often called contract of sales or land contracts.

Institute for Real Estate Management (IREM®) An association of real estate management professionals, a source for education, resources and information, and membership for real estate management professionals.

Intensity of land use A measure of neighborhood change. A change of land use intensity in time will act to increase or decrease the supply of real estate.

Interest rate risk The risk that market interest rates will change, especially upwards, resulting in possible loss in value of an investment.

Internal Rate of Return (IRR) The rate of return on the funds invested, identical to the discount rate, yield rate, or interest rate. Technically, it is the rate that discounts the future cash flows to just equal the amount of money initially invested.

Investing The act of giving up present consumption, in order to use the saved funds to generate future benefits.

Investment characteristics Key differences between investments, setting alternatives for investors to choose from.

Investment choices The important issue in investments: what choices are available and how to rate them.

Investor A person who invests personal funds to buy property for a personal investment portfolio.

Investor trust The amount of confidence that investors have with the information upon which they based their investment decision.

Labor A factor of production. The human effort that is used to transform raw materials into finished products or to perform services.

Labor force participation rate The percentage of the total population that works at a paid job.

Labor-oriented industries Those that choose locations primarily to obtain access to low-cost labor.

Lagging indicators Economic and financial-market indicators which tend to show a change in the business cycle only after the economy has already changed.

Land A factor of production. The natural resources: trees, minerals, air, and water—as well as the surface of the earth.

Land development Subdividing and preparing the land for building.

Law of demand The lower the price, the more that consumers will buy. The higher the price, the less they will buy.

Law of supply The lower the price, the less that producers will produce. The higher the price, the more they will produce.

Leading indicators Economic and financial indicators which tend to show a change in the business cycle before (ahead of) the cycle.

LEED® certification A widely recognized green building certification system, establishing standards to promote design, construction, and maintenance practices that reduce negative environmental impacts of buildings.

Limits on choice A key investment concept: at any one time, there is a limited choice of available properties, which affects the investor's buying strategy.

Linear (axial) growth Growth of cities in a linear form, drawn by linear transportation systems, such as streetcars and subways.

Linear strips Retail districts, usually on both sides of a major arterial road, drawn by exposure to the heavy traffic.

Linkage The interrelationship that exists between some businesses and others, causing them to benefit from a location close to one another. Diamond merchants, auto dealers, and fashion retail stores are each examples.

Liquidity An important investment characteristic–the speed, cost, and ease of converting the investment into cash.

Live-work housing Housing that is designed to serve both as residential space and also work space for artists, crafts people, and other very small businesses. Often developed in old industrial buildings, and industrially zoned sites. These are usually complexes, with a number of units where a dwelling unit is combined with a ground-floor shop, store, or craft area.

Local community forces The social, economic, legal and physical forces that cause changes in the use and value of local properties.

Local market Properties that are advertised primarily through the local newspaper, brokers, or word of mouth, as contrasted with properties that are sold by regional or national advertising programs.

Location The sum of all of the characteristics of a particular place and its surroundings, including proximity to transportation, employment, shopping, and desired cultural facilities, and the influence of any nuisance that is found in the area.

Long-term secular trends Economic changes that occur over an extended period of time, perhaps 50 years or more.

Management The supervision needed to oversee an investment.

Market economy An economic system where the majority of decisions about the production and distribution of goods and services are made by private individuals in competitive markets.

Market rents What the space or units would rent for if new tenants were sought.

Market A place where buyers and sellers meet to bargain and exchange goods and services at negotiated prices.

Market-clearing price The price at which all of the goods in the marketplace at one time are sold.

Market-oriented industries Industries which seek a location as close as possible to their customers. A neighborhood market is an example.

Measure of value One of the functions of money: it is used to measure or compare the worth of unlike items.

Medium of exchange One of the functions of money: it allows people to exchange goods and services, without the need to revert to a barter (or swap) system.

Minerals Natural compounds that are formed through geological processes.

Monetary policy The use of controls on the supply and cost of money as a means of controlling the economy. Increased cost of money will show down an inflationary economy, while low interest rates will stimulate a weak economy.

Multiple nuclei A model of the growth and shape of larger communities, with the growing city forming multiple high-value clusters, about major intersections and the former downtowns of suburbs that are absorbed into the growing city.

Multiplier effect The ratio of new local jobs that are created for every new basic job. The ratio varies with the size of the community.

Multiyear analysis An analysis over multiple years of the expected income from an investment.

Negative declaration A finding by a governmental body that a proposed project or action would not have a significant impact on the environment, thus eliminating the need to prepare an Environmental Impact Study.

Neighborhood A cluster of properties of relatively similar land use and value.

Neighborhood boundaries The line or area where the location starts to change. Sometimes, a clear line formed by a lake, river, marsh, freeway, or a similar distinct barrier to development. Other times, only defined by the gradual change in the properties over several blocks or more.

Neighborhood centers A retail shopping center, usually anchored by a supermarket, with a few other stores such as a drugstore, laundry, and small restaurants.

Neighborhood cycle The theory that neighborhoods go through a predictable cycle as they age, and are regenerated.

Neighborhood obsolescence Neighborhoods that decline to the point of properties being abandoned.

Net Sale Proceeds The amount of money the investor is estimated to net, after close of escrow and payment of capital gain or income taxes on the sale, when the property is sold at the end of the holding period.

Net Spendable Income See After-Tax Cash Flow.

New construction A home or other property that hasn't been occupied, where the seller is typically the builder.

No-growth policy A social or political policy to restrict the growth of a community's population, by restrictions on zoning or availability of utilities. Motivated by a desire to reduce the impacts of growth and change.

Nodes A point on a transportation route where movement slows or branches. This often allows easier access to cargo than elsewhere, leading to community growth. Some nodes form solely to service the transportation system, as the railroad watering stops that became towns.

Nonresidential construction Consists of retail and office buildings, industrial plants, and institutional buildings such as schools and libraries.

Open-market operations The actions of the Open Market Committee of the Fed, in buying and selling government securities in the open market, in order to expand or contract the amount of money in the banking system.

Opportunity costs The unrealized, potential earnings that the money tied up in unimproved land might have earned if invested elsewhere.

Other Income Sources of property income, other than rent, such as vending machine income, storage or parking space income, and so on.

Overhead costs The continuing costs that a developer incurs, regardless of project delays. These include such items as rent on the developer's office, bank payments and maintenance expense on office equipment, and fixed salaries for office workers.

Passive loss rules An income tax law that states that real estate losses can only offset what is known as passive income.

Permits and quotas Permissions required from the government to grow some crops, including tobacco, cotton, and sugar beets, and to produce fresh milk.

Personal income A measure of personal income: total income earned by all individuals, after business taxes have been paid, but before personal taxes are paid.

Physical forces The physical forces that impact real estate values. These include the effects of time and the elements including the weather—from routine fading and settling to the sudden tornado or flood—as well as earthquakes, slides, soil creep, and fault creep.

Police power The constitutional right of the government to regulate private activity, in order to promote the general health, welfare, and safety of society.

Political conflict An unresolved disagreement between two groups over some issue.

Political forces The political forces that impact real estate values. These range from taxation to education and include the effects of a radical city council on a conservative neighborhood, and a traditional city council on an unorthodox neighborhood.

Pollution Introduction of harmful substances or products into the environment.

Population growth The increase in the population of a defined area.

Poverty Too little income to be able to pay for safe and sanitary housing and a nutritious diet.

Power center A retail shopping center, usually with a cluster of separate retail buildings, often big-box stores, with adjacent parking areas.

Preservation The process of reducing neighborhood deterioration, by encouraging maintenance, remodeling, and renovation of existing buildings.

Price supports A government subsidy used to maintain prices at a certain level. Usually applied to agricultural products, in order to stabilize or support farm income.

Prime rate The rate of interest that a bank charges its best, large customers, such as major corporations.

Private benefits The rewards of a decision or event that are enjoyed only by a particular individual or business and not by society as a whole.

Private costs Those expenses of a project that are paid by the project investor(s).

Private deed restrictions Restrictions on the use of private property that are agreed to by the owners of a group of properties.

Product market In economics, a market where businesses sell goods and services to individuals and households.

Productivity growth The growth in output, over time, for a given labor force.

Progressive tax A tax that takes a larger percent of income as income increases.

Property rights The collection of rights to own, use, sell, etc. property. The government retains some rights.

Property tax A tax that is collected from the owner or user of each privately owned parcel of land.

Proportional tax A tax where the percentage of tax remains the same when the taxpayer's income increases.

Proximity One of the two main forces, along with accessibility, that influence where businesses try to locate in a community.

Public works construction refers to the building of streets, sewer systems, highways, bridges, and public projects other than buildings.

Purchasing power risk The risk of possible loss in the purchasing power of investment funds due to inflation.

Rate of exchange The rate or price at which the currency of one nation can be converted into the currency of another.

Real estate Land, that which is affixed to the land, that which is appurtenant to the land, and that which is immovable by law.

Real estate economics The study of how the actions of people affect real estate use and value.

Real GDP Gross Domestic Product adjusted for inflation.

Recession A period of general economic decline; typically defined as a decline in GDP for two or more consecutive quarters.

Recreational subdivisions A residential subdivision located in a recreational area, rather than as housing for workers or for retirees.

Regional centers Retail shopping centers that are large, planned projects with enclosed malls and several major "anchor" department stores.

Regressive tax A tax that charges a declining percent of income, as income increases.

Regional planning Urban planning executed by a regional government agency.

Rehabilitation cycle The phase in the neighborhood cycle where the neighborhood comes back into favor, with increasing renovation and remodeling.

Rent controls Governmental controls on the rents for residential housing, or mobile home sites. Usually also restrict most evictions of tenants to allow owner-occupancy.

Rent, wages, interest, profits The payments made to individuals for the use of the factors of production: land, labor, capital, and entrepreneurship.

Reserve requirements The amount of funds that banks that are members of the Federal Reserve System must hold in reserve against the deposits made by their customers. This money must be in the bank's vaults or at the closest Federal Reserve Bank.

Residential construction Construction of single-family dwellings, condominiums, and multifamily apartments.

Resource market In economics, a market where sellers of land, labor, capital, and business management or entrepreneurial skills meet buyers.

Resource processing plant A plant to process raw materials in order to obtain valuable ores or products. If bulky, low-valued materials are being processed, the plant needs to be located close to the mine or origin of the raw materials, to minimize transport cost.

Return of investment The recapture or recovery of the original investment funds. Contrast with return on investment.

Return on investment The profit on the original invested funds, the payment for the use of the funds and the risk of the investment. The ratio of the money gained or lost on an investment relative to the amount of money invested.

Reversion See Net Sale Proceeds.

Risk The danger that the expected benefits of an investment will not be obtained; a result more negative than what was expected.

Risk of legal change The risk that new laws might be passed, with a negative impact on an investment's ability to produce income.

Risk of social change The risk that social changes could influence supply or demand and have a negative effect on the earnings of an investment.

Sales tax A tax levied on a sale of goods or services, as a percent of the sales price.

Scientific method A structured process of defining a question, developing data that is relevant to the question, testing the data to see what light it sheds on the question, and concluding whether the data collected answer the question as posed. If necessary, reword the question, seek added data, and repeat.

Seasonal fluctuations Short-term changes in business and economic activity that generally repeat at about the same time each year, result from either weather or custom.

Secondary industries Local companies that produce goods and services for use by people within the community or region being studied.

Secondary employment Employment at secondary industries.

Secondary markets In real estate finance, markets where existing loans are sold, from the originator to an investor, or from one investor to another.

Sensitivity analysis An investment analysis in which the estimates of future income, expenses, financing, or other investment variables are changed, one at a time or in combination, usually in order to see the effect upon the expected profits from the investment. Can be done manually, or as a statistical technique, varying many inputs.

Single tax theory A theory of taxation, where it is proposed that the full value of the land should be taxed, which it is argued generates enough revenue so that no other form of taxation would be required. Improvements to the land would not be taxed.

Slow growth policy See No growth policy.

Social benefits Rewards from a project or private investment that accrue to all of society, not just to the individual or businesses that invested in the project.

Social costs The expenses generated by a private project that are paid by society as a whole rather than by the individual or business investors.

Social forces The social forces that influence the use and value of real estate, including a variety of lifestyle and age factors.

Socialism A theory or system of social or economic organization that advocates the vesting of the ownership and control of the means of production and distribution, of capital, land, etc., in the community as a whole.

Soil banking The government pays the farmer for not planting an allotted number of acres.

Soil productivity The capability of the soil for producing a specified quantity of particular types of plant produce per unit area.

Solar power The use of the rays of the sun to produce either electric power, or hot water.

Special assessment bonds Bonds that are sold by a government agency, in order to make infrastructure improvements to benefit a specific area, to be paid off by special assessments against the benefitted property.

Specialization The degree to which a particular building is adapted to one specific use. The trend in the real estate industry to narrow one's efforts to a specific category of work, rather than trying to cover all of the different fields of real estate work.

Standard of deferred payment One of the functions of money: used to describe what a debtor owes a creditor. If you buy now and pay later, the amount that you owe is expressed in money.

Store of value One of the functions of money: a way to store or save up wealth.

Structural unemployment Unemployment caused by some fundamental changes in the economy rather than the normal ebb and surge of the business cycle.

Subdivision regulations Regulations that real estate developers must follow to obtain approval for a new subdivision.

Supply The total quantity that sellers are willing to sell at a given time at certain prices.

Telemobility The ability to use electronics and technology to bring the experience to the person, rather than requiring the person to go to the experience. Examples include on-line shopping, working from home, and video-conferencing.

Tight-money policy A course of action undertaken by the Federal Reserve to constrict spending in an economy that is seen to be growing too quickly, or to curb inflation when it is rising too fast.

Time value of money A dollar in hand today is worth more than a dollar in hand tomorrow.

Topography The surface features of a place or region on a map, indicating their relative positions and elevations.

Traditional economy In economics, a society that chooses to continue doing things as they have been done in the past.

Transfer tax A state or local tax that is paid when property is sold, usually as a percent of the sales price.

Transportation The movement of people and goods from one location to another, a major influence on the location, shape, and economic success of communities.

Transportation service towns Communities which perform services for transportation systems, along transportation routes.

Trend A continuing movement in one direction of some physical, economic, or social measurement.

Turnover rate The percentage of housing units which change occupants each year, or, alternatively, the percent that change owners each year.

$25,000 real estate exception to the passive loss rules An income tax rule, which allows a qualified rental property owner to use up to $25,000 of passive real estate rental losses to offset active or portfolio income each year, after first offsetting any passive income.

Unemployment The state of a person who is not employed, but wants to be.

Unemployment rate The percentage of the total workforce that is unemployed and is looking for a paid job.

Urban planning To plan or study how to anticipate and achieve community goals in light of social, economic, and physical resources and needs.

Visibility An investment which, because of the building, the occupants, or the co-owners, is likely to receive more attention from the public or the press.

Water A clear liquid, essential for most plant and animal life and the most widely used of all solvents.

Wind power The use of the wind to generate electricity, or to pump water.

Zoning The use of the police power by governments, to restrict how land can be used. Often, zoning ordinances divide land into designated use districts. In zoning's simplest form, these districts are divided into ones for residential, commercial, or industrial use.

Index

Ability-to-pay tax philosophy, 337–38
Accessibility
    community land-use
        patterns and, 182, 280
    proximity vs., 186–87
Accessibility, farmland
    markets, 308
Active income, defined, 461
Active-in-management test,
    passive loss exceptions
    and, 462
Adjustable rate mortgages
    (ARMs), 97
Advertising, effects on
    demand, 23
Affordability, housing shortages
    and, 247
Affordability index,
    236, 237, 242–43
After-tax cash flow, real estate
    investment and, 438
Aging, of neighborhoods,
    216–23
Agricultural Foreign Investment
    Disclosure Act, 310
American Recovery and
    Reinvestment Act (2009), 391
Annual debt service, real estate
    investment and, 437
Apartment buildings, as real
    estate investment, 452–53
Appeal, defined, 370
Applied real estate economics,
    477–89
Architectural review, defined,
    370
Assessments, skills upgrades
    for, 351
Asset bubbles, 59, 112–15
Automatic stabilizers, 67
Automobile cities
    emergence of, 283

Balance of payments, interna-
    tional trade and, 27, 47
Balance of trade, international
    trade and, 27, 46
Banks, as depository institutions,
    80–81

Barlowe, 195
Basis, income tax on investment
    and analysis of, 457–60
Bay Area Rapid Transit
    System (BART), 187
Before-tax cash flow, real
    estate investment and analysis
    of, 435–37
Benefits
    analysis of, 418–19
    of government regulation,
        40–41
Benefits-based tax
    philosophy, 337–38
Big box centers, 282–83
Boeing family, 290
Boot, in real estate investment,
    468
Boundary problems, in older
    rural homes, 319
Break-bulk point, city
    locations and, 153
Break-cargo point, city
    locations and, 153
"Bubbles"
    asset, 59
    managing, 502–04
Budget deficits, 62, 336
Budget surplus, 62
"Build-and-They-Shall-Come
    Syndrome", 406–08
Building codes, housing
    market and, 255–56
Building construction. *See*
    Construction
Building permits, 411–14
"Built to suit" construction
    process, 399
Bundle of rights, defined, 3
Bureau of Land Management,
    309
Burgess, 182
Business cycles
    demand for business real
        estate and, 271–73
Business location factors,
    community growth and,
    160–61
Business real estate
    characteristics of, 267–71

economic issues and,
    271–76
property taxes and, 275, 344
Business Week, 49
Buyers, in business real estate,
    275

California
    construction trends in, 390
    population and demo-
        graphics about, 164
    real estate trends in, 406–08
California Coastal Zone
    Conservation Act, 378
Capital, as factor of production,
    18
Capital equipment, 18
Capitalism
    basic principles of, 13–14
    defined, 11
    imperfect markets and,
        39–41
    mixed, 14–17, 39–43
    private land-use controls
        and, 362
Capitalization rate, real estate
    investment and, 443–44
"Cash for Clunkers"
    program, 63
Center town, analysis of, 194
Central business district (CBD),
    trends in, 280–83
Certainty, in tax policy, 337
Change
    anticipation of, 502–528
    in commercial land-use
        patterns, 279–85
    land-use patterns and
        principle of, 179
    national change, impact on
        real estate of, 484
    neighborhoods as barom-
        eters of, 208–16
    patterns of industrial
        location and, 291–92
Checking accounts, 79
Circular flow of economy,
    19–20, 25–26, 43, 44
Circular land-use patterns, com-
    munity growth and, 183–84